The Normative Basis of Fault in Criminal Law:
History and Theory
Adekemi Odujirin

DATE DUE

While a functi _____ ent roots,
theoretical and _____ ury. In this
book, Adekem _____ e: one
contextual and _____ he result is
a study that tra _____ tifying and
exploring the _____ ne.

Beginning _____ develop-
ment of the co _____ cholarship.
He considers t _____ utions of
Locke and Ho _____ rs, notably
Bentham and

A major coi _____ aw, this
study will be c _____ throughout
the common-l:

ADEKEMI ODU _____ d his
doctorate in la

Demco, Inc. 38-293

D0366294

ADEKEMI ODUJIRIN

The Normative Basis of Fault in Criminal Law: History and Theory

UNIVERSITY OF TORONTO PRESS
Toronto Buffalo London

© University of Toronto Press Incorporated 1998
Toronto Buffalo London
Printed in Canada

ISBN 0-8020-4304-6 (cloth)
ISBN 0-8020-8132-0 (paper)

Printed on acid-free paper

Canadian Cataloguing in Publication Data

Odujirin, Adekemi
    The normative basis of fault in criminal law: history and theory

    Includes bibliographical references and index.
    ISBN 0-8020-4304-6 (bound)   ISBN 0-8020-8132-0 (pbk.)

    1. Criminal liability.   I. Title.

    K5065.O38 1998   345'.04   C98-930525-2

University of Toronto Press acknowledges the financial assistance to its publishing
program of the Canada Council for the Arts and the Ontario Arts Council

This book has been published with the help of a grant from the Humanities and Social
Sciences Federation of Canada, using funds provided by the Social Sciences and
Humanities Research Council of Canada.

To my parents,
Mustafa A. Odujirin
and
Abeni A. Odujirin

Contents

After all, the truth about Right, Ethics, and the state is as old as its public recognition and formulation in the law of the land, in the morality of everyday life, and in religion. What more does this truth require ... [than for] it to be grasped in thought as well; the content which is already rational in principle must win the *form* of rationality and so appear well-founded to untrammelled thinking. Such thinking does not remain stationary at the given, whether the given be upheld by the external positive authority or the *consensus hominum*, or by the authority of inward feeling and emotion and by the 'witness of the spirit' which directly concurs with it. On the contrary, thought which is free starts out from itself and thereupon claims to know itself as united in its innermost being with the truth.

Hegel, *The Philosophy of Right* (Preface)

Preface

Some problems are endemic to criminal jurisprudence. One is whether the strict liability offence fits into the lattice of the criminal law. Another is whether corporate entities are amenable to the criminal sanction. Yet another is whether negligence can sustain responsibility in the criminal law. Any attempt to solve the theoretical issues raised by any of these and other related questions has to grapple with, and transcend, the answers proffered by analytical criminal jurisprudence. The objective of this book is to dissolve the perennial problems of the legitimacy of strict liability offences and negligence in the criminal law. However, I will add, for purposes of clarity, that this book does *not* argue for strict criminal liability or negligence-based criminal liability. Rather, it shows that the strict liability offence and negligence are not as incompatible with penal law as analytical jurisprudence makes them to be.

Analytical jurisprudence is less than two hundred years old, and analytical criminal jurisprudence is even younger; indeed, the latter is a product of the twentieth century. Yet the theoretical conclusions reached by analytical criminal jurisprudence have become so firmly established that it is difficult to imagine that things could be otherwise. Specifically, analytical criminal jurisprudence limits the notion of wrong in criminal law to intentional or reckless breach of legal duty or obligation. This delimitation effectively excludes negligence and strict liability offences from the purview of the criminal law.

The thesis of this book is that the determination of wrong made by analytical criminal jurisprudence is not the only basis for arriving at juristic conclusions. Analytical jurisprudence generally, and analytical criminal jurisprudence in particular, conceives legal history and legal theory in a way that confines legal scholarship to the analysis and exposition of the formal rules and principles of law. Yet, while analytical jurisprudence is free to derive fundamental legal concepts from ample and mature systems of positive law and, on the basis of such materials, elaborate coherent conceptual conclusions, it is not absurd to ask whether those conceptual conclusions themselves tell all there is.

Analytical jurisprudence insists that its conceptual conclusions are the quintessence of rationality. If one grants the limited role that analytical jurisprudence assigns to theory, and if one accepts its conception of legal history – that legal history consists essentially of the sum total of the finite and definite intellectual constructs (concepts) embedded in developed systems of positive law – then it will be impossible to deny that analytical conclusions invariably represent the peak of rationality. But to take the legal experience of 'developed' societies as constitutive of the totality of legal experience is to abbreviate legal history. As well, the role that analytical jurisprudence assigns to theory is not incontrovertible. Untrammelled legal history and legal theory can unveil juridical conclusions that transcend the analytical position. My argument is that the conceptual conclusion reached by analytical criminal jurisprudence is not necessarily the only basis for arriving at jurisprudential determinations.

This book emanates from a doctoral thesis I submitted to the University of Toronto. I am grateful to professors Bruce Chapman and Jim Phillips not only for supervising the original research work but also for their continued interest in my well-being. Professor David Beatty deserves special thanks for the same reason. I am also grateful to Professor Denise Reaume for reading and commenting on the materials of chapters 5 and 6 and to Curtis Fahey for editing the book. I thank, too, Canada Law Book for establishing the Alan Marks Medal at the Faculty of Law, University of Toronto. The substance of this book won that medal in 1994 and prompted me to take a second look at the work. I am particularly grateful to the Humanities and Social Sciences Federation of Canada and the Social Sciences and Humanities Research Council of Canada for the financial subvention that made publication of this book possible.

To my children, Adenike Toluani and Abeni Adeyinka, and their mother, Adunni Oluyemisi, I owe a special debt. Not only did they tolerate my constant disappearance from home but they also cheerfully put up with the seemingly unending clatter of my keyboard.

ADEKEMI ODUJIRIN

THE NORMATIVE BASIS OF FAULT IN CRIMINAL LAW

Introduction:
Criminal Law or the Law of Crimes

This book traverses ground that stretches from pre-Norman England to contemporary English-speaking societies. Its subject-matter is the idea of legal wrong. It begins with an account of how the idea was understood in the intellectually unsophisticated society of Anglo-Saxon England, combining this with the related issue of the basis of responsibility for wrong acts. After tracing the fortunes of these two issues in Anglo-Norman England when wrong was bifurcated into civil and criminal wrongs, it pursues the same themes from the time when the latter class began to assume a distinct intellectual character in late Anglo-Norman times through early modern England when it became a clear and distinct concept. This culminated in the moral conception of crime which was incorporated into the common law in the seventeenth century. The moral conception of crime emphasized the necessity of the presence of wrongful or unlawful intention (*mens rea*) before a particular unlawful act could be punished as a criminal wrong. As well, it defined *mens rea* as a precise and direct intention on the part of the defendant to bring about the unlawful consequences of an act. With the advent of analytical jurisprudence in the nineteenth century, the moral conception of crime became the legal concept of crime.

Analytical jurisprudence concentrates exclusively on explicating the concept of law and other fundamental legal concepts common to developed systems of positive law or those embedded in particular developed or mature legal order(s). This tends to freeze the meaning of the legal terms and concepts that had survived in the legal habitat and that were, therefore, part of the legal lexicon at the time the analysis and systematization of positive legal knowledge were carried out. The resultant 'analytical and moral dogmatism'[1] holds that the conceptual meaning of the word 'crime' determines the perimeters of the criminal law. This book shows that the analytical criminal jurisprudential position is inadequate. It is inadequate because it takes a part only but represents it as the whole of legal experience.

To make this point, the present study adopts a historical approach. Its brand of historical analysis is untrammelled by any grand philosophical or historiographical assumptions: it eschews the pretensions of the universal legal historian, and it avoids the evolutionary or romantic premises of historical jurisprudence. As well, it does not pick or choose between the legal ideas of unsophisticated and those of sophisticated societies.

It is often said that the common law mind is more attuned to resolving practical problems than to untying theoretical knots. Nevertheless, common law scholars occasionally forsake the practical for the theoretical field. For instance, in the early part of this century it was vigorously debated whether or not tort law was grounded on any general principle. Those who denied that there was such a general principle based their belief on the conviction that it was impossible to reduce to a single formula the common law principles of tortious liability.[2] The opposite belief was informed by the conviction that the common law of tort was grounded on a general principle of liability.[3]

The apparent sterility of such academic debates gives a misleading picture of the importance of the issues at stake. For the point of such debates is the all–important issue of whether we should operate with a plurality of concepts in a given area of the law or whether we should operate with a single concept. If we take the pluralist path, the mansion of the law will be sufficiently capacious to accommodate the totality of legal experience. If, on the other hand, we opt for the conceptualist position, we will be monotheorists.

With reference to the criminal law, the adoption of the pluralist position would mean that it (the criminal law) is a sort of bank where one can keep and operate a variety of accounts, one of which is the concept of intentional wrong. The adoption of the conceptualist position would make the criminal law a strange sort of bank where one can keep and access a single account, that account being the concept of intentional wrong. Analytical criminal jurisprudence takes the latter position. It holds that 'crime' is synonymous with intentional wrong, and that the criminal law should not harbour any other notion. In apparently tautological terms, this means that criminal law is criminal law, and nothing else. Specifically, analytical criminal jurisprudence maintains that the concept of negligence and the notion of strict liability offences are alien to the legal concept of crime.

As a descriptive claim this is unobjectionable, but as a prescriptive stance it is insufferable. I believe that criminal jurisprudence should encompass the totality of legal experience. Negligent wrongdoing and strict liability offences are integral parts of legal experience. Therefore, an adequate criminal jurisprudence should be sufficiently elastic as to accommodate these notions. Insofar as analytical criminal jurisprudence fails to embrace these notions it is inadequate.

The historical analysis leads to the conclusion that the pluralist position displays a degree of fidelity to the facts of legal history that cannot be matched by the analytical position. The latter is conceptualistic. It binds the intellect and constrains our choice. Indeed, it insists that we are not at liberty at all, for there is only one way and that is the narrow road paved by analytical criminal jurisprudence. This book finds that legal history teaches a different lesson. It teaches that we have 'free hands,'[4] and that our freedom is freedom within the law – law with a capital 'L.' Thus, while the analytical position argues for the 'criminal law,' the pluralist position argues for the 'law of crimes.' This book shows that the concept of negligence and the concept of strict liability offences are not necessarily repugnant to the idea sheltered by the concept of crime.

Ironically, analytical criminal jurisprudence itself relies on legal history. One of the central points of this book is that analytical criminal jurisprudence is underpinned by an abbreviated legal history, in three distinct though related ways. First, its legal history begins with the advent of intellectual sophistication generally, and of legal sophistication in particular. Second, it is not comparative in any sense of that term: it not only limits its historical knowledge to a single system of mature positive law but also shuns the 'adolescent' legal ideas of Anglo-Saxon and Anglo-Norman England which preceded legal sophistication. Third, the last chapter in its legal history was written in the first half of the nineteenth century. In short, analytical criminal jurisprudence derived the materials for its criminal theory exclusively from the criminal law as it crystallized under the common law between the seventeenth and the first half of the nineteenth centuries. This cannot and does not represent the totality of legal experience.

To capture the totality of legal experience, legal theory must entertain a more expansive notion of legal history. Specifically, it must take into consideration two other periods of legal history. These are the period before the advent of intellectual sophistication and the period following the advent of analytical jurisprudence. In order to do that, this book begins with Anglo-Saxon England and takes the story up to the turn of the twentieth century.

The book consists of nine chapters. Chapters 1 and 2 cover the first of the two grounds neglected by analytical criminal jurisprudence. While chapter 1 identifies the meaning attached to the idea of wrong in Anglo-Saxon England, chapter 2 ascertains the basis of responsibility for wrongs in Anglo-Saxon society. Chapter 3 picks up the story at the point where chapter 2 stopped. It is divided into three parts. The first part discusses the principal institutional device used to transform the law of wrongs in Anglo-Norman England. This is the notion of the King's Peace, allegation of breach of which was used as a pleading device for converting trespasses into 'pleas of the Crown,' that is, crimes. The second part discusses the growth of intellectual and legal sophistication in the twelfth and thirteen centuries. Intellectual sophistication gave rise first to a political conception of crime and later to a moral conception of crime. The third part of chapter 3 outlines these two conceptual models and emphasizes that the latter, which fastened on the mental element or *mens rea*, triumphed under the common law. The origin, formation, and crystallization of the doctrine of *mens rea* is the subject-matter of chapter 4. Chapter 4 concludes that substantive criminal law is encapsulated in the maxim: *actus non facit reum nisi mens sit rea*.

The generality of this maxim suppressed certain distinctions found in the law. Specifically, it suppressed the distinction between *mala in se* and *mala prohibita*. Chapter 5 focuses on the role played by this distinction in the common law of crimes. The chapter is divided into two parts. The first part looks at criminalization through the prism of the common law mind. It suggests that the peculiar common law view of legal history, which holds that the common law is of immemorial origin, gave meaning to and determined the use to which it was put under English law. Although the distinction has a hoary pedigree, English law did not take cognizance of it until the fifteenth century. Originally, the distinction was based on the supposed inherent differences between crimes grounded in nature or divine law and those that derived their illegal character from human or positive law. In other words, the distinction followed the philosophical distinction between natural and positive laws. But, in the course of the development of the common law, common law crimes were elevated to the same status as *mala in se* and the phrase *mala prohibita* acquired a restrictive meaning peculiar to English law: it denoted those things that the King prohibited for his own convenience. Chapter 5 underscores the fact that, while the distinction had moral and political significance, it did not have any jurisprudential implications: the only legal significance it had was that the Crown could license and/or dispense *mala prohibita* but not *mala in se*.

The second part of chapter 5 considers the philosophical basis for the distinction as it was canvassed in the eighteenth century by Sir William Blackstone. It points out that, properly understood, Blackstone did not put the distinction to any jurisprudential use. At any rate, the philosophical basis for the distinction was exploded by juridical positivists, notably Bentham and Austin in the early nineteenth century. With the banishment of the distinction from juristic thought, there was no longer any theoretical basis for distinguishing one class of offences from another. Yet it is common knowledge that a new class of offences – the so-called regulatory offences – developed in the course of the nineteenth century. Chapter 6 identifies the substantive reasons for the emergence of this species of offences.

Juridical positivism came hand in hand with a new approach in jurisprudence. To be precise, it witnessed the adoption of the analytical approach in legal science. Chapter 7 discusses the decisive role played by analytical jurisprudence in the formation of the legal concept of crime. It first discusses the advent, and determines the nature, of analytical jurisprudence. It then gives an account of the analytic meaning of legal wrong enunciated by Austin, and the analytic meaning of the concept of crime under the common law elaborated by analytical criminal jurisprudents. Next, it pinpoints the definitional method employed by analytical criminal jurists in fashioning a definitive meaning of crime. This is the essentialist method of definition, which makes intention or recklessness the essence of crime. It concludes by noting that the conceptual meaning of crime rules out both negligence and strict liability from the sphere of criminal law.

Chapter 8 is an extensive consideration of the influence of the analytic method in criminal jurisprudence. I argue in this chapter that analytical criminal jurisprudence results in mental myopia since it sees its own creation as the quintessence of rationality. By confining legal scholarship to conceptual analysis, analytical jurisprudence makes it impossible for criminal theory to address and possibly solve such perennial problems as whether negligence and the strict liability offence can be accommodated by the criminal law. The chapter offers alternative explanations for the exclusion of these notions from the criminal law, and it concludes that their continued exclusion is due entirely to the desire to maintain the purity of the analytic, conceptual, or scientific – all interchangeable terms – meaning of crime.

Chapter 9 makes a number of important points. First, it exposes the strategic moves that enable analytical criminal jurisprudents to reduce criminal theory to 'a chanting of tautologies.'[5] Second, it refutes the analytical criminal jurists' implicit assumption that their view of legal history captures the totality of legal experience. Third, it shows what an accurate picture of the totality of legal experience would look like. The chapter concludes by showing that the analytical jurists' conception of essences as objects that can be recovered through conceptual analysis is at best only a partial truth. For there is another, non-analytic sense in which concepts have essences. In a human science such as law, the function of such non-analytic essences is not the *descriptive* or analytic one of distinguishing one concept from another, but the *prescriptive* or normative one of distinguishing 'right' from 'wrong.' The normative function of the analytic essence of crime – *mens rea* – is that it is wrong to impose condign sanction on a legal actor for breach of a legal duty or obligation except when the act was intentional or reckless. As well, chapter 9 pinpoints the normative function of 'free will' and 'act,' and it concludes that none of them warrants the exclusion of negligence or strict liability offences from the purview of the criminal law. Their exclusion is dictated solely by the conceptualistic assumptions of analytical criminal jurisprudence.

1

The Idea of Wrong in Anglo-Saxon Law I

In the latter part of the nineteenth century, a new school of jurists arose whose main preoccupation was to establish the autochthonous character, continuity, and unity of Western legal categories. They attempted to do this by investigating 'the legal institutions of all Aryan peoples' and by endeavouring 'to reconstruct an Aryan Urrecht in which the roots of modern law were to be found.'[1] The underlying faith of this genre of historical analysis was that the legal history of any of those peoples was no more than an illustration, though a very important illustration, of a linear and universal movement which culminated in modern legal ideas.[2] They conceived legal history as a mine for the embryology of modern or contemporary legal concepts and categories.[3] Legal history was to them the mother of modern legal concepts and categories.

Legal historians took a different tack. Knowledge of the past had convinced some legal historians of the extravagance of the idea of universal history generally, and universal legal history in particular. This made them sceptical about the thesis of the historical jurists. Of course, they were not against theory but they eschewed the species of legal theory based on questionable speculative historical fantasies. Instead, they insisted that any generalization must be confined to the ascertained or ascertainable facts about particular legal orders. Legal history was to them more a nursery than the mother of modern legal concepts and categories. The great English legal historian F.W. Maitland[4] epitomized the second approach.

Maitland[5] warned against the hazards inherent in the assumption that the seeds of modern legal concepts and categories are to be found in earlier ages. Even the use or occurrence of legal terms which are distinctly understood in a developed system of law could not warrant the inference that the underlying notion was grasped by its 'barbarian' user. Nor was it safe to assume the antiq-

uity, at least insofar as a particular society was concerned, of the legal categories which have come down to us from earlier times. As he put it:

We must not be in a hurry to get to the beginning of the history of law ... the history of
law must be a history of ideas. It must represent, not merely what men had done and
said, but what men have thought in bygone ages ... if ... we introduce the *persona ficta*
too soon, we shall be doing worse than if we armed Hengest and Horsa with machine
guns or pictured the Venerable Bede correcting proofs for the press; we shall have built
upon a crumbling foundation.[6]

Maitland prescribed an antidote against the errors to which a belief in the antiquity of our legal concepts and categories may lead, namely to read 'our history
backwards as well as forwards.'[7]

In all probability Maitland himself was not unaware of the fact that there is as
much danger in reading our history backwards as there is in reading it forwards.
Each may lead to the same sort of perceptual error. If we read our history forwards, it is not unlikely that we will see the legal ideas of earlier times as mere
precursors of contemporary legal concepts and categories. If we read it backwards, we are likely to impose upon past ages adumbrations of the legal concepts and categories of later ages or ascribe to them a level of intellectual
advancement which they did not make or blame them for failing to make distinctions which were either unknown to them or were not considered important.
In both cases, we fail to confront the past age on its own terms. More precisely,
'by looking at pre-modern law from our theoretical vantage point, we run the
risk of studying the past not on its own terms, but as nothing more than the
inchoate, imperfect incidence of what was to come later.'[8] The Scylla of reading legal history forwards should be avoided without falling into the Charybdis
of reading legal history backwards. In short, 'We must try to avoid analysing
their thinking through application of our own intellectual categories or search-
ing in the past for evidence of ideas that interest us, but never existed, (consciously or not) for the subjects themselves.'[9] One way to avoid these pitfalls is
to attempt to immerse ourselves in the moral, political, and social climate that
prevailed in the society in question at the time the relevant ideas were elaborated on or put into practice. But this leads to a head-in-the-sand position.
Accordingly, we will adopt a Janus-headed approach, or, more accurately, we
will proceed like the ornithological specimen which, while flying forwards,
continually looks backwards. In other words, we will fix our gaze simulta-
neously in both directions.

This chapter explores the idea of wrong embedded in Anglo-Saxon laws. The
analysis is based entirely on evidence contained in Anglo-Saxon dooms. In

other words, the idea of wrong is discussed in the context of the various acts prohibited in Anglo-Saxon laws, the commission of which attracted compensation, reparation, fines, or capital punishment. The chapter does this without any interpolations derived from either the intellectualized theories of old civilizations or the sophisticated legal ideas of contemporary times; in explicating the idea of wrong, we shall deploy a selective anthology of acts regarded as wrong by a society unequipped with the acute analytic apparatus characteristic of sophisticated legal systems.

It is pertinent to pause here to explain why it is necessary to begin with the idea of wrong in a society as remote to contemporary English-speaking societies as Anglo-Saxon England. One of the leading criminal law scholars of the present century[10] has opined that the modern criminal lawyer need not go beyond Sir Edward Coke. This means that a student of the common law of crimes will not lose anything by ignoring the history of the criminal law before the seventeenth century. While it is true that a clear, general, and distinct law of criminal liability did not emerge until after the sixteenth century,[11] a legal theorist's insights would be greatly enriched by a perusal of the history of legal ideas before they were moulded into the cast-iron shapes of theoretical thought. This requires the student to start from at least the twelfth century. But I propose to begin earlier still.

There are, at least, two reasons why it is necessary to go farther back than that 'most legal of all the centuries.' First, it is important to remind ourselves that the process of isolating, identifying, and declaring certain acts or their consequences as wrong has been a slow and gradual one; there is no reason to assume that most of the acts that are now generally stigmatized as wrongs have necessarily been viewed this way. A nodding acquaintance with ancient history shows that, with the probable exception of homicide, there is hardly any wrongful act which was not sanctioned by the practice of one ethnic or political group or another in its relationship with other ethnic or political groups.[12] In intra-ethnic or intra-group relationships, however, even the most savage society had its own set of wrong acts[13] and none sanctioned the killing of its own members for sport.[14] It was through the mediation of custom (law) that various acts became classified and condemned as wrong. As a matter of fact, the manners or mode of life and the range of activities available in a particular age necessarily act as a constraint on the type and number of acts which are perceived as injurious. Of course, we can talk only about 'the ages'[15] we know, and reasonable people may disagree on the wisdom of premising the idea of wrong on experiential foundation. But the 'golden age' of mankind (when it is supposed that human beings neither knew nor did wrong) is irrelevant for our purposes. We should, therefore, content ourselves with explicating the idea of wrong as it was understood by men operating within what the later Middle Ages would call the second kind of nature, that is, 'the lower nature of the world and man.'[16]

Second, the approach adopted here highlights the fact that 'the law came because of offences.'[17] Without becoming embroiled in speculation about the original state of mankind or man-in-society, we assume that wrongs or offences were discovered by experience; wrongs are acts that experience showed to be detrimental to peaceful co-existence and survival in the face of external forces. Sidetracking Edward Jenks's assumption that many acts that later became wrongs were once freely practised in and sanctioned by society,[18] we insist only on the epistemological standpoint that the wrongness of such acts was taught or discovered by experience. Undoubtedly, as Jenks himself points out, the destructive effects of the acts were 'apprehended to be the judgment of the gods upon *evil* practices, no less than the thunderstorm and the earthquake.'[19] The recognition of the evil nature of a given act and its description as a judgment of the gods are complementary, not contradictory. For ancient and/or unsophisticated societies did not make the distinction between cosmos – the natural world order – and nomos, the world of man.[20] Indeed, among the Germanic peoples, the first set of wrongs was construed as being against the gods or, after conversion to Christianity, against God.[21] This is generally true about ancient communities:

The penal law of ancient communities was not a law of 'crimes,' (Crimina), but of 'wrongs' (delicta) or torts. Offenses that are now regarded as crimes were treated as torts – not only theft (furtum) but also assault, violent robbery, trespassing, libel and slander, and, more frequently than not, even homicide. According to Athenian laws, ... sins were also punished as torts. This was because offenses against the gods were established in the first ordinances; those against another fellow were the second one, and the idea of an offence against the state was the last to appear within the criminal law, usually in a separate text. Only then did the earliest notion of crime appear.[22]

The above passage bristles with all the technical legal terms of sophisticated legal systems – 'penal,' 'delict,' 'torts,' 'libel,' 'slander,' 'state,' and so on. As noted earlier, we have to eschew such terms and confine ourselves instead to the word 'wrong.' This word lacks the distinct legal connotations of 'delict,' 'torts,' and the like[23] but retains something of the moral undertone that it had in pre-modern legal contexts.

The structure of the chapter is as follows. Without referring to the wrong acts themselves, we consider whether the idea of wrong embedded in Anglo-Saxon laws was 'substantive' or 'procedural.' This is followed by a short description of the nature of 'unsophisticated' thought. Next, we consider the idea of wrong as manifested in Anglo-Saxon laws, and, lastly, the nature of the wrong acts. 'Anglo-Saxon society' means England between roughly 600 and 1066 A.D.

Wrongs: Substantive or Procedural?

The main sources for the idea of wrong among Germanic peoples generally, and Anglo-Saxons in particular, are the materials generated by nineteenth-century historical scholarship. However, the fruits of this scholarship bear the tell-tale signs of their intellectual milieu. On the one hand, the literature is permeated with the romantic idealism which characterized the general intellectual move-ment in that century, and, on the other, the materials are shot through with the attempt to identify the historical roots for the justly lauded and proud achieve-ments of the English people. There were, of course, many different strands and strains in the intellectual skein of the nineteenth century. But the most pervasive was the idea of evolution, which formed, as it were, 'the great hinterland of belief'[24] of that age. This was manifested in legal scholarship in the form of 'legal evolution.' The historical school of jurisprudence derived much strength from the idea.[25]

P. Stein has described the term 'legal evolution' as 'a group of theories which claim to explain change not merely in historical terms, but as proceeding according to certain determinate stages, or in a certain predetermined man-ner.'[26] The wealth of legal historical materials unearthed in the nineteenth cen-tury was interpreted against the background of these evolutionary premises. Caution is therefore required when reliance is put, as it must be, on the available literature. For, although facts are facts, the selection and structural arrangement of facts are often such as to make them speak the language of the historian rather than the language of the time in which they occurred.[27] For instance, one of the fundamental assumptions of nineteenth-century historical scholarship was that the history of law and government is a history of the growth of the power of society over and at the expense of the power of the individual, of the displacement of private power, and of the ascendancy of public power.[28] This assumption is meaningful only if it is remembered that it was made against the background belief that, unless the advancing tide of democratic reforms was confined within manageable limits, the much cherished rights or freedom of the individual would be swept away. Consequently, it was fervently believed that the pedagogical function of historical scholarship was to expose the dangers which lurk in a threatened eclipse or loss of the immemorial rights of English-men or in the dwindling of private power.[29] The polity, the constitution, and, needless to say, the course of legal history were viewed against the backdrop of these assumptions.[30] Thus, J.L. Laughlin asserts:

In the most primitive period of German society, and when through the doctrine of self-help, the individual himself exercised active judicial powers, the punishment of crimes ... lay without the jurisdiction of courts – which did not indeed exist. The German was himself judge and warrior; he levied execution and exacted blood for blood by the sovereign powers vested in himself by that most democratic of all constitutions. The archaic German procedure ... is essentially and radically, characterized by the absolute independence ... by which the individual enforces his right.[31]

Purporting to go back to the earliest period of history and society, such a view of legal procedure is coupled with a nostalgic note of regret for the loss of such 'absolute independence.' Sometimes, however, the community is perceived as tacitly consenting to the procedure:

The community's reaction to anti-social behaviour was governed and dictated by a simple basic drive: *revenge*. In its earliest stages, the group determined that the account to be settled between victim and wrongdoer was a private affair. It was to the victim to extract vengeance; neither the clan, the tribe nor the community as a whole would interfere ... the injured party was therefore victim, judge and executioner ... the burden of protecting his person and property was his and his alone ... private revenge was the initial form of vengeance.[32]

In short, it was generally accepted that, 'the earliest view which we obtain of political society shows us in each case the same system prevailing for the redress of wrongs and punishment of offences, namely, a system of private revenge and personal redress of injuries. Each person avenged, in whatever manner he thought right, a wrong done him by another and the customs of the tribe sanctioned his doing so with impunity.'[33]

Whether the above picture of the enforcement of rights in early society is an accurate portrayal of the legal procedure of unsophisticated societies in general or merely a generalized account of legal procedure based on observations of particular, historical, and unsophisticated societies, the historians of this process of legal procedure were so much concerned with what they took to be its political significance that they tended to downplay or overlook the substantive legal rights that it enforced. For, unless both the individual or clan and the tribe or society as a whole perceived revenge, self-help, or personal redress as a mere process for remedying wrongs, the individual could not possibly by the sheer might of his strength alone (or, as it is said at a later stage, the combined force of the individual and his kinsmen),[34] successfully wreak vengeance on the aggressor. In other words, a shared understanding of 'right' and 'wrong' constituted a hidden substructure upon which was erected the whole process of self-help or revenge; an idea of wrong predated and underlaid the process for obtaining redress. And, while the conditions, constraints, and encrustations from the past and the limitations of a particular age would perforce be evident from the type and number of acts which were perceived as wrong, it is doubtful whether 'the mind of the primitive'[35] differs in any significant respect from the mind of the so-called 'modern' man.

But in the zeal to integrate historical facts into the lattice of their historiographical framework, historical jurists of the nineteenth century allowed the process to overshadow the substance; the substance was submerged under an avalanche of cultural, political, and legal idealism. It has been pointed out that procedure occupied an insignificant place in Anglo-Saxon laws, and this was precisely because these laws served more as clarifications of customs or rulings on customary practices than the expression of a complete body of laws[36] or the expression of the arbitrary will of a political sovereign.[37] By overemphasizing the procedural advantage purportedly enjoyed by the individual in early law and society, nineteenth-century historical jurists failed to draw attention to the fact that private revenge or self-help was only the remedial process which clothed the substantive idea of wrong and its expression in the manifold number of wrong acts. In short, the evolutionary premises of much nineteenth-century historical scholarship engendered an insidious underestimation of the moral sensibilities of men in so-called primitive societies. Naturally, Anglo-Saxon England was considered 'primitive,' or, as we prefer to say, unsophisticated for this purpose. It is necessary to pause here to highlight some pertinent characteristics of unsophisticated thought.

The General Nature of Unsophisticated Thought

This chapter is concerned with the idea of wrong as manifested in the regulation of the actions of members of the same political society, not in the regulation by members of one political group of the actions of those who were perceived as strangers or outsiders. All modern authors agree that the morality in the two cases is markedly different.[38] For instance, writing in the middle of the first century before Christ, Caesar reported that among the German tribal groups 'no discredit attaches to predatory expeditions outside the tribal boundary.'[39] In the Middle Ages, Thomas Aquinas read Caesar's observation as meaning that the Germans did not consider it wrong to steal.[40] This reading must have been prompted by the universalized and absolute morality which the scholastics wanted to promote. A not dissimilar perceptual standpoint is the practice of interpreting the morality of a foreign society from the perspective of the morality of one's immediate society or, which is the same thing, the universalization of the moral concepts of one's immediate society coupled with a belief that the moral concepts of the former are unknown in the other society.[41] This is not to deny that there are some things which are 'absolutely prohibited' and which 'we are obliged to avoid forever.'[42] It merely re-emphasizes that different socio-economic, religious, and political arrangements do give rise to different conceptions of things absolutely prohibited; for these are the sources from which stem legal principles and rules.[43]

As pointed out earlier, in unsophisticated societies life is a structured whole, unseparated and unseparable from the natural order. Further, what is perceived as the natural order is itself determined by the religious, socio-economic, and political practices of a society. A corollary of this is that acts which tend to disturb the natural (social) equilibrium are condemned as wrong. Indeed, it is the religious, social, economic, and political-institutional arrangements of a society, whether primitive, medieval, or modern, which alone enable us to identify acts that are discountenanced and, therefore, regarded as wrong.

The morality of any political society or group is inevitably concerned with fashioning legal rules to promote 'social arrangements for continued existence, not with those of a suicide club.'[44] It follows that however much societies differ, and, however warlike, savage, or barbarous a given society may be, the legal system almost invariably affords 'minimum forms of protection for persons, property and promises.'[45] One of the distinctive features of unsophisticated societies is that such minimum forms of protection for persons, property, and promises are construed in absolute terms. This is so even when the 'masks of the law'[46] are used, for, in unsophisticated societies where the fortunes of life were such that a slave could, within living memory, become an influential figure, there could be no room for metaphysical inventions such as Aristotle's[47] notion of 'slave by nature' or, for that matter, the Judeo-Christian doctrine[48] of slavery as an integral part of a divinely ordained political, economic, and social world. Hence, in unsophisticated societies, the masks of the law were never so opaque as to obscure the humanity of those who were unfortunate enough to fall into the lowest classes in the society, that is, slaves and servants.[49] Of course, as will be seen shortly, in Anglo-Saxon England compensation for wrongs done to slaves or servants were paid not to the victims themselves but to their owners, but there is nothing in the laws to warrant the inference that slaves and/or servants were left to the whimsical caprices of their owners or masters.[50]

Though this feature is shared by unsophisticated and some sophisticated societies alike, the former tends to be imbued with a strong conviction in symmetry usually derived from the order in the physical world; the order in the physical world is projected into the moral and political life. In early societies with strong and centralized religion, the socio-economic, political, and legal institutions and practices are often gathered under the mantle of divine mandate.[51] However,   in early societies with no centrally organized religion, the existing socio-economic, political, and legal institutions are perceived primarily as reflecting the best or most advantageous or natural order of things. This was the case with the Germanic tribesmen described by Caesar.[52] In both cases we are confronted with a status-based socio-political and legal-economic model. (History does not extend beyond such a model[53] and, with the probable exception of the flicker of light in the eighteenth century, philosophy, as well as literature, affords no counter-example.[54]) The model continued to obtain even after the latter class of societies had been 'converted from polytheism to monotheism, from chaotic Nature-worships to "the religion of the book."'[55] Until the later Middle Ages, the Church, the great moral impresario in European societies, 'was almost wholly integrated with the social, political and economic life of society. It did not stand opposite the political order but within it. Religion was united with politics and economics and law.'[56] The Church undoubtedly influenced the polity and policy of the law, but Anglo-Saxon laws, beginning with those made by the Kentish King Aethelberht in 602 A.D. or thereabouts, were 'only slightly inoculated by the Canon Law.'[57]

When the Germanic tribesmen first appeared in 'real history'[58] they were still a rude and barbarous people. And they were still very much in a rude and barbarous state when those who coveted the English island (or, as tradition says, those who were invited by the war-weary Britons) – the Angles, Saxons, and Jutes – invaded Britain. The idea of wrong entertained by men still in a barbarous age may be of interest to students of comparative social anthropology,[59] but it is of little or no relevance to the crystallized idea of wrong entertained by the same people long after they had ceased to be nomadic huntsmen and largely become a settled, sedentary, or agricultural people. Neither the roots nor the foliage of Anglo-Saxon laws and institutions are to be sought in the woods of Germany, as many a historian avidly sought to prove in the last century. For, however excellent may have been the features of what were proudly called 'Germanic institutions,' they were fashioned and fitted for men who were principally nomadic people, unaccustomed to agrarian or fixed permanent settlements, with each tribe led by its warrior-chiefs.[60] Kingship, as a political institution, developed in Anglo-Saxon England, and its development was made possible by the circumstances of the migration to the British island, the subsequent long drawn-out wars with the Romano-Britons, and internal strife and restlessness.[61]

It cannot be gainsaid that Anglo-Saxon laws contain large amounts of identifiable customs and practices and modes of dealing with wrong acts and wrongdoers dating to an earlier place and age. But we reject the supposition that the people had merely changed soils, fitfully received a new religion (with not infrequent relapses into heathen practices),[62] and added new activities to their vocations without any corresponding changes in their manners, laws, customs, and institutions. It may well be that the changes in the customs and modes of dealing with wrongdoers were not as dramatic as the transformation in political institutions, but to assume that later Anglo-Saxon manners, customs, and institutions were mere replications of those described by Tacitus six hundred years earlier is to ascribe too much resilience and tenacity to things which, by their very nature, change in tandem with the changing fashions of society. On the other hand, to assume that certain features or mode of legal procedure mark a particular age as one stage or another in an evolutionary process is as inimical to a proper understanding of the age as the one that posits static institutions.[63] It is against this background that one must examine the idea of wrong as manifested in Anglo-Saxon dooms – as laws were then called.

Wrong and Wrong Acts in Anglo-Saxon Laws

In later Anglo-Saxon England, when the people were neither the fiery men depicted by Tacitus nor yet what the Romantics would call effeminate landtillers, 'the evils most frequently calling for remedy were manslaying, wounding and cattle-stealing.'[64] Although private war was still recognized as a lawful means of settling disputes (and indeed continued as such until well into the Anglo-Norman era), by the time we first catch a glimpse of Anglo-Saxon dooms 'the sword of punishment had been wrested ... out of the hand of the vindictive individual'[65] and public authority had been so far consolidated that it could be said that 'Anglo-Saxon justice was directed from above.'[66] By the time of the Danish invasions (in the ninth century onwards), public authority, even in case of killing, forbade vengeance before or when the offender offered acceptable compensation.[67]

Ever since attention was first directed at Anglo-Saxon legal institutions, laws, and customs, scholars have been struck by the extreme minuteness of the tariff system of compensation for all manner of injuries found in the 'laws of the earliest English kings.'[68] We have already noted that Anglo-Saxon England was a status-based society. The amount of compensation payable for wrongs done to the person or property of individuals varied according to the status of the victim. From the *wergild*[69] (payable by a slayer) to the *wite* (payable for breach of the peace or violation of the protection of the person who had control over the place where the wrong was committed) to the *bot* (payable as compensation to the person wronged), the compensation or fine was carefully calibrated to accord with the status of the victim on the one hand and the magnitude of the harm on the other. For instance, while 'theft of God's property and the Church' attracted twelvefold compensation, theft of a bishop's property attracted elevenfold compensation; a priest's, ninefold; a deacon's, sixfold; a clerk's, threefold. Breach of the peace of a church or a meeting place attracted twofold compensation (Aethelberht 1). 'If a thumb is struck off, 20 shillings shall be paid as compensation. If a thumb nail is knocked off, 3 shillings shall be paid as compensation. If a man strikes off a forefinger, he shall pay 9 shillings compensation; middle finger, 4 shillings; a "ring finger," 6 shillings; a little finger, 11 shillings; for the nails of each of the above-mentioned fingers, 1 shilling' (Aethelberht 54, 55; Alfred 56–60). 'For the slightest disfigurement, 3 shillings, and for a greater 6 shillings' (Aethelberht 56). The laws are also replete with examples where the status of the offender called for a higher fine or compensation than would ordinarily be the case.[70] The important thing to note, however, is that while the scale of compensation was variable, and could in fact be changed by legislation, the wrongs that attracted compensation were neither the product nor the subject of legislation, in the modern sense of the word.[71] Nor were they entirely the product of spontaneous custom. Rather, they were an amalgam of customs and rulings in individual cases. Indeed, it has been pointed out that the details of the laws betrayed their origin in arbitration or rulings in actual cases.[72] (We will return to this issue in the next section.) The fact that compensation was payable for such an exhaustive number of minutely detailed harms testifies to the extensiveness of the idea of wrong in Anglo-Saxon England. To what degree the *extensiveness* of the idea of wrong was due to the influence of the Christian religion cannot be determined.

Reference has already been made to the fact that in unsophisticated societies the law affords a modicum of protection for persons, irrespective of the status of the individual in the social hierarchy. This is amply illustrated in the extant laws of the earliest English kings: Aethelberht 10 provides for fifty-shillings compensation (presumably to the king) 'if a man lies with a maiden belonging to the king.' If she is a grinding slave, twenty-five shillings; and if she is a slave of the third class, twelve shillings (Aethelberht 11). Cap. 16 of the same laws provides that 'if a man lies with a commoner's serving maid, he shall pay 6 shillings compensation; if he lies with a slave of the second class, he shall pay 50 sceattas compensation; if with one of the third class, 30 sceattas.' Cap. 89 fixes the sum to be paid for robbing a slave on the highway at three shillings. And cap. 85 provides that 'if a man lies with the woman of a servant, during the lifetime of the husband, he shall pay a twofold compensation.' Although this clause did not say so, a portion of the 'twofold compensation' probably went to the servant-husband of the woman. Alfred 25 stipulates five-shillings compensation and a fine of sixty shillings 'if anyone rapes the slave of a commoner,' and if 'a slave rapes a slave, castration shall be required as compensation'! Whatever may have been the drawbacks of a status-based society, these and several other provisions scattered throughout the laws are sufficient to support the conclusion that there was an understanding that it was unacceptable for such wrongs to be inflicted upon even slaves and servants.

Of course, one might retort that had no provision for the payment of compensation in those cases been made, it would simply have meant that the persons who would have been entitled to receive compensation would have been compelled to take steps to avenge the wrongs. But that is to shift the problem a step back, for, as noted earlier, if there was no agreement that an act was wrong, the question of private revenge or self-help would not arise; self-help was only a matter of procedure not substance.

The detailed descriptions and large number of the acts that attracted compensation or fine in one form or another warrant two overriding conclusions. The first is that the laws were designed for the express purpose of assuring the wholeness or physical integrity of the individual. The second is that the laws were informed by a related conception of what the legal rules should be in order to conserve or preserve the wholesomeness of the community. As far as the Anglo-Saxons were concerned, the individual and the community were pre-existing entities; they did not engage in such speculations as whether the individual is prior to the community or vice versa. In short, it did not occur to them to pose the kind of question about the individual or the community that would nowadays be instantly recognized as a chicken-and-egg issue. Nor were they given to abstractions. In other words, there is nothing to suggest that there was at that time any conception of hypostatized or abstract creatures called 'individual' and 'community.' Rather, these terms referred to concrete individuals and the concrete community.

The twin notions of wholeness and wholesomeness capture the realization that, within the limits of one's acquired social status, the integrity of the person and the safety of the property of the individual are to be preserved inviolate. Applied to the community, these notions meant that civic tranquillity and freedom from external aggression were a sine qua non for the peaceful co-existence and continued well-being of members of the community as a viable political unit. Any act that diminished significantly the physical integrity of the person and the security of property, or that was manifestly antithetical to the conservation of the wholesomeness of the community, was considered a species of wrong. The main object of Anglo-Saxon laws was the promotion of peace, order, and stability.

The manifestation of these ideas is copiously exemplified in the laws. There were provisions for compensation for such obvious wrongs as homicide, theft, and robbery. Compensation was payable for any injury or harm which in any significant way detracted from individual honour and dignity. A few examples will suffice. Compensation was payable for seizing a man by the hair,[73] if a bone was laid bare or damaged,[74] if an ear was pierced or lacerated or struck off,[75] if the nose was pierced or lacerated,[76] and if the thumb or any of the four other fingers or toes or their nails was wounded.[77] For the slightest disfigurement,[78] for striking another on the nose with the fist, whether or not it left a bruise,[79] compensation was payable. Indeed, the laws were so detailed that each tooth had its own price.[80] Thus, the compensation for wounding varied according not only to which limb or part of the body or organ was wounded but also to the length or depth of the wound.[81] As well, the laws extended protection to livestock. For instance, it was a wrong to fleece one's own sheep before midsummer[82] – an obvious protection for sheep from cold.

The same notions of wholeness and wholesomeness undergird the provisions for payment of compensation for damages and injuries done to another's property. Again, a few examples will suffice. If a freeman broke the fence round another man's enclosure or made his way into a fenced enclosure and/or if any property was seized therein, or if anyone damaged the enclosure of a dwelling,[83] compensation was payable. Compensation payable for injuries done to the oxen or cow of another was as carefully graded as that for injuries done to individuals.[84]

The homestead was as much protected as the peace of every freeman, and any act that could lead to a disturbance or breach of the peace, private or public, attracted compensation. Thus, 'if the King calls his liege to him and anyone molests them there, or if one man slays another in the King's premises or slays a smith in the King's service or a messenger belonging to the King,'[85] the offender was to pay compensation. The fine for breaking into the fortified premises of the King was 120 shillings; into those of an archbishop, 90 shillings; into those of a bishop or of an ealdorman, 60 shillings; into those of a man whose *wergeld* was 1200 shillings, 30 shillings; into those of a man whose *wergeld* was 600 shillings, 15 shillings. The fine for breaking through a commoner's fence was 5 shillings.[86] In Alfred's laws, to fight or draw one's weapon in the King's hall attracted capital punishment, unless 'the King is willing to forgive him.'[87] Violating the King's protection, or that of an archbishop, bishop, or ealdorman, all attracted both compensation for the wrong to the injured person as well as a fine for the violation of the protection of the person who had control or guardianship over the place or the victim.[88] To fight at a meeting in the presence of an ealdorman of the King, or to disturb the meeting by drawing a weapon or to fight in the house of a commoner, also attracted fines.[89]

It is clear from the foregoing examples that, however unruly the people may have been,[90] and however frequently people may have defied the law or perpetrated one kind of wrong or another with apparent impunity,[91] there was a consensus (at least among the leading members of the society)[92] that such acts diminished the wholeness and wholesomeness of the individual and the community, and, accordingly, were wrong acts. Assuredly, Anglo-Saxon laws did not attempt absolute prohibition of the enumerated wrong acts; rather, the laws provided that if such things were done then the offender or aggressor would be liable to pay compensation to the victim as well as assuage the hurt feelings of the man-of-authority, or, as in the later laws, pay the ultimate penalty of death unless the King spared his life. Thus, the idea of wrong was tied to any act that actually or potentially detracted from the wholeness or wholesomeness of either the individual or the community. It follows from this that the number or type of wrong acts was not fixed. In short, the notion that the law should preserve the integrity of the individual and promote the safety and tranquillity of the community made possible a progressive elaboration and prohibition of any act that was inimical to the attainment of such goals. The compiler of the laws of King Henry I succinctly captured the problem when he noted that, because there were many ways of doing or going wrong and so much profusion of evil, and because new tricks for inflicting injury were continually being devised, it was impossible for the laws to anticipate all wrongs.[93] The most cursory examination of the later Anglo-Saxon laws supports this assertion.

In the Germania described by Tacitus, there was virtually no commercial activity. As well, in cases where compensation was an acceptable settlement for wrongs, such compensation was paid in horses or cattle – a clear indication that coinage was unknown. However, by the time of the first English dooms, pecuniary mulct had replaced compensation in kind, and commerce grew steadily in the course of the centuries.

In Anglo-Saxon England, no less than in modern times, trade could not thrive unless commercial transactions were secure and promises were accorded protection by the law. Nor could economic activities prosper if the means of exchange were subject to the vagaries of moneymakers. We are accustomed to standard state-backed money but the situation was different in early times: 'At its beginning, the only coins in general circulation were small pieces bearing designs which were determined by the fancy of individual moneyers ... In the course of Offa's reign [in the eighth century] this informal currency was superseded in every part of England but Northumbria by a new type of coin ... bearing almost universally the names of the king and the responsible moneyer.'[94] Base money is certainly detrimental to commerce. The introduction of money and the development of rudimentary commerce, therefore, called for laws to regulate such activities.

Accordingly, beginning with slender provisions in the earlier laws, provisions relating to the regulation of commerce and coinage rose to a profusion of detailed and repeated rules by the early eleventh century. Initially, the law was content to require sales transactions to be carried out before witnesses[95] or to promote good faith by ensuring that the subject matter of sale transactions (principally cattle) was wholesome and without any concealed blemish.[96] The later laws go so far as to require a man who sets out to make any purchase to inform his neighbours of the object of his journey and, on his return, to declare who was present as witness when he made his purchases.[97] Piracy, which used to be the pastime of many tribesmen, was increasingly frowned upon: merchant ships were protected from pillage.[98] The whole of IV Aethelred deals with the regulation and control of commerce and fines for evading tolls and dues. In Canute's time, any sale transaction that involved anything over four pence in value had to be witnessed by four trustworthy men, whether the purchase was made within a town or in open country.[99]

Coining and counterfeiting made their appearance as wrongs as soon as coinage became the exclusive preserve of limited and identifiable political authorities.[100] Thus III Aethelred provides that 'every moneyer who is accused of striking false coins, *after it was forbidden*, shall go to the triple ordeal; if he is guilty, he shall be slain.' And the law was further strengthened under IV Aethelred, which, as observed above, dealt exclusively with commercial topics. The influence of Christianity is particularly noticeable in VIII Athelred 17, which forbade Sunday marketing. Weights and measures, which could not conceivably have been the subject matter of law in a non-commercial society, also made their appearance in the extant laws as soon as standard though crude weights and measures were established in order to discourage dishonest trade practices.[101]

The Nature of Anglo-Saxon Wrongs

The foregoing discussion has deliberately avoided a sophisticated or romantic explication of the moral sentiments discernible in Anglo-Saxon dooms. In particular, it avoids the sort of exposition that leads to debates over whether the Anglo-Saxons distinguished between crime and tort, private and public wrongs, and among the proper functions of compensation, fines, and punishments.[102] So far as we can see, these analytical categories were neither known nor employed by Anglo-Saxons themselves. Moreover, as Sally Moore points out, while the features of the law that such debates focus on undoubtedly existed in Anglo-

Saxon society, 'the meanings which they are given are in terms of a traditional conception of the developed legal arrangements and their opposites in pre-industrial systems.'[103] The evolutionary premiss or the romantic fervour of those who participate in such controversy skews their elucidation of the acts whose commission attracted compensation in Anglo-Saxon England. But what is the nature of these wrongs? Did these wrong acts exemplify 'a customary idea of wrong'?

Commentators differ on this issue. There are at least three different approaches. The first school of thought is represented primarily by students of comparative anthropology, who combine the theoretical framework of the idea of legal evolution with the postulates of the positivist theory of law. They see legal history through the prism of the political institutional arrangements through which laws are filtered into the society.[104] Therefore, they are inclined to conceptualize all laws (including early laws) as legislation, in a strictly positivistic sense of the word, and to dismiss with the wave of a hand any reference to any substantive concept of right found in some of the early dooms.[105]

The second school of thought is distinguished by a fervent desire to demonstrate the indigenous character of the wrongs found in Anglo-Saxon dooms, particularly in the earliest ones. It asserts that the idea of right found in Anglo-Saxon dooms is peculiar to the people, in a Savignyian sense of that phrase. Consequently, students of this school discount any external influence, especially the impact of the Christian religion and the role of kings, on the content of these laws.[106]

The third approach is neither wholly Austinian nor wholly Savignyian. Rather, it concedes that the wrongs found in the dooms were wrongs and were recognized as such long before they were collected or reduced into written form. It also recognizes the changes brought about by the presence of new factors such as kingship and its role as a political institution, as well as the introduction and institutionalization of a new religion.[107] But these undeniable historical facts are sometimes downgraded when, as in the case of A.W.B. Simpson, it is concluded that the first English dooms were aspirational only, 'not a compulsory and enforceable set of regulations.'[108]

A.S. Diamond is representative of the first school of thought. He dismisses the references to *aew, aewe* – the Anglo-Saxon word for 'right'[109] – which occur in the laws of Hlothere and Eadric, and also in those of Ine, as 'later superscriptions to the laws.'[110] He claims that, though a Kentishman of the time of Aethelberht was familiar with the idea of law or right, in all probability he understood it in customary terms only, that is, doing that which was customarily right, rather than that which was morally right or demanded by a moral law.[111] It seems that this is a clear instance of the type of erroneous conclusion which arises whenever the legal ideas of one age are forced into the mould of thought of another. Diamond collapses his own working version of juridical positivism into a cosmological and epistemological standpoint. He then attempts to make the facts fit into the procrustean bed of his theoretical framework. Thus, that 'which is customarily right' is transformed into that which has been duly legislated by the political sovereign, not that which is thought to be morally right or is culturally right. Yet, in the absence of any evidence to the contrary, there is no compelling reason to accept this definition of that 'which is customarily right.' The dooms were drawn from existing custom or usages; however, in bygone days and from the perspective of the people, the notion was that laws were conceived by kings either spontaneously or through divine prompting.[112] As well, that the kings and their advisers also believed themselves to be doing the will of God on earth (at least after the piecemeal introduction of the Christian religion) may be surmised from the fact that in most cases it was the Church's support for the institution of kingship that facilitated the transformation of kingship from a military institution into an essentially political one.[113] The position of tribal military chieftains must have been precarious, especially during the incessant wars with Gallo-Romans, but by the time of the extant dooms 'the pagan-war chief of early times has developed into the Christian leader of a Christian people';[114] at least, that is the impression given by the dooms. It would be rash, therefore, to dismiss the notion that what was customarily right was, at the same time, construed or understood as what was morally right.

Those who adopt what we have called a Savignyian approach maintain that in Anglo-Saxon England a man could 'find the law by examining his own conscience' and that the laws merely 'reminded the conscience.'[115] This raises at least two problems. First, Savignyian commentators refuse to ascribe any creative role to the institutional processes through which laws become crystallized. Like the evolutionary theory to which it is closely associated, the Savignyian approach postulates that the law develops by itself spontaneously from the consciousness of the people. According to this school of thought, then, what we usually call 'law-makers' or 'law-men' are but mere amanuenses, that is, passive transcribers of custom. But was that ever the case? The answer to that question must be in the negative. Secondly, the claim that the law merely reminds the conscience contains a hidden form of circularity. For the law that is found by examining the conscience is itself the product of custom, and the wrongs that the laws exhort the conscience to abhor are in turn customary wrongs!

None of these approaches tells the full story. What later became reduced into written dooms were largely, though not wholly, the cumulative result of the exercise initially of arbitral and later of legislative functions. Sir Henry Maine reminds us that the most ancient courts established by mankind were arbitral in nature,[116] and, in spite of the gradual consolidation of central political authority, in Anglo-Saxon times the idea of separating the legislative from the judicial or arbitral powers was unknown.[117] It follows, therefore, that the end product of a joint exercise of legislative and judicial or arbitral functions cannot be appropriately described in conventional positivist, evolutionist, or historicist vocabulary.[118]

A.W.B. Simpson's suggestion that the first written law, 'the laws of Ethelbert,' was designed 'to provide, in the form of fixed money payments, an alternative to retaliation and the feud' is clearly correct, but to attribute this change to the ameliorating influence of the new Christian religion claims too much. In particular, it is misleading to assert that the first English doom was meant to introduce the new idea that it was not wrong to take money instead of blood.[119] Compensation for lesser wrongs used to be made in horses and cattle, but that was long before money became generally known and its use widespread.[120] By the time of the written dooms, the 'primitive' conscience had become so thoroughly accustomed to being salved by gold that compensation for injuries had come 'to be treated in a perfectly business-like fashion.'[121] Simpson is surely right in alluding to the momentous entry of the Christian religion into Anglo-Saxon society, but he seems to have unduly magnified the extent of its immediate influence.

Conclusion

From earliest times, human beings grouped in tribal bands have held ideas about 'right' and 'wrong.' The Teutonic tribal communities that one encounters in the pages of history have all crossed the divide separating the Cyclopean or the Hobbesian construct from a political state, thereafter becoming small tribal societies with definite procedures for remedying wrongs done to individuals on the one hand and the community on the other. Anglo-Saxon England was no exception. It was a tribal society imbued with all the characteristics peculiar to societies that had made the transition from a nomadic and chilvaric lifestyle to a pastoral and agricultural one. The introduction of a new religion, so different from the erstwhile heathenism practised by the people, combined with an incipient feudal structure to wreak dramatic changes in the legal and political institutions of Anglo-Saxon England. Assuredly, changes in the mode of dealing with wrongs and wrongdoers were not as profound as the changes in political and legal institutions. The system of compensation in kind for wrongs that prevailed in Germania had been replaced by a system of pecuniary compensation in Anglo-Saxon England. And, instead of customary ideas of right and wrong which used to be transmitted orally and carried by the various tribesmen in their sporadic migrations, the history of Anglo-Saxon laws opens with the written laws of Kent, which 'say little about rights, much about wrongs.'[122]

But there is no reason to believe that the wrongs spelled out in the written laws of those days sprang out, like the bird of Minerva from Jupiter's head, spontaneously from the cranium of a Hobbesian sovereign. Rather, they were the cumulative result of a long process of customary practices, arbitration in individual cases, and legislative activities of the leading members of society. They manifest a markedly anthropocentric idea of wrong characteristic of unsophisticated societies bent on fostering internal cohesion, peace, and tranquillity. Consequently, the idea of wrong was tied to anything that actually or potentially detracted from the wholeness or wholesomeness of the individual or the community. This made possible a continual augmentation of the list of wrongs or wrong acts.

In contrast to the historical interpretation set out here, the trend in historical scholarship, so far as it relates to the idea of wrong in Anglo-Saxon times, has been to structure and interpret the facts of legal history in a way that would ensure that the evolutionary assumptions of the investigators are invariably vindicated. The idea of wrong discernible from the surviving materials is somewhat overshadowed by the attempt to chart the course of an assumed progressive movement from the rudimentary moral ideas of early times to the mature moral sentiments embedded in modern legal concepts and legal categories. From a procedural point of view, the course of legal history is viewed largely as the story of the process by which the individual was stripped of the power to enforce his own right and the consequent monopoly of that power by public authorities.

The position from a substantive standpoint is more ambiguous. On the one hand, those who emphasize the procedural advantage purportedly enjoyed by the individual in early law end up saying very little on the nature of the substantive rights and, therefore, the idea of wrong that lurked in the interstice of self-help, revenge, or retaliation. On the other hand, those who claim that such rights as were enforced by the individual were spontaneously generated by custom fail to articulate how the substantive rights became crystallized and enforced as such through the instrumentality of identifiable political institutions.

The tenor of the foregoing discussion is that, however much the Anglo-Saxon mind may have been conditioned and constrained by the particular historical circumstances of the age, all remedial processes (be they self-help, revenge, arbitration, or public intervention) 'proceed[ed] from the notion of a right emphatically recognized by the community.'[123] At the time when it was the individual (either alone or aided by his kinsmen) who enforced his rights, both the individual and the community understood and perceived self-help as 'the collection of what is due, the correction of a wrong.'[124] When the individual was gradually stripped of the power of private redress, and the power to enforce rights was deposited with and exercised by public authorities, the underlying principle was the substitution, in place of the anarchist system of private redress, of a mode of enforcement that was more conducive to the promotion of civic cohesion and tranquillity. As the Anglo-Saxons became more and more accustomed to a settled lifestyle, to agriculture and commerce, private interests coalesced with public interests to strengthen the hand of public authorities.

It is manifest that the number of wrongs progressively increased in Anglo-Saxon England. It is equally certain that the remedy for most wrong acts was monetary compensation. What is not evident from Anglo-Saxon laws is whether the occurrence of a wrong act invariably attracted compensation. For instance, was a person liable to pay compensation even though he accidentally knocked out another's tooth? Or was he liable to make amends if, and only if, he caused the injury deliberately or negligently?

One of the stylistic features of Anglo-Saxon laws is that they are couched in the conditional form. With few exceptions, the laws eschew imperative language. Some commentators have taken this as evidence that the dooms were not the handiwork of a Hobbesian sovereign.[125] We have already advanced reasons why it would be misleading to perceive Anglo-Saxon laws through the prism of the imperative theory of law.

The conditional form also betrays the fact that the laws were not concerned with ascertaining the circumstances or discriminating between different circumstances in which a wrong act occurred for the purpose of determining liability to make compensation. In other words, the dooms are silent on one of the perennial issues in the idea of wrong, namely, the question of the basis for responsibility for wrong acts. To use the same example as before, while it is one thing to know that it is wrong for a person to knock out another's tooth, it is quite another to say that he is liable to compensate the victim for that wrong act. The former question focuses on what is meant by wrong or wrong acts; the latter focuses on the basis for holding a person responsible for the wrong act he commits. The two issues may be treated, jointly or severally, as raising moral or legal questions; but, while one raises a 'non-technical' question (Is X a Y?), the other poses a 'technical' one (How Y is X?). Put differently, a moral or legal order is a prerequisite for a technical approach to moral or legal issues. This chapter has been concerned with the first of these issues.

2

The Idea of Wrong in Anglo-Saxon Law II

Until recently, the question of the basis of responsibility in Anglo-Saxon law was addressed by two groups of jurists. The first group was led by Henry Wigmore,[1] the second by Henry Maine.[2] Both groups approached the issue with a strong conviction that early law possessed a measure of doctrinal unity comparable to that which modern law is taken to display. They therefore sifted through the legal materials of Anglo-Saxon society for evidence that would disclose the sole organizing principle of responsibility. Not surprisingly, they found the object whose existence they had predicted: in Anglo-Saxon England 'a man acts at his peril.' For instance, Pollock and Maitland maintained that Anglo-Saxon society had neither the means nor the inclination to distinguish between intentional and non-intentional wrongs. According to them, all that was required for responsibility in Anglo-Saxon society was that the actor had, in a crude 'but for' theory of causation, inflicted harm or injury on another.[3]

They marshalled many arguments in support of this supposed rule. First, they claimed, by way of general observation, that early law was one of torts not crimes, and that its main purpose was to compensate the victims of harm. Second, they stated that the notion of crime could not and did not arise until two conditions were satisfied. These were (a) the emergence of a centralized political authority and the construal of a species of wrongs as being primarily offences against the public at large, to be prosecuted and punished as such by public authority; and (b) the refinement and adoption of a discriminatory attitude towards intentionally or negligently inflicted harm on the one hand and accidentally caused harm on the other. Underlying the writings of the first group of jurists referred to above was an implicit assumption that neither of these two conditions was satisfied in early societies generally and Anglo-Saxon society in particular.

Although it was seldom made explicit in their writings, the first group was particularly influenced by certain philosophical assumptions. These were assumptions about the origin and nature of political society and the nature and character of man. Such unarticulated assumptions significantly coloured their interpretation of the course of legal-historical development. For instance, Wigmore arrayed a dazzling amount of evidence to support the theory that liability in early law was strict or absolute because, among other factors, man was, until comparatively recent times, only slightly better than a beast. John McLaren's summation of the tenets of the beliefs of this group of jurists can hardly be surpassed:

[T]hese jurists characterized 'primitive' man as living in a Hobbesian twilight, unable to bridle his passions, largely devoid of reason and intellect, the slave of barbaric superstitions, terrified by witchcraft, and, insofar as he was able to devise rules by which to govern himself, caught in a vicious cycle of rigid, formalistic, and immutable injunctions. In particular, he was incapable, either because of the dominance of his negative emotions, or because of the limitations of his own ingenuity, of distinguishing between the intentional, negligent, and the purely accidental causation of harm in deciding the basic issue of liability or the secondary question of its degree. As a consequence, liability was absolute. From these dark chapters of legal history mankind liberated himself as, with his gradual transformation into a civilized being, reason was progressively substituted for animalistic urges and fault was developed by the courts as its juridical manifestation.[4]

Many members of this group of Anglo-American historical jurists and legal historians were obsessed with the idea that the modern legal concepts and categories represent not just a phase but the ultimate or final step in an evolutionary process that started from a complete lack of morality. They saw their task as consisting essentially in demonstrating the absolute superiority of modern moral and legal categories. In order to do this, they found it necessary, logical, and expedient to explicate the theory of the 'wild beast in his den'[5] in all its nakedness. In short, they stripped man of all reason and intellect. Once the beast was so denuded the thesis could then be maintained, without necessarily showing at what point in the evolutionary process the creature acquired reason and intellect, why the meaning of modern legal concepts and categories represents the triumph of a set of superior moral ideas over earlier and necessarily inferior legal concepts and categories. To those who subscribe to this account of the state of man and early legal and moral ideas, the inevitable conclusion is that 'strict' or 'absolute' liability prevailed in early law generally and Anglo-Saxon England in particular.

The second group of jurists, 'the opposing camp of relativists,'[6] shrunk from the galling depiction of man as an essentially beastly creature, devoid of reason and intellect. Instead, they subscribed to a modified set of evolutionary assumptions. They insisted that it could not be maintained, without doing violence to historical facts, that the state of man at a particular epoch in any way resembled the picture painted by the other school, or, even if it did, that this phase belonged to prehistoric times. To them, man has always been man, and, although his reason and intellect may remain largely dormant, not sharply developed, or clouded by irrational and superstitious beliefs, it is preposterous to argue that man was at any historical point largely devoid of reason and intellect. Hence, they concluded that it is absurd to insist that early law did not distinguish at all between intentionally and non-intentionally caused harms. Again, McLaren offers an unsurpassable precis of the kernel of thought of this group of jurists:

... [T]his group of jurists was ready to credit 'primitive' man with possessing a modicum of common sense which manifested itself in variations in emotional response depending upon the moral quality of the injuror's actions. In the words of Holmes' pungent metaphor, 'even a dog distinguishes between being stumbled over and kicked.' Accordingly, there was some perception of the distinction between harm willfully, negligently or accidentally caused ... [But] their acceptance of the proposition that the fault of the actor was a relevant factor was not erected into an article of faith. Rather it was characterized as a recognizable element in the largely undifferentiated strains which came together in the 'primitive' reaction to injurious conduct ...[7]

Notwithstanding the differences between these two groups, one thing stands out clearly, and that is that their respective theses revolved around the affirmation or denial of the proposition that early law was imbued with a single unifying principle of responsibility. This leads to obvious difficulties. In the first place, it casts the issue in terms which suggest that early law was necessarily organized after the fashion of law in modern societies. The insidious effect of such an approach is that it compels the investigators to probe the question and couch their answers *as if* early societies employed the same analytical tools in addressing the moral and legal issues of their time. Second, it allows the investigators to limit themselves to a purely technical question, namely '*how* "primitive" man ordered his relations, as opposed to *why* he ordered them in a particular way.'[8] The restrictive scope permitted by the technical nature of the question could shield from view certain circumstances or situations which would have shown that 'some apparent examples of absolute liability can in fact be regarded as cases in which there is a well-understood danger of intentional killing'[9] or harm. Third, the evolutionary assumptions of the investigators has the pernicious result of committing them in advance to a particular way of looking at early societies. Because their underlying assumption was that the course of legal history has necessarily been towards more and more refinement of legal principles, they thought only as they *could* and not necessarily as the evidence dictated. For instance, even a cautious writer such as Winfield, who conceded that 'there is no reason to suppose that in early times English law had any subtle analysis of the mental element in liability,'[10] nevertheless felt himself compelled to say that the Anglo-Saxon legal order sometimes groped 'its way along with a subconscious grasp of the differences between "intent," "negligence," and "unavoidable harm."' And he concluded that in the end it failed 'to apply very consistently such dim ideas as it possess[ed].'[11] The main object of the disputants was to demonstrate that the course of legal development has been necessarily a movement from lower to higher stages of development, and this made it impossible for them to put the issues involved in their proper context.

The difficulties raised by this approach provoked reactions from later commentators. These varied from attempts to reinterpret the data supplied by the foregoing groups of jurists in the light of evidence from contemporary 'primitive' societies to modifications and sometimes outright rejection of the conclusions reached by the earlier authors. A review of the literature and a survey of the reactions generated by new evaluations and facts from comparable contemporary 'primitive' societies reveal that there are at least five different though not necessarily exclusive ways of looking at the issue of the basis of liability in early law generally, and Anglo-Saxon law in particular.

First, some scholars hold that in early law liability was 'absolute' or 'strict,' that is to say, that Anglo-Saxon law did not make any distinction whatsoever between intentionally, negligently, or accidentally inflicted harm. Henry Wigmore[12] is the most ardent upholder of this thesis. The second way of looking at the issue is an attenuated version of the one just mentioned. These scholars hold that, generally speaking, Anglo-Saxon law did not make a distinction between wilfully and accidentally caused harm and, therefore, that liability was by and large strict or absolute.[13] The third group of scholars sees traces of the beginning of the idea of responsibility based on the presence or absence of intention in Anglo-Saxon law but they do not go as far as saying that this was in any way determinative.[14] Rather, they see 'intention' as a mere 'intensifier of punishment.'[15] A fourth group maintains that intention originally played a large role in establishing responsibility in early law and that strict or absolute responsibility was a consequence of a relapse into barbarism or of the litigiousness or covetousness occasioned by the advent of a system of pecuniary compensation.[16] Finally, there are those who claim that it is altogether inappropriate to foist on early law and 'primitive' societies the analytical scheme of modern legal refinements. They insist that the modern 'sole-basis of liability approach' is utterly unsuitable for the explication of early law. As well, they maintain that the phenomenon of strict liability which the earlier investigators purportedly discovered in early law merely illustrates the pre-modern notion of the moral basis of responsibility. John McLaren,[17] G. MacCormack,[18] and Sally Moore[19] fall into the last category. Their approach is more illuminating and allows for better appreciation of the facts. It underlies what follows.

Like many other 'primitive' societies, Anglo-Saxon England was originally a tribal, agricultural society where private war or feuding were lawful means of redressing wrongs.[20] Initially, the tribe – a group of kinsmen – was the institutional unit of legal action and legal responsibility. All legal wrongs were wrongs not against the individual as such but against the family as a whole.[21] The legal system was thus originally a system of tribal justice.[22] Strictly speaking, there was no 'criminal law';[23] the 'primitive' conception was one of wrongs and nothing else.[24]

Like the Hebrew law, which began as a tribal system of justice and ended with individual personal responsibility,[25] Anglo-Saxon society and laws began as a tribal system and were later leavened by Judeo-Christian teaching.[26] The kinship or tribal structure (which indeed never blossomed fully in Anglo-Saxon England as it did in other communities on the continent[27]) gradually gave way to a feudal society.[28] Feudalism, of course, implies a stratified social system based on a tenurial relationship between landowners (lords) and their tenants.[29] And 'as feudalism and Christianity changed the organization of the society, the blood-feud was suppressed and replaced with a system of compensation: the *wer*, *wite* and *bot*.'[30] The influence of the Church in developing the idea of responsibility was particularly noticeable. The combined effect of the feudal structure, with its concomittant notion of fealty, and Christianity was a shift from group to individual responsibility.

But the pertinent question is not really whether responsibility was personal or individual or group-based. Rather, the question is: what was the basis for responsibility for wrongs? It is generally agreed that, at the period with which we are now concerned, legal liability was not based on what is called 'moral fault' in contemporary criminal jurisprudence. However, assuming that we insist on casting the issue in terms of the presence or absence of 'moral fault,' the real question is: what was understood by that term, whether applied to a group or the individual? That question ought to receive a very short answer but for the fact that the term 'moral fault' is ambiguous.

The majority of commentators claim that the term 'moral fault' can have only the meaning attached to it in contemporary Anglo-American legal literature, that is, 'intention' or 'negligence.' They therefore speak of 'liability without fault' or 'strict (or loosely of absolute) liability where a person is held liable for damage he has caused even though there has been no intent or negligence on his part.'[31] They almost always condemn as morally and conceptually indefensible or intellectually immature any incidence of legal liability that is not strictly based on the presence of the strictly psychological fact of intent or the not-so-purely-psychological fact of negligence.[32] When combined with evolutionary assumptions, the logical outcome of this is that thoroughgoing legal evolutionists consign pre-modern law to the 'age of barbarism' while the less drastic legal evolutionists see only adumbration of moral fault as a basis for legal liability in Anglo-Saxon law. We have alluded to the shortcomings of these evolutionary paradigms in the second chapter. The strictures offered there apply *mutatis mutandis* to the issues explored in this chapter.

In an illuminating article,[33] H.L.A. Hart has subjected the concept of 'responsibility' to a critical analysis. He distinguishes and clarifies four senses in which the word 'responsibility' is used. These are 'role responsibility,' 'causal responsibility,' 'liability responsibility,' and 'capacity responsibility.' Role responsibility arises when the question of a person's answerability for the performance or non-performance of a set of well-defined duties that fall within that person's 'sphere of responsibility' is at issue. To determine whether or not a particular person is responsible in this sense, we first have to know the duties attached to the role, position, or office the person occupies, and then evaluate the action in the light of what is expected of the role-actor. Hart adds that 'role responsibility' may arise in a moral or a legal context. 'Causal responsibility' asserts one's causal connection or relationship with an event or state of things and is more properly called 'liability-responsibility.' 'Liability-responsibility,' in turn, may be either 'moral-liability-responsibility' or 'legal-liability-responsibility.' The essential difference between them is that one covers a narrower ground than the other: 'legal-liability-responsibility' might impose sanctions in circumstances in which it would be considered improper do so so under 'moral-liability-responsibility.' Further, 'legal-liability-responsibility' may be used restrictively to denote 'liable to punishment or liable to pay compensation or make reparation.' Likewise, 'morally-liability-responsibility' can be used restrictively to mean that 'a person is morally blameworthy or morally obliged to make amends for his conduct so far as this depends on certain conditions: these relate to the character or extent of his control over his own conduct, or the causal or other connection between his action and harmful occurrences or his relationship with the person who actually did the harm.'[34] The fourth type, 'capacity-responsibility,' refers to the possession of certain normal mental and physical capacities, and it constitutes 'the most important criteria of 'moral-liability-responsibility.' Thus, 'moral-liability-responsibility' straddles all the four different senses of 'responsibility.'

It is unfortunate that the analysis comes from and proceeds along a legal-positivist perspective, a perspective that maintains a rigid distinction between law and morals and that allots a larger place to the former than to the latter. Nevertheless, and with this reservation in mind, if we transpose Hart's exposition of 'moral-liability-responsibility' to Anglo-Saxon law, we will see the fundamental cleavage that separates the modern from the pre-modern understanding of the concept of responsibility.

There is no denying the fact that Anglo-Saxon law did not make any subtle analysis of the mental element in liability. At the same time, though, numerous instances in Anglo-Saxon law show incontrovertibly that some attention was paid to the actor's state of mind. But it is incorrect to describe liability in Anglo-Saxon law as 'strict' or 'absolute.' Or, to put it differently, the basis of liability in Anglo-Saxon law could be described as 'strict' or 'absolute' only if we insist on addressing the question of responsibility in early law in terms of what Sally Moore calls the time-honoured issue in jurisprudence, that is to say, the relationship between intention and responsibility.[35] As Hart's analysis of the concept of responsibility suggests, that method collapses the issue of responsibility into the question of legal liability. In other words, the issue of responsibility is made synonymous with the question of liability to punishment. In modern Anglo-American criminal jurisprudence, the question of liability is limited to 'whether or not an accused person satisfied some mental or psychological condition required for liability or whether liability was "strict" or "absolute," so that the normal mental or psychological conditions were not required.'[36]

The question was neither raised nor answered in that form in Anglo-Saxon law. Rather, 'what occurs is that an injury is considered in the context of all the circumstances under which it is inflicted and it is the combination of circumstances which determines the response or penalty. Embedded in the circumstances is the offender's state of mind.'[37] The response depended on the totality of the circumstances of the case, for in early law 'the process is not so much one of distinguishing between liability and non-liability as between different degrees of liability.'[38] Earlier scholars did not advert to this difference in approach. This is obvious from the use to which they put those passages[39] that show quite clearly that Anglo-Saxon law was not unaware of the differences between intentionally and non-intentionally inflicted harm. Instead of seeking the significance of those passages or rather what those passages and phrases meant to those who wrote and used them, they saw them as a 'queer collection, which show to a modern age a good deal of muddling of intent with negligence, or perhaps even with inevitable accident.'[40] It will be more profitable if we see such passages and phrases as showing what those who wrote or used them understood or meant by 'responsibility.'

Because in modern criminal law the meaning of the word 'responsibility' is inextricably intertwined with the issue of the presence or absence of intent or negligence, modern legal writers tend to use the words 'liability' and 'responsibility' interchangeably.[41] Clearly, this cannot be applied to Anglo-Saxon law for a number of reasons. First, because the modern conception of crime was foreign to early law, it would be mistaken to think of Anglo-Saxon laws as dealing with crimes or even with 'torts.'[42] Second, the Anglo-Saxon notion of responsibility was not restricted to the narrow question of determining the presence or absence of a specific range of psychological or not-so-psychological facts as intention or negligence. Third, as a corollary of the second point, the purpose of legal sanction in Anglo-Saxon times – in contrast to the modern era – was neither exclusively punitive nor compensatory. For instance, liability might be imposed 'as a means of assuaging the resentment of those who have been injured or damaged in a social situation in which injurer and injured must go on in a continuing social relationship.'[43] Or, as the compiler of the laws of Henry I puts it, compensation might be payable and determined 'on grounds of compassion and intended to repair any violation of honour.'[44] But whether liability was imposed because the circumstances revealed that apparently blameless conduct was in fact blameworthy, as insurance against retaliatory action, or to compensate the sufferer of harm or to restore or guarantee social harmony, emphasis was placed on a 'causal' relationship between a person's action and the harmful occurrence. If there existed a causal connection, the overriding moral principle was that 'men must pay for all the evil they do.'[45]

Let us recall our discussion of Hart's analysis of the different senses of the term 'responsibility.' There, we saw that 'causal responsibility,' should be more properly called 'liability-responsibility,' which may be either 'moral-' or 'legal-liability-responsibility,' and that 'moral-liability-responsibility' straddled the four different senses of responsibility. Since the distinction between law and morals was unknown to early law, it follows that (if we were to isolate a single test of responsibility in Anglo-Saxon law) 'causal responsibility' (in the 'moral-liability-responsibility' sense) was at once the necessary and sufficient condition for legal liability in Anglo-Saxon England.

The Anglo-Saxon notion of 'causal connection' was expansive. A person was liable to pay compensation for causing death or injury in any circumstances in which it could not be said that the victim 'was not through his agency further from life or nearer to death.'[46] The instances of such circumstances given in the *Leges Henrici Primi* are very instructive:

if anyone, by the dispatch of another, is the cause of his death while on the errand; if anyone sends for a person and the latter is killed while coming; if anyone, when summoned to a place by a person, suffers death there; if anyone's weapons kill a person when they have laid on the spot by the one who owns them; if anyone throws them down, whether the person who has been killed or someone else, and they cause harm; if anyone on being summoned to a place, is transfixed on someone's weapons wherever they have been laid; if anyone frightens or stirs a person so that in falling from a horse or something else he suffers some harm; if anyone, being brought to witness a public exhibition of a wild beast or a madman, incurs some injury at their hands; if anyone entrusts a horse or other thing to a person and then some harm befalls him; if a person's horse, when goaded or struck under the tail by someone, runs into anyone else.[47]

It is not hard to see that each of these instances represents particular situations in which the question of responsibility had to be determined. The next clause in the same section of the laws makes it clear that the extent of liability, the amount of compensation, varied according to the circumstances of each case. As well, if we disabuse our minds of the modern position, it would not be difficult to see the presence of an element of control or causal or other connection between a person's action and the harmful occurrences in each of the enumerated illustrations. We may well view the Anglo-Saxon conception of 'control' or 'causal relationship' as being too loose or elastic. But that would not change the fact that, to the Anglo-Saxons, the existence of such slight degree of control or causal relationship was sufficient to ground moral responsibility. Further, since early societies tied law and morals together, their notion of 'legal-liability-responsibility' coincided with their understanding of 'moral-liability-responsibility.' Moreover, since the purpose of legal sanction was neither exclusively punitive nor solely compensatory, there was no compelling reason why the issue of liability should be limited to ascertaining the presence or absence of intention or negligence. Hence, there arose liability in every case in which a person could be shown as having had a hand in the causation of an injury. In Maitland's quaint phrase, liability was imposed in all cases where 'a distinct voluntary act'[48] resulted in death or injury to another.

This shows that Anglo-Saxon law did not lack well-defined legal principles. However, it also shows that the principles embedded in Anglo-Saxon laws were of a different character and mould from the legal principles of modern law. The unity of broad moral ideas and legal principles that characterized unsophisticated societies is a feature unknown in modern law; the broad meaning of moral-liability-responsibility has been displaced by narrow, restrictive, and analytic connotations of the same notion. And, because modern law prides itself on the success it has achieved in separating law and morals, modern writers are prone to expound pre-modern law *as if* the dichotomy between law and morals has always been part and parcel of the rhetoric of legal scholarship. A corollary of this is that thoroughgoing legal evolutionists consign Anglo-Saxon law to the age of barbarism and superstition, and half-hearted legal evolutionists fail to detect a wholly unobnoxious principle of responsibility in Anglo-Saxon law.

Both are unsatisfactory. In the first place, their evolutionary assumptions falsify the state, character, and behaviour of human beings in 'primitive' societies, and this vitiates the whole enterprise. Fixation with the evolutionary framework has meant that little attention has been paid to the actual sociological context in which the so-called principle of 'strict' or 'absolute' liability operated. Secondly, evolutionists overlook the possibility, adverted to by Oliver Wendel Holmes, Jr, that intention played a large role in liability in early times and that the so-called strict liability rule was a comparative latecomer in the legal arena. As well, they overlook the possibility that the substitution of pecuniary compensation for compensation in kind engendered litigiousness on the part of sufferers of injuries,[49] and that in some cases arbitrators may have been induced to impose liability as well as token fines for the sole purpose of restoring social harmony. Lastly, the evolutionists do not notice that, as the use of money became widespread and wealth was increasingly possessed, 'pecuniary mulcts became legal impunity'[50] and so in some cases the focus of adjudication shifted from an emphasis on restoring social harmony through monetary compensation to imposing stringent punitive sanctions. This must have led to a consideration of the presence or absence of intent or negligence. It is not surprising, therefore, that the second group of jurists are able to discern traces of 'moral fault' as a basis for liability in Anglo-Saxon law. Moreover, since the nature of the wrongs themselves or the circumstances in which many wrong acts were committed were such that in many cases the presence of 'moral fault' could not be ruled out, and since the purpose of legal sanction in early law was neither strictly punitive nor exclusively compensatory, we may justly conclude that 'primitive' man 'often ha[d] good functional reasons for stringency in the fixing of legal responsibility.'[51] To expect otherwise is to fail to confront early law in general, and Anglo-Saxon law in particular, on its own terms.

We saw in the last chapter that the Anglo-Saxons did not classify wrongs into civil and criminal offences. Here, we have noted that they did not distinguish between compensation, fine, and punishment. There is general agreement on these two points, but there is less agreement on the test for establishing responsibility in Anglo-Saxon law. In this chapter we have explored the various approaches to the question of the principle of liability in Anglo-Saxon law. We have rejected as inadequate both the thoroughgoing evolutionists' perspective, which brands early law with a supposedly indelible mark of 'absolute' or 'strict' liability, and the historical relativists' position, which sees Anglo-Saxon society as groping erratically towards the recognition and establishment of the principle of moral fault, in the sense of intention or negligence, as a basis of legal responsibility. Instead, we have embraced the approach first broached by Moore, and later independently articulated by McLaren and MacCormack, which decries the evolutionary assumptions of earlier writers and allows for a contextual examination of the basis for responsibility in Anglo-Saxon law. We maintain that the concept of 'responsibility' had a wider and different moral import in Anglo-Saxon society than the restrictive, narrow, and technical meaning it assumed in later times. The concept was not understood during the Anglo-Saxon era in terms of its relationship with the psychological fact of intention. Moreover, unlike in modern times when its main function is punitive or compensatory, the legal sanction under the Anglo-Saxon legal order served multiple purposes, which ranged from punitive to conciliatory. We conclude that, while Anglo-Saxon law did not lack a principle of responsibility, it is misleading to explicate its principle of responsibility as if its laws possessed a doctrinal unity characteristic of the laws of later times.

3

The Idea of Wrong under
the Common Law I

The lineaments of the idea of wrong in Anglo-Saxon England sketched in the preceding chapters show that Anglo-Saxon law made no distinction between civil and criminal wrongs. They show as well that Anglo-Saxon law assigned no definite functions to compensation, fines, or punishment. Later, in Anglo-Norman England, a bifurcated model of wrongs emerged. This was due partly to changes in the socio-political and institutional structure caused by the Norman Conquest and partly to the advent of intellectual sophistication. The legal and political institutions which were responsible for the development of the common law[1] as a system of positive law originated in the Anglo-Saxon period. But these institutions assumed definite shape only after the Norman Conquest.

The realization that Anglo-Norman legal and political institutions owe something to Anglo-Saxon times has given rise to what I call a scholarship of continuity. Although the common law developed after the Norman Conquest, the scholarship that elaborated its continuity dates from the seventeenth century onwards. Beginning with Sir Matthew Hale's *History of the Common Law of England*[2] in that century, legal historians and other writers on the development, form, and nature of the common law share the notion that a thread of continuity runs through the fabric of the common law. Perhaps this frame of mind has been dictated by intellectual and political expediency, but the belief in continuity has not necessarily been a figment of the scholarly imagination; it is real.[3] It is particularly so in the case of the common law of crimes. In short, the institutional base of the common law goes back to the scaffolds erected in Anglo-Saxon England.

It suffices for our purposes to refer to the notion of the King's Peace, which singularly determined the course taken by the common law of crimes: some wrongs were early construed as constituting affronts to the person or authority of the King. This is the subject-matter of the first part of this chapter; we shall

call it 'the procedural conception of crime.' The second part gives a brief
history of the beginnings of legal science in the eleventh century, and it underscores the role played by the science of law in the intellectualization of the
common law generally and, in particular, the common law of crimes. Institutional developments coupled with intellectual sophistication resulted in the
formulation of the idea of criminal wrong. The third part traces the contours of
two models of crime under the common law. We will call them the 'political'
and 'moral' conceptions of crime. Although both models require a mental state
for legal liability, I emphasize that what constitutes 'mental state' under the
former is different from the meaning of the same phrase under the latter. In sum,
this chapter explores the reasons for the shape assumed by the concept of crime
under the common law.

Procedural Conception of Crime

The King's Peace

From an institutional point of view, the idea of the King's Peace is the most
important contribution made by the Anglo-Saxon law to the common law of
crimes. We noted in chapter 1 that kingship developed in Anglo-Saxon England
and that its recognition by the Church fostered political thought. The tendency
was to confound what we would now call the state with the personality and
authority of the King. However, since Anglo-Saxon England was essentially a
feudal society, the extent of the King's authority had to be demarcated from that
of the other 'under-kings.' In Anglo-Saxon England, every determinate legal
authority had its own peace, breach of which entitled the owner to compensation or fine. Indeed, the idea of peace was an important instrument of control in
Germanic societies generally.[4] It assumed enormous proportions in Anglo-
Saxon England. In Roscoe Pound's words,

the idea [was] that certain places, certain times, certain persons are exempted from private war and that a wrong done in such a place, at such a time or to such a person [was] a
breach of the peace or protection or guardianship of the authority responsible for order
therein or for protection thereon. Any wrong done in such a place at such a season or to
such a person thus entitled the person or authority concerned to compensation.[5]

The idea of peace assumed three forms in Anglo-Saxon England. First, it
meant a state of peacefulness, safety, and security that surrounded households.
This form 'developed from the early meaning of the word *mund*.' That word
'originally meant "hand" or "palm,"' but it later acquired a technical, legal

meaning. It came to connote 'the power and protection exercised by the head of a household over the members of the household and guests.'[6] This was the means by which the sanctity of the homestead was guaranteed from very early times; it was the foundation of the legal concept of peace and order.[7] Second, the peace referred to a general non-legal state of peacefulness. Finally, and most important for our present purposes, the third form of peace was called *mund* or *grith*, and it belonged specially to the King. It meant, in the first place, the peace of the King's household, and, in the second, the King's hand-given *mund* or *grith*, which he could confer as he pleased on any specified individual or place. In D. Feldman's words, it was, 'an authority which could be extended anywhere in the kingdom to specified people for special purposes. The King could grant his peace under his hand to anyone he chose. Any assault on them in their travels would be regarded as a direct affront to the King's own personal peace, as if it had happened in his own residence.'[8]

As time went on, royal power gained more and more ground and so increased its prestige. And the more prestigious the royal power became, the more frequently the King exercised the right to grant, sell, or confer his peace on a number of specified persons, including traders and merchants, in order to ensure their safe conduct within the realm.[9] This device laid the foundation for the eventual extension of the King's Peace to the whole realm of Anglo-Norman England.[10]

The idea of peace, coupled with the feudal theory of autonomous personal allegiance,[11] brought into existence what F.M. Stenton[12] aptly calls a system of private justice in Anglo-Saxon England. Legal authority, the right to adjudicate, including the right to impose and collect fines and compensation for wrongs, could not and was not monopolized by a single central authority. As Feldman succinctly puts it, in Anglo-Saxon England, 'the maintenance of law and order was not normally seen as a concern of what we would now call central government.'[13]

The gradual extension of the King's Peace did not immediately give rise to any theory of the overweening political authority of the King. Breach of the King's Peace was not conceived as an offence against the public or state as such. Rather, it was seen as an offence against the personal authority of the King:

[N]o conception of benefit to the community seems to have entered into the composition of the king's or chief's peace. The circle within which injury or disturbance was to be compensated to him was a privilege to him, a support of his dignity, a lucrative perquisite that he and his immediate surroundings should be free from disturbance. That was all. Each chief and king jealously guarded any interference with such immediate jurisdiction from without, or sought to increase its scope.[14]

Thus, prior to the Norman Conquest, the King's Peace – breach of which gave rise to the 'pleas of the Crown' – covered only acts of violence and injuries done to persons or at places or at particular times or seasons that were specifically or specially protected by the royal power.[15]

The Conquest and the centralization policy of the Norman kings perfected the nascent Anglo-Saxon feudal structure. The result was that 'England was swiftly transformed into the most royal of the feudal monarchies.'[16] With the King as the chief landlord, it did not take long before royal jurisdiction was formally extended to the whole realm. This considerably enhanced the royal power.[17] Consequently, 'the various forms in which the King's special protection had been given before the Conquest disappeared, or rather merge[d] in his general protection and authority until it eventually swallowed up that of all the under-kings.'[18] The result was that all serious wrongs became a breach of the King's Peace and a felony.[19]

In early Anglo-Norman law, the distinction between felony and trespasses was of a procedural nature. Any wrong cognizable in the King's court was a plea of the Crown and it was easy to convert a trespass to a felony. All that needed be done was to insert in the plea the words *vi et armis* and *contra pacem nostram*.[20] From a theoretical point of view, however, there was as yet no conception of crime as a wrong or injury to the public or to the King in his capacity as the symbol of the commonwealth:

The only contemporary significance [of describing a trespass as a plea of the crown] was that the King took the profits instead of some local franchise holder. When it is said that the breach of the King's peace is a plea of the Crown it does not mean that the whole field of trespass in which this allegation is generally made is part of the criminal law; it simply means that the plaintiff wants to sue in the King's court and the King's court had devised a convenient technicality for inviting him to do so.[21]

The concept of crime as an offence against or punishable by the sovereign authority was an intellectual creation, and it did not emerge until learned men deployed the legal terms and categories derived from the scientific study of Roman law in systematizing the laws and customs of England.[22]

Wrongs, Sins, and Crimes

The transformation of the Anglo-Saxon private justice system into the Anglo-Norman system of royal justice was not achieved solely through the political process. Nor can the history of the process of transformation be broken into clear-cut periods without doing violence to the end result. The process is best seen from the viewpoint of 'overlapping histories.'[23] In such histories, one discerns the influence of the Church as well as that of Roman law. We advert here to an aspect of the influence of the Church on the idea of wrong.

The formative decisions of the common law system were made by King Henry II's justices between 1166 and 1179.[24] At that time the revived interest in classical legal literature had not been sufficiently orchestrated for its results to be applied in practice.[25] It is also important to add that, until well after the intellectual renaissance of the twelfth century, the Church was an integral part of the feudal socio-political, economic, and legal order[26] and, as a result, was not willing to initiate changes that could have far-reaching repercussions for the law. Nevertheless, the law was never devoid of the influence of the Church. This is primarily because until 1166, when the Constitution of Clarendon severed the jurisdiction of secular courts from ecclesiastical authorities, church and state worked hand in hand. Indeed, secular and ecclesiastical pleas were heard by more or less the same personnel, the majority, if not all, of whom were clerics.

In the determination of such causes, the ecclesiastics emphasized questions of moral and individual responsibility as distinct from the general or customary rules of liability to pay compensation to victims of wrongs. The emphasis on individual responsibility played a major role in transforming the idea of responsibility held by the English people. More precisely, it resulted in the shift from group to individual responsibility. As T.F.T. Plucknett puts it, the Church had 'brought with it moral ideas which were to revolutionize English law. Christianity had inherited from Judaism an outlook upon moral questions which was strictly individualistic. The salvation of each separate soul was dependent upon the actions of the individual.'[27] The cooperation between secular and ecclesiastical authorities was so strong that, generally speaking, all sins were regarded as crimes and all crimes were sins. F. Barlow makes the point succinctly:

the intensity of the penetration of royalty by religious sentiments varied ... according to the times and the persons. In the Anglo-Saxon period it probably reached its height with Edgar (959–975), a King who carried out the policy of his bishops, restored monasticism and passed laws against vice. The interpenetration ... (or, if you like, confusion) was such that all sins became crimes, and all crimes sins.[28]

Consequently, there were two kinds of liability:

[O]n the one hand, the sinner who broke the law was ... considered to be not only a sinner but also a criminal, a lawbreaker and hence liable not only to repent but also to pay a price for the violation of the law ... on the other hand, the law-breaker, the criminal, was also a sinner, whose guilt consisted not only in the fact that he broke the law but also, and more significantly, in the fact that he voluntarily chose to do evil. Thus there was a strong emphasis on the moral ... quality of his act, that is, his sinful state of mind when he committed it.[29]

It seems that, if a sinful state of mind was not present at the time the injury or wrong was done, the accused person would not be adjudged a sinner (liable to do penance) but rather would be regarded merely as a wrongdoer, who, according to customary rules, was liable to make amends to his victim. Penance had a history going as far back as the eighth century, and, although the collected dooms of Anglo-Saxon Kings made no mention of penance, in all probability penance operated side by side with the customary remedy of monetary compensation. Indeed, a recent study of the influence of the Church on the laws and customs of England concluded that 'it may be that to look at the Anglo-Saxon law Codes is to see only half of the liability that any person incurred when he committed homicide, or perjury, or any other criminal act.' The same study suggested that in Anglo-Saxon England 'the doing of penance' may have been 'as requisite as the paying of compensation.'[30]

Be that as it may, the cooperation between church and state had a salutary effect on the polity and the laws: it made the duty to obey the law and to conform to customs a moral duty. As John Kemble puts it, 'by slow degrees, as the State itself became Christianized, the moral duty became a legal one.'[31] A corollary of this was that the law became suffused with Christian institutional morality. Acts that offended against the institution of marriage (for example, bigamy), property rights (such as theft, robbery, and brigandage), personal integrity (rape, assault, homicide) were regarded as breaches of God's laws.

Nevertheless, a large bulk of offences were seen primarily as wrongs against the victims or against one's neighbours. When a wrong amounted to breach of fealty or of the peace of a distinct legal authority, it was seen as a wrong done to the relevant authority:

A crime was not generally conceived as an offense directed against the political order as such, or against society in general, but rather as an offense directed against the victim and those with whom he was identified – his kinfolk, or his territorial community, or his feudal class. It was also an offense against God – a sin ... crime was considered for the most part to be an offense against other people – and at the same time an offense against God – rather than an offense against an all-embracing political unit, whether the State or the Church.[32]

As noted earlier, one of the immediate consequences of the Norman Conquest was that the sphere of the King's Peace became co-extensive with the whole realm. Within a century after the conquest, ecclesiastical jurisdiction was severed from secular power. For the first time, it became necessary to distinguish between wrongs punishable in ecclesiastical courts and those punishable by secular authorities. However, the basis for assigning wrongs to the two different jurisdictions did not have much to do with the character of the acts as sins.[33] The distinction was procedural. Any act that could be prosecuted or punished by the secular authority was regarded as a secular offence; those punishable by ecclesiastical authorities were regarded as ecclesiastical offences. But the idea of sin had already made inquiry into the state of mind of the wrongdoer both necessary and indispensable for establishing responsibility in ecclesiastical causes. It also led to the requirement of *mens rea* in the common law of crimes. This in turn was made possible by the revival in classical legal knowledge and a renewed interest in canon law.

Before making reference to the intellectual ferment that led to the emergence of legal science and the transformation of the law of wrongs, we will refer briefly to one other aspect of the 'overlapping histories' of the common law of crimes. This is the category of offences known as 'botless' wrongs.

Botless Offences

We saw in chapter 2 that in Anglo-Saxon England every person had a 'price' (*wer*) and every injury had a fixed amount of compensation (*bot*). Likewise, the breach of the peace of any authority was emendable with fines or compensation (*wite*). However, from early times certain wrongs were deemed so heinous or so grave that they were not redeemable by compensation, monetary or otherwise. In the language of the time they were 'botless' offences. Yet, as time went on, more and more erstwhile botless offences became emendable. It is said that this was due to the ameliorating influence of the Church on the law; the Church had a distaste for bloodshed.[34]

The type and number of emendable crimes, however, fluctuated with the times. For instance, during the period of the Danish invasions in the ninth century, the necessity to have as many able-bodied fighting men as possible led to the relaxation of the law. Consequently, 'crimes which had ceased to be emendable became emendable once more.'[35] That trend continued throughout the late Anglo-Saxon period, and 'on the eve of the Conquest many bad crimes could still be paid for with money.'[36] But the Hobbesian cast of the period[37] immediately before and after the conquest caused a dramatic change in policy. Characteristic punishments such as hanging, burning, drowning, stoning, mutilation, castration, and flogging featured regularly in the annals of the time.

The anonymous author of the *Leges Henrici Primi*[38] listed the unemendable pleas of the time. They consisted of *hus breche* (house-breaking), arson, manifest theft, palpable murder, treachery towards one's lord, and violation of the peace of the Church or the protection of the King through the commission of homicide. Apparently, the nature of these offences is such that it is inconceivable that their occurrence could be the result of anything but conscious, deliberate, or premeditated actions. In short, the belief that certain offences or the manner or ways in which they are perpetrated is so flagrant and sufficiently repulsive and disruptive of the legal peace that the only proper amends for them is punishment goes back to pre-conquest times. And when, following the Norman Conquest, the King's Peace was extended over the whole realm and so all serious offences became pleas of the Crown, a further distinction was made between the class of wrongs that were not only a breach of the peace but also of such magnitude that a conviction entailed the loss of life or limb or the forfeiture of worldly goods.

These were called felonies. Every felony was a trespass but not every trespass was a felony. Although it is not easy to ascertain the precise meaning of the word 'felony,'[39] F. Pollock and F.W. Maitland argue that we can offer a rough conjecture if we saturate ourselves in the political and legal climate of the thirteenth century. According to them, 'every crime that can be prosecuted by appeal, and every crime that causes a loss of both lands and goods and every crime for which a man shall lose life or member and every crime for which a fugitive can be outlawed is a felony.'[40] For our present purposes, it is sufficient to underline the fact that the nature of this class of offences or the manner in which they were usually perpetrated was such that they were almost invariably committed intentionally or deliberately. As F.B. Sayre puts it, 'the early felonies were roughly the external manifestations of the heinous sins of the day.'[41] In other words, felonies carried on their faces the tell-tale signs of what a sophisticated legal age would unhesitatingly call 'malice aforethought.' It is to the source of that legal sophistication that we must now turn.

Foundations of Legal Science

The Norman Conquest ushered in a series of legal and political mechanisms which ultimately resulted in the attainment of unity in the law. The process received a boost from the intellectual progress – particularly the revival of classical legal learning – that occurred in Europe generally at the very time when the Normans were establishing their suzerainty over England. As Pollock and Maitland put it, 'the Norman Conquest takes place at a moment when in general history in Europe new forces are coming into play. Roman law is being studied, for men are mastering the Institutes at Pavia, and will soon be expounding the

Digest at Bologna; Canon law is being evolved and both claim a cosmopolitan domain.'[42] The impact of the development in intellectual activity on legal institutions and ideas was spectacular. However, we cannot attempt to underscore its significance for the idea of wrong without first tracing the history of the revival of classical legal studies.

The Intellectual Ferment[43]

Until about 1000 A.D., Europe remained in what is known as the 'Dark Ages.' The Dark Ages were indeed very dark in the intellectual history of Europe, since, outside the tamed intellectual activity of the monasteries, nothing that could be rightly designated intellectual took place between the period following the collapse of the Roman empire in the third quarter of the fifth century and the eleventh century. Eventually, the impetus to intellectual activity came from the Crusades. From the time of the first Crusades in the eleventh century onwards, the people of Europe were rudely awakened to a new reality. The Crusades brought them into contact with classical antiquity, and a once intellectually quiescent people became thirsty for knowledge. Of course, knowledge of classical antiquity had never become extinct in southern Europe, but the direction or flow of knowledge had been largely determined by a religious order which held an extremely pessimistic view of human nature. In terms of classical legal materials, Roman law had been applied in some areas of southern Europe before the Crusades, and law was studied as part of the general curriculum in the Pavian and Ravenna schools in the eleventh century. However, it was not until the emergence of the Bologna School in the second half of the eleventh century, and its rise to pre-eminence in the next, that law became a 'purely professional study for a special class of professional students' and 'men of good birth and good position – beneficed and dignified ecclesiastics or sons of nobles – flocked from the remotest parts of Europe to the lecture-rooms at Bologna.'[44] Englishmen were not left out.[45]

Law was first cultivated as a science before it was pursued as a profession. This is no doubt surprising; however, it ceases to be so when one realizes that the scientific study of the law at Bologna was based not upon the divergent legal customs of the divergent peoples of Europe but on the Roman law.[46] The recovery of the full texts of Justinian earlier in the eleventh century prompted the systematic study of the *Corpus Iuris Civilis*, and this initiated the institution of a regular curriculum of legal education.

The scientific research work of Bolognese scholars falls into two periods. The first commences with the work of the reputed founder of the school, Irnerius or Warnerius, in the early part of the twelfth century and ends about the middle of the thirteenth century with the labours of Accursius (1182–1260). The writers in this period are known as the Glossators, from the method of the gloss or textual interpretation that they adopted in their scientific study of Roman law texts.[47] The second period, that of the post-Glossators or Commentators, began in the second half of the thirteenth century. It flourished throughout the Middle Ages and endured until the nineteenth century in the form of the humanist pandectists.[48]

The Nature of the Scientific Study of Law

The aims of the scholars who worked in the two periods mentioned above differ from one another. The Glossators viewed Roman legal texts as the 'primary and pure sources of the law.' They therefore limited themselves to the task of expounding or making textual interpretations of Justinian texts. The post-Glossators, on the other hand, approached their task with a philosophical frame of mind. Whereas the Glossators had believed that the Roman legal texts themselves should be the basis of study and practice alike, and were not particularly interested in adjusting law to fact,[49] the post-Glossators boldly sought to and did extract fundamental legal and political concepts from the Roman legal materials. They also went a step further. They endeavoured to harmonize the law in the books with the socio-political realities of their time. Walter Ullmann succinctly explains the differences between the two sets of scholars:

In modern terminology, the Glossators may be styled analytical jurists: the paramount aim of their legal science was analysis, pure and simple, purporting to explain the Roman law from within itself in purely legalistic terms ... the merely legal interpretation of the Roman texts was completed and concluded by the Glossators. The task which remained ... was the philosophic interpretation of the Roman law, the penetration into the intricate mechanism behind the law, and the exposition of universally valid, general principles. With this aim in view, the Commentators extended the sphere of legal science and studies from the mere interpretation of individual legal rules to the investigation and presentation of the fundamental principles, notions, and sources of the law.[50]

The Roman legal texts neither addressed their subject matter after the fashion of Greek speculative thought nor suggested that law could be a subject for abstract thought.[51] Moreover, although Roman legal texts were dotted with legal terms and concepts, Roman law lacked the concept of a concept. In the hands of the post-Glossators, however, the notion of a concept was born.[52] Thus came into currency such legal concepts as 'right,' 'tort,' 'crime,' and so on. These concepts received a typically medieval tinge. In other words, they acquired certain nuances which reflected the moral and political assumptions that pervaded the intellectual climate of the time.[53]

The Nature of the Influence of the New Learning

We know that in Anglo-Saxon England wrongs were perceived as offences directed against specific persons or particular legal authorities. That this conception of wrong survived the Norman Conquest is not surprising, for, aside from the refined barbarity that masqueraded as feudal legal principles, the Normans themselves had no system of jurisprudence to import into England,[54] any more than the Teutons had brought learning and thought across the English Channel. The extension of the King's Peace to the entire realm, with the consequence that any trespass could be contrived into a plea of the Crown, did not immediately alter that position. The impetus for a change came as part of the package from the intellectual ferment which has been briefly sketched above.

The scientific study of the law by the post-Glossators or Commentators had the full benefit of a full-grown scholastic method.[55] 'Scholasticism' has a wide meaning, and it is not easy to enumerate all its peculiar characteristics. But, however wide its meaning may be, it will not be inaccurate to identify it with the criteria proposed by David Knowles.[56] According to Knowles, scholasticism is characterized by 'a close connection between philosophy and religion, and a close dependence upon ancient philosophy, especially as presented by Aristotle, and this philosophy is regarded as a corpus rational of natural truths which are ascertainable and valid in their degree as is the body of revelation.'[57] The scholastic method, then, is essentially a hermeneutical activity. It requires its practitioners to seal themselves up in the universe discovered within their own library, and the books in that library constitute their 'cognitive authority.'[58]

True to the earmarks of scholasticism, 'for the doctors of the new study the books of Justinian were sacred, the sources of authority from which all deductions must proceed.'[59] They had their own predilections too. For instance, 'the early Bologna doctors were all staunch imperialists.'[60] And the post-Glossators, schooled as they were in the law of the later empire, 'inclined to the monarchical point of view.'[61] Moreover, the library of the Bolognese scholars was a mansion with many capacious rooms. This is especially true in the case of the post-Glossators, whose work had a lasting influence on medieval legal ideas and institutions. The post-Glossators took within their ambit not only the scientific study of Roman law and its harmonization with the social and political realities of medieval Europe but also enacted law and customs as well as the newly evolved canon Law.[62] This enabled them to evolve a comprehensive philosophy of law:

the post-Glossators ... harmonized or attempted to harmonize law with the social and political realities ... Furthermore, since the compilation of the Corpus, the body of positive law had grown considerably, both by enactment and by customs, two sources of law which received only scanty consideration by the Glossators. The Commentators ... viewed these sources as parts of the legal order as a whole, and devoted considerable space in their writings to the scientific explanation of municipal statute and gradually developed customs. Lastly, the newly created Canon law and the feudal laws were adequately treated ... Thus, for the first time in the history of European jurisprudence a philosophy of law was created.[63]

That philosophy of law conceptualized legal and political ideas from the point of view of a ruler. It was, however, the ruler who was at one and the same time empowered and bound by the two kinds of nature known to the intellectuals of the time. These were the unchanging and changeless 'nature of the fundamental natural law,' and the changing and changeable 'lower nature of the world and man.'[64] Government and regular legislation were necessary in the second type of nature, and the Prince was to it what God was to the former type of nature. In the post-Glossators' scheme of things, the polity was a moral entity overseen by a monarchy and worthy of the highest endeavours of man. Moreover, it was believed that, in devising new laws to meet the exigencies of the changing lower nature of the world and man, human reason participated in the higher natural law.[65] It follows, therefore, that 'God and nature directly approved the public law that was administered by princes'[66] for the preservation of the polity.

Nevertheless, the earthly power remained subordinate to God and the higher nature, for it was accepted that positive laws ought not 'to violate the moral commands of God embodied in the higher natural law; God and the higher nature remained superior to and a limitation of the State and the *ius civile.*'[67] Or, as Otto von Gierke put it, 'it was never doubtful that the highest Might, were it spiritual or were it temporal, was confined by truly legal limitations.'[68]

When the crop of men who had received their legal training from the civilians and canonists were confronted with the task of systematizing the laws and customs of England, they naturally adopted the perspective of their tutors. To put the point starkly, the men who laid the foundations of the common law system were what we would emphatically call natural law theorists.

We need not pause here to consider in detail specific aspects of the teachings of the civilians and canonists which bear directly on the criminal law.[69] The determinative point is not what the Roman jurists themselves or their interpreters understood particular concepts to mean; but rather what their pupils took such concepts to mean. And this can be ascertained from the institutional writers and the principal historians of the common law.

On the other hand, it is generally agreed that the influence of classical legal science on the common law was felt more particularly in the basic legal vocabulary which was deployed in structuring and systematizing the laws and customs of England.[70] Roman legal concepts and categories supplied the form into which was poured the laws and customs which evolved in and was administered by the King's courts throughout the realm. Indeed, all the institutional writers resorted to Roman legal concepts and categories in elucidating the common law:

> Beginning with Glanvill and Bracton in the twelfth and thirteenth centuries, then beginning again after 1600 with John Cowel, Henry Finch, Matthew Hale, and Thomas Wood, and culminating in W. Blackstone's famous Commentaries, then beginning once more with John Austin, T.E. Holland and their American and Commonwealth counterparts, these authors all borrowed their terminology and structure wholly or partly, directly or indirectly, from a Roman scheme of classification.[71]

More specifically, like all legal history, the history of the common law of crimes is 'a winner's history.'[72] In fact, the institutional writers, especially the early ones, give us 'but one side of a many-sided story, and that side the king's.'[73] It is, as we have seen, the history of the process by which the King's Peace swallowed up all other peaces and thus resulted in the triumph of the King's power over the power of all the erstwhile authorities within the realm. The King's jurisdiction simply superseded that of all others.

The King's advisers and officers were recruited from 'the best educated men in the realm.'[74] It follows that the legal system that was forged in the alembic of the King's courts under the auspices of the Angevin royalty was shaped and moulded by the moral, political, and legal ideas which these educated men had imbibed from their study of Roman and canon law. In short, while it is true that law was first cultivated as a science before it was pursued as a profession, the common law itself is a plant which sprang from and grew on the native soil of England but was partly nourished with water drawn from the troughs of Roman law.

The deployment of scientific legal concepts and categories in systematizing the rude and unstructured idea of wrong prevalent in England indirectly transformed the idea itself. Put differently, the end product participated, so to speak, in the fundamental legal principles immanent in Roman law from which the structural elements had been taken. What emerged was a legal system in contrast with a mere legal order, and institutional writers sought to guide the unlearned along the path of a learned and structured articulation of the laws and customs of England. Henry de Bracton, who gave 'English jurisprudence its first typical expression'[75] and who produced 'the greatest legal work of the whole Middle Ages'[76] by 'using Roman bricks for the construction of an English edifice,'[77] explicitly stated this as his general aim.[78] It is, therefore, not presumptuous to confine ourselves to the concept of crime enunciated under the common law.

The Concept of Crime under the Common Law

We noted earlier that, although concepts were not unknown in Roman law, classical legal science lacked the concept of a concept. We added that the scholastic activities of the commentators led to the invention of the concept of a concept, and that the meaning attached to the concepts so fashioned was coloured by the moral and political assumptions of the time. This was an indirect reference to the distinction made familiar by some contemporary moral, political, and legal philosophers, namely, the distinction between 'concept' and 'conception.'[79] A brief description of the distinction is necessary for the purposes of what follows.

To ask questions of 'right' or 'wrong' is to invite meditation on moral issues. To attempt to provide reasoned answers to such questions is to engage in moral philosophy. Moral philosophy takes place at two planes: abstract and concrete. At the abstract or general theoretical level, 'concepts' are the tools of the trade. At the concrete or definitive theoretical level, 'conceptions' constitute the wares of moral discourse. Conceptions come into existence when a particular concept (form) is invested with a given meaning (content). By marrying (or synthesizing) content with form, moral philosophers arrive at particular definitive meanings of abstract concepts, and this allows them to proceed to treat forthwith such moral concepts *as if* they have been invested with the only meaning (content) they could possibly bear. In other words, any attempt to treat moral issues scientifically presupposes not only the acceptance of the existence (real or nominal) of certain moral concepts but also the belief that the theory which one embraces captures the true meaning of such conceptual forms. The scholars who avidly devoured Roman law, and who sought to harmonize law with the social and political realities of their time, shared these sentiments. Indeed, as pointed out earlier, they regarded their sources as *ratio scripta*.

The Political Conception of Crime

The conception of crime that the civilians encountered in their sources was a thoroughly mature and political one. Crime was depicted as an offence against the sovereign authority and punished as such by 'public criminal law.'[80] When coupled with the Roman legal principle (as tempered by medieval political and legal philosophy) that 'the Sovereign is the fountain of all Justice and the depository of all Grace,'[81] it led to the conclusion that 'crime' is not and cannot be a wrong for which the appropriate remedy is satisfaction or compensation to the victim.

The conception of crime as a wrong against and punishable by the sovereign authority found a congenial home in Anglo-Norman England. It will be recalled that the centralizing policy of the Norman kings had resulted in the extension of the King's Peace over the whole realm. This set the political stage for the reception of the idea that crimes are wrongs punishable by the sovereign authority. In this way the conceptual framework derived from Roman legal science was harmonized with the historical and political realities in England. Once the King's jurisdiction had been enlarged to encompass the whole of England, allegations of breach of the King's Peace became the fictional touchstone with which trespasses were converted into offences against and punishable by the sovereign authority.[82]

However, it would be a mistake to suppose that it was all fiction. Many trespasses did impinge upon the King's Peace. In particular, the class of offences that at least since the time of Canute, had been 'botless' and were regarded as pleas of the Crown were flagrant breaches of the King's Peace. The subsequent history of the development and crystallization of common law crimes consists largely of the process by which more and more trespasses or wrongs were absorbed into the category of breach of the King's Peace either through the pleading device or by legislative fiat. As W.J.V. Windeyer succinctly puts it, 'the history of the development of criminal law is the history of the King's peace.'[83]

The conception of crime as an offence punishable by the sovereign authority supplanted the erstwhile belief that offences were primarily wrongs against specific individuals or particular legal authorities. The twelfth century marks the watershed. In the words of the oft-cited passage from J.W. Jeudwine, 'in that most revolutionary of all the centuries ... the Western world suddenly ceased to regard murder, arson, rape and theft as regrettable torts which should be compensated by payment to the family – such and other serious offences came to be regarded ... as crimes against society at large to be prosecuted by the community through its chief.'[84] Yet it is not altogether accurate to describe the changes in legal orientation that occurred in the twelfth century as having effected the transformation of the enumerated offences into 'crimes against society at large.' The transformation was not as earth-shaking as that. What seems to have taken place was that the enumerated offences ceased to be seen as wrongs done to individuals; instead they were perceived as wrongs punishable by the political sovereign. Again, it would be an exaggeration to assert that in the twelfth century the system of compensation disappeared with 'marvellous suddenness.'[85] Recent research has revealed that the transitional process was much more gradual and traces of the old system persisted long after the twelfth century.[86] Nevertheless, decisive changes in legal orientation did occur in the twelfth century. This is manifest from the institutional writings on the common law, which began with Glanvill.[87]

Writing before the time of legal memory, Glanvill opened the first book of his *Treatise* with the words: 'Pleas are either criminal or civil.'[88] He then enumerated the criminal pleas of the time that belonged to the Crown, adding that they were all 'punished by death or cutting off of limbs.' Significantly, he merely listed the criminal pleas of the Crown and stated the punishment without adverting to the basis for establishing criminal responsibility. But, with the exception of the omnibus 'plea of breach of the lord King's peace,' (which Glanvill did not give any separate discussion in the short chapter[89] he devoted to criminal pleas), it is evident that the nature of such offences was such that they would be, in most cases, the result of conscious, deliberate, or purposeful action.

Be that as it may, by the thirteenth century legal knowledge had attained a level of sophistication hitherto unknown. Although it may be that the use of distinct legal terms by an early institutional writer did not necessarily mean that such legal concepts were already distinctly grasped or applied as such in practice, Bracton's *Treatise*[90] suggests that a more sophisticated conception of crime was in the background. We refer here to the idea that crime is a species of *peccatum*.

In the generic sense, *peccatum* means 'sin against men, laws and gods.'[91] At the concrete level, it means the transgression of the lines of right action or conduct 'drawn by gods, men and State.'[92] In this triad, sin against the gods (or, after the inception of Christianity, God) comes first, sin against men comes second, and sin against the state comes last. Maine pointedly underscored this when he remarked that 'the conception of offense against God produced the first class of ordinances; the conception of offense against one's neighbour produced the second.' The conception of offense against the state or community was the last to emerge.[93]

This source-oriented outlook betrays two patterns of thought, one of which has persisted into modern times. First, the fact that the first set of wrongs was conceived as transgression of the lines of right action believed to have been drawn by gods or God explains the tendency to identify sin with crime. This tendency persisted well into the medieval period; indeed, it is discernible from the writings of medieval jurists.[94] Second, the source-oriented outlook explains the view that laws are binding because they emanate from a rightful or recognized political authority. This view has admittedly persisted into modern times. However, whereas in pre-modern times the lines of right conduct delineated by the triumvirate legal authority – God, man, and state – were severally and jointly recognized and reflected as such in moral, political, and legal thought, in modern times legal philosophy seems to have annihilated the first two authoritative sources. The result is that we are left with a single, sole legal authority, the state. This has enabled legal positivists to carry to its ultimate limits the startling proposition that the Hobbesian-like sovereign is the exclusive determiner of right and wrong.

Let us leave aside for the moment the extravagances of the Austinian conception of law. Instead, we will immerse ourselves in the intellectual milieu of the Middle Ages. On doing so, we immediately realize that the conception of crime as a species of *peccatum* was predicated on a number of unarticulated but general axioms of thought.

In the form that the idea assumed under the aegis of Christianity,[95] it meant culpable or blameworthy deviation from the lines of right conduct drawn by God, man, and state. Obviously, this assumes knowledge of right and wrong, which is, in turn, based on the totality of medieval moral, political, and legal thought. To attempt to enumerate the axiomatic beliefs of that age will take us far away from the main subject of this book. Suffice it to say that the conception of crime as a distinct species of *peccatum* was coloured and shaped by the moral climate of the later Middle Ages. This meant, for instance, that it was assumed that law and morals coincide, or, to put it more elegantly, that there was no separation of law and morals. On the contrary, later medieval jurists attempted to cover 'the whole field of morals with legal precepts by conforming existing precepts to the requirement of a reasoned system of morals.'[96] Indeed, the separation of law and morals is itself a twentieth-century phenomenon.[97] More precisely, this idea of crime presupposes that the rights and duties delineated by public law and enforced by public institutions reflect universal ideas of right and wrong.

We observed earlier that medieval philosophy of law conceived legal institutions, rules, and principles from the point of view of the ruler, though a ruler subject to a higher law. Parallel to that, this idea of wrong perceives crime from the standpoint of the subject bound by the laws of God, man, and state. Further, it indirectly sets limits on the power of the political sovereign authority to prosecute, convict, and punish individuals accused of wrongdoing. It does this by stipulating that 'a crime is not committed unless the intention to injure exists.' We shall call it the moral conception of crime.

Early attempts to put the moral conception of crime into practice gave rise to conflicts with the earlier and prevailing political conception. At the formative period of the common law of crimes, the conflict between the political and the moral conceptions of crime in turn led to a failure to appreciate fully the nature of crime. This delayed the distillation of the distinctive elements of crime. For instance, the political conception of crime required an accused person to meet stringent conditions before he or she could resort to the claim of self-defence. The conditions were not as stringent under the moral conception of crime, for it recognized that individuals had the natural right of self-defence. Instead of applying rarefied rules of self-defence derived from the legal materials of a bygone age, the rule of self-defence fashioned by the moral conception of crime focused on the circumstances in which the act was committed in order to determine whether the defendant was merely exercising the right to self-defence. Thomas Green[98] has amply shown that, during the early common law period, the official rules for self-defence were so strict that many self-defenders would have ended up on the gallows were it not for the fact that juries often resorted to pious fraud. I suggest that the official rules of self-defence were strict precisely because they were fashioned with an eye on the political conception of crime.

The moral conception of crime was closer to (though not identical with) the 'societal' perception of crime than the latter was to the political conception of crime. And, since society was actively involved (primarily through the jury of presentment and the trial jury)[99] in the adjudicatory process, jury behaviour synchronized more with the societal perception of crime than with the political conception of crime. Consequently, the community's standard of liability not infrequently diverged from the official standard. The result was that the jury frequently nullified the law.[100] The existing legal rules were very much shaped by the political conception of crime; practice, or rather jury behaviour, was closer to the moral conception of crime. The clash between the official and the societal standards illustrate the fact that 'in daily use the classical doctrines sometimes did violence to the popular conscience.'[101] Both sought to enforce 'legal' standards, and both standards could be ventilated through public institutions. The moral conception eventually displaced the political conception of crime and modified the societal one.

The moral conception of crime was derived from the 'Canonistic scholarships as regards the idea of "peccatum."'[102] Its central theme was the notion of *culpa*, in the technical sense of 'guilty mind' or blameworthy state of mind. The canonists were the first to inquire into the moral quality of acts which constituted factual sins. Like the civilians, they insisted that, before a person could be held criminally accountable for his wrong acts, there must be a psychical connection between the actor and the wrongful act. They took a further step: they emphasized the normative aspect of intention and stipulated that it is the intention to do a harmful act that makes an actor liable to the penal sanction. In other words, they were concerned with the pre-eminently moral issue of whether the defendant's wrongdoing resulted *not* from the will or intention to do wrong. This notion culminated in the emergence of the intellectual hobby horse of criminal jurisprudence – *mens rea*. The canonists' elucidation of the moral conception of crime was unnecessarily encumbered by the ecclesiastical purposes for which they wrote. But it was given precise and extensive formulation by one of the post-Glossators, Lucas de Penna. Relying on Ullmann's pellucid exposition,[103] we shall briefly outline this conception of crime.

The Moral Conception of Crime

De Penna 'postulated a close interrelationship between criminal, crime and punishment.'[104] In this triad, the central and controlling position was occupied by the word 'crime.' He advanced the idea that every crime is an offence committed against society in general and thus constitutes a public wrong.[105] It follows from this that 'the prosecution of criminals is the concern, not of private citizens but of society ...[and] accordingly, fines imposed upon criminals flow into the coffers of the State and are not to be considered as a means whereby the wronged party obtains satisfaction.'[106] Sounding uncannily modern, he considered 'the external wrongful act,' the factual sin or actual wrong deed 'merely as a symptom of the criminal's state of mind – it is the internal attitude of the offender not his external act, which constitutes crime.'[107] In short, 'Lucas's view of crime is subjectively oriented. The ... unlawful character of the external act is not a sufficient basis upon which to estimate its criminal character. The decisive element is the individual's intention,'[108] that is, 'the evil intention of the wrongdoer.'[109]

It is immediately clear that, like the political conception of crime, the moral conception of crime is not concerned with the intractable question of what acts are or ought to be criminalized. On the contrary, the moral conception assumes that the 'criminal' knows which acts are wrong, according to the line of right conduct drawn by God, man, or state. In other words, this view of crime does not require us to enter into such debates as to whether, for instance, adultery is wrong or whether it should be criminalized. Nor does it require us to pose such questions as whether the political sovereign authority was right in criminalizing (say) poaching or in enacting sumptuary laws. Issues raised by such questions fall outside the pale of both the political and the moral conceptions of crime. Both rest on the premiss that, according to the laws of God, Man, or state (as the case may be), adultery, poaching, and violation of sartorial regulations are legally prohibited acts.

What constitutes an evil intention? De Penna answers: '[T]hat intention must be considered as evil which is detrimental and destructive both from the moral and religious and from the social point of view.'[110] He links the evil intention of the wrongdoer with the question of punishment: the presence of the evil intention suffices to make the perpetrator liable to 'punitive treatment.' At first glance, this does not have anything to say about the entirely different penological issue of the purpose and appropriate type of punishment.

However, because de Penna postulates a close connection among criminal, crime, and punishment, he has to introduce penological issues into the exposition of the moral conception of crime. To him, the primary purpose of punishment is to correct the wrongdoer by 'directing him to ethically good actions.'[111] This, in turn, makes him insist that 'the motive of the perpetrator is the sole element which designates his act as wrongful.' Since 'the chief concern of the punishment is the criminal himself,' he insisted that 'the punishment should be commensurate to the criminal's motive.'[112] According to him, 'wherever the motive of the delinquent expresses no evil intention no reason can be adduced ... to inflict punishment on him.'[113]

The word 'motive' is ambiguous. But it had definite meaning in pre-modern times and, as de Penna suggests in the passage above, was not infrequently used as a synonym for 'intention.' In brief, the Middle Ages distinguished between 'good' and 'bad' motives or 'evil' and 'good' intentions. In practical terms, the use of the one or another indicates the approbation or disapprobation, or legality or illegality, of the action so described. Approbation or disapprobation here does not refer to any subjective or divergent opinions on or about right and wrong. Rather, they refer to what were regarded as absolute or universal ideas of right and wrong. An action was good if, and only if, the actor was impelled by a motive which was not merely good in given circumstances but absolutely good. Likewise, an action was bad if the actor was impelled by a motive which was universally and absolutely bad. Thus, it is the goodness or badness of the motive or intention which impresses an act with a moral character. This is starkly reflected in language for we often employ different words to describe factually identical actions or passions.[114]

We are accustomed to ascribing to Bentham[115] and the Utilitarians the notion that no action is good or bad in itself but rather that it is the consequences of a given act which enable us to determine whether an act is good or bad. It is less well known that Bentham also opined that the distinctive element which converts a wrong act into a criminal offence is 'the state of the offender's mind with reference to the obnoxious event,' and that this is 'relative to intentionality and consciousness.'[116] De Penna quite clearly made the same point when he insisted that 'the offender's action presents itself as criminal precisely because it springs from an *unlawful* intention, *not because it is harmful and unlawful in itself.*'[117] This is not, of course, to say that medieval jurists were Benthamites before Bentham; they certainly were not. But it points to an unexpected similarity between their respective philosophical assumptions. This is the notion that the moral quality of an act does not belong to the realm of ordinary facts, but to the realm of law.

The determination of the legal quality of an act takes place at two levels. At the first level, we are faced with the pre-eminently general issue: 'Is X wrong?' At the second level, we are faced with the particular issue: 'Is this X wrong?' Both are legal questions. To use a specific example, that 'homicide is wrong' belongs to a first-level legal judgment; that '*this* homicide is wrong' belongs to a second-level legal judgment. In the present context, the fundamental difference between medieval jurisprudents and Benthamites is that, while the former recognized at least three sources of law, God, man, and state, legal positivists recognize only such decrees as emanate, mediately or immediately, from the state. Nevertheless, both would concur in the proposition that it is wrong to do what the law reprobates.

The pertinent question then is: What exactly does the law reprobate? It is a platitude that 'ought presupposes can.' The law cannot prohibit human beings from erring any more than God can make two plus two equal five. Nor, it appears, can the law forbid the occurrence of the psychic state in which human actions ordinarily take place. The law, therefore, stays within the realm of possibility, and it reprobates neither the factual wrong deed nor the factual psychic state in which human actions ordinarily take place. Instead, the law reprobates the doing of harmful acts in an unlawful state of mind. If we use the words 'intention' and 'motive' interchangeably, it becomes clear that the motive to do what the law does not condemn cannot give rise to an unlawful intention so as to make the act a crime, at least not when, as was the case in pre-modern times, law was thought to coincide with morals. To take a particular example, provided one keeps within the parameters of lawful self-defence, the intention to ward off an unlawful attack cannot amount to an unlawful intention so as to convert a killing done in self-defence into culpable homicide. The self-defender acts with a good motive.

Whether a harmful act was committed intentionally is a question of fact. Whether the intention is legally innocuous, or, as de Penna would have put it, 'detrimental and destructive from the moral, religious and social point of view,' is a question of law. Remembering that the purpose of the factual inquiry is not to determine whether a given act amounts to a crime, the factual question is always: 'Did the defendant intentionally do what he did?' The moral or legal question is always invariably: 'Why did the defendant intentionally do what he did?' An affirmative answer to the first question is a prerequisite for posing the second question; the second question would not arise unless the first receives an affirmative answer. It is the answer to the latter question that will enable the adjudicator to determine not only whether the act in question is wrong but also how wrong the act is from a moral or legal point of view. In short, the factual question raises the issue of the conditions of imputability[118] while the legal question raises the issue of the conditions, degrees, and extent of responsibility. Medieval jurists rightly regarded them as two distinct issues.

In one sense, both the question of fact and the question of law are moral questions: one poses a 'legal-moral' or extra-legal question, the other poses a 'moral–legal' or 'intra-legal' question. An act cannot possibly amount to a crime unless the two questions are answered in the affirmative. But the moral conception of crime regards the first question as a non-legal issue. It holds that the conditions of imputability are relatively settled or uncontroversial. It takes the inquiry into the moral quality of the act as its starting point. Consequently, the question 'whether X intentionally did what he did' is not conceived, in this schema, as raising moral issues. The only moral issue is whether the accused did what he did in an unlawful state of mind, or, which is here the same thing, whether he was actuated by an unlawful or a bad motive.[119] Thus, what was a question of fact when the purpose of the inquiry was to ascertain whether an act could be imputed to the actor became a question of law when the purpose was to determine whether (and, if so, to what extent) the actor was liable to 'punitive treatment.' Nor did the pleonastic men of the Middle Ages hesitate to employ two different words to denote 'intention' when the purpose of the inquiry was not to establish individual responsibility but to determine the extent of responsibility. Hence, de Penna used the phrase 'evil intention' when talking about crime but switched to 'motive' when talking about punishment.

That de Penna was, in all probability, following a conventional practice in employing two apparently different words to describe what is, in reality, a single legal category becomes clear when we consider his view on the determinative factor in fixing punishment. In strict conformity with the subjectively oriented view of crime, he insists that 'the constitutive element of crime [that is, the evil intention of the perpetrator] warrants the infliction of varying *degrees* of punishment upon criminals who have committed superficially identical crimes.'[120] An example will make the point clearer: one person killed because he wanted to avenge a previous homicide; another killed because he caught his adulterous wife and her paramour *in flagrante delicto*; yet another killed because he wanted to facilitate his own escape from a robbery scene. From an observational point of view, they all intentionally committed homicidal acts. From a moral-cum-legal point of view, however, the robber's action is not only wrong but also more reprehensible than that of the unfortunate cuckold; the avenger's act may not even be illegal at all.

A person is either liable or not liable. Consequently, liability is indivisible. But responsibility *is* divisible. Thus, while an evil intention suffices to establish liability to punishment, the type and/or degree of punishment must vary according to the degree of responsibility discernible from the totality of the circumstances in which the wrongful act was done. As de Penna puts it, 'responsibility varies according to certain circumstances which influence the formation of the evil intention ... wherever the internal freedom of motivation is decisively influenced and restricted by circumstances which lie outside the individual's personality, his responsibility is diminished in proportion to the influence of those circumstances.'[121]

The external stimulus may have exerted such an overbearing influence on the offender that he ought not to be subjected to 'punitive treatment.' Unlike the notion of liability, the notion of responsibility is not monolithic: 'In the opinion of Lucas, the notion of responsibility is flexible and elastic: the perpetrator's responsibility may be diminished by certain accompanying circumstances, which, when they exist in sufficient strength, may completely neutralize the freedom of motivation, and consequently lead to exculpation.'[122]

The notion that 'external circumstances may exercise such a decisive influence on the formation of the intention that the motivation is no longer free,' and that in such a situation 'the individual cannot be held in any degree responsible for his action,'[123] points to another fundamental difference between the moral and the political conceptions of crime. Whereas the moral conception of crime separates the conditions of imputability from the conditions of responsibility, the political conception conflates the two. The result is that, while the former regards the requirement of evil intention as a positive requirement for responsibility, the latter regards intention as a negative requirement for liability. Put differently, while the moral conception of crime insists that an evil intention is the constitutive element in crime, the political conception starts from the opposite position that 'the wrongful act [is] the constitutive element' of crime.[124] Thus, the task in the one case is to ascertain whether there is any reason for holding the accused liable and, if so, to determine the extent of his responsibility. The task in the other is to ascertain whether there is any reason for not holding the defendant liable. Of course, under the two regimes, 'intention' is a necessary element for liability. But, whereas the former fastens on the morality or rather immorality of the intent, the latter fastens on the factual or purely psychical notion of intent.

When it came to the issue of the extent or degree of punishment, the fact that the political conception of crime favoured a psychical test for liability led to insuperable difficulties. One of the immediate consequences of the Norman Conquest was that capital punishment was substituted in many cases where pecuniary compensation or fine had hitherto been the proper remedy.[125] Capital punishment did not allow for the kind of graded punishments which the canonistic writers as well as de Penna had in mind when formulating the moral conception of crime. For instance, while ecclesiastical authorities had a bewildering number of punishments which were carefully calibrated to fit different degrees of guilt or fault manifested by criminous clerks who commit homicides, 'English law hardly knew what to do with a slayer who was not guiltless but [who] did not deserve to be called a felon and put to death.'[126]

As noted above, the societal perception of wrongdoing was closer to the moral conception of crime than it was to the political conception of crime. This is not to say, however, that the societal concept of wrongdoing coincided with the moral conception of crime. In other words, it was not the moral conception of crime that was, strictly speaking, reflected in jury behaviour. Further, although we know that Bracton's *Treatise* is replete with the assertion that it is the intention to injure which makes the crime, and that he attempts 'to anglicise the learning of his Italian masters,'[127] it is nevertheless not entirely clear whether he conceptualized 'intention' in accordance with the moral or the political conception of crime or strictly in conformity with the 'societal concepts of criminal liability.'[128] The correct answer is probably that he construed 'intention' sometimes according to the one, on other occasions according to the other, and on still others according to the societal concept of liability.[129] However, one thing is clear and that is that Bracton's definition of capital crimes was derived from classical sources.[130] This means that, in Bracton's view, a person could not be visited with capital punishment unless he intentionally did the felonious act. Be that as it may, when it came to punishment 'the English law of Bracton's day could command a scale of only three alternatives: acquittal, pardon or the gallows.'[131] Acquittal occurred when the accused was not guilty, that is, the criminal act was not committed intentionally; pardon, when though the criminal act was committed intentionally, the circumstances were such that 'the community did not believe the defendant deserved to be hanged.'[132] Pardon often entailed forfeiture of worldly goods and was, therefore, 'a quasi-sanction.'[133]

A conception of crime such as de Penna's which intimately links crime with both the criminal and the punishment, and which rigorously applies the principle that 'it is the "why," the motive, which impresses upon actions the mark of criminal character,'[134] is bound to recognize different shades of guilt. It follows that it will also recommend inflicting varying degrees of punishment, not only upon criminals who commit apparently identical crimes, but also upon those who commit different crimes in identical situations.

De Penna insists that any such differentiating factor must be outside the personality of the actor, and 'his responsibility is diminished in proportion to the influence of those circumstances.' Such external or extraneous factors may serve to enhance or to mitigate the punishment. In some cases (such as 'necessity,' 'duress,' and 'self-defence') the influence of the external factors may be deemed so overwhelming as to 'completely neutralize the freedom of motivation,' and, therefore, 'exculpate the offender from all criminal responsibility.'[135] The notion that factors external to the personality of the individual may exculpate the offender from all criminal responsibility requires some clarification.

There is no need to enter into a lengthy discussion of the list of the extenuating, aggravating, or neutralizing circumstances given by de Penna.[136] It suffices to underscore the point that, in his scheme of things, the fact that intention to injure exists is determinative neither of the question of liability or of the choice of the type or degree of punishment. A person may have intentionally inflicted injury on another or intentionally done an act which, viewed superficially, amounts to a violation of the law. Yet, when the totality of the circumstances is taken into account, the act may not amount to 'intentionally-doing-what-the-law-forbids.' In such a situation, we travel back, so to speak, to our starting point. In other words, we move 'anti-clockwise' from the conclusion in an argument to its premise. The argument assumes this form: 'D is not liable to punishment because he is not a criminal. He is not a criminal because he did not commit a crime. He did not commit a crime because he did not do the wrong act in an evil state of mind.' In short, when de Penna wrote about 'circumstances which completely neutralize the freedom of motivation and which may suffice to exculpate the offender from all criminal responsibility,' it should not be thought that, in such cases, liability is first established only to be negated by the unfree motivation. Rather, de Penna's argument is just a convenient, prosaic expression of the core principle of liability under the moral conception of crime, namely, that the evil intention of the wrongdoer is the constitutive element of crime. It is the evil intention that makes the defendant into a criminal liable to punishment. We cannot tell whether the intention is an unlawful or an evil one until all the factors that 'caused' the defendant to act as he did have been considered in the round.

To conclude, behind the moral conception of crime stands the picture of an individual personality or subject who not only knows which acts are wrong but also recognizes that he is bound in conscience to abstain from transgressing the lines of right action drawn by God, man, and state. The willingness to abide with the law in a particular situation is a personal and subjective fact; what the decrees of God, man, or state require in any given situation is a general and objective fact. The latter is independent of the private moral values of individual citizens or subjects; the former can exist only as individual subjective facts. The moral conception of crime is not concerned with the specific contents of the law of God, man, and state; on the contrary, it takes them as given. Rather, it concerns itself primarily with the internal, subjective fact. It insists that we should endeavour to ascertain, in every case, whether the defendant's action springs from an unwillingness to structure his external action to conform with the demands of the law, and, if so, to determine the extent of his responsibility.

Willingness or unwillingness to obey the law is a factor that is 'personal' to the individual; it does not lie outside the individual's personality. But the reasons 'why' are factors outside one's personality. Under the regime of the moral conception of crime, the existence of the personal factor is a sine qua non for liability while the reasons for the unwillingness to abide with the law may attenuate or aggravate legal responsibility. These issues assumed a particular form in England, and the solution proffered under the common law is given expression in the doctrine of *mens rea*.

4

The Idea of Wrong under the
Common Law II

The science of law that was derived from Roman law and that paved the way for the emergence of the moral conception of crime lays claim to universality. However, in adopting and applying the legal concepts and categories derived from classical texts, local moral attitudes and sentiments intruded into and largely coloured the meanings which such universal legal terms bear in different jurisdictions.[1] As a result, the mere fact that Rome is the home of many common law criminal terms is not in itself a sufficient basis for assuming that these terms retained their pure Roman meanings under the common law. Indeed, English law did not receive substantive principles from Roman law.

Nevertheless, the intellectual impact of the legal terms and categories that the legists derived from Roman law indirectly affected their signification under the common law. Although some scholars deny that the genesis of the common law rule of liability for crimes is to be found in Roman law,[2] there is, as we saw in the preceding chapter, little doubt that Roman legal terms and concepts were deployed in the service of common law of crimes. This alone is sufficient reason why we cannot avoid alluding to Roman legal ideas.

The signification of common law criminal terms was determined by the mutual influences and reactions of Roman legal scholarship, canon Law, and the mores of the English people as expressed in jury behaviour. When, as a result of the emergence of 'juridical nationalism,'[3] Englishmen became provincial and, subsequently, the common law became the subject of professional monopoly, Roman legal terms and categories acquired and retained local (common law) meanings. But the constant deployment of Roman legal terms and categories by 'lawyers, judges and legal academics,' in a never ending attempt 'to portray in a single work the whole of the common law,'[4] often leaves the impression either that the content of these legal terms and categories was wholly derived from Roman law or that their *true* meanings are to be found in Roman law.

A corollary of this is that any divergence between the locally fashioned meaning and that derived from Roman legal science will likely be resolved in favour of the latter. (The Aristotles of common law,[5] such as Sir Matthew Hale, Chief Justice Coke, and Sir William Blackstone, can fairly be acquitted of this charge.) The insidious result of such a 'cognitive posture' is that Roman legal terms and concepts which had been relieved of their non-moral characteristics by canonistic learning are surreptitiously restored to their facile Roman meanings. By this device, legal theorists, specifically positivists, have been able to insist 'on a precise and a morally neutral vocabulary for use in the discussion of law and politics.'[6] That, well into the nineteenth century, law, politics, and morals were neither separated nor (if separated) kept in watertight compartments has been emphasized by many historians of medieval and pre-nineteenth century scholarship.[7]

The common law rule is that a person is not criminally liable unless she or he did the wrong act in a certain state of mind called *mens rea* or guilty mind.[8] The rule is encapsulated in the maxim: *actus non facit reum nisi mens sit rea*. This maxim or its equivalent made its first appearance in an English legal text as early as the twelfth century. The anonymous author of the *Leges Henrici Primi* resorted to the maxim while discussing the crime of perjury.[9]

P.E. Raymond,[10] among others, has suggested that the correct interpretation and significance of the maxim, in the form in which it appeared in the *Leges Henrici Primi*, turns on a passage in which St Augustine enunciated a subjective notion of *mens rea*. However, rather than beginning this chapter with Augustine, we will endeavour to trace 'the phases in the development of criminal *mens rea*'[11] by offering a short excursus on the theoretical distinction between criminal and penal law. The significance of this distinction for criminal *mens rea* is then underscored. Lastly, an attempt will be made to isolate the distinctive features of criminal *mens rea*, and it is here that reference will be made to Augustine. The chapter concludes with Chief Justice Coke's adoption of the subjective meaning of *mens rea* in the seventeenth century.

Penal and Criminal Law

At first glance, the adjective 'criminal' in the phrase 'criminal *mens rea*' appears otiose. But it is not. This is because the notion of *mens rea* features prominently not only in criminal but also penal laws. Both criminal and penal laws have one thing in common, 'punishment.' Indeed, as we saw in the preceding chapter, the notion of punishment is intimately connected with the concept of crime; in the majority of cases, criminal liability results in the infliction of punishment. This makes criminal law look similar to, if not identical with, penal law. But however similar penal and criminal laws may appear to be, there is an analytical difference between the two. Whereas penal law deals with the whole field of punishment, criminal law deals with a small (but an exclusive) segment of punishment. Put differently, while all criminal law is penal, not all penal law is criminal: 'The terms *Criminal Law* and *Penal Law* are by no means identical ... Penal Law is a term of wider signification than Criminal Law; it means that branch of law which deals with punishment. All Criminal Law is Penal in its nature, that is, it effects its ends by means of punishment, but all Penal Law is not Criminal.'[12] It is this difference between criminal and penal laws that distinguishes criminal *mens rea* from another form of *mens rea* which suffices to ground penal liability generally but not criminal liability. In Roman law, criminal *mens rea* or what came to be known as such was called *dolus*; penal *mens rea* or what came to be known as such was called *culpa*.

Significance of the Distinction between Criminal and Penal Law

Before considering the meaning of *dolus* and *culpa*, we must underscore the importance of the distinction between penal and criminal law for the signification or the ambit of criminal *mens rea*. In the first place, the recognition of the distinction would forestall the likelihood of confusing cases falling under the ordinary or general head of penal law with those belonging to the extra-ordinary or special (criminal) law. Medieval scholars were not unaware of the distinction between criminal and penal liability but they did not explicitly underline the difference between them. As a result, institutional writings of the time sometimes give the impression that their authors were not aware of the theoretical distinction between penal and criminal liability. This leads to apparent ambiguity in their works, a fact that Bracton's *Treatise* illustrates.

Bracton started by defining *injuria* as anything done wrongfully. He then divided *injuria* into two classes, namely, *delicta* and *maleficia*. He distinguished *delicta* from *maleficia* on the basis of the 'will and intention' with which they are perpetrated. 'Will and intention,' he wrote, 'are the marks of *maleficia*, and the major and minor crimes arise *ex maleficio* while delicts arise *ex delicto* as trespasses when mean and measure are not observed.'[13] In other words, Bracton explicitly confined *dolus* to crimes. Indeed, Bracton asserted repeatedly that a crime was not committed unless the intention to injure existed. Yet, when considering homicide by misadventure, he deemed it necessary to add that the offender would not be liable unless there was *dolus* or *culpa*. The implication is that *culpa* could support criminal liability. But this inference flies in the face of the emphatic statement that 'it is will and purpose which distinguish *maleficia*.' The better inference is that such inconsistencies are more apparent than real. They are due partly to the fact that both the political and the moral conceptions of crime probably featured side-by-side in Bracton's scheme of things, and partly to the fact that he did not explicitly make the theoretical distinction between penal and criminal liability. Or the explanation may be that Bracton was not simply 'a lawyer who set down legal stipulations and legal theory pure and simple.'[14]

In the second place, the realization that penal law is the genus of which criminal law is a species, and that medieval jurists were conscious of it (even though they did not deign to explicitly formulate the theoretical distinction between them), obviates the necessity of having to decide whether or not *culpa* was a sufficient basis for criminal (as opposed to penal) liability under Roman law. For, whatever the position may have been in classical times,[15] and whatever the position may be in contemporary times,[16] it is the position taken in medieval juristic thought that determined the course of legal development on this issue. And it is abundantly clear from the literature that, throughout the medieval period, *culpa* was not considered a basis for criminal liability.[17]

Two Forms of *Mens Rea*: *Dolus* and *Culpa*

Dolus and *culpa*, then, are the forms that *mens rea* assumed in Roman legal texts. They are convenient shorthand words for states of blameworthiness, guilt, or fault. In the former case, it is the state of a person's mind that has to be blameworthy; in the latter, it is the character of a person's conduct. When the Bolognese scholars mined Roman legal texts and extracted from them universal legal terms and concepts, they took over the two forms of *mens rea* found in Roman law.[18]

We saw in the last chapter that the conceptual formulation of crime made intention an element of crime. Medieval jurists carefully kept and restricted each of the two forms of *mens rea* to its proper functions: *dolus* or any of its numerous equivalents such as 'prava intentio, malus animus, malitia'[19] was confined to the criminal branch of the law; *culpa* was restricted to the penal branch of the law. Medieval jurists never thought that the latter could be a sufficient basis for criminal as opposed to penal liability. Neither the civilians nor the canonists nor the common lawyers entertained the belief that *culpa* could lead to the infliction of what Bentham[20] aptly called 'extra-ordinary species or degree of punishment,' namely, 'death, mutilation, imprisonment, or loss of one's worldly goods.'[21]

Criminal *Mens Rea*: *Dolus*, Malice, Intent

What, then, is criminal *mens rea*? In Roman law *dolus* means strictly fraud, intention, intentional wrong;[22] it 'implies deceit, concealment, clandestinity.'[23] However, *culpa* could also mean 'blame of every kind and so include *dolus*.'[24] Or, as Austin puts it, *culpa* means 'negligence, heedlessness or temerity' and so includes 'indirect and sudden intention.'[25] Nevertheless, in deferential parlance, a distinction was drawn between *dolus* and *culpa*. Rather than cast a veil of mystery on these words, 'the ingenuity of the first masters of language'[26] clarified them by maintaining a sharp distinction between the two. To use D.A. Stroud's terminology, *dolus* denotes full intention while *culpa* denotes imperfect intention.[27]

We can be more exact. In Roman law, *dolus* signified 'willful and designed injury done to another.'[28] It was clearly distinguished from *culpa*: 'In Roman criminal law an effect is said to have been caused *dolo*, whenever the will of the agent was consciously directed towards the attainment of the effect, *when the effect was directly aimed at by him* ... *culpa* meant negligence, lack of skill, blameworthy conduct (*malum exemplum*), recklessness.'[29] It is important to emphasize the phrase 'directly aimed at by him' because, as H.D.J. Bodenstein rightly points out,[30] the Bolognese jurists who took over the concepts of *dolus* and *culpa* from the Romans were careful enough to confine *dolus* to its narrow meaning. To expect otherwise from men who regarded Roman law as *ratio scripta* will be to underrate their dependence on classical legal materials.

In English Law, the word 'malice' performed the function of the Roman *dolus*. English law required malice in murder, but, as Austin puts it, this merely means that 'the murder should be intentional.'[31] Since, according to Austin, '*dolus* includes direct and indirect intent,' this way of putting the issue assimilated indirect or oblique intention into *dolus*. As already noted, the Roman legal term *dolus* excluded indirect intention, and there is no reason to suppose that the legal science based on Roman legal materials did otherwise.[32] Whatever nuances may have been bestowed on 'malice' in the deeply religious society of the Middle Ages, juristic thought served more to expound than to expand its meaning.

The quintessence of 'malice' in common law of crime is *malice prepense* or malice aforethought. Pollock and Maitland suggest that, when the term *malitia* first came into use in English law, it hardly signified a state of mind; rather, it meant wrongdoing.[33] Or, as Sayre puts it, 'malice was construed in its popular sense as meaning general malevolence or cold-blooded desire to injure, and referred to the underlying motive rather than to the immediate intent of the actor.'[34] To make *malitia* refer to a state of mind, some qualifying adjective like *praemedita* or *ex cogitata*, was needed.[35] When this was done, the phrase 'designated a purely psychical element, and referred to the immediate intent of the actor.'[36] In other words, the phrase *malice prepense* initially referred to 'the relation between the psyche of the agent and his act and its consequences.'[37] During the formative period of the common law of crime, all felonious homicides were punishable and a homicide was felonious if it was committed intentionally.[38] If the psychical element was present, the defendant was punishable; both excusable and justifiable homicides were felonious. Indeed, until after the fourteenth century, it was always necessary to obtain pardon in the case of justifiable or excusable homicide.[39]

This brings us back to the distinction made in the last chapter between the political and the moral conceptions of crime. While under the former criminal *mens rea* denoted 'the relation between the psyche of the agent and his act and its consequences,' under the latter it included also 'his state of mind regarding the unlawful nature of his conduct.' In the one case, the presence of the psychical element was sufficient for criminal liability; in the other, the psychical element was only a necessary but not a sufficient condition for liability.

The institutionalization of the moral conception of crime, and its cognate meaning of 'malice' or criminal intent, can be dated to the early part of the seventeenth century. Specifically, it can be attributed to Sir Edward Coke. Sayre has pointed out that 'in his *Third Institute*, which was completed in 1628,' Coke 'found it impossible to restrict the meaning of *malice prepense* to its popular, purely psychical sense.'[40] This is at once a testimony to the hold of the political conception of crime and a tribute to the soundness of the moral conception of crime with its concomitant concept of criminal *mens rea*. In short, it would not be an overstatement to say that the political conception of crime held sway until the seventeenth century. The arguments of Jerome Hall,[41] who assumed that a single conception of crime – the moral conception or at least something akin to it – has always prevailed in common law criminal jurisprudence, are unpersuasive. They are unpersuasive precisely because Hall did not see that the moral conception of crime was preceded by the political conception. As we have argued, the two conceptions of crime are not identical, and criminal *mens rea* did not have the same meaning under both regimes. Indeed, recent research into jury behaviour in pre-modern criminal trials has confirmed that, while the official interpretation of such terms as malice or *malice prepense* inclined to the purely psychical element of intent, the jury was more sympathetic to the societal notions of criminality.[42] In other words, the jury looked not so much to the psychical aspect of intent as to the circumstances which brought the psychical fact into being – an attitude that was not asymmetrical with the moral conception of crime. The common law of crimes was considerably influenced by juries' moral and idiosyncratic convictions. The most cursory glance at the writings of the principal historians of the common law will bear this out. But we shall confine ourselves to Coke's *Third Institute.*

Writing at a time when *malice prepense* had acquired a technical connotation and was used to distinguish the capital crime of murder from other forms of punishable but lesser homicide, Sir Edward Coke described *malice prepense* as 'when one compasseth to kill, wound, or beat another and doth it *sedato animo.*' He added that 'this is said in law to be malice aforethought, prepensed, malitia praecogitata.'[43] In other words, in Coke's time, what distinguished murder from manslaughter was the environment in which the intention to kill was formed. If the intention to kill was formed on a sudden falling out or provocation it would still be malice but not *malice prepensed.* As Coke put it,

some manslaughters be voluntary, and not of malice forethought, upon some sudden falling out. And this for distinction sake is called manslaughter. There is no difference between murder and manslaughter; but that the one is upon malice forethought, and the other upon a sudden occasion, and therefore is called chance-medley. As if two meet together, and striving for the wall the one kill the other, this is manslaughter and felony.[44]

Coke described murder as 'when a man of sound memory and of the age of discretion, *unlawfully* killeth an reasonable creature ... with malice forethought either expressed by the party, or implied by law.'[45] The presence of the word 'unlawfully' shows quite clearly that not all intentional killings were malicious or unlawful. In short, under the common law the psychical element of intent was a necessary but not a sufficient condition for criminal *mens rea.*

Yet the phrase *mens rea* is often used by writers to denote the threshold requirement for criminal liability under the common law without adverting to the difference in its meaning when used in the context of the political conception of crime. This oversight enables some commentators to write as if the history of *mens rea* under the common law commenced with Bracton in the thirteenth century and led directly to Sir Edward Coke and Sir William Blackstone, in the seventeenth and eighteenth centuries respectively. Even such a discriminating analyst as Sayre[46] (who perceptively pointed out that 'malice' had a purely psychical meaning during the medieval period) freely used the phrase 'guilty mind' to describe the beginning and end-product of a process which began in the twelfth century and which culminated in the crystallization of the so-called general defences.

The position taken here is that the moral conception of crime was not formalized in English law until it was embraced by Sir Edward Coke in the seventeenth century. Since the idea of criminal *mens rea* or 'guilty mind' embedded in the common law of crimes was derived from the conjoint influence and mutual reactions of Roman legal scholarship, canonistic learning, and native moral sentiments and attitudes, it is appropriate at this juncture to refer to the reputed source of the common law doctrine of *mens rea*.

The Subjective Notion of *Mens Rea*

Although the intellectual history of the idea of *mens rea* goes back to the moral philosophy of Plato and Aristotle,[47] and was manifested in Roman law in the form of *dolus*, it is to St. Augustine that we owe the ethical notion of *mens rea*. As Maitland has pointed out,[48] the phrase *mens rea*, which has become a permanent feature on the legal landscape, was filched by the anonymous author of the *Leges Henrici Primi* from the great ecclesiastical writers, Gratian and Augustine.

In formulating the idea of moral blameworthiness, Augustine enunciated a thoroughly subjective notion of *mens rea*. Using the example of a person who knowingly swears a false oath, Augustine maintained that 'nothing makes the tongue guilty but a guilty mind.' When one swears falsely, nothing but the knowledge or belief that one is swearing a false oath makes the false oath maker a wrongdoer. It is immaterial that the true state of things or facts coincide with what the false swearer represents or believes it to be. He is a perjurer if he affirms as true (or false) what he knows or believes to be false (or true). What damns him, what makes his action morally reprehensible, is the fact that he knowingly asserts as true (or false) what he knows or believes to be false (or true). Perjury, lying on oath, is not only a transgression of the laws of God but also a violation of the laws of man and state. It springs from an intention to deceive, which is a bad motive, an unlawful intention. Moreover, it is irrelevant that it is in the selfish interest of the false oath maker to affirm as true (or false) what he knows or believes to be false (or true). The blameworthiness of his mind or the goodness or badness of his motive or the lawfulness or unlawfulness of his intention does not depend on the dictates of his private interests but on the dictates of an objective law. The passage is a very long one, but it is worth quoting in full:

For men swear falsely, when either they deceive or are deceived. For a man either thinks that to be true which is false and swears rashly, or he knows or thinks it to be false and swears it as true; and no less in wickedness. But these two false swearings which I mentioned differ. Suppose a man to swear, who thinks what he swears to be true; he thinks it to be true and yet it is false. He does not intentionally swear falsely, he is deceived, he takes this for true which is false, does not knowingly offer an oath for a false thing. Suppose another, who knows it to be false and says it is true; and swears as though what he knows to be false were true. See ye how detestable a monster this is, and fit to be exterminated from human intercourse? All men detest such things. Suppose another, he thinks it to be false, and swears as though it were true, and perhaps it is true. For example, that you may understand, 'Has it rained in this place?,' you ask a man, and he thinks it has not rained, and it suits his purpose to say, 'It has rained'; but he thinks it has not; You say to him, 'Has it really rained?,' 'Really,' and he swears; and yet it has rained there but he does not know it, and thinks that it has not rained; he is a false swearer. The question is how does the word proceed out of the mind. Nothing makes the tongue guilty but a guilty mind.[49]

One thing stands out clearly from the above passage. It is that Augustine maintained a clear-cut distinction between the objective and the subjective wrong. The author of this passage was not much concerned with the objective wrong; the passage simply assumes that perjury is wrong. This is manifest from the laconic declaration: 'all men detest such things.' A corollary of this is that any 'subjectiveness' in the notion of *mens rea* which derived from the idea of moral blameworthiness enunciated in the above passage cannot possibly have anything to do with the objective wrong. On the contrary, it will concentrate exclusively on the subjective wrong, that is, the state of the mind of the actor in relation to the wrong act.

This was precisely what happened. The common law concept of *mens rea*, which has its source in the Christian idea of sins of the mind,[50] is thoroughly subjective. The Christian idea of sins of the mind itself was predicated on the assumption that law is necessarily moral and that the duties imposed by the law bind the conscience. Whether the legal duty was imposed by god, man, or state, or, which is the same thing, whether the crime in question falls into the category of *mala in se* or *mala prohibita*,[51] that is, whether the act is considered wrong in itself or wrong because conventional law says so, criminal legislation binds the conscience. Consequently, as in Roman law,[52] common law *mens rea* presupposes, on the part of the defendant, knowledge of the unlawfulness of the act. Or, as Herbert Packer[53] puts it, the idea of *mens rea* includes the notion of awareness of wrongdoing on the part of the actor. It was assumed that the individual conscience readily recognized the binding force of laws in general, and criminal law in particular. The main issue in criminal proceedings was to ascertain whether or not the breach of the duties imposed by the law emanated from the mind of the actor.

As in modern criminal jurisprudence,[54] medieval jurisprudents postulate a moral agent endowed by its Creator with free will. Although a pessimistic view of human nature was one of the unarticulated premises of pre-modern thought,[55] medieval law was rooted in a firm belief that human beings had the capacity to choose between acting lawfully and acting unlawfully. They set apart for special blame the mind that deliberately or intentionally chose to act unlawfully when it could and ought to have chosen to act lawfully. In short, that 'ought presupposes can' was as fundamental to medieval metaphysics as it would be for Immanuel Kant and most modern moral, political, and legal philosophers. Again, as in modern law, the aim of the criminal law was not to compel the individual to choose to act non-criminously. Then, as now, the general aim of the criminal law was, as H.L.A. Hart puts it, 'to announce to society that [the prohibited] actions are not to be done and to secure that fewer of them are done.'[56] From at least the seventeenth century onwards, the emphasis (under the common law) was not so much on the psychical element of intent as with the normative or moral aspect. The culprit's action must manifest contempt for or defiance of the law.

In the absence of a confession, contempt for or defiance of the law can be inferred only from the totality of the circumstances in which the crime is perpetrated. It is necessary to add here that it was not until 1851 that litigants became competent to give evidence on their own behalf in civil cases, and it was nearly half a century later that accused persons became competent to testify on their own behalf in criminal prosecutions.[57] It is not unlikely that, in some cases, the adjudicator would make the wrong inference, but it is a fatal error to mistake an erroneous inference about a subjective fact for unconcern about the actual mental attitude of the actor,[58] or, to put it another way, to assert that the law favoured objective standard for legal liability.[59]

Just as the Roman legal term *dolus* says nothing about the moral status of acts punishable by public criminal law, the subjective notion of *mens rea* does not have anything to say about the moral status of the prohibited acts. Rather, it is concerned exclusively with the question of whether an alleged criminal act was perpetrated in an unlawful state of mind. And, under the moral conception of crime – which, as we have seen, was incorporated into the common law – an unlawful state of mind does not mean the purely psychical state in which human actions ordinarily take place. Rather, it refers to a specific, precise, and direct intention to engage in an unlawful act. The law cannot and does not attempt to forbid human beings from erring but it can and does attempt to enjoin human beings, acting as free moral agents, to refrain from erring in circumstances in which they could and ought to conform with the law.

The refinement of common law of crimes occasioned by the adoption of the moral conception of crime and the subjective notion of *mens rea* facilitated the attempt to *define* the circumstances in which moral blame could attach. This, in turn, led to the delimitation of the meaning of the phrase 'guilty mind.' To quote Sayre:

[T]he conception of blameworthiness or moral guilt is necessarily based upon a free mind voluntarily choosing evil rather than good; there can be no criminality in the sense of moral shortcoming if there is no freedom of choice or normality of will capable of exercising a free choice. After the twelfth century, new general defences begin to take shape such as insanity, infancy, compulsion, or the like based upon lack of a guilty mind and thus negativing moral blameworthiness.[60]

This is a tortuous way to go about proving 'lack of moral blameworthiness.' The point of such defences as 'insanity, infancy, compulsion' is not so much to 'negative' moral blameworthiness as to show that they are instances in which the issue of moral blame or guilty mind cannot be raised at all. 'Normality of will' and the capacity or ability to exercise it are prerequisites, not the requisites, for establishing moral blame.

It is the moral aspect of intention, its essentially ethical connotation, that makes common law *mens rea* mean 'an evil mind.' And it is this that clearly distinguishes a formal *mens rea* (or *mens rea* under the political conception of crime) from a substantive *mens rea* (or *mens rea* under the moral conception of crime). As G.O.W. Mueller succinctly puts it,

the imposition of criminal liability does not follow every finding of an act and a *mens rea*, or rather seeming *mens rea*, for not every form of *mens rea* also has its substance ... *Mens rea* does not lie ... if the actor had a ground of a justification for his act, or acted by order of the law. Thus in murder, we prohibit the killing of a human being with the intent to kill, but admit exceptions to the rule ... such as the killing at war-time, the killing in self-defence ... etc. As the law does not deem these instances of killing evil, the defendant who kills under such circumstances with intent to kill, though he acted with a form of *mens rea*, intent, has not had the substance of *mens rea*, an evil mind.[61]

From at least the seventeenth century onwards, the common law embraced the substantive notion of *mens rea*. It did not undergo any significant transformation until the nineteenth century.[62]

The distinction between formal and substantive *mens rea* parallels the distinction recently made by George Fletcher[63] between wrongful conduct and wrongdoing. According to him, 'wrongful conduct' 'is a purely formal concept, defined by the incompatibility of the act with the norms of the legal system.' 'The concept of wrongdoing,' on the other hand, 'is material or substantive,' and pertains to the attribution of responsibility for the wrongful conduct to the defendant.[64] In other words, Fletcher drew a sharp line between a formal and a substantive definition of crime.

The substantive notion of crime deals with the definitional elements of crime.

An alternative name for substantive definition of crime is substantive criminal law or the general part of the criminal law. The general part of the criminal law is or should be 'topic-neutral,' that is, the determination of what acts are or should be criminalized does not fall within the ambit of substantive criminal law. Rather, it is concerned exclusively with the conditions under which liability can attach, irrespective of the character of the acts or harms that are prohibited by a given criminal legislation.[65]

One of the distinctive characteristics of the moral conception of crime is that it favours a substantive definition of crime. The moral conception of crime was a product of a moral philosophy that has a distinctively (Judeo-Christian) natural law flavour. It conceives *mens rea* as a metaphysical brake on the power of the political authority to fix the definitional elements of crime and to prosecute, convict, or punish the subject for crimes. In contrast, the political conception of crime was a product of a political theory that was decidedly secular. Consequently, under the political-conceptual model, the power to determine the definitional elements of crime is not ordinarily subject to any constraints other than those expressly or impliedly recognized by the political authority itself. Thus, while the moral-conceptual model necessarily defines crime in substantive terms, the political-conceptual model favours a procedural definition. Nevertheless, under both conceptual regimes, crime would invariably be an objective fact. Or, to use George P. Fletcher's auspicious phrase, what acts are incompatible with the norms of the legal system can be ascertained at any given point in time by examining the corpus of the laws of a given political unit.

Such laws usually contain provisions relating to 'the attribution of responsibility for the wrongful conduct to the defendant.' It is customary to dichotomize the conditions for attributing responsibility for the wrongful conduct to the defendant into the mental and the physical elements or *mens rea* and *actus reus* respectively. The latter is often defined residually as all the elements of an offence except the mental part. As already noted, *mens rea* may refer to either a formal or a substantive *mens rea*. In other words, what constitutes *mens rea* depends on the prevalent conception of crime. The thrust of my argument is that, from the seventeenth century onwards, the common law embraced the moral conception of crime along with the substantive notion of *mens rea*.

The moral conception of crime leaves untouched the role of the political authority in promulgating, prosecuting, and enforcing penal laws. Unlike the political conception, however, it fetters the legislative power of the sovereign by laying down certain conditions for the application of the criminal sanction. These are that the act must be imputable to the defendant and the defendant must be culpable or blameworthy. To be criminally blameworthy the actor must have directly intended to do the crime.

The common law position, then, is that no act can be a crime unless it is also a moral wrong. 'Moral wrong' is an ambiguous phrase; it means different things in different contexts. Here, it means that an unlawful act alone is not sufficient to make a person a wrongdoer: the unlawful act must have been done in a particular state of mind called *mens rea*. And *mens rea* means unlawful intention, in the quintessential sense of wilful and direct intention to engage in an unlawful act. The moral conception of crime thus presupposes a free individual who deliberately violates the legal norm. In the apt words of Owen Fiss,[66] 'the concept of wrongdoer is highly individualistic. It presupposes personal qualities: the capacity to have an intention and to choose. Paradigmatically, a wrongdoer is one who intentionally inflicts harm in violation of an established norm.' That is the sum of the common law position on criminal wrongdoing.

5

Crimes and the Common Law Mind

In the last two chapters we outlined the theoretical assumptions that shaped the concept of crime under the common law, namely, the moral conception of crime and the subjective notion of *mens rea*. In this chapter we will pursue two other assumptions that informed the common law of crimes. These are that crimes are divisible into *mala in se* and *mala prohibita*, and that while the former does not change, the latter is continually changing. The chapter traces the historical formulation of this distinction under the common law and outlines the use to which it was put by the common law mind.

The discussion is divided into two parts. The first part considers criminalization[1] from the perspective of the common law mind. It suggests that the peculiar common law view of legal history which holds that the common law is of immemorial origin gave meaning to the bifurcated categories of *mala in se* and *mala prohibita*. Though the historical justification for the distinction disappeared in the aftermath of the Glorious Revolution, William Blackstone resuscitated the distinction in the eighteenth century. The second part analyses the form and explores the philosophical justifications for the distinction as canvassed by Blackstone in the eighteenth century and its subsequent explosion following the birth of 'juridical positivism.'[2] Its explosion meant the disappearance of the theoretical basis for distinguishing between one class of offences and another.

Over the centuries, a growing consciousness of the fact that 'all human activities are historical: that is to say, conditioned by time and place,'[3] coupled with the desire to avoid the absolutist tendency of Roman law,[4] led common lawyers to take an avowedly anti-civilian stance.[5] At the same time, it prompted them to put increasing emphasis on the origin of the common law in immemorial unwritten law. The result was a form of common law hermeneutics that purported to assign the common law a pedigree as ancient as the Angles, Jutes, and

Saxons themselves.[6] The common law was regarded as the ancient and fundamental law of the land,[7] as 'second nature' in Richard Hooker's apt phrase,[8] and
was used as a bulwark against the indiscriminate and extravagant political and
legal powers claimed by sovereigns in Tudor and Stuart England.[9] In the result,
'by the early 1600s the belief that the common law was merely an expression of
immemorial custom had become an article of faith.'[10] The attendant 'intellectual insularity'[11] fashioned a potentially efficacious weapon which curtailed and
controlled the political sovereign's legal powers.

When applied in criminal law, the intellectual character of the common law
as 'a kind of secondary law of nature'[12] enabled the most outstanding common
lawyer in pre-revolutionary England to assimilate common law offences into
the category of *mala in se*.[13] This meant, among other things, that when common law offences were declared by statutes the political sovereign authority
could not abrogate such statutes or diminish their content or change the legal
character of the offences themselves: common law offences were rooted, as it
were, in immutable law. But the designation of a particular offence as *malum in
se* did not have criminal jurisprudential implications: both *mala in se* and *mala
prohibita* were offences. Thus, notwithstanding the apparent latitude enjoyed by
the legislative authority in creating or declaring new offences, and despite the
bifurcation of crimes into *mala in se* and *mala prohibita*, English law was able
to remain faithful to the theoretical presuppositions of the moral conceptual
model of crime.

Criminalization and the Common Law Mind

The growth of crimes consists more in the gradual process by which hitherto
unprohibited or legally neutral or indifferent acts, conducts, and activities were
brought under the cognizance of the criminal law than in changes in the character of the acts, conducts, and activities themselves. From the second half of the
twelfth century, when legislation became a regular feature of the legal landscape,[14] the criminalization process was accelerated by the determined effort of
the monarchy to enhance its own legal authority and to suppress all manifestations of lawlessness.[15] By the seventeenth century, numerous offences had been
created or declared by statutes. Indeed, offences created by statutes constituted
the bulk of the 'pleas of the crown,' as crimes used to be called.

That the majority of offences had been created or declared by statutes was
not lost on the men of the seventeenth century who saw the common law as the
accumulated wisdom of ages of judging. For instance, Sir Edward Coke explicitly remarked that 'the pleas of the crown are for the most part grounded upon
or declared by statute laws.'[16] However, they articulated the 'pleas of the

crown' in a way that was consistent with their working belief that the common law was politically and legally the ancient and fundamental law which stood above the King and, perhaps, controlled Parliament. In their scheme of things, Parliament was as ancient as the common law itself; common lawyers early aligned themselves with Parliament.[17]

Nearly half a century ago, T.F.T. Plucknett[18] pointed out that much of the common law was ultimately of legislative origin. In spite of the belief in the immemorial origin of the common law, the common law mind of the seventeenth century was keenly aware of this. But it was also conscious of the fact that not every statute[19] had been made by Parliament. A typical example would be a law made by the King in the exercise of his prerogative powers. Consequently, a distinction between offences that were declared by parliamentary statutes or deemed acts of Parliament and those created by other statutes loomed large in their minds. Offences created or declared by the former were *prima facie* common law offences while those declared by the latter were not, being regarded rather as penal statutes.[20] Of course, both amounted to 'pleas of the crown,' but to the common law mind their respective legal character was different.

In this section of the chapter, we will deploy the structural apparatus fashioned by the peculiar historical sense possessed by the common law mind in explicating the classification of offences into *mala in se* and *mala prohibita*. Taking three specific examples, we shall briefly outline 'the reason and cause'[21] for criminalizing the enumerated acts, conduct, or activity, and we will emphasize the determinative role of the common law mind in investing these offences with the legal character they had in English law. The three examples are unlawful hunting, sumptuary regulation, and such 'fiscal offences' as counterfeiting, smuggling and forestalling.

Unlawful Hunting

We noted in the previous chapters that late Anglo-Saxon England was an embryo feudal society and that the nascent feudal structure was rapidly brought to perfection by the Normans. To the common law mind, Anglo-Saxon England had been a land of freedom. The centralizing policies of the Norman kings, with the concomitant engrossment of political and judicial powers, created a congenial atmosphere for the belief in the 'free Anglo-Saxons.'[22] The conquest was perceived as having ruptured the ancient constitution and disturbed the political and legal equilibrium that obtained in Anglo-Saxon England. All the political and legal developments subsequent to the conquest were construed as the gradual process by which the English people redeemed or emancipated themselves from the Norman yoke. According to the common law mind, the conquest subjected or attempted to subject the English people to a 'complete and well concerted scheme of servility.'[23] The forest laws, which vested property in all game in the king, epitomized such a 'concerted scheme of servility.' Indeed, Blackstone ranked the forest laws among the violent alterations of the English constitution made by the Normans.[24]

Although there was a royal forest before the conquest, the forest law did not pre-date the Normans' arrival on English soil.[25] As Blackstone puts it,

in the Saxon times, though no man was allowed to kill or chase the King's deer, yet he might start any game, pursue and kill it upon his own estate. But the forest laws vested the sole property of all game in the King alone; and no man was entitled to disturb any fowl of the air, or any beast of the field, of such kinds as were specially reserved for the amusement of the sovereign without express licence from the King by a grant of chase or freewarren.[26]

The first forest law was made by William the Conqueror.[27] His successors expanded it into a code to protect the trees and wild animals within the forest boundaries. By the time of Henry I, the pleas of the forest, as offences against the forest laws were called, were numerous.[28]

Breach of the forest laws attracted severe and brutal punishments such as castration, loss of eyes, and cutting off hands and feet. In the twelfth century, the rigorous enforcement of the forest laws occasioned many insurrections and upheavals of the barons and principal feudatories.[29] In the fourteenth century, property qualifications were introduced for hunting rights.[30] However, although the forest laws were later momentarily revived by the Stuarts,[31] by the end of the sixteenth century they had almost ceased to be enforced. They ultimately fell into desuetude. But, in Blackstone's fine phrase, the forest laws sired a bastard offspring – the game laws.[32]

The device by which kings granted franchises to landowners conceded to the grantees the right to hunt deer and game within parks, chases, and warrens. However, pleas of the forest were cognizable only in the King's court. As a result, even the holder of a franchise could not punish offences committed against the rights conferred by such a licence on his own authority; pleas of the forest were pleas of the Crown.[33] When the forest laws became obsolete, the game laws were enacted and frequently augmented to 'ensure that the hunting of game, particularly hares, partridges and pheasants was the exclusive privilege of the landed gentry.'[34]

This is not the place to traverse the whole gamut of the history of the game laws.[35] It suffices for our purposes to underscore their effects on criminal law.

The right to hunt, based on the view of Genesis that 'animals were made for man,'[36] was perceived by Englishmen as a natural right. When the forest laws first made the exercise of that natural right a legal offence, the enforcement of the laws was naturally 'embarrassed with too many inconveniences.'[37] It never sank into the consciousness of 'the people' that unlawful hunting was really wrong. How could what was thought to be an assertion of an immemorial or natural right against the Jacobean forest and game laws constitute an offence? It follows that poaching was wrong only because it was prohibited by and for the convenience of the King, and, subsequently, for the convenience of the landed gentry. As has been pointed out by several scholars the belief that poach- ing was not wrong formed the context in which the poacher operated. The inveterate belief that hunting was not wrong in itself, that is, that it contradicted neither the law of God nor the common law (at least as far as it related to landowners), when digested by the common law mind became acts that were merely prohibited.

The history of the game laws is revealing for another reason. It affords an excellent illustration of how a morality, born of extraordinary circumstances, gives rise to new laws. The game laws were eventually reformed.[38] The result was a return to the supposed common law position, namely, that game was the property of the proprietor of the land on which they were found. But, even before the laws were reformed, the reckless activities of poachers, fuelled by the active connivance of commercial men, had led the landed gentry to realize that some species of game faced extinction. Since the game preserver was invariably the rich landed aristocrat, and since he could and did regard highly both the hunted and the hunting animals, he had cultivated the habit of treating animals with tenderness and love. Of course, we are painting with a broad brush here. In sharp contrast, plebeians had all along been engaged in reckless poaching, hunting down game with fiendish relish. Moreover, members of the labouring classes, who, in their quotidian toils, had to deal with animals were not known to be better than poachers in their attitude to animals. Ill-treatment or cruelty to animals was likely not particularly irksome to such people, but it probably did offend the sensibilities of members of the privileged classes.

In many human societies, cruelty qua cruelty would be regarded as wrong. But whether a particular cruel act would be regarded as so offensive as to be condemned by public law depends largely on the moral attitude of the members of the politically dominant group. For it is the prevailing opinion among such a group that determines a society's positive public morality.[39] Although it incubated for a long time, the positive public morality eventually discountenanced cruelty to animals, and this was manifested in legislation.[40] Thus, a morality that probably originated from what was an accident of history came to be enshrined in the law. If cruelty is wrong in itself, and it was this that formed the palimpsest upon which was etched the law prohibiting cruelty to animals, it might be denied that the common law mind played a dispositive role in fixing the character of offences against the forest/game laws. Nevertheless, it is one of the paradoxes of legal history that the belief that the hunting of wild animals was not proscribed by the ancient law – a belief that fostered mordant hostility to the forest laws – determined the legal character of the offences created by the forest/game laws. That character was that such offences were not common law crimes. They were mere *mala prohibita*.

Sumptuary Laws

The romantic idea that Anglo-Saxon England was a land of freedom and liberty is not necessarily incompatible with the recognition that it was made up of different social classes, namely, 'nobles, freemen and villeins.'[41] Nor is the belief in the 'free Anglo-Saxons' irreconcilable with the notion that the law could differentiate between classes in the social strata. Indeed, as we saw in chapter 1, Anglo-Saxon law explicitly recognized the distinctions between persons as well as between social classes. All this would be readily granted by the common law mind. What the common law mind would reject is the belief in an hierarchical universe which is reflected in the microcosm called society and which stipulates that a man's place in the society is fixed at birth. The common law mind would unhesitatingly attribute any traces of such a belief that may be found in English law to the invidious influence of 'the authority of Justinian in law and of Aristotle in philosophy.'[42] In other words, while the common law mind would deny that it was the spirit of the common law to keep individuals perpetually buried within the social class into which they were born, it would at the same time concede that the law could distinguish between classes and regulate the actions of individuals insofar as such conduct constituted public evil.

Whatever the common law mind would say, medieval English society was thoroughly imbued with the principle of hierarchy.[43] Whether the common law is of immemorial origin (as Lord Coke and others maintain) or whether it evolved only after the Norman Conquest (as modern historians assert), the function of the rules of law in England during the later Middle Ages was the preservation of the feudal socio-economic and political system.[44] Of course, whether particular conduct such as an individual's manner of living or dressing is perceived as constituting a public evil and, therefore, a proper subject for legal regulation depends largely on the state of economic development in the society in question. Later Anglo-Saxon and early Anglo-Norman England were predominantly agricultural. They were able to produce goods only for the domestic market, and what manufacturing there was was also focused mainly on domestic consumption.[45] As well, there was little commercial activity. The end result was a society without a significant amount of wealth. And, since there was not much wealth, the opportunity for private luxury, extravagance, or ostentation was minimal or non-existent: 'consumption was automatically limited by the prevailing poverty.'[46]

The situation changed gradually after the conquest, and by the fourteenth century private luxury was so common that the political authorities deemed it necessary to enact sumptuary laws. F.E. Baldwin[47] has enumerated the factors responsible for the change. In the first place, the constant liaison between the courts of France and England led to the importation of costume and styles into England from the continent. Second, England made considerable progress in the manufacture of clothes and in the arts of goldsmithing and jewellery-making. Third, and most important, successes in wars with foreign countries brought considerable wealth and articles of luxury into England:

[T]he development of extravagance and luxury during the fourteenth century was largely, if not primarily, due to England's successes in foreign wars ... Great quantities of garments lined with fur, of fine linen, jewels, gold, silver plate and rich furniture, the spoils of foreign cities, were brought into England. There was hardly a gentlewoman in the land who hadn't in her house some spoils from Caen, Calais and other French cities. At Poitiers the English were said to have been so laden down with valuable booty that they despised military equipment and, at the taking of Harfleur, even the camp followers placed no value on gowns trimmed with fur. Those Englishmen who had gone to Alexandria brought home with them cloth of gold, velvets and precious stones.[48]

The increase in wealth and the availability of costly articles led to ostentatious display of luxury and extravagance both in the dressing and living habits and in the manners of men and women. As individuals strove to outdo each other, it became apparent that the stability of the social order was in jeopardy. As Baldwin writes,

as a result of this flood of costly articles, the ladies of England became haughty and vain in their attire ... Nor was this haughtiness of attire confined to the ladies. The knights too endeavored to outstrip each other in the brilliancy of their appearance, and the lower classes followed the example of the nobility in their manner of living as well as in dress, thus transgressing one of the fundamental, though unwritten rules, of medieval society, namely, that every man should 'keep his place.'[49]

In order to ensure that every man kept his proper place in the social hierarchy, the political authorities resorted to sumptuary legislation. The first sumptuary law that regulated in detail the sartorial appearances and costumes of the English people[50] not only attempted to curb extravagance in dress but also did so in a way that recognized and preserved class distinctions. In medieval and early-modern English society, apparel proclaimed the man as well as the woman:

Few things often help us more effectively to realize the regimentation of medieval and early modern society in England than do sumptuary laws of the period. Every costume was to some extent a uniform revealing the rank and condition of its wearer. [The 1365 statute] serves to preserve and accentuate natural differences in dress and thus to bolster up the class distinctions on which they were founded. In taking up the various classes one by one, from the lowest to the highest, it grants to each one a few more privileges with regard to dress than it had accorded to the class next below it. It also makes distinctions within a class, the wealthier members of the group being allowed to indulge their taste for finery to a greater extent than their poorer brethren.[51]

Nevertheless, the laws cannot be comprehended merely as manifestations of a determined attempt to preserve the social pyramid. It may even be that, like many other laws,[52] sumptuary laws had economic purposes, though economic purposes as perceived and understood by men whose idea of the function of law was the perpetuation of the contemporary socio-economic and political order.[53] Indeed, it has been pointed out that sumptuary laws were part of the scheme devised by Edward III to promote prosperity in fourteenth-century England.[54] And, while it would be rash to rule out the influence of (Christian) ethical ideas,[55] the regulation of personal conduct continued to be justified for a long time on social, economic, and political considerations.[56]

However, the wisdom and efficacy of sumptuary laws came to be doubted.[57] Indeed, Blackstone, who was not used to castigating the common law, expressed terse reservations about the wisdom of such laws: 'It may still be,' he wrote, 'a dubious question how far private luxury is a public evil and as such cognisable by public laws.'[58] All traces of sumptuary laws were wiped out from the statute books in the nineteenth century.[59]

Having briefly outlined 'the reason and cause' behind sumptuary legislation, we turn to the next question: What was the legal character of breaches of such statutes? At least one legal scholar, who perceived sumptuary laws as a species of 'regulatory offences,' concluded that they were 'derelicts on the waters of the law.'[60] This is not altogether satisfactory. Although J.E. Starrs recognized that the conscience of a society changes with time, and that this is often reflected in its laws, he looked at regulatory statutes generally, and sumptuary laws in particular, as products of an unsound jurisprudential outlook.[61] Thus, he expressly denied that 'the laws prescribing the attire to be worn by various classes of society had sought to remedy some public evil.'[62] But if we immerse ourselves in the jurisprudential outlook of medieval and early-modern England, we come to the opposite conclusion. That indiscriminate display of extravagance and luxury as well as unrestrained freedom of consumption constituted 'public evil' was the background belief against which the authorities set out to enact sumptuary laws. The makers of such laws regarded unrestrained extravagance and luxury as contrary to what may be called the law of natural classes. However, it is inconceivable that they would have deigned to put sumptuary laws on the same pedestal as breach of the fundamental natural law, for nothing could be clearer than the fact that garments are artificial contrivances. Further, since the distinction between *mala in se* and *mala prohibita* was firmly ingrained in the law,[63] transgression of sumptuary laws would naturally fall into the latter category.

At any rate, the decisive factor is not the opinion that sumptuary laws were mere 'flotsam and relics of an era through which our legal system has grown in its process of enlightenment.'[64] Nor is it how the makers of the laws would have classified them. Rather, the determinative factor is what the common law mind would say. As noted earlier, the existence of different social classes would not be necessarily repulsive to the common law mind. It is, however, one thing to recognize different social classes, and quite another to concede that the law could interfere with the personal conduct of members of such classes. To the extent that sumptuary laws attempted to keep men and women perpetually in the social classes into which they were born, the common law mind regarded these measures as repugnant to the spirit of the common law. In fact, the decline of interest in sumptuary legislation in England[65] coincided with the period when the common law mind crystallized and the law was beginning to turn away from the artificial and arbitrary separation of people favoured by such legislation. To the common law mind, sumptuary laws could not be anything but unnecessary legislative interference with the personal liberties of men and, perhaps, women. As such, they punished what was neither wrong in itself nor wrong at common law. In other words, sumptuary offences were *mala prohibita*.

Fiscal Policy and Crimes

At its inception, pecuniary mulct was probably seen as a convenient way by which a balance could be struck between the less grievous crimes or less vicious criminals and their punishments. But fines had a meretricious effect on the criminal law. This was due largely to the fact that their use brought fiscal considerations into the criminal justice system.[66] The fiscal interest of the Crown in the administration of criminal law became paramount in the period following the Norman Conquest when the King's Peace, and, therefore, the King's criminal jurisdiction covered the whole kingdom. Specifically, the fiscal element in the administration of criminal law ultimately shaped and determined the political attitude[67] to regulatory statutes. In discussing the corrosive influence which fiscal considerations had on criminal law, we will focus our attention on the effect which the deployment of regulatory statutes in the service of the King's fiscal policy had on the classification of the relevant offences.

Before the conquest, the revenue of the King was derived from his vast possession in land, the demesne and the folkland. In both cases rent was paid in kind, that is, in goods and services. Fines and charges imposed in the King's court constituted another source of revenue. Obviously, the revenue realized from fines could not have been considerable because there were many legal authorities beside the King who exercised judicial functions in Anglo-Saxon times. A fumage, a sort of tenement rate, was also payable to the King. Apart from these permanent sources of revenue, 'taxes' were levied, usually in periods of emergency or imminent peril, by the supposed embryo parliament – the witenagemot.[68]

The transformation of England from a nascent feudal society to a mature and 'most royal of all the feudal monarchies'[69] did not immediately give rise to any new form of taxation, whether direct or indirect. But the revenue generated from pecuniary mulcts in the administration of the criminal law increased considerably.[70] Additionally, the Kings started to exercise, probably for the first time, certain rights such as purveyance, pre-emption, and prisage.[71] Moreover, the incidents and casualties of the mature feudal system brought from the continent, such as wardship and livery, became entrenched and rigidly enforced. The exercise of the prerogative rights was also a good source of revenue: 'Other sources of revenue springing from the King's prerogative or his right to the demesne existed in – grants of liberties and charters to towns and guilds; composition for tallage, a head which strictly falls within the revenue from the demesne; and grants to individuals of markets, fairs, parks, and monopolies.'[72] Virtually all of these prerogative rights, the existence of which was never doubted, were used as fiscal instruments by kings in the subsequent centuries. It was not until after the Civil War and the Glorious Revolution in the seventeenth century that some of the prerogative rights of the King were either abolished or whittled down by Parliament.

Direct taxation or tax on moveables was introduced for the first time in 1188.[73] By the thirteenth century it had become a regular fixture in the constitutional and legal arrangement of the polity.[74] Taxation was unpopular from its inception. No matter how unabrasive its effects might be, taxpayers never liked to part with their property in the name of taxation. Dr Johnson tells us that taxation is a spiteful and hateful thing; Edmund Burke asserts that 'to tax and to please, no more than to love and be wise, is not given to man.'[75] So loathsome was taxation that, although pre-modern men believed that oaths carried spiritual sanction,[76] they had no scruples about prevaricating when it came to taxation: 'In ancient, as in modern times, oaths have ever been little regarded.'[77] Neither the lawmakers themselves, except the King and his officers, nor the general populace were happy about this indirect way of depleting their coffers. When, in the course of the centuries following the Norman Conquest, kings frequently resorted to taxation, especially during wars with foreign nations, taxation bore heavily on the subjects. The administration of taxes worked relatively smoothly only when the tax was not too burdensome, as was the case in the early periods, or, as in the later periods, when the relationship between the King and the leading social classes was cordial.[78]

The incidence of taxation was felt by virtually all segments of the society, except the Crown itself.[79] Opposition to taxation was widespread.[80] The poor resented many levies and taxes on movables; landowners and farmers did not like taxes on immovables; excise duties were resented not only by the peasantry but also by agriculturists and tradesmen. Merchants and tradesmen were happy about port duties[81] only to the extent that such payments assured the safe conduct of their ships on the seas and of their goods on the King's highways.[82] The administration of taxes itself bred much corruption.[83] Consequently, tax evasion and such related activities as smuggling and counterfeiting were indulged in without remorse.[84] The attitude still persists in modern times.[85]

Yet, notwithstanding the fact that tax evasion and the like were common, as well as the reality that 'taxation is the creation of statute and not of common law,'[86] the common law mind would not hesitate to designate tax-related offences as common law crimes. For coining was early monopolized by the Crown, and, as was noted earlier, port duties were ancient sources of revenue for the King. Indeed, counterfeiting the King's coin amounted to a high treason,[87] and smuggling has always been regarded as a very serious offence, a felony.

The common law mind also classified forestalling, ingrossing, and regrating[88] as common law crimes.[89] In fact, Sir Edward Coke characteristically traced the existence of these offences to pre-conquest times and appropriately called them *mala in se*. Since these commercial practices were 'highly criminal at common law,'[90] and since, as noted earlier, the legal character of common law offences could not be affected by Parliament, forestalling should have remained a crime. Surprisingly, however, by 1850 forestalling had ceased to be a crime in English law.

Among other reasons, this was perhaps due to the fact that, from the thirteenth century onwards, the primary purpose for enforcing the common law rules as well as statutes against such commercial practices was to generate revenue for the King rather than to protect the public against the rapacity of tradesmen. We have seen that resentment of taxation was widespread and that the people had no qualms in engaging in activities that circumvented the fiscal demands of the King. When the rules against forestalling and other practices were put to fiscal use, they naturally fell into disfavour: resentment of taxation left a permanent impress on the criminal law. In order to put the metamorphosis of these common law crimes into its proper perspective, it will be necessary to outline briefly the general moral outlook of late-medieval and early-modern English society.

One of the essential functions of the government in medieval English society was to regulate the economic activities of individuals in order to harmonize private with the public interest.[91] Medieval authorities did not consider it wise to leave the determination of the quality and prices of goods and services to the superintendence of an invisible hand. On the continent, this function was performed solely by local authorities, but in England, where strong central government early emerged, it was performed, jointly and severally, by the central and local authorities, that is, governmental authorities and the guilds.[92] Both authorities were impelled by a well-defined moral ideal:

[T]he ideal aimed at by medieval state was a moral ideal – honest manufacture, a just price, a fair wage, a reasonable profit. Commerce and industry were regarded as a series of relations between persons not as a mere exchange of commodities. The acceptance of this moral ideal naturally led men to think that modes of manufacture, prices, wages and profit could be and ought to be definitely fixed by reference to the definite and fixed standard of right and wrong by which all human actions must be measured.[93]

This moral ideal gave rise to the promulgation of numerous regulatory laws:

Between the thirteenth and sixteenth centuries, all the major trades and industries became subject to detailed rules and regulations designed to guarantee to the consumer the good quality of products. An extra-ordinarily large number of regulations was made laying down with the most pedantic minuteness of detail, what the quality should be of the most important products in every day life: wine offered for sale was to be pure, with no water in it; bread was to be made of good flour sifted in the prescribed manner; candles were to be of good wax, without resin or tallow; candle-wicks were to be of good cotton; ginger, saffron, indigo and pepper were to be unadulterated.[94]

While the motive of the government was to protect the public and that of the crafts and merchant guilds was to discourage unfair competition among their members,[95] both parties subscribed to the moral ideal of the medieval state.[96] Consequently, throughout the medieval period, the law never acquiesced in the multifarious acts of deception and frauds and the artificial means of raising the market prices of commodities devised and practised by men of commerce. On the contrary, such practices provoked strong moral condemnation and were severely punished.[97] In sharp contrast to the *caveat emptor* rule in later times, when it came to guaranteeing the quality of goods, the rule was *caveat consules*.[98] As long as the pursuit of the medieval moral ideal was the paramount justification for enacting and enforcing regulatory statutes, the rules could be construed as merely declaratory of the common law. However, beginning in the sixteenth century, the regulatory ideal came under increasing attack, and by the middle of the eighteenth century the medieval moral outlook had been displaced.[99]

But long before that happened, regulatory statutes had been put to fiscal use, and, imperceptibly, the fiscal interest came to dominate the enforcement of such laws. For instance, the practice of informing, by which the informer shared with the King the proceeds from fines, made regulatory laws particularly odious in the eyes of the people.[100] In fact, from the sixteenth century onwards the primary purpose for enacting and administering regulatory statutes was to generate revenue for the Exchequer.[101] One example suffices to illustrate this point. In the reign of Henry VIII, a statute[102] entitled 'Proclamations for the prices of victuals viz., the pricing of them, and proclaiming the prices' was passed, ostensibly for the purpose of combatting the frequent increases in the prices of some named victuals. But the remedy it prescribed was manifestly designed more to raise revenue than to curb the mischief. The statute provided that, on the complaint of one of His Majesty's subjects that any of the named victuals was being sold at above the normal price, the lord chancellor would set (by proclamation) and tax the reasonable prices of such victuals. It then enjoined all farmers, owners, broggers, and other victuallers 'to sell to such of the King's subjects as would buy them at such prices as shall be set and taxed by such proclamation'! Is it not clear that the original objective, namely, to make victuals or necessaries accessible to the people, had been diluted by the desire for revenue? In fact, the subordination of the protection of the public to the fiscal interests of the Exchequer started as early as the thirteenth century with the enforcement of laws against food adulteration: 'The thirteenth and fourteenth centuries saw the enforcement of the Assize of Ale to have assumed very much the character of an excise duty ... an increase in public revenue was of more importance than an increase in public health in the administration, during the fifteenth and sixteenth centuries, of laws prohibitive of the adulteration of food.'[103] The displacement of the moral ideal of the medieval state and the subordination of the protection of the public interest to the fiscal needs of the King in the enforcement of regulatory statutes combined to corrode the attitude of the people to this species of regulatory offences. The result was that the character of regulatory offences changed dramatically. In discussing this issue, we will concentrate on the offence of forestalling.

As emphasis shifted from the paternalistic objective of making qualitative goods available at reasonable prices to generating revenue for the Exchequer, the public came to regard the laws 'as a curse.'[104] Also, since foreign and itinerant merchants enjoyed a partial exemption from the rule against forestalling,[105] this must have fostered the belief that those practices were not really wrong. Finally, and more important, the ascendancy of the individualistic impulse coupled with the diffusion of commercial morality radically affected the way governmental authorities themselves perceived regulatory laws.

Individualistic strains had always existed side by side with the corporative system prevalent in the medieval period.[106] From the fifteenth century onwards, the individualistic spirit was brought into prominence by the unprecedented growth of towns, and what Plummer christened 'bastard feudalism.'[107] From the twelfth century when the towns started receiving charters,[108] to the fifteenth century, when the old feudal structure began to give way before a rising middle class, one of the great objects of the townsmen and guilds when they acquired power through charters was to prevent the import of foreign manufactures and control exports.[109] The charters conferred on them the monopolistic right to control and regulate the commercial affairs of the town.

But the practice whereby the King granted mercantile concessions to traders releasing them from local customs barriers posed serious threat to guild merchants. As well, it weakened the monopoly powers conferred by charters bought by townsmen from the same kings. Eventually, the multiplication of such mercantile concessions broke down the protective system of the English towns,[110] and this enabled the great mass of traders throughout the country to assert freedom of traffic. In these circumstances, a growing number of free tradesmen must have come to hold the view that the practices of forestalling, regrating, and ingrossing were not morally wrong but rather normal commercial strategies.

The significance of this point is that when commercial morality began to gain a toehold in society the attitude of men of commerce to regulatory rules also began to intrude into the law. The process was facilitated by a change in political theory which occurred in the seventeenth century. Towards the end of that century, the conception of society as an organic corporative unit was discarded. Its place was taken by an atomistic conception of society in which everybody was on his own. This spelled the death knell for the paternalistic legal rules of the medieval period. By the second half of the eighteenth century, the moral economy of provision, which required regulation and supervision of the economic activities of subjects in medieval and early-modern English society, had been displaced by a new political economy – that of the free market. As E.P. Thompson puts it, 'the breakthrough of the new political economy of the free market was also the breakdown of the old moral economy of provision.'[111]

Laws, says L.O. Pike, are nothing unless they are obeyed, and they are worth little unless obeyed in the spirit as well as in the letter.[112] He might have added that the spirit in which laws are made also determined the way they would be interpreted. Merchants, tradesmen, and townsmen had come to perceive the laws against forestalling and other such commercial practices as at best a necessary evil. As we have seen, in the enforcement of such rules emphasis had shifted from protecting the public to making money for the Exchequer. Consequently, neither the public, in whose interest the rules were made in the first place, nor the tradesmen, against whom the laws were enforced, could discern anything except the revenue objective in regulatory rules. This made such rules obnoxious. Thus, when the philosophical outlook which insisted on such legal restrictions was crushed and replaced by one that was partial to the spirit of economic individualism and benign to commerce, conscience was at last relieved of the constraints imposed by the early regime. Nevertheless, the laws prohibiting forestalling remained on the statute books, but the tongue with which they were read and the spirit with which they were applied were that of the new commercial morality – a morality that did not perceive such monopolistic practices as forestalling, ingrating, and engrossing as wrongful acts.[113] For practical purposes, the statutory prohibitions became dead letters, and before long the relevant statutes were repealed.[114] However, this left untouched the common law rules. When, at the turn of the nineteenth century and in the face of an acute shortage of goods and high prices, the common law rules were invoked to punish these commercial practices, Parliament intervened and abolished the common law rules.[115] Such was the chequered history of an offence that the common law mind had regarded as *mala in se*.

We have seen that the distinction between *mala in se* and *mala prohibita* was ingrained in English law. The common law mind in pre-revolutionary England absorbed common law offences into the category of *mala in se*. This was so whether such offences were declared or created by statute or whether they were contained in judicial precedents. Of course, these two pigeon-holes – *mala in se* and *mala prohibita* – were invented by the canonists. In their scheme of things, offences in the former category were breaches of the fundamental, Judeo-Christian-flavoured, natural law. A corollary of this was that the legal character of such offences could in no way be affected by positive law. To the common law mind in pre-revolutionary England, common law offences had exactly the same attributes and legal status as offences that contravened natural or divine law. Indeed, as already noted, the common law itself was elevated to the same pedestal as nature. Thus, the common law was invested with a moral halo, and this made common law crimes sacrosanct. Put simply, Parliament could not change the common law any more than it could change the fundamental natural law.

The triumph of the parliamentarians in the Glorious Revolution effected a change in the nature of parliamentary power. The early common lawyers would have conceded that Parliament was supreme, but they would have emphatically denied that it was omnicompetent,[116] or that it could change the common law. But after the revolution, parliamentary power was shorn of its legal and ethical constraints. Consequently, parliamentary supremacy metamorphosed into an Hobbesian sovereign legislative power. The Hobbesian conception of sovereignty represents the conventional wisdom not only of many political theorists but also of most modern common lawyers, from Lord Mansfield (1705–93) onwards.[117] The transformation of parliamentary supremacy into parliamentary sovereignty paved the way for the lawmakers to tinker with the common law. The common law crime of forestalling was abolished by Parliament in the exercise of its newly forged plenary powers.

This is not to say, however, that the law was divested of the distinction between *mala in se* and *mala prohibita*. On the contrary, these categories were so deep-seated in the law that it was impossible for them to be blown off by such a sidewind. Although virtually all offences known to the law attracted capital punishment in the eighteenth century, many offences were nevertheless regarded as 'evils merely prohibited.'[118] If anything had changed in the common law of crimes, it was that the veil of the common law could be pierced such that an offence that had hitherto been regarded as a *malum in se* could be shown to be a *malum prohibitum*. In fact, these categories were given a new lease of life by Blackstone, but this a subject for the next section.

The Form and Significance of the Distinction between *Mala in Se* and *Mala Prohibita*

The Historical Justification for the Distinction

Whatever its origins,[119] the distinction between *mala in se* and *mala prohibita* was recognized in English law as early as the fifteenth century.[120] What follows is an attempt to pinpoint the significance of the distinction in English law from the time when it was first judicially noticed to the eighteenth century when it appeared in William Blackstone's *Commentaries.*

In a concluding note to his *Principles of Morals and Legislation*,[121] Bentham remarked that aside from the civil and penal laws, 'every complete body of law must contain a third branch [namely] the constitutional.' He might have added that both the constitutional and the penal laws fall into the larger category of public law. We have already alluded to the fact that criminal law is a species of penal law, and that although medieval writers did not make it explicit in their writings, they were conscious of the distinction between criminal and the penal laws. Since criminal law is a chip from the penal block, it follows that the criminal law falls into the category of public law. Within the latter category, the constitutional comes first in order of priority. As such, it is not surprising to find that the penal, *a fortiori* criminal, law depends on the constitutional in much the same way that the criminal law itself depends on an established system of 'rights and duties in the spheres of private law and public law.'[122] This is the case with the distinction between *mala in se* and *mala prohibita*. Its significance in the law can be understood only against the background of the constitutional theory and practice within which it was elaborated.

By the fifteenth century, it was settled constitutional law that the King had the power to grant dispensations in respect of penal law. But the scope of this power was limited. It extended only to non-common law offences. As we have seen, non-common law offences clearly excluded offences against natural or eternal law. The modern reader will no doubt have difficulty in understanding or determining the content of such offences, but in the scholastic atmosphere of the Middle Ages such an exercise would not have been problematic.[123] Be that as it may, it cannot be supposed that the phrase 'non-common law offences' had exactly the same import that it came to have in the 'classical common law theory'[124] that took shape in post-revolutionary England. However, it was established early on that the dispensing power could be exercised only in respect of penal statutes. The emphasis here is on 'penal statutes,' and, to hazard a definition, a penal statute is a statute, whether made by King or King-in-Parliament, which attached penal consequences to an act that was punishable neither at common law nor by divine or natural law. Such statutes usually redounded to the King's benefit; and, of course, like most public fines and forfeitures, the profits that accrued from the enforcement of such statutes went to the King. The power to dispense with these statutes resided in the King from early times, and, its use having been restricted to *mala prohibita* offences, it survived – unquestioned and unchanged – until the seventeenth century.[125]

When the Latin phrases, *mala in se* and *mala prohibita* made their first appearance in judicial decision it was appropriately within the context of delimiting the scope of the dispensing power possessed by the King. In 1496 Chief Justice Fineux employed the phrase *mala in se* for the purpose of confuting any supposition that the King could exercise the dispensing power in respect of offences against the eternal law or the law of God. A decade earlier, it had been said that the King could not dispense with offences 'against the common law,' for such a dispensation would be 'against common right.'[126] Moreover, one of the early panegyric writers on the common law, Sir John Fortescue, had stated that any supposition to the contrary would be 'against reason.'[127] Hence, the tentacles of the dispensing power could not reach an offence if its exercise would jeopardize or compromise a private (natural) right or a public (common law) right.[128] The eternal law and the yet-to-be-immemorial common law occupied the same pedestal even in the fifteenth century. As an anonymous writer declares:

Inasmuch as the common law was based on the 'law of reason,' there was no essential difference between the position of Fortescue and Fineux. The King could not dispense with the common law, but no more so could he with any other act offensive to that 'eternal law' of nature or of reason with which the common law was believed to be so intimately connected, and which before the time of St. Germain [the sixteenth century] included a condemnation of acts ... offensive to the morality of the church.[129]

Chief Justice Fineux used *mala in se* as a catchphrase which embraced offences against eternal law as well as offences against the common law, and *mala prohibita* to describe 'those things which the King for his own convenience prohibited.'[130]

The King there referred to means the kings beginning in 1066 with William the Conqueror. This is so for a number of reasons. First, as noted above, it was not until after the conquest that the power to legislate came to be vested in and wielded by the kings. Second, the phrase 'those things which the King for his own convenience prohibited' possibly refers to things prohibited by the King in the exercise of his prerogative (legislative) power. Third, and perhaps most important, the leaders of the intellectual and political movements that culminated in the 'classical common law theory' derived as little as possible from William the Conqueror.[131] Rather, they assigned the common law a pedigree older than the Normans, and they saw most of the political and legal developments subsequent to the conquest as mere restorations of the ancient and fundamental law of the land. Thus, whatever any of the Kings beginning with William prohibited for his own convenience amounted to *mala prohibita*.

In this sense, *mala prohibita* were legion in 1496, and they grew steadily in the ensuing centuries. Between the fifteenth century, when the distinction was judicially recognized in English law, and the eighteenth century, when Sir William Blackstone wrote, the issue was neither whether a *malum prohibitum* was devoid of moral content nor whether or not *mala prohibita* were binding on the conscience. The significance of the distinction between the two classes of offences was simply that, while the King could license *mala prohibita*, he could not exercise the dispensing power in respect of *mala in se*.

The dispensing power survived the Glorious Revolution; the Bill of Rights[132] did not abolish it suddenly but rather 'killed it off by degrees.'[133] For all practical purposes, however, the dispensing power disappeared from the law in the seventeenth century. In other words, the historical justification for the deployment of the distinction between *mala in se* and *mala prohibita* ceased to exist in the seventeenth century. The distinction was resuscitated by William Blackstone; however, because, as with Edward Coke and most common lawyers in the seventeenth and early eighteenth centuries, Blackstone's jurisprudence was in the 'Judeo-Christian tradition,'[134] he did not present the distinction in its historical garb. That would have been anachronistic. Rather, he revived the philosophical justification for the distinction. This changed the form and significance of the distinction between *mala in se* and *mala prohibita* in the common law of crimes. It was the philosophical foundation for the distinction that was debated in legal theory in the following century.

Blackstone on the Distinction between Mala in Se *and* Mala Prohibita

Blackstone's discussion of the distinction between *mala in se* and *mala prohibita* is to be found in section two of the introductory chapter to the first book of his *Commentaries*. The section is entitled 'Of the Nature of Laws in General.' There, Blackstone espoused the natural law–natural right philosophy current in the intellectual circles of the time. As his discussion was necessarily a prelude to the exposition of the laws of England, it was necessarily an eclectic commentary on the philosophical basis of law. Until recently, scholars were wont to dismiss this portion of the *Commentaries* as a mere 'bit of rhetoric embodying fragments of inconsistent theories.'[135] However, contemporary writers now emphasize the importance and significance of natural law theory for a proper understanding of Blackstone.[136] For our purpose, two points emerge clearly from Blackstone.

First, to Blackstone, there are two sources of law – nature/God and human – each of which gives rise to different types of law. He calls the body of law that originates from the lawgiver in a polity *municipal law*, which he defines as 'a rule of civil conduct prescribed by the supreme power in a state commanding what is right and prohibiting what is wrong.'[137] The laws that originate from nature/God are natural/divine laws, and the legislative competence of 'the supreme power in a state' does not extend to the rights, duties, and wrongs founded in nature or revealed in divine law: they are rights that human beings have by merely being *in esse*, duties that we perform by virtue of being humans, and things that we abhor because they are wrong in themselves:

Those rights ... which God and nature have established and are therefore called natural rights ... need not the aid of human laws to be more effectually invested in every man than they are; neither do they receive any additional strength when declared by the municipal laws to be inviolable. On the contrary, no human legislature has power to abridge or destroy them ... Neither do divine or natural duties ... receive any stronger sanction from being also declared to be duties by the law of the land ... The case is the same as to crimes and misdemeanors that are forbidden by the superior laws, and there-fore styled *mala in se* ... which contract no additional turpitude from being declared unlawful by the inferior legislature. For that legislature in all these cases acts only ... in subordination to the great lawgiver, transcribing and publishing his precepts ...[138]

The common law is a species of municipal law,[139] and, insofar as it deals with things that 'are naturally and intrinsically right or wrong,' it 'has no force or operation at all.'[140] In other words, since such rights, duties, or things do not derive their quality of rightness or wrongness from human laws, they do not exist as *positive* rights, duties, or wrongs. Further, they do not and cannot exist merely at the sufferance of 'the supreme power in a state.' In short, like pre-1688 common law thinkers Blackstone distinguished between natural and positive laws, but, unlike Coke, he did not identify the common law with natural law.[141] Although the common law was *sui generis*, it was nevertheless a species of positive law. Accordingly, it dealt with, and could dispose of things indifferent in themselves. Nonetheless, Blackstone considered himself primarily as an expositor of the municipal laws of England, and so he opined that all offences ought to be considered 'as deriving their particular guilt, here punishable, from the law of man.'[142]

Secondly, since Blackstone employed the Latin phrases *mala in se* and *mala prohibita* primarily in the introductory chapter to the *Commentaries*, it is not to be expected that he made and used the distinction for any purpose other than to underscore its utility in philosophical analysis. Put differently, Blackstone did not attach any criminal jurisprudential significance to the distinction. Wherever the phrases appear in the *Commentaries*,[143] the context makes it clear that they are used in the philosophical sense. Thus, while it is true that Blackstone revived the distinction between *mala in se* and *mala prohibita*, it is erroneous to maintain that, in the process, he made Chief Justice 'Fineux's'[144] modest contribution to fifteenth century politics a basis for a pretentious classification – to be utilized for all purposes.'[145] Blackstone was as innocent of 'juridical positivism,'[146] as the men of the fifteenth century, and, the historical justification for the distinction having disappeared long before he wrote, he did not employ the phrases in the same sense and context in which Fineux had used them in the fifteenth century nor did he put the distinction to a general jurisprudential use. With him, the distinction was philosophically important, and the moral and political implications it entailed were meaningful only in a non-positivistic legal regime such as that which prevailed in Blackstone's days.

This is brought out clearly in the passage where Blackstone launched into a short disquisition on the obligation to obey the law. He affirmed that 'human laws are binding upon men's consciences.' But he circumscribed that general proposition by insisting that it ought to be understood with this restriction, namely, that

> it holds ... as to *rights*, and that when the law has determined the field to belong to Titius, it is matter of conscience no longer to withhold or to invade it. So also in regard to *natural duties*, and such offences as are *mala in se*. [For] here we are bound in conscience, because we are bound by superior laws, before those human laws were in being to perform the one and abstain from the other. But in relation to those laws which enjoin only *positive duties*, and forbid only such things as are not *mala in se* but *mala prohibita* merely, annexing a penalty to non-compliance, here ... conscience is no farther concerned, than by directing a submission to the penalty in case of our breach of those laws: for otherwise the multitude of penal laws in a state would not only be looked upon as an impolitic, but would also be a wicked thing; if every such law were a snare for the conscience of the subject ...[147]

The nature of Blackstone's binary jurisprudence is such that, as in the case of common law and equity after the Judicature Acts, the waters dripping from the two cisterns of law – natural/divine and human – flow into the same channel but without intermingling. Hence, while the subject is under a political obligation to obey all laws, only such portions of the law as are sanctioned, directly or indirectly, by natural or divine law bind the *natural* or *religious* conscience of the subject. The natural or religious conscience is pre-political in a supremely non-positivistic sense. The infringement of natural rights or the shirking of natural duties or the failure to abstain from doing intrinsically wrong things constituted a breach of the natural bond between man and man, and a denial of God's authority. And so, to Blackstone, while the breaching of natural rights and duties and the doing of *mala in se* are *moral offences*, the breaching of positive rights and duties and the doing of *mala prohibita* are not. In short, both the distinction and the use to which it was put by Blackstone make it clear that he 'meant two entirely distinct sets of acts, treated of by two entirely distinct sets of Laws.'[148] It follows, therefore, that when Blackstone wrote that the conscience of the subject is in no way affected by breach of 'prohibitory law,' he used the phrase 'prohibitory law' in the distinctive sense of laws that forbid or prohibit things that are indifferent in themselves. In his scheme of things, *mala in se* were 'illegal because they were immoral: because, in other words, they had been forbidden by a Divine law, which no human authority could possibly abrogate or abridge even if it desired to do so.'[149] In contrast, *mala prohibita* were illegal not because they were immoral but because they were prohibited by human laws, and they concerned morally indifferent rights, duties, and things. Blackstone's use of the distinction between these two categories of offences did not have any jurisprudential ramifications.

From Blackstone to Austin

We have seen that the historical justification for the division of crimes into *mala in se* and *mala prohibita* in English law ceased to exist in the seventeenth century. As well, we have seen that the bifurcated model was resuscitated by Blackstone in the eighteenth century. Here we will explore and adduce reasons for the form in which the distinction was revived by Blackstone, and highlight the fate suffered by the distinction at the hands of the two leading legal positivists of the nineteenth century – Jeremy Bentham and John Austin.

It has been suggested that no appreciable advance was made in English common law philosophy between St Germain in the late sixteenth century and Sir William Blackstone in the middle of the eighteenth century. This is not strictly correct. As we have already noted, the common law mind crystallized in the early seventeenth century, and the classical common law theory that it fashioned assumed a definite shape before the end of that century; it was to receive the imprimatur of the first Vinerian professor in the next. Although the *Commentaries* contain several elements of the classical common law theory, it is nevertheless necessary to distinguish between the pre-revolutionary common law mind and the common law mind in the age of 'the Whig Supremacy'[150] – for two reasons.

First, modern moral and political philosophy in general,[151] and, in particular, the moral and political theory of John Locke that underpinned or justified the Glorious Revolution 1688, and that greatly influenced the course of legal and political development in the subsequent years, did not belong to the Judeo-Christian natural law tradition to which Edward Coke, 'the great fountain of Whig principles'[152] in pre-revolutionary England, had belonged. Second, the revolution marked the beginning of the ascendancy of the aristocratic element in the polity. In fact, it inaugurated 'the perpetuation of collective leadership of the nation in the form of a propertied aristocracy.'[153] The ascendancy of a propertied aristocracy greatly shaped the penal policy furthered by the law.[154]

As we have severally noted, before the revolution the law was heavily spiced by the moral and political precepts of (Judeo-Christian) natural law.[155] The structure of offences was such that some were taken to be offences against natural or divine law, others as offences at common law, and still others as offences created by penal statutes. The pre-revolutionary common law mind regarded the first two as *mala in se*, and this view implied that the political sovereign authority was impotent to affect the legal character or to diminish the content of such offences. After the revolution, the political sovereign power was transformed into a more or less Hobbesian construct.[156] Nevertheless, the deistic strand in the intellectual climate of the eighteenth century[157] ensured that a place was carved out in legal theory for natural right, with its correlative natural duties and wrongs. Consequently, the distinction between natural and positive law or between natural and acquired rights[158] was maintained in moral, political, and legal philosophy throughout the eighteenth century. Parliament did not attempt to change the bifurcated model of crime; it merely displayed a 'sinister fecundity'[159] by proliferating capital offences.

Blackstone was neither a philosopher nor an historian, but he borrowed liberally from both the old (Judeo-Christian) natural law and the new natural rights theories.[160] Moreover, he subscribed, wholeheartedly, to the Whig construction of English legal and political history.[161] Thus, the *Commentaries* as a whole, and specifically Book Four, which deals with 'Public Wrongs,' can be understood only against the background of the eclectic natural law–natural rights theory and the Whig historical vision that permeate the work. As we have seen, that background warrants the conclusion that it is a mistake to represent Blackstone's resuscitation of the distinction between *mala in se* and *mala prohibita* as having inaugurated a jurisprudential innovation.

Blackstone's influence was more intellectual than practical,[162] and his work made Englishmen begin to look at the law as a science.[163] The scientific approach in the study of law culminated in the emergence of the textbook tradition[164] in the nineteenth century. Unlike the nineteenth-century common law tradition, which was profoundly Austinian,[165] Blackstone's jurisprudence rested on a bipolar *episteme*. On the one hand, there is the law of nature; on the other, there is human law. The former was prescribed by the Creator, God, for the creature, Man, and it was comparable with the principle of motion infused by God into the physical world; the latter was made by a human lawgiver. The law of nature both constrains and regulates man's free will:

[A]s God, when he created matter and endued it with a principle of mobility, established certain rules for the perpetual direction of that motion; so, when he created man and endued him with freewill to conduct himself in all parts of life, he laid down certain immutable laws of human nature whereby that freewill is in some degree regulated and restrained, and gave him also the faculty of reason to discover the purport of those laws.[166]

The precept of the law of nature is simple: 'man should pursue his own happiness.'[167] The actual demands of this moral precept were discoverable by pure reason. Mankind had lost its pristine purity at the Fall; however, in his infinite kindness, God had interposed 'at sundry times and in divers manners' and caused specific laws of nature to be promulgated 'by an immediate and direct revelation.' Such revealed laws of nature are found in the Holy Scriptures, and are called 'divine law.' These laws did not, however, exhaust the whole field of human activities: they 'laid down only such laws as were founded in those relations of justice that existed in the nature of things antecedent to any positive precept.' In short, the natural/divine laws were ontological baggage.

The case is different with human law. Human laws are concerned with and limited to regulating or legislating on 'a great number of indifferent points in which both the divine law and the natural leave a man at his own liberty.'[168] The power to legislate on such things resides in the supreme authority in a state, and such things become right or wrong, lawful or unlawful, as the sovereign decides.[169]

The fideistic basis for any species of law was rejected by Bentham. Instead, he embraced the principle of utility and expounded a thoroughgoing juridical positivism. In the nineteenth century utilitarianism was to juridical positivism what the snail is to its shell: when one moves, it necessarily drags the other along and in the same direction. Utilitarianism is the secular counterpart of the Genesis cosmogony. Like the Biblical story, it purports to begin in the beginning: 'In the beginning there was a moral and legal void. Of course, there was Nature, and, implicitly, Mankind. Nature put mankind in an hedonic garden, and endowed mankind with the faculty of reason with which to discover which actions give more pleasure than pain. Reason appropriately fathomed the principle of utility. Any action that accorded with the principle of utility was good: it could and ought to be legal or at least it ought not to be illegal. Any action that did not accord with the principle of utility was wrong: it could and ought to be illegal or at least it ought not to be legal. Mankind fell when reason forsook the principle of utility and embraced such arrant principles as "asceticism," "sympathy," "antipathy" and "the will of God."'[170] Bentham is the Newton of moral science as well as the Luther who endeavoured to carry out the reformation of jurisprudence or legal theory.[171]

Utilitarianism is both rationalistic and hedonistic. As Bentham puts it, its object is to 'rear the fabric of felicity by the hands of reason and of law.'[172] It is also experiential. In tune with the modern epistemological postulate that the mind is a *tabula rasa* which receives its basic knowledge from sense impressions, Bentham assumes that reason has no contents of its own: it is experience alone that furnishes reason with the data from which it grasps and educes the actual demands of the principle of utility. In Bentham's view, the principle of utility modulates all our moral and legal ideas:

Nature has placed mankind under the governance of two sovereign masters, *pain* and *pleasure*. It is for them alone to point out what we ought to do, as well as to determine what we shall do. On the one hand the standard of right and wrong, on the other the chain of causes and effects, are fastened to their throne. They govern us in all we do, in all we say, in all we think: every effort we can make to throw off our subjection, will serve but to demonstrate and confirm it.[173]

With these words, full of monarchical metaphors, Bentham converted, in one stroke, the question of right and wrong, ethics, or the province of censorial jurisprudence, into an epistemological question, namely, 'how do we know that any action whatsoever is right or wrong?' Of course, the answer he gave was that the rightness or wrongness of any action depended on whether it was conformable to the principle of utility. And, 'an action may be said to be conformable with the principle of utility when the tendency it has to augment the happiness of the community is greater than any it has to diminish it.'[174]

Utilitarianism, then, takes the moral categories of 'right' and 'wrong' as given. And, having converted the moral question of 'what is right or wrong?' into the epistemological question of 'how do we know what is right or wrong?' it proceeded to give a practical, and perhaps irreproachable, answer to that epistemological question and triumphantly announced that it had answered the moral question. Further, it made utility coordinate with truth. In this circuitous way, utilitarian ethics is made the moral theory par excellence, and so the enunciation of a moral and legal science could proceed apace. This harks back to the point made earlier, namely, that any attempt to treat moral issues scientifically presupposes not only the acceptance of the existence of certain moral concepts and categories but also the conviction that the theory one embraces captures the true meaning of such concepts and categories. In short, like most moral philosophies, consequentialism in general and utilitarianism in particular, is inevitably involved in conceptualism, that is, it holds that its concepts 'are operative in the sense that they correspond to elements of the real world.'[175] This is the first leg on which Bentham and his followers stand.

With the principle of utility grounded in nature, and not God, and human reason assigned the role of secreting the actual requirements of the principle, it follows that all laws originate from reason. In legal positivist thought, legislative powers belong to the sovereign in any polity. Hence, all laws originate, mediately or immediately, from the will or reason of the political sovereign authority. This is the second leg on which Bentham and his pupils stand.

In the scheme of positivist-utilitarian legal philosophy, there is no room for such dichotomous categories as natural/positive rights, natural/positive duties, and intrinsically wrong/good things: all things are indifferent in themselves, and they become good or bad by virtue of their utility. Nor is there any room for such niceties as the distinction between the natural and the positive conscience of the subject. If the subject is encumbered with any such excess baggage, juridical positivism relieves the citizen of it, substituting in its place the conscience of the individual whose duty is to obey punctually the behests of the political sovereign.[176] It is not surprising, therefore, to find that Bentham excoriated Blackstone for both making and using the distinction between *mala in se* and *mala prohibita*.[177] Bentham dismissed these phrases as meaningless, and concluded that 'there is no ground for distinction with respect to any sorts of acts whatsoever.'[178] In short, the philosophical justification for the distinction between *mala in se* and *mala prohibita* in the law was exploded by Bentham.

Juridical positivism came to its own in the work of John Austin. As a positivist, Austin inevitably rejected the distinction between natural and positive laws. He comprehended all rules worth the appellation of law as positive law, that is, rules of action set by a political superior for political inferiors. Austin was also the founder of analytical jurisprudence. In contrast to the twentieth-century turn in analytical philosophy[179] as manifested in analytical jurisprudence,[180] he was not enamoured with neo-Darwinian linguistic analysis of legal concepts. And in contrast to the philosophy of ordinary language which confines itself to the conservative task of clarifying the existing moral concepts or to determining the present usage of legal concepts, Austin did not eschew all references to the history of the legal ideas and concepts that he subjected to penetrating analysis. Accordingly, we find that he had something to say on the origin and function of the distinction between *mala in se* and *mala prohibita* in the law. In fact, he takes us back to Roman law.

Austin pointed out that the distinction between *mala in se* and *mala prohibita* derived from another distinction made in Roman law, namely, the distinction between *jus gentium* and *jus civile*. However, he explicated the latter mainly for the purpose of showing that, if (as he held) the true test for our moral and legal ideas was general utility, then the purported distinctions between *jus gentium* and *jus civile* 'are absurd, or are purposeless and idle subtilties.'[181] This resonates with Bentham's position. Austin believed that the classical jurists introduced into Roman law the distinction between natural and positive laws or *jus gentium* and *jus civile* more as an ostentatious display of 'their acquaintance with the ethical philosophy of the Greeks, than because [they thought] it was a fit basis for a superstructure of legal conclusions.'[182] Nevertheless, he found that one legal conclusion was drawn from 'this curious distinction' by Roman lawyers. It is that

the persons, *quibus permissum est just ignorare*, cannot allege with effect their ignorance of the law, in case they have violated those parts of it which are founded upon the '*jus gentium*.' For the persons in question are not generally imbecile, and the *jus gentium* is knowable *naturali ratione*. With regard to the *jus civile* or to those parts of the Roman law which are peculiar to the system, they may allege with effect their ignorance of the law.[183]

He then added that the distinction between crimes *jus civile* and crimes *jus gentium* 'coincides with our distinction between *malum prohibitum* and *malum in se*; and the distinction is reasonable. For some laws are so obviously suggested by utility, that any person not insane would naturally surmise or guess their existence; which they could not be expected to do, where the utility of the law is not so obvious.'[184] Elsewhere, he reiterated the gist of the above-quoted passage and expatiated on the use to which modern writers put the distinction.[185]

On the whole, Austin was inclined to reject the distinction;[186] he concluded by pointing out that 'no legal consequence has been built on this last distinction, by any of the systems of positive law which have obtained in modern Europe.'[187] There is no better way of saying that the distinction between *mala in se* and *mala prohibita* did not have any jurisprudential implications.

The distinction between *mala in se* and *mala prohibita* could be considered from two standpoints, namely, an hermeneutic and a philosophical point of view. The first affords an internal rationalization for the bifurcated model of crimes while the latter provides this model with an external justification. The internal rationalization hinges on an historical accident in the development of the common law. This is the constitutional power of dispensation possessed by the King. The dispensing power was exercisable in respect of laws made for the benefit or convenience of the King. The licensing of non-compliance with or breach of such laws did not ordinarily affect the common law rights of the subject. Between the fifteenth century, when the distinction was judicially recognized, and the seventeenth century, when the dispensing power became a dead letter, the phrase *mala prohibita* was used primarily to designate this class of offences. During the same period the phrase *mala in se* was used to denote common law crimes as well as offences against natural or divine laws. When the dispensing power disappeared from the legal scene in post-revolutionary England, the distinction between *mala in se* and *mala prohibita* ceased to have any meaningful ramifications in the law. As we have seen, however, Sir William Blackstone resuscitated the distinction in the eighteenth century, and he did so by reverting to its external or philosophical justification. This was the epistemological belief that, whereas *mala in se* derive their wrongness or illegal status from natural or divine laws, *mala prohibita* owe their illegal status to conventional or positive laws. Whatever else the common law might be, it was obvious to Blackstone that the common law was not a part of natural or divine laws. Consequently, common law crimes are offences against positive laws. In other words, crimes at common law that were not at the same time crimes against natural or divine laws are, properly speaking, *mala prohibita*.

The root of the philosophical justification for the distinction is to be found in the ethical philosophy of the Greeks. From the Greeks it passed into Roman law, and from there it migrated into the Western intellectual tradition. But whether it was Greece or Rome or England, the distinction did not entail jurisprudential conclusions; it had only moral and political implications. The sole legal inference that seemed to have been drawn from the distinction was the one made by Roman lawyers – in certain circumstances, ignorance of the law could be claimed in respect of crimes *jus civile* but not crimes *jus gentium*. Neither the pre-revolutionary common law mind nor the common law mind in the age of the Whig supremacy nor the acutely analytical mind of John Austin made the distinction a basis for jurisprudential conclusions. Bentham rejected the distinction in its entirety, and he was followed in this respect by Hans Kelsen,[188] who unhesitatingly declared that all crimes are *mala prohibita*. If the distinction continued to be made in the law, its use ought to have been confined to its philosophical function. But we shall see in a subsequent chapter that the distinction still plagues criminal jurisprudence.

6

The Re-emergence of Regulatory Offences

One of the salient points made in the preceding chapter is that the regulatory ideal which prevailed in medieval and early-modern England was displaced in the eighteenth century by a new political economy. The ascendance of free-market ideas sounded the death knell for regulatory laws generally and common law regulatory offences in particular. As well, the explosion of the distinction between *mala in se* and *mala prohibita* meant that there was no longer any theoretical basis for distinguishing between one class of offences and another.

It is well known that a species of offences often generically referred to as 'regulatory offences,' and that Sayre baptized as 'public welfare offences,'[1] emerged in the course of the nineteenth century. The purpose of this chapter is to underscore the 'substantive reasons'[2] that accounted for the emergence of regulatory statutes in the nineteenth century and, along with them, regulatory offences. In my discussion of the issue, attention will be focused entirely on certain aspects of the history of factory legislation in the first half of the nineteenth century. I have selected early factory legislation because it was the labour and conditions of work in the cotton manufacturing mills that called into being 'the first essay in industrial regulation'[3] in the modern period.

The Laissez-faire Background

The appearance of Adam Smith's *Inquiry into the Nature and Causes of the Wealth of Nations* in 1776 is usually taken as marking the formal abandonment of the principle of mercantilism which sanctioned state regulation of and incessant intervention in the economic activities of individuals in the society. As well, its publication is taken as having ushered in the principle of natural liberty. Although the term was not used by him, Smith is nevertheless generally regarded as the 'first great exponent in England of the principles of *laissez-*

faire, and the subordination of government and law to the enterprise and initiative of the individual.'[4]

Smith theorized that, in the process of pursuing his own self interests, the individual would be led by an invisible hand to contribute to, and unwittingly promote, the public interest. It was believed that the pursuit of private economic interest, untrammelled by restrictive legal rules, would ineluctably promote the public interest. It was therefore considered improper for the government to interfere with the natural economic system for the purpose of promoting what it considered to be the public interest.

Nevertheless, since Smith himself was 'a professor of moral philosophy turned economist,'[5] he introduced one important qualification to the operation of the principle of natural liberty. This was that the individual should be at natural liberty 'as long as he does not violate the laws of justice.'[6] It is unnecessary to spell out what he regarded the 'laws of justice' to be.[7] It suffices to say that they required that the individual would not sacrifice duty to his fellow human creatures at the altars of profit. The point here is that, when Smith wrote what was later relegated to the status of the Old Testament of political economy,[8] he did not make use of the construct known as the 'economic man.'[9] If he had any notion of the 'economic man' it did not occur to him to send such a creature 'into the streets like a man of flesh and blood to make laws for his fellow men.'[10] In short, although Smith was one of 'the high-priests of the commercial society,'[11] and although the moral agent in his system of thought was notoriously a self-centred being, he believed that each individual should have a 'disinterested interest in the survival and welfare'[12] of others.

However, either because they lacked the catholicity of their predecessor or because they held a highly optimistic view of human nature, or for both these reasons, the succeeding generation of political economists freed Smith's moral agent from the shackles of the laws of justice. Thus, 'economic man' emerged as a completely amoral and egoistic entity. Under the principles of natural liberty and of laissez-faire, the onslaughts of 'economic man' were supposed to move unconstrained by any governmental regulatory legislation. The new political economy was shorn of all intrusive moral imperatives to the extent that even humanitarian laws were to be deprecated.[13] As T.W. Arnold states,

[T]he 'economic man' ... [was] invented to explain why moral and humanitarian ideas cannot be pushed too far ... All he needs is intelligent selfishness, and under the great economic principles his sins will all cancel each other, and everything will work out for the best ... all that he needs to do is to follow his self-interest intelligently ... the economic man is an automaton, who needs only to be wound up and set going.[14]

In formulating the principles of the new political economy for 'a new genera-tion of merchants and industrialists,'[15] Smith's successors regarded the erst-while 'laws of justice' as 'the injunctions of indignant moralists.'[16] To them, the principles of natural liberty and laissez-faire constituted the rules of justice of a natural order.[17] From the late eighteenth century until well after the middle of the following century, those who had the power to decide whether the state should intervene in the socio-economic activities of individuals (and if so, how) all subscribed to the basic tenets of the new political economy.[18] Laissez-faire was the battle cry of the merchants and industrialists. As well, it was the official slogan during the decades that witnessed the emergence of the new industrial pattern in England.[19]

Some commentators hold the view that the adoption and long reign of the principle of non-interference were due primarily to the soporific effect which the ideas of the classical economists had on their contemporaries. Whatever may be said for or against that belief,[20] there can be but little doubt that the operation of the principle of natural liberty in the pursuit of economic activities and of laissez-faire in political economy during the early decades of the indus-trial revolution gave rise to horrendous socio-economic and moral conditions. It was in the cotton manufacturing mills that Parliament first intervened to protect 'pauper apprentices' from the appalling conditions under which they worked. This was in 1802.[21] It heralded the advent of modern regulatory laws.

The Factory Regulatory Laws

The 1819 Act

Modern regulatory laws did not really begin until 1819, when the first Factory Act[22] was passed.[23] Further legislation followed in 1825, 1831, 1833, and 1844. The 1833 act marked an extensive departure from the principle of laissez-faire and constituted the first real interference with the liberties of millowners.[24]

The evils that the first factory law was intended to combat can be gleaned from the confines of its provisions.[25] But a better appreciation of the mischiefs aimed at by the law is gained through an historical perspective. Between 1802 and 1819 pauper apprentices had ceased to be the bulk of the children employed in the cotton manufacturing mills. While the older water mills were located in the hinterlands, the invention and deployment of the steam engine had made it possible for large cotton mills to be situated in urban areas. As a result, a large number of children, mostly children of the poor, had been eagerly sought and recruited by manufacturers to work in the mills. This new crop of children labourers was not covered by the 1802 act, and so the master manufacturers were able to recruit tender-aged children and work them as many hours a day as they liked.[26]

How effective was the 1819 act? The available evidence suggests that, like the 1802 act, its provisions were not taken seriously by millowners, and were largely ignored.[27]

The 1833 Act

The accuracy of this observation was substantiated by the royal commission that investigated the conditions of work in the factories in 1833. Although this commission was not unsympathetic to the cause of the factory owners and the principle of laissez-faire, it was nevertheless overwhelmed with the evidence of total disregard of the existing legislation. It found that

in country situations the existing law is seldom or never attempted to be enforced, that in several principal manufacturing towns it is openly disregarded, that in others its operation is extremely partial and incomplete and that even in Manchester where the leading manufacturers felt an interest in carrying the Act into execution as against the evasions practised by the small mill-owners, the attempt to enforce its provisons through the agency of a committee of masters has ... been given up.[28]

The commission concluded that

on the whole ... the present law has been almost entirely inoperative ... and has only had the semblance of efficiency under circumstances in which it conformed to the state of things already in existence, or in which that part of its provisions which are adopted in some places would have equally been adopted without legislative interference, as there is reason for presuming ... that such provisions have actually been adopted in the progress of improvement in other branches of manufacture unrestricted by law.[29]

The widespread evasion of the provisions of the law was in no way limited to factory owners. Parents, overseers, and sometimes the children themselves often had reasons for conniving at the evasions. The commission's report also attested to this.[30] The individual interests of the several participants ran counter to the spirit of the law.[31] The law enforcers had to have recourse to the services of informers and agents provocateurs.[32]

The debilitating effects of long hours of toil on children labourers[33] and the poor conditions in which they worked were also considered by the commission. In this regard, the commission found that whether the factory be in the pure air of the country or in the large town; under the best or the worst management; and whatever be the nature of the work, whether light or labourious; or the kind of treatment, whether considerate and gentle or strict and harsh; the account of the children when questioned as to its feelings of fatigue is the same. The answer always being 'sick-tired, especially in the winter nights' ... 'So tired when she leaves the mill that she can do nothing,' 'Often so tired she could not eat her supper.'[34]

The commission found that one of the stumbling blocks in the way of effective administration of the earlier factory legislations was the difficulties encountered by prosecutors in establishing violations of the law. As one experienced witness explained to the commission

under existing law 'you have got to produce the parents to prove the actual age of the child ... then you've to produce a person who worked near the child in the same room to prove that on the day named in the information, the child worked more than the legal hours ... then, with reference to Sir John C. Hobhouse Bill [the 1825 Act], if you lay the information against the master, the overlooker or manager can still depose that he received orders from the master not to work children more than is allowed by the act and his oath to this effect is still sufficient to cause the information to be quashed.[35]

Having given due consideration to the totality of the evidence, the commission did not hesitate to recommend that 'it should be declared unlawful to employ any child of the prescribed age without a certificate from a surgeon or medical man resident in the township where the mill or factory is situated, who shall certify that ... he believes it to be of the full strength and usual condition of a child of the age prescribed by the legislature, and fitted for employment in a manufactory.'[36] Further, seized of the evidence of continual breaches of the law, the commission also recommended that 'as one security against children being worked beyond the time prescribed ... the proprietor of a mill shall be liable to a penalty on proof of a child having been within the mill more than [the prescribed hours].' It added that 'this provision would obviate many technical difficulties, and the necessity of obtaining the evidence of workmen in the mill or of parties interested, and would facilitate conviction.' It also recommended a system of certified age testimony; it had no misgivings in stipulating that 'the onus should be thrown on the mill-owner of proving that any of the children or young persons in his employment are duly certificated.'[37]

Perhaps the most important innovation recommended by the commissioners, and that was reflected in the law, was the appointment of a corps of inspectors empowered to enforce the provisions of the factory laws. Admittedly, this recommendation was made at the instance of 'certain eminent manufacturers' who were probably more interested in putting regulatory legislation to strategic uses[38] than to ensuring effective implementation of the law.[39]

As usually happens with the recommendations of all such commissions, the ensuing act did not incorporate all the measures recommended. Nonetheless, the act abolished night work for all persons under eighteen years of age (section 1) and limited the length of work for such persons to twelve hours in any one day or not more than sixty-nine hours in any one week (section 2). It prohibited the employment of children under nine years old (section 7), and it progressively limited the employment of children under eleven, twelve, and thirteen years of age to a maximum of forty-eight hours work in a week and not more than nine hours in any one day. The act introduced the system of certified 'strength and appearance' before a child could be employed. The relevant section reads:

[F]rom and after the expiration of six months after the passing of this Act it shall not be lawful for any person to employ, keep, or allow to remain in any Factory or Mill any child who shall not have completed his or her Eleventh Year of Age without a certificate [issued by a surgeon or physician] certifying such child to be of ordinary strength and appearance of a child of the age of Nine years, nor from and after the expiration of Eighteen months after the passing of this Act any child who shall not have completed his or her Twelfth year of age, without a certificate of the same form nor from and after the expiration of thirty months after the passing of this Act any child who shall not have completed his or her thirteenth Year of Age, without a certificate of the same form, which certificate shall be taken to be sufficient evidence of the ages respectively certified therein.

The effect of this provision was that, from the appointed dates, no child of the named ages could be employed in any factory to which the act applied unless the requisite certificate was presented. Offences against the act were addressed in the punishment sections. For instance, section 31 provides that

if any Employer of children in any Factory or Mill shall, by himself or by his servants or workmen, offend against any of the provisions of this Act, or any order or Regulation of an Inspector made in pursuance thereof, such offender shall for such offence ... forfeit and pay any sum not exceeding Twenty Pounds, nor less than One Pound, at the discretion of the Inspector or Justice before whom such offender shall be convicted: Provided nevertheless that if it shall appear to such Inspector or Justice that such offence was not wilful[40] nor grossly negligent such Inspector or Justice may mitigate such Penalty below the said sum of One Pound, or discharge the Person charged with such offence.

Through the semi-annual reports of inspectors vested with the power of enforcing its provisions the 1833 Act opened 'a window on industrial conditions' in England.[41] The inspectors' reports leave no doubt that, like the earlier legislation, the 1833 Factory Act did not meet the ready favour of manufacturers, overseers and, indeed, the parents of children operatives. In some manufacturing districts, it was completely ignored.[42] Manufacturers continually succumbed to the temptation to work the protected children beyond the limits imposed by the law for the extra profits which thereby accrued to them. As W.G. Carson succinctly explains:

[V]iolation of the law's pivotal provisions with regard to hours of labor in this period was a calculated response to economic exigency, a response which reflected perfectly rational, if illegal, choices from within a range of possibilities ordained by the industry's employment structure, organization and economic reasoning. Indeed, 'calculational' was precisely the term that was used in protracted evidence to the Select Committee of 1840 in relation to both overworking and many other kinds of offenses against the act ... According to Superintendent Trimmer ... for example, some mill owners had even told him that it answered their purpose better to pay the occasional fine rather than to obey the law.[43]

The provisions requiring a surgeon's or physician's certificate were early rendered nugatory, since 'certificates were tendered from cow-doctors, dentists and various persons by no means qualified for the work.'[44] More ingenious ways of evading the law were devised and practised by manufacturers, overseers and children:

[T]here was a well-known and often practised fraud of sending the older and stronger children to the doctor, and passing the younger ones into the factory with the certificates thus obtained. One certificate in this way might serve for a hundred children. In Glasgow a boy was known to have driven a regular trade with age certificates; he would present himself to one doctor after another and sell his certificates for a shilling or two.[45]

Transgressions of the law were so rampant and the justices were so lenient in penalizing proven violations of the law – they almost invariably imposed the least fine – that it became a joke in some districts that manufacturers would break the law and pay 'the sovereign remedy!' It was not long before the need for further legislation was accepted.

In a section-by-section commentary on the operation of the 1833 act, a select committee appointed in 1840 attested to the multifarious ways by which the provisions of the law were set at nought. For instance, on the section that allowed millowners to recoup time lost on account of short or excess water or breakdown of machinery, one inspector testified that

at a certain mill, he found that the people had been working over time. It was entered on a particular day, so many hours lost in virtue of the 4th section and in consequence of an extra-ordinary accident. On questioning the hands, I said, 'You lost so much time on such a day?' – Yes, Sir,' 'What was the cause?' – 'There was a dinner to Mr. O'Connell, and we had a holiday.' And, therefore the fracture to the steam engine was coincident with the holiday and the gentleman who owned the mill had the credit of giving a holiday and at the same time recovered the time afterwards, by virtue of the 4th section.[46]

With reference to sections 30 and 31 (both punishment sections) one inspector told the committee that 'if the offence is thrown upon the overlooker, the over-looker admits the case rather than run the risk of losing his situation, as he expects would be the case if he were not to admit it. That is to say, he thinks it better to admit that he has been guilty of the offence than run the chance of los-ing his place.' In calling for the invariable vicarious liability of the master for the acts of his servants, another inspector informed the committee that

the tendency of this opening for shifting the responsibility from the master to the work-man [section 31] is to induce the former, the man of education, character, and station, to represent himself ... as having no knowledge of the proceedings of his work-people ... so that he may escape responsibility himself, although he is the person who ultimately prof-its by the evasion of the law, who can hardly be really ignorant of the acts of his work-people ... The unavoidable responsibility of the master would also lead him to cultivate a better understanding with his work-people, to take a greater personal interest in them and to remove the feeling of distrust which it is said frequently prevailed between them.[47]

In introducing a new Factory bill in the House of Commons in 1844, Lord Ashby, the indefatigable parliamentary champion of factory legislation for sev-eral years, was able to declare, without any fear of being contradicted, that

factory labour has no longer an unquestionable pre-eminence of ill fame; and we are called upon to give relief not because it is the worst system, but because it is oppressive ... Sir, I confess that ten years of experience have taught me that avarice and cruelty are not the peculiar and inherent qualities of any one class or occupation – they will ever be found where the means of profit are combined with great and, virtually irresponsible power – they will be found wherever interest and selfishness have a purpose to serve, and a favourable opportunity.[48]

He most appositely affirmed that 'apart from considerations of humanity which nevertheless should be paramount, the State has an interest and a right to watch over and provide for the moral and physical well-being of her people: the principle is beyond question; it is recognised and enforced under every form of civilised government.'[49] Thus, although operating against the background belief that laissez-faire was the rule while regulation could only be an exception, regulatory laws had come to stay.

This somewhat staccato excursion into the advent of, and reception given to, early factory regulatory legislation, which could be parallelled by others,[50] is perhaps sufficient to illustrate the substantive reasons for the re-emergence of regulatory statutes and 'regulatory' or 'public welfare offences.' It shows, as well, that the self-centred 'economic man' was not a figment of the imagination of the classical economists; the latter merely provided the theoretical underpinning for free reign of economic individualism. The fact that the free reign of economic morality would lead inexorably to insuperable problems was early recognized by discerning minds. For instance, in 1833 a Member of Parliament expressed the view that he did not think that the masters of factories tortured the children in their employ wantonly and gratuitously; rather they mistreated child workers for reasons of profit.[51] The history of the enforcement of factory laws amply confirmed that violations of the law were mostly motivated by economic considerations.

From the perspective of the 'economic man,' regulatory laws created duties which rested on no firm ethical substratum. The moral idea that 'you must not seek without restraint your own profit and well-being but must be careful that in so doing you do not injure others'[52] was not recognized by men in the new industrial order. It was a matter of indifference to the manufacturer qua manufacturer whether the consumer lived or died; it was a matter of indifference to many employers if the employee was maimed, or, if through the negligence of a co-worker he lost his legs and arms to the industrial machine: the doctrine of common employment, fashioned for a pre-industrial society, overly protected the employer.[53] Workers were randomly and accidentally killed during work; many consumers were poisoned and many more made ill by adulterated food.[54] Ecological damage and health hazards resulting from manufacturing activities were seen more as signs of a healthy and buoyant economy or as industrial equivalents of Malthus's natural checks on population than as raising moral problems.[55] The absence of consensus among doctors and scientists on the exact effect of 'noxious vapours' on health left much room to manoeuvre.[56] The passions united with the intellect to suppress interest in the survival and well-being of others. If it was possessed at all, the minimal modicum of altruism which H.L.A. Hart[57] called 'limited altruism' was resolutely kept in abeyance by men to whom profit was a north star.

It remains to add, by way of conclusion, that the recurrent breaches of the law, the innumerable difficulties encountered in enforcing regulatory laws, and the observed readiness on the part of 'the people' to violate or circumvent the law led to the adoption of strict liability in the case of regulatory or public welfare offences.[58] The common law mind would have subsumed these regulatory offences under the rubric of *mala prohibita*. As already noted this categorization would not have had any jurisprudential ramification. The important point to note here is that regulatory offences re-emerged in the course of the nineteenth century.

7

Analytical Jurisprudence and the Criminal Law

The preceding chapters outlined several aspects of the formation of the concept of criminal wrong under the common law. The legal concepts and categories found in the common law of crimes assumed definite shape in the seventeenth and eighteenth centuries. Until the nineteenth century, writers on the common law of crimes were content with describing crime as a public wrong and with merely depicting the twin elements of crime as 'vicious will,' 'evil mind' or *mens rea*, and 'vicious act,' 'unlawful act,' or *actus reus*. They did not attempt to reduce these terms to clear and distinct analytic meanings. In the nineteenth century, the most important aspect of the work done within the sphere of criminal law was analytic. Indeed, the first half of the nineteenth century witnessed the birth, and the second half saw the ascendance, of analytical jurisprudence. The aim of this chapter is twofold. First, it determines the conceptual meaning of criminal wrong enunciated in analytical jurisprudence. Second, it establishes that the concept of crime embraced by analytical criminal jurisprudents was precisely the same as the one which crystallized under the common law in the seventeenth and eighteenth centuries.

Austin is regarded as the father of analytical jurisprudence. It is well known that he propounded an imperative theory of law; however, it is unnecessary for the purpose of this chapter to review Austin's theory of law. Indeed, as will be argued shortly, an excursion into Austin's theory of law is irrelevant to the task of ascertaining the analytic meaning of wrong. Hence, this chapter sets for itself the limited task of identifying the general notion of wrong and the meaning of the concept of crime under the common law explicated by analytical jurisprudents. The latter is a species of the former.

In what follows, we will briefly consider the advent, and determine the nature, of analytical jurisprudence. As well, we will pinpoint the difference between Austin and succeeding analytical jurists. Then, we will explicate the analytical meaning (specifically, Austin's determination) of the general notion of 'wrong' or 'injury.' Next, we will determine the specific meaning of criminal wrong under the common law. Lastly, we will show how analytical criminal jurisprudence established a closed meaning of the concept of crime.

The Advent and Nature of Analytical Jurisprudence

'Everyone,' says W.L. Morison,[1] 'writes the history of jurisprudence for himself.' It would not be inaccurate to say that the history of jurisprudence since the second half of the nineteenth century has been the history of, and sometimes the reaction to, Austin's conception of the jurisprudential enterprise. Hence, a preliminary determination of the nature of Austinian jurisprudence is indispensable for a proper understanding of the idea of legal wrong (of which criminal wrong is a species) which was elaborated in legal theory following the adoption of the analytical method in legal philosophy.

Although the full text of his *Lectures* did not appear until 1863, the first English text on jurisprudence was written by Austin[2] in 1832. The nineteenth century was the scientific century par excellence. Among other things, the scientific outlook required the enquirer to identify and separate the subject matter of enquiry from all others and to accurately capture in *thought* such isolated phenomena. In writing the *Lectures*, Austin adopted the method which made possible the identification and concentration on the study of law as a phenomenon separate and distinct from all other cognate phenomena such as morals and politics. This is the analytical method. The strictly apolitical and amoral bent certified Austin's approach as 'a scientific methodology for the study of law.'[3]

Prior to writing his text, Austin took a trip to Germany which was then the acclaimed 'center of Civil law studies.'[4] Just as in the thirteenth century Bologna had led its legal scholars indirectly to Rome,[5] so did the German civilians lead Austin ultimately back to Roman law. It was probably in Germany that Austin imbibed the classical Roman lawyers' notion, as reflected by Gaius,[6] that jurisprudence or the philosophy of law must concern itself with positive, and not with divine or natural, law.[7]

The influence of Roman law on Austin is inestimable.[8] Indeed, it has been said that 'Austin naturalised many Pandectist ideas and passed them off as universal legal concepts.'[9] Nevertheless, in laying down the program for jurisprudence in the English-speaking world, Austin was not subservient to Roman law. On the contrary, he regarded Roman law as merely the leading exemplar of 'the ampler and maturer systems of law,'[10] and the latter served as the mine from which he quarried the legal terms that are *sine qua non* for the coherent articulation of any system of positive law. As he puts it, Roman law was not 'to be resorted to as a magazine of legislative wisdom, [for] the great Roman lawyers [themselves] were, in truth, *expositors* of a positive or technical system [of law].'[11]

Austin described the coherent exposition of 'the principles, notions, and distinctions which are common to systems of [ample and mature positive] law,' as general jurisprudence or the philosophy of positive law.[12] According to him, this task necessarily requires the identification and careful analysis or determination of the meaning of the leading terms which are *necessarily* employed in the science of law[13] in contradistinction to the science of ethics or politics.[14] In other words, the philosophy of law entails two expository exercises, conceptualization and systematization. It unifies in the latter and universalizes in the former. Austin thus confined the philosophy of law to conceptual analysis and the systematization of the materials of positive law. General jurisprudence or the philosophy of law is in no way evaluative; it does not seek to criticize the law, whether from within or from without. Rather, its task is purely expository or analytic. Austinian jurisprudence is known under the sobriquet of 'analytical' jurisprudence.

It is difficult to sever analytical jurisprudence from the *theory* of law professed by an analyst or the school of jurisprudence to which he or she belongs. Nonetheless, it is important to note that analytical jurisprudence cannot be identified with a particular school or theory of law.[15] Particular theories of law or schools of jurisprudence, no less than analytical jurisprudence, often result in the formulation of definitive meaning of law and other fundamental legal terms. Of course, neither the definition supported by a school of law or that supports a particular theory nor that which results from conceptual analysis can 'settle any fundamental question.'[16] Nevertheless, since the analytical approach is esteemed the scientific method par excellence, the definitions of law and legal concepts fostered by conceptual analysis are more likely to command our assent than those fostered by particular theories or schools of law. Therefore, it is necessary to keep separate and distinct the definition of law and other legal concepts fostered by a particular school or theory of law from the definition of the same phenomena generated by analysis. Further, the definition of law and other legal concepts proffered by a particular analytical jurist should not be identified with law and legal concepts themselves. In H.L.A. Hart's more ponderous words, it is a mistake to fail 'to distinguish between, on the one hand, *law* and *legal concepts* and, on the other, *theories* of or about law, and *definitions* of legal concepts.'[17]

The analysis of legal phenomena can be carried out independently of a theory of or about law. Nor do we have to underwrite the definition of law and legal concepts by the theory of law we somehow happen to hold. Gerald J. Postema[18] recently made a similar point when he pointed out that one might accept and defend a particular legal theorist's conception of the jurisprudential enterprise but reject the theory of law embraced by that theorist. In short, like analytical philosophy generally, analytical jurisprudence is 'ethically and politically neutral *formally.*'[19]

It is a core assumption of analytical jurisprudence that law and 'legal concepts can be sharply separated, for purposes of analysis, from the practical context within which they live.'[20] Some commentators distinguish between Bentham and Austin by denying that the former embraced this core assumption of analytical jurisprudence.[21] We are inclined to the contrary view; indeed, the suggested distinction is untenable. First, the analytical approach in jurisprudence was made respectable by both Bentham and Austin. Secondly, both Bentham and Austin realized that legal words and terms 'taken by themselves are the work of abstraction, the produce of refined analysis.'[22] Bentham maintained that 'every man who speaks, speaks in propositions, the rudest savage, no less than the most polished orator.'[23] Austin was as emphatic as Bentham on this point. According to him, legal terms are but 'short marks for long series of propositions.'[24] The real distinction between Bentham's and Austin's analytical vision seems to be that while Bentham was more interested in 'censorial' jurisprudence, and so was less consistent in following his own injunctions that analysis of legal phenomena must remain detached from ethics, Austin was more interested in 'expository' jurisprudence and hence was more consistent in pursuing the analytic meaning of law and other legal concepts. To what extent he succeeded in doing this is an entirely different question.

Analytical jurisprudence regards legal words and terms as shorthand representations of otherwise lengthy lexical discourse. Put differently, analytical jurisprudence treats leading legal words and terms as propositional idioms. The primary task of the analytical jurist consists essentially in casting such propositional idioms into conceptual forms, and in enhancing the understanding of such concepts by making explicit and capturing the complete thought systems fossilized in or symbolized by the linguistic labels that stand for them; his secondary task is to deploy these structural elements in systematizing the materials of the legal order. It may be that this makes analytical jurisprudence 'compatible with very great iniquity'[25] but, again, that is a different matter. At any rate, criminal jurisprudence has been and continues to be carried on in accordance with these tenets of analytical jurisprudence.

It has also been suggested that analytical jurisprudence involved a priori considerations of or about the meaning of law and legal concepts.[26] As well, it has been suggested that conceptual analysis is necessarily prior not only to the exposition but also to evaluation of the law.[27] The latter assertion is unexceptionable, but only a misunderstanding of the nature of analytical jurisprudence could lead to the claim that it entails a priori considerations of the meaning of law and legal concepts. Analytical jurisprudence is post-reflective. As such, the concept of law and other legal concepts an analyst deploys in expounding the law are not formed a priori but a posteriori. In addition, analytical jurisprudence is 'pre-interpretive.'[28] This means that it does not countenance subjective interpretation of law and legal concepts. Nor does it aspire to mirror some platonic legal forms. On the contrary, it is quite content with accurately ascertaining the meaning of law and legal concepts in 'ample and developed systems of positive law' and with systematizing such legal phenomena. To depict analytic concepts as 'Platonic' or (which is the same thing) characterize analytical jurisprudence 'as a legal version of Plato's theory of Forms'[29] is merely to call attention to the 'objectivism' which is the hallmark of all scientific enterprise.

A weak Austinian jurisprudence would restrict itself to the formulation of the concept of law and the fundamental legal concepts of a particular system of developed positive law, as well as to the systematization of the materials of the particular system of developed law with which it deals. In other words, a weak version of Austin's analytical jurisprudence would confine itself to the examination and exposition of the legal experience of a single developed positive legal order.

Analytical jurisprudence as practised in English-speaking societies, especially since the second half of this century, fits into the picture of a weak version of analytical jurisprudence. Accordingly, the professed aim of the dominant analytical approach in the common law jurisdictions has been to elucidate the concept of law and other legal concepts embedded in the positive legal orders within the common law orbit. Of course, analytical jurisprudents in these countries proffer definitions of law and legal concepts but, following the 'linguistic turn,' they arrive at such definitions on the basis of acute analysis of the language of the common law. Austin's comparative conceptual framework is simply superseded by the conceptual framework revealed by philosophical analysis of the language of law in the common law system. Unlike Austin's philosophical analysis, contemporary analytic inquiry into law and legal concepts 'does not pursue a [universal] definition, but rather an account of a concept that is already implicitly defined in our [legal] language.'[30]

In other words, one of the points of departure between Austin and his contemporary followers is that, while the former concentrated on analysing the concept of law and determining the meaning of the fundamental legal terms that were common to the systems of developed positive law he deemed worthy of philosophical enquiry, the latter focus on analysing the concept of law and determining the meaning of the fundamental legal terms embedded in a particular system of mature positive law. Austin would have underlined this difference by calling his followers particularists.[31] Though it was possible for Austin to universalize the analytic meanings of the legal concepts which are indispensable for systematizing, expounding, and understanding sophisticated systems of positive law, his successors are compelled to restrict any generalizations to the ascertained facts of the particular system of law with which they deal. This is usually the Anglo-American law.

Be that as it may, analysis is not a method for augmenting knowledge; rather, it is a method for understanding and systematizing actual or potential knowledge. Analytical philosophy does this by clarifying the meanings of concepts and terms and by systematically exploring their implications.[32] As such, analytical philosophy assumes that 'knowledge in any sphere must be based on knowledge.'[33] While the older tradition assumed that such foundational knowledge was pre-existent, modern analytical philosophy assumes that any foundational knowledge must be empirical, that is, the product of human observation and thought, not a supposed deliverance of divine or natural intelligence. Accordingly, analytical jurisprudence presumes an empirical foundation for law.

Austin gave general jurisprudence a solid empirical foundation[34] by deriving the data for a science of law from 'the positive systems of law of all civilized European Nations.'[35] After identifying and isolating the leading terms from this empirical data, he subjected them to rigorous analysis and then proceeded to make the universalistic[36] claim that the analytic meanings of such necessary terms (concepts) are the ultimate basis on which legal science must rest.[37] In short, the essential difference between Austin and his successors is not that Austin strove after some Platonic legal forms while the latter do not, but that Austin was basically a comparativist while his followers are particularists. Thus, while he could and did take the bold step of making a universalist claim for the concept of law and the meanings of those legal concepts which he deemed absolutely necessary for a proper exposition of any developed system of positive law, this course was not open to his successors. Austin's successors domesticate (or, if you please, emasculate) general jurisprudence by limiting their field of observation, so to speak, to a particular (single) system of positive law. By this device, 'the quest for fundamental legal notions and their clarification and arrangement was relativized.'[38]

The upshot was a tendency to elevate the concept of law in the Anglo-American legal system and the meanings of the fundamental legal concepts embedded in it to a normative position.[39] This has the deplorable result of defanging the philosophy of law, for it internalizes the positivist-inspired belief that the task of the jurist consists merely in 'a purely legal elucidation or explanation of concepts.'[40] Or, as David Sugarman puts it, 'exposition, conceptualization, systematization and the analysis of existing legal doctrine became equated with the dominant tasks of legal education and scholarship.'[41]

Insofar as the criminal law is concerned, one of the purposes of this chapter is to demonstrate the fundamental identity of the weak and robust forms of analytical jurisprudence. We also show that contemporary analytical criminal jurisprudence is enmeshed in the moral conception of crime discussed earlier. In other words, we contend that analytical criminal jurisprudence is a form of scholasticism in legal science. More precisely, we maintain that contemporary analytical criminal jurisprudence operates against the background belief that the conceptual framework for the law of crimes which crystallized in the seventeenth and eighteenth centuries is the ultimate formal basis for criminal law.

This is not to suggest that analytical criminal jurisprudence is monolithic. On the contrary, analytical criminal jurisprudents may be divided into two classes, namely, normative and descriptive analysts. Whether a particular criminal law scholar falls into one category or the other does not depend solely on the school of law to which he or she belongs. Rather, it depends on whether that scholar employs the key phrases in the definitional elements of crime – 'guilty mind' or *mens rea* and 'guilty act' or *actus reus* – in normative or descriptive senses. We shall presently touch on this distinction.

Earlier we outlined the conception of crime which was incorporated into the common law.[42] It is appropriate to examine here Austin's explication of the general notion of legal wrong, for it was his formulation of this notion that defined the boundaries for subsequent analytical work in this area of the law.

The Analytical Meaning of Legal Wrong

The 'Font': Austin on Wrong or Injury

It is conventional to divide the law into two branches, namely, private and public, and to subsume the criminal law under the latter. Austin refused to make any such distinction.[43] Nevertheless, he did regard the distinction of wrongs into civil and criminal wrongs or private and public delict as analytically necessary in the exposition of a developed system of law.[44] But he did not mince words in stating that there is no theoretical difference between these classes of legal wrongs; the distinction between them is procedural. In words that have since been mimicked partly by C.S. Kenny[45] and partly by Glanville Williams,[46] Austin insisted that

the differences between crimes and civil injuries is not to be sought for in a supposed difference between their tendencies, but in the difference between the modes wherein they are respectively pursued, or wherein the sanction is applied in the two cases. An offence which is pursued at the discretion of the injured party or his representative is a civil injury. An offence which is pursued by the Sovereign or by the subordinates of the sovereign, is a crime.[47]

Austin used the terms 'injury' and 'wrong' interchangeably, and he depicted them alternatively as 'breach of Obligation or Duty by commission or omission.'[48] He stated emphatically that 'every wrong supposes intention or negligence on the part of the wrongdoer,' and that these notions (intention and negligence) in turn implied 'will' and 'motive.'[49] An attempt to elucidate the latter concepts inescapably took him into the realm of the philosophy of mind.[50]

It is unnecessary to follow Austin through the labyrinth of the philosophy of mind which underly his articulation of 'intention' and 'negligence.' For our purposes, it suffices to say that until well into the present century, legal scholars explicated criminal legal terms and words against the background of Cartesian dualism. Cartesian dualism divided the human person into two: body and soul or mind. The mind was distinct and separate from the body, and so the processes of the mind were sharply distinguished from those of the body. As a result, the only way to fathom mental processes was to draw conclusions from overt human acts.

To Austin, the term 'act' meant volitional or willed movement of the body.[51] 'Volition' is an antecedent desire for bodily movement, and to will an act is to desire those bodily movements. The dominion of the will could not and did not extend to the mind.[52] In his own words,[53] an act is no more or less than 'a voluntary movement of the body, or a movement which follows a volition':

'To *will*,' is to *wish* or *desire* certain of those bodily movements which immediately follow our desires of them. A '*determination* of the will,' or a '*volition*,' is a wish or desire of the sort. A 'motive determining the will,' is a wish *not* a volition, but suggesting a wish which is ... The bodily movements which immediately follow our desires of them, are the only human *acts*, strictly and properly so called ... the bodily movements in question are the only events which we *will*.[54]

Austin distinguished between 'act,' properly so called, and its consequences: the latter are separate and often flow from the former.[55] Only acts are, strictly speaking, willed; their consequences cannot be willed. According to Austin, the consequences of willed muscular movement (that is, act) are either intended or not intended. If a consequence of an act is expected then that consequence is intended.[56] This sharp distinction between acts and their consequences closely mirrored the distinction between 'body' and 'mind' in the then prevalent philosophy of mind.[57]

It has been pointed out that the philosophy of the nature of action which underlay Austin's exposition has become obsolete. However, this does not mean that the *idea* which Austin grappled with in demarcating 'act' from 'consequence,' and in defining an act as a voluntary muscular movement that is separate and distinct from the motions of the mind, has also been ejected from legal topography. In contemporary criminal jurisprudence the necessity of separating an 'act' from its 'consequences' is given expression in the requirement of 'causative responsibility for liability.'[59]

This is a digression, albeit a necessary one. Having distinguished between an act, that is, 'the bodily movements which immediately follow our desires of them' and 'consequences' (which may be intended, foreseen, or not foreseen), Austin proceeded to remark that the force of the established linguistic practices compelled him to speak simply of 'acts' when he meant 'acts and their consequences,' and also to speak of consequences as *willed* when, in fact, he meant that they (the consequences alone) were the object of *intending*.[60] In short, clarity demands that 'will' and 'act,' which are not, in Austin's schema, mental phenomena, should be kept separate from such mental phenomena as 'intention,' in all its variegated connotations, and 'negligence,' in all its manifestations.

What, then, is it to intend? Austin maintained that to *expect* or *contemplate* a consequence of an act is to *intend* that consequence,[61] or, alternatively, to *desire* a consequence is to intend it.[62] Thus, to desire an act does not necessarily mean that its consequence is also desired or intended. Such a conclusion could arise only from confusing 'will' with 'intention':

When I will an act, I expect or intend the *act* which is the appropriate object of the volition. And when I will an act, I may expect, contemplate, or intend some given event, as a certain or contingent *consequence* of the act which I will. Hence ... the frequent confusion of Will and Intention. Feeling *that will implies intention* ... numerous writers upon Jurisprudence ... employ 'will' and 'intention' as synonymous or equivalent terms. They forget *that intention does not imply will*; or that the appropriate objects of certain intentions are not the appropriate objects of volitions. The agent may not intend a consequence of his act. In other words, when the agent wills the act, he may not contemplate that given event as a certain or contingent consequence of the act which he wills.[63]

It is obvious that, in strict conformity with the tenets of the prevailing philosophical speculation as to the dual nature of the human person, Austin sharply distinguished between the activities of the body and those of the mind. 'Intention' may be a present intention to act in the future.[64] But only an intention that is manifested in or followed by an illegal consequence attracts legal notice; a 'present intention to act in the future' alone is as irrelevant for legal purposes as the presence of conduct unaccompanied by intention.

According to Austin, intention could be manifested in three principal modes: '[Fir]st, the agent may *intend* a consequence; and that consequence may be the *end* of his act. [Seco]ndly, ... he may desire that consequence as a *mean* to an end. [Thi]rdly, he may *intend* the consequence, without desiring it.'[65] A killing done in any of these circumstances would be an *intentional* action or rather an intended homicide.[66]

'Negligence' denotes 'injurious' or 'culpable' omissions or breach of duty: 'the party who omits, is said to "*neglect*" his duty. The omission is ascribed to his "negligence." The state of his mind at the time of the omission, is styled "negligence."'[67] Austin's explication of the meaning of 'negligence' involved a discussion of two cognate but separate terms - 'heedlessness' and 'rashness.' 'Negligence' and 'Heedlessness' are alike in that both involve inadvertence to the consequences of one's act; both differ from 'rashness' or 'temerity' in that the latter involves advertence to the probable mischief of one's act. It is better to let Austin himself speak:

The party who is negligent *omits* an act, and breaks a *positive* duty: The party who is heedless *does* an act, and breaks a *negative* duty ... The states of mind which are styled 'negligence' and 'heedlessness' are precisely alike. In either case, the party is inadvertent. In the first case, he does *not* an act which he was bound to do, because he adverts not to it. In the second case he *does* an act from which he was bound to forbear, because he adverts not to certain of its probable consequences. Absence of a thought which one's duty would naturally suggest, is the main ingredient in each of the complex notions which are styled 'negligence' and 'heedlessness.'[68]

In the case of 'rashness' or 'temerity,'

the party ... *thinks* of the probable mischief; but, in consequence of a missupposition begotten by insufficient advertence, he assumes that the mischief will not ensue in the given instance or case ... The radical idea denoted is always this. The party runs a risk of which he is conscious; but he thinks (for a reason which he examines insufficiently) that the mischief will probably be averted in the given instance.

Austin concluded his analysis with a consideration, and rejection, of the tendency of civil lawyers to equate, in certain cases, 'rashness,' 'heedlessness,' or 'negligence' with intention. In his view, the latter ought to be distinguished from the former at all times, for 'intention is a *precise* state of the mind, and cannot coalesce or commingle with a different state of the mind.'[70] He was emphatic in maintaining a distinction between these two classes of states of mind:

'[T]o intend,' is to believe that a given act will follow a given volition, or that a given consequence will follow a given act. The chance of the sequence may be rated higher or lower; but the party *conceives* the future event, and believes that there *is* a chance of its following his volition or act. Intention, therefore, is a state of consciousness. But negligence and heedlessness suppose *un*consciousness. In the first case, the party does *not* think of a given act. In the second case, the party does *not* think of a given consequence ... The party thinks, or the party does *not* think, of the act or consequence. If he think of it, he *intends*. If he do not think of it, he is *negligent* or *heedless*.[71]

Austin concluded that any suggestion that one class could run into another or that there was an intermediate state between the two classes could have arisen only as a result of confusing a question of fact, that is, the existence of a particular state of mind, with the evidentiary issue of how to ascertain precisely the relevant state of mind:

The state of a man's mind can only be known by others through his acts: through his own declarations, or through other conduct of his own. Consequently, it must often be difficult to determine whether a party *intended*, or whether he was merely negligent, heedless, or rash. The acts to which we must resort as evidence of the state of his mind, may be *ambiguous*: insomuch that they lead us to one conclusion as naturally as to the other ... But the difficulty which belongs to the *evidence* is transferred to the *subject of the inquiry*. Because we are unable to determine *what* was the state of his mind, we fancy that the state of his mind was itself *indeterminate*.[72]

It was noted earlier that the elaborate excursion into the realm of the philosophy of the mind which led directly to the analysis of 'intention,' 'negligence,' 'heedlessness,' and so on was necessarily a prelude to the determination of the meaning of the legal concept of wrong or injury. Before Austin defined this general legal notion, he divagated once more to analyse 'duty,' 'sanction,' and 'physical compulsion.'[73] After this, he prefaced his discussion of injury or wrong with an analysis of the concept of 'guilt' or 'imputability.' We can dispense with the former set of concepts, but reference to the latter is indispensable.

'Guilt' or 'imputability' means that a person has violated a duty or broken an obligation by acting in a way that is inconsistent with such legal duty or obligation.[74] Hence, a wrong or injury is 'an act, forbearance or omission of such a character, that the party is *guilty*: And, to be *guilty*, is to have acted, forborne, or omitted, in such wise, that the act, forbearance, or omission, is an *injury* or *wrong*.'[75] 'Guilt' and 'imputability' are equivalent, and so they can be used interchangeably. Thus,

[i]f the act, forbearance, or omission, be an *injury* or *wrong*, and if the party be therefore *guilty*, the act, forbearance, or omission, together with such of its consequences, as it was the purpose of the duty to avert, are *imputable* to the party. And if the act, forbearance, or omission, together with such of its consequences as it was the purpose of the duty to avert, be *imputable* to the party, the party has broken or violated a duty or obligation.[76]

The terms 'injury' and 'guilt' are, therefore, contradictions of the word 'duty' or 'obligation':[77] a guilty act is an act that is imputable to the agent, and an imputable act amounts to an injury that is in turn a breach of duty or obligation. It thus follows that for there to be 'guilt' or 'injury,' or before there can be breach of duty or obligation – all of which are equivalent terms - there must be added to the whole grill another ingredient. This is the element of 'intention' or 'negligence.' The rationale is obvious: legal sanction operates on the 'will.' And, since the latter is inseparable from intention and negligence,[78] the presence of either of these ingredients is essential for the existence of guilt, injury, or breach of duty:

Whether the act, forbearance, or omission, constitute an injury or wrong; or whether the party be placed by it in the predicament of guilt or imputability; or whether it constitute a breach of duty or obligation; *partly* depends upon his *consciousness*, with regard to *it*, or its consequences, at and before the time of the act, forbearance, or omission. *Unless the party intended, or was negligent, heedless, or rash, the party is not placed by it in the predicament of guilt or imputability; nor is it a breach or violation of duty or obligation.*[79]

Austin stated emphatically that 'intention, negligence, heedlessness, or rashness is *of the essence* of injury or wrong; is *of the essence* of breach of duty; is a *necessary condition precedent* to the existence of that plight or predicament which is styled guilt or imputability.'[80] These mental phenomena – intention, negligence, heedlessness, or rashness – are quite clearly different and distinct from volition, and they are as necessary for imputability, guilt, or breach of duty or obligation as volition is necessary for the existence of an act.

We have already alluded to the fact that Austin rejected the division of law into private and public law, and that he further insisted that the distinction between civil and criminal wrongs is procedural, not substantive. Having shown the interconnectedness of the various terms that enter into the idea of legal wrong, he exposed the confusion that a contrary view (which insists on a theoretical distinction between private and public wrongs) engenders in legal science. He pointed out that lawyers in general, and presumably common law writers in particular, were in the habit of using 'guilt' or 'culpa' in a restrictive sense to mean 'the state of the party's mind.'[81] This usage tended to limit the notion of legal guilt to 'intention,' and it confined intentionally caused harm to directly intended consequences of an act. Austin found this objectionable. According to him, the legal concept of guilt 'denotes the intention of the party, or his negligence, heedlessness, or rashness,'[82] and he triumphantly cited passages from the writings of German civilians to support the preferred meaning. He concluded by stating that while it would be necessary to distinguish between the various types of intention and negligence, 'a general expression for culpable *intention*, and for the various modifications of *negligence*, tends to confusion and obscurity rather than to order and clearness.' Consequently, it would not be advisable to talk of them *collectively.*[83] That, in a nutshell, is the kernel of the analytical meaning of 'wrong' or 'injury': it denotes intentional, negligent, heedless, or rash breach of legal duty or obligation. This meaning of legal wrong holds irrespective of the source of such legal duties or obligations or the authority that enforces them.

The Rivulets: Two Types of Analytical Criminal Jurists

Criminal jurisprudence is 'becalmed on a painted ocean of controversy.'[84] The controversy is between 'normative' and 'descriptive' theorists,[85] but, consistent with the nomenclature adopted earlier, we shall call them 'normative' and 'descriptive' *analysts* respectively. This is a more apposite appellation because, as the ensuing discussion will make clear, they both end up at the same theory of criminal law. Nevertheless, it is proper to emphasize the differences between them.

First, as the names suggest, descriptive analysts use law and legal concepts in a descriptive and normatively neutral sense while normative analysts are wont to use them in a value-laden or moral sense.[86] Secondly, descriptive analysts are almost always avowed legal positivists, while normative analysts are seldom, if at all, self-conscious legal positivists. However, since, as already noted, legal analysts take little precaution against confounding law and legal concepts with *their* theories of law and the definitions of law and legal concepts favoured by such theories,[87] their *definitions* of the concept of wrong are often determined by the *theory* of law which underlies their legal scholarship.

Nonetheless since analytical jurisprudence presupposes the existence of law and legal concepts, we find that the divergence in their underlying theories of law does not have devastating implications for analytical criminal jurisprudence. Consistent with the analytic vision, analytical criminal jurisprudence assumes the prior existence of legal wrongs, that is to say, it assumes that the acts in question are legally prohibited acts. Put differently, analytical criminal jurisprudence is not concerned with the definition of crime dictated by a particular theory of law nor is it concerned with specific crimes. Neither the one nor the other is susceptible to the analytical method. The analysable issue is the definition of crimes in general. In other words, the analytical notion of wrong or injury is concerned exclusively with a technical question: What are the conditions for liability for legally prohibited acts? We have already seen that Austin's analysis dealt with this question.

Whatever may be said for or against the division of law into private and public laws, English law regards crimes as public wrongs. The application of the analytical method to this species of wrongs under the common law shows that its analytic meaning is narrower than that of Austin's. The disparity is due to the ahistorical posture of the father of analytical jurisprudence. The difference lies essentially in the fact that, whereas Austin included 'negligence' as a basis for legal liability generally, contemporary analytical criminal jurisprudents have had to exclude it from the purview of the criminal law for the simple and obvious reason that the common law notion of criminal wrong did not include it.

Although legal history supplies the foundation for legal theory,[88] analytical jurisprudents are wont to see the subject-matter of legal history as different from that of legal science, and historical jurists are not always interested in analytical jurisprudence. While the former concentrate on identifying and elucidating persistent legal concepts and notions, the latter are concerned sometimes with the evolution of such legal concepts, sometimes with the history of legal ideas, and sometimes with the history of legal institutions. This does not exhaust the differences between analytical and historical inquiries into law and legal phenomena but it underlines the fact that a sort of division of labour exists here: analytical and historical approaches provide answers to different questions.[89]

Nevertheless, some legal writers engage in both historical and analytical studies. This was especially so in the nineteenth century, and such historical-cum-analytical jurists were keenly alive to the dangers inherent in pursuing one to the exclusion of the other. In the latter part of the nineteenth century, legal historians such as the Victorian Austinian Fitzjames Stephen,[91] whose lingering Toryism[92] prevented him from embracing the neutral description of crime as simply 'an act or omission which the law punishes,'[93] wondered aloud whether 'crime' was a definite or technical legal term; Stephen's doubt was echoed by Pollock and Maitland.[94]

From the point of view of the common law, it seems that the doubt expressed by Pollock and Maitland could have arisen only within the context of a legal-historical inquiry which limited itself to the history of English law before the fifteenth century. And Stephen's soliloquy cannot be understood unless it is viewed against the background in which it was made. That background was the re-emergence and proliferation of regulatory offences in the latter part of the nineteenth century, coupled with a hard-headed insistence that 'such offences differ in many important particulars from those gross outrages against the public and against individuals which we commonly associate with the word crime.'[95] This belief occasioned a hiatus in the criminal law. In a development reminiscent of the division of crimes into *mala in se* and *mala prohibita*, crime was bifurcated into common law and statutory offences.[96]

Following the ascendance of what we earlier characterized as a weak version of Austinian jurisprudence, the analytical scalpel was brought to bear on English criminal law. Unsurprisingly, the new analytical jurists had no difficulty in rejecting Austin's refusal to treat 'crime' as a distinct legal concept, for, as noted earlier, their conception of the role of the analyst was such that his task was strictly limited to identifying and describing accurately the fundamental legal concepts embedded in a particular system of developed positive law. The result was the exhumation and exposition of the concept of crime which had crystallized under the common law in the seventeenth and eighteenth centuries, with its attendant 'neolithic'[97] premises.

Earlier, we characterized the common law notion of crime as the moral conception of crime. That characterization still holds good. It is, however, necessary to enter a caveat here. The common law concept of crime is susceptible to divergent interpretations. It has so far been interpreted differently by legal positivists and non-positivists. The imperative theory of law commits some analytical jurists to the position that the will of the sovereign is the ultimate authority for law. In England, the *ipsissima verba* of the triumvirate parliamentary institution makes a law. From the positivist's theoretical viewpoint, this means that the formal criminalization of an act is conclusive as to its criminal status; the moral, socio-economic, religious, and political factors that led to its criminalization do not enter into the legal inquiry. Consequently, when positivists analyse the precepts and doctrines of a developed legal system, they find only fundamental legal conceptions devoid of any moral content.[98] Needless to say, legal positivists do not regard any act as intrinsically wrong; and so, like Austin himself, they invariably proffer a procedural definition of crime.[99]

The second way in which the common law concept of crime has been interpreted discriminates between laws which prohibit morally wrong things and those which forbid morally indifferent things. In other words, writers in this group find it difficult to embrace the notion that there are no intrinsically wrong acts. However, from an analytic, as opposed to a theoretical, point of view, they conceive crime in material or elemental terms. Such analysts as Jerome Hall, H.M. Hart, Herbert Packer, Peter Brett, C.K. Allen, and, in more recent times, George P. Fletcher and Michael S. Moore make the definition of crime turn not simply on the fact that a particular result of human conduct has been declared criminal by the legislature but on whether certain essential components are present. It is interesting to note parenthetically that, although most of these writers are not legal positivists, their approach has a closer intellectual affinity with Austin than the other school of thought.

It is unnecessary for our purposes to enter into a lengthy discussion of the differences between these two definitional standpoints, for, as noted earlier, it is sufficient for analytical purposes if there is agreement about the fact that a particular concept is a legal concept. Analytical criminal jurisprudents assume that 'crime' is a concept under the common law. The only issue, therefore, is to ascertain its meaning; and this does not depend on the definition of that concept favoured by either positivism or natural law theory. We hope to show in the next section that the two schools of thought converge in limiting the concept of criminal wrong to intentional or reckless breach of legal duty or obligation, and that they are supported by history.

The Analytic Meaning of (Common Law) Criminal Wrong

At first sight, this task requires us to traverse an already-covered ground, that is, it seems to involve a discussion of the moral conception of crime. But it cannot be overemphasized that analytical inquiry into the meaning of a legal concept ought to be conducted free of the theory of law which undergirds its formation. The searchlight should be focused on the concept shorn of its moral or political underpinnings. The discussion here exhibits the end result of the application of the analytical method to the notion of crime embedded in the common law. It presents an account of the process by which a descriptive picture of the moral conception of crime unencumbered by any moral and political theory, was developed.

The process was simple. We have already referred to the fact that the maxim *actus non facit reum nisi mens sit rea* runs through the common law of crime, at least until the nineteenth century. It has also been noted that the common law notion of *mens rea* had a strong ethical connotation. This was, of course, a reflection of the moral and intellectual outlook that informed its formation. Premodern doctrinal analysis was carried on in an intellectual climate that dealt with a moral agent whose actions were not supposed to be self-centred. As well, it was assumed that the moral agent not only knew but also accepted the fact that he had a moral (which was at one and the same time a political and legal) duty to refrain from engaging in wrongful or injurious acts. The common law thus presupposes an ordinary, though initially not necessarily, adult mind[100] which not only can but does make correct moral choices in contradistinction to merely self-centred, rational choices. Behind this presupposition lay another assumption, namely, that the individual conscience readily recognized the binding force of such moral-political-legal duties.

Modern moral and political philosophy disputes the assumption that the individual conscience necessarily acknowledged the binding force of such moral- political-cum-legal duties. It was Thomas Hobbes who took the first and decisive step to break with the older tradition. Observational evidence had convinced Hobbes that the assumption was not descriptively true. He felt that both the ancient and medieval moral philosophers had dissipated their energy in the futile attempt to moralize law, of appealing always to the individual conscience. To Hobbes, they had spoken endlessly, and apparently vainly, against the hard fact that the individual conscience did not provide a common or uniform standard of morality. In his view, human beings, as rational creatures, do whatever they consider to be in their own selfish interest; men's actions are calculated to secure themselves from the predation of others. It follows, in Hobbes's schema, that the individual conscience is a shifting quicksand which cannot provide a solid basis for measuring or establishing what is morally right: 'Such is the nature of man that every one calls that good which he desires, and evil which he eschews; and therefore through the diversity of our affections, it happens that one counts that good, which another counts evill; and the same man what now he esteem'd for good, he immediately looks on as evill; and the same thing which he calls good in himselfe he tearmes evil in another.'[101]

Hobbes (and he convinced most modern moral and political theorists)[102] took the asocial, solitary man – the creature who pursued with unflagging assiduity the singular aim of self-preservation – as the Newtonian counterpart of his moral, political, and legal theory. Through remorseless logic, he arrived at the conclusion that the sovereign legal authority is the determinant of not only what is right and what is wrong but also of when any particular act or omission is wrong or is 'by reason blameable.' As he explained,

men may agree indeed in some certaine generall things, as that theft, adultery, and the like are sinnes, as if they should say that all men account these things evill to which they have given names which are usually taken in an evill sense; but we demand not whether theft be a sinne, but what is to be term'd theft, and so much therefore as in so great a diversity of censurers what is by reason blameable, is not to be measur'd by the reason of one man more than another, because of the equality of humane nature, and there are no other reasons in being, but onely those of particular men, and that of the City [public authority], it follows, that the City is to determine what with reason is culpable: So as a fault that is to say, a SINNE is that, which a man do's, omits, sayes or wills, contrary to the Laws.[103]

Hobbes distinguished between sin and crime and, like many other philosophers, he not only regarded intention as a necessary component of crime but also insisted that intention had to be manifested in overt (illegal) act:

Crime is a sinne consisting in the committing (by Deed or Word) of that which the Law forbiddeth, or the Omission of what it had commanded. So that every Crime is a sinne; but not every sinne a crime. To intend to steale, or kill, is a sinne, though it never appeare in Word, or Fact ... *but till it appear by some thing done, or said by which the intention may be argued by a humane Judge, it hath not the name of crime.*[104]

Hobbes could not have agreed more with Blackstone when the latter wrote that 'to constitute a crime against human laws, there must be, first, a vicious will; and secondly, an unlawful act consequent upon such vicious will.'[105]

Well into the seventeenth century, the requirement of 'will' was regarded as raising the question whether a particular act(ion) was volitional, voluntary, or wilful. Hobbes was the first to delimit the question more narrowly and definitively. He converted it into the specific question of ascertaining when a particular action could be described as intentional. He rejected the definition of 'will,' commonly given in his own time,[106] which made it a causal agent for action.[107] Instead of making 'will' a causal agent of action, and thus (according to him) confounding intentional with rational action, he cast the moral concepts of his predecessors into the mould of mechanistic thought. In his own words, he 'snuffed and purged them from ambiguity.' By this device, he arrived at what he called 'exact definitions'[108] of such words and concepts. To him, the question of 'will' was not a matter of locating 'volition' or determining 'the antecedent of action,'[109] as it would still be for John Austin and others in the nineteenth and twentieth centuries. Rather, it was a question of ascertaining the presence of the psychological fact of intent. And this could be discerned from that paradigmatic activity of the mind called 'deliberation.'

Unlike the ancients and their medieval followers, he put 'will' not at the beginning of 'deliberation' but at the end of it:

In Deliberation, the last Appetite, or Aversion, immediately adhering to the action, or to the omission thereof, is that we call the WILL; the Act (not the faculty) of Willing ... The definition of the Will, given commonly by the Schooles, that it is a rational appetite, is not good enough. For if it were then could there be no Voluntary Act against reason. For a Voluntary Act is that, which proceedeth from the Will and no other. But if instead of a Rational Appetite we shall say an Appetite resulting from a precedent Deliberation, then the definition is the same as I have given here. Will therefore is the last Appetite in Deliberating.[110]

Thus, 'the act of willing' is performed by the mind, and it is directed to what, as we have seen, Austin called 'the consequences of an act.'

The last Appetite or Aversion, in turn, depends entirely 'on foresight of the good and evil consequences and sequels of the actions whereof we deliberate.' This itself depends on how far we are able to see through a long chain of consequences.[111] If we couple this with the claim that what is good or evil varies with different individuals at different times or even in the same individual under different circumstances, such that only the reason of the City could provide an unvarying uniform standard, it leads straight to the conclusion that the domain of the law is not the *forum internum qua* the seat of morality but the *forum internum qua* the seat of human actions, that is law is not concerned with the subjective evaluation by the individual of the goodness or badness of his acts but with what could be deduced about *individual* mental attitude to legal rights, duties, and obligations as manifested in external or visible action. By this device, Hobbes deftly turned the question of the presence of legal guilt from the erstwhile inquiry into the willingness or readiness to make morally sanctioned choices to an inquiry into the willingness to structure our behaviour to conform with our (externally imposed) legal duties and obligations. Thus, except where legal duty coincides with moral duty, legal guilt would not be synonymous with moral guilt.

The fact to be established is the blameworthiness of the action: the agent must have intended to act in breach of legal duty or obligation. This is a cognitive matter. For it requires that one perceives the 'good and evil consequences of the doing or omitting the thing propounded.' Further, it requires that a choice be made: it has to be 'a last inclination or appetite.' The presence of such a cognitive state may be proved by showing that the agent directly aimed at the proscribed consequences, or it may be inferred from the fact that he acted despite the fact that he foresaw the occurrence of the forbidden consequences of his act.

We have spent so much time on Hobbes's exposition for three reasons. First, it was once believed that acquaintance with his work was indispensable for a thorough understanding of the theoretical background of English law.[112] Second, the analytical tradition in English law goes back to him. Indeed, Austin paid glowing tributes to Hobbes's speculative thought.[113] More precisely, when allowance is made for the difference between them on the present subject matter – Hobbes did not speak about negligence – both arrived at similar conclusions. Lastly, Austin's successors have narrowed down his ideas by excluding 'negligence' from the purview of criminal theory. In short, analytical criminal jurisprudence has turned full circle: it has reached exactly the same conclusions as Hobbes. Contemporary analytical criminal jurisprudents describe *mens rea* as 'awareness of facts which make conduct criminal,'[114] 'the intention to cause or foresight of, result of the act,'[115] 'knowledge of circumstances or foresight of consequences,'[116] or simply 'intention' and 'recklessness.'[117] In explicating this requirement, criminal law scholars do not necessarily employ identical terms and phrases. But it seems that there is general agreement that 'the bottom of the psychological kit [has been] reached' so that 'one may substitute various synonyms'[118] for 'intention' and 'recklessness.' However, the phrase 'foresight of consequences' has given rise to much controversy.

Specifically, the question has been asked whether it was not a mistake to base criminal responsibility on foresight of consequences.[119] The short answer is that it is a palpable error to construe 'foresight of consequences' as equivalent to intention. But it is suggested that that was not its original meaning. The test reflects the clarity brought into legal science by a shift from pre-modern political and legal philosophy, which invests all laws with a moral halo, to their modern equivalents, which divest legal science of such epistemological pretensions. Whatever may be the differences between descriptive and normative analysts of criminal law, both are empirically minded, and they are committed to the singular goal of elucidating the general principles and concepts embedded in existing, positive law.

It has been said that English law has never been a slave to any particular abstract speculation about the nature and basis of law.[120] As well, it has been pointed out that the idea that human beings are naturally wicked was not an integral part of Hobbes theory.[121] Nevertheless, modern political and legal philosophy embraces the 'bad man'[122] view of the human actor. As such, it was a good and reasonable working assumption that an agent who foresaw the occurrence of a forbidden result, effect, or consequences of an act or omission *and* who did not abstain from the conduct or take necessary and adequate precautions to prevent its occurrence evidenced his inclination to bring about such result, effect, or consequences.

Whether an actor was inclined to bring about the forbidden consequences or result of an act is a question of fact to be ascertained in each case. In other words, it could not have been a substantive principle of law that foresight of consequences was equivalent to intention; that is to say, whether foresight of consequences evidenced an inclination to bring such consequences about depended on the facts of each case. The presence of intent is always a question of fact; whether such an intent constitutes *mens rea* is a question of law. The latter can not be dissolved into a mere evidential point. 'Foresight of consequences' is a necessary but not a sufficient condition for *mens rea* in English law. Indeed, it was not until about four decades into the twentieth century that it was first propounded and, subsequently, accepted as a simple statement that 'what is required to establish liability is merely foresight of consequences.'[123] That formulation quickly became the ruling orthodoxy, and, in spite of trenchant criticisms,[124] it is still not infrequently reiterated in academic circles.

Be that as it may, the analytic approach reveals that the concept of criminal guilt in English law entails a 'subjective' and 'cognitive' standard of liability. This is why the dominant approach in criminal jurisprudence has been described as upholding a 'cognitive theory of mens rea.'[125] Clearly, the subjective/cognitive theory of criminal guilt cannot admit 'negligence' as a basis for criminal liability. With the exception of legal scholars strongly influenced by the civil law tradition,[126] or those who, like H.L.A. Hart,[127] seek the extension of the standards of responsibility found in ordinary life to law,[128] or those who suggest its adoption on utilitarian grounds or as a legitimate extension of the principle of *mens rea*,[129] analytical criminal jurisprudents resolutely exclude 'negligence' from the sphere of criminal law.[130]

The subjective/cognitive basis of criminal guilt is supported by legal history, and criminal law scholars continually emphasize the importance of upholding it.[131] Nevertheless, scholars cling to it not because it happens to have been historically given. Rather, it is because they are firmly convinced that the subjective/cognitive notion of criminal guilt is not an adventitious property of crime but an embodiment and reflection of rationality in juridical science. At this point one encounters the idealistic streak in analytical criminal jurisprudence.

The Conceptualist Sting

The foregoing discussion confirms the commonplace knowledge that the concept of crime is composed of two elements: *mens rea* and *actus reus* or guilty mind and guilty act. From an analytical point of view, the latter is a descriptive label which sums up the motions of the human person directed at and which brought into existence certain proscribed actions; the former denotes the motions of the human person aimed at and which achieved some proscribed consequences of an act. Strictly speaking, the specific proscribed actions themselves are not constitutive parts of the analytic meaning of the concept of crime. The content of the legal concept of crime is not really certain enumerated or specific crimes but the further concept of intentional unlawful action. It follows that Stephen[132] erred when he denied that *mens rea* or 'guilty mind' had a general meaning merely because the phrase could be used in the context of divergent crimes. 'Guilty mind' is 'guilty mind' whatever the specific proscribed consequences of the act, and 'guilty act' is 'guilty act' whatever may be the particular proscribed action.

'Intent' and 'act' in themselves do not constitute human actions such as stealing, killing, burning, and so on. Although people do witness such things or see someone steal, kill, or burn down an edifice, nobody has ever seen theft, homicide, or arson any more than anyone has ever seen 'rights.' In other words, such human actions which are juristically known as theft, murder, arson, and the like and which, linguistically, are jointly or severally referred to as 'crimes,' are exemplars of what Bentham regarded as 'fictitious moral entities.'[133] As fictitious entities they are neither 'directly perceptible nor knowable by inference based on perception.'[134] The referents of juristic concepts are not physical entities. In Bentham's positivistic vocabulary, they are 'a sort of vapours which during the course of the legislative process are as it were generated and sublimed.'[135]

As already noted, 'intent' and 'act' are generic terms for certain motions or activities of the human person. Unlike human actions, they are real entities. As real entities, they are either directly or indirectly perceptible, and they constitute the irreducible, analytic contents of the concept of intentional action. Thus, the concept of crime ultimately directs the analyst's attention to the activities of the human person that are perceptible either directly or inferentially. An accurate description of the phenomenon that we call 'crime' requires a set of terms which reflect the difference between those activities of the human person that are directly perceptible and those that are only inferentially perceptible. In short, the nature of the concept of crime requires that we split the human person into two. As well, clarity demands that we employ different words to describe each aspect.

Traditionally, mind (or soul) and body have been used to reflect this; it is conventionally known as Cartesian dualism. As originally formulated, dualism entailed the reality of the mind,[136] but in this century behaviourists have reduced the mind to a ghost. Nevertheless, it is suggested that, as an analytic necessity, dualism does not inexorably involve the reality of the mind. Mind may be real or it may be a mere 'ghost in the machine'[137] of the human body; the analytic enterprise is not affected one way or the other. Indeed, normative analysts of criminal law such as Peter Brett[138] and George P. Fletcher,[139] and descriptive analysts such as Hyman Gross[140] expressly maintain 'an antirealist position about minds.'[141] Whatever may be its significance in other fields of inquiry, the reality of the mind is not an integral part of analytical criminal jurisprudence. Nevertheless, this book subscribes to the realist position.[142]

The notion of mental states enables us to elaborate on a malady plaguing analytical criminal jurisprudence. Analytic work is dual in nature: it involves both 'resolution' and 'composition.'[143] As the word suggests, 'resolution' requires the breaking of a concept into its parts while 'composition' requires an analyst to reconstruct the whole from its parts. Hence, the analytical jurist's task is not completed as soon as he or she has succeeded in resolving a legal concept into its component or irreducible parts. Resolution is merely the way down. The way up is to compose the whole from the parts. Hence, analytical criminal jurisprudents have not been content with resolving the concept of crime into its component parts. They have taken the further step of composing it from the bottom upwards. In other words, they have had to frame a *definition* of crime. And they do so in conceptualist terms, that is, they hold that the meaning of the word 'crime' generated by conceptual analysis can be generalized.[144]

They have been aided in this task by the essentialist method of definition. This method of definition requires an inquirer to select one out of several properties or components of a particular concept as the essence – real or nominal – of that concept. An essential property is an attribute of a concept that is regarded as its central, universal, and indispensable formal element. The definition of the concept is then framed in such a way that its meaning will invariably include the definitive or universal attribute. In short, the essentialist method of definition 'consisteth principally in *right* limiting of the significations of such Appellations or Names as are of all others the most Universal: Which Limitations serve to avoid ambiguity and equivocation in Reasoning.'[145] It fixes the meaning of a word, term, or concept and decrees that the stipulated meaning should be the ultimate basis from which any rational argument must commence and end. In other words, such a definition provides a 'scientific' or formal basis for expository work. The essentialist method of definition is as old as Aristotle;[146] the difference between the ancients and the moderns is that, while the latter regarded such essences as nominal, the former have taken them to be real.

In an attempt to establish a science of criminal law, analytical criminal jurisprudents have resorted to this method of definition. And they invariably seize on *mens rea* or guilty mind as the essence of crime.[147] The essentialist method was employed by the father of analytical jurisprudence himself, John Austin. While pointing out that an 'essential part is not the complex whole of which it is an essential part,' Austin insisted, in his rather archaic language, that 'intention, negligence, heedlessness or rashness, is *an essentially component part* of injury or wrong ... intention, negligence, heedlessness or rashness, is *of the essence* of injury or wrong; is *of the essence* of breach of duty; is a *necessary condition precedent* to the existence of that plight or predicament which is styled guilt or imputability.'[148]

The dominant trend in contemporary analytical criminal jurisprudence takes the same 'essentialist' position. The difference between them and Austin is that, while the latter's notion of legal guilt includes negligence, the former excludes it. The end result is an intellectual standpoint that finds liability for crimes based on negligence offensive to a sound system of reasoning.

A *fortiori*, the essentialist definition of crime rules out strict liability in criminal law. Although some analysts do not see any insuperable difficulty in the way,[149] the dominant trend in analytical criminal jurisprudence has been that strict liability or the strict liability offence is 'irrational,' 'arbitrary and unreasonable,'[150] a 'noxious weed'[151] that 'cannot be brought within the scope of penal law.'[152] Consequently, they maintain that strict liability has no place in criminal law, and that it should be excluded in principle from the sphere of penal law.

The scope of penal law is regarded as coterminous with criminal law. Hence, criminal liability is defined as liability to penal or punitive sanction. Since analysis of the concept of crime reveals that the notion of guilt in the criminal law is restricted to intentional or reckless infraction of the law, it follows that only 'affirmative state of mind'[153] is sufficient for penal liability. This framework makes it difficult to rationalize punitive sanction on any other ground.[154] Indeed, there has been intermittent calls for the constitutionalization of the subjective/cognitive standard for criminal liability.[155] Criminal jurisprudence smarts under the conceptualist sting.

This chapter began with a brief exposition of the nature of analytical jurisprudence. Although the analytical tradition in legal philosophy goes back to Hobbes, and was considerably furthered by Bentham, it was John Austin who delineated the program for analytical jurisprudence in the English-speaking world. Like analytical philosophy generally, analytical jurisprudence is primarily concerned with facilitating the understanding of the existing body of knowledge; it is, if at all, only tangentially involved with the increase of knowledge. Thus, analytical jurisprudence aims at giving accurate description of the structural elements of law and at systematization of legal phenomena. It consequently limits itself to the task of identifying and clarifying fundamental legal concepts, notions, and distinctions and providing a coherent exposition of the materials of positive law. Moreover, only such pervasive concepts, notions, and distinctions as are found in developed systems of positive law are taken into consideration by analytical jurisprudents. This indirectly but effectively excludes from the purview of the philosophy of law the legal ideas, notions, and principles of unsophisticated legal regimes. Specifically, analytical jurisprudence disregards the idea of wrong which prevailed in Anglo-Saxon and early Anglo-Norman England.

Analytical jurisprudence consigns to a pre-intellectual period everything that preceded the emergence of recognizable or distinct and sophisticated legal concepts, principles, and notions. We have suggested that a definitive notion of crime did not crystallize in English law until the seventeenth century, and that it was the moral conception of crime that was incorporated into the common law. A corollary of this was that the common law fastened on the moral meaning of intention as the basis for ascribing criminal responsibility. This is encapsulated in the maxim *actus non facit reum nisi mens sit rea.*

Since analytical jurisprudence aspires to elucidate law and legal concepts in descriptive or morally neutral vocabulary, it had to slough off or somehow disregard the moralistic premises of the common law notion of crime. In other words, analytical criminal jurisprudents are enjoined to explicate the common law concept of criminal wrong without any regard to the moral or political theory that supported its original formulation. This is so not only because Austin's theory of law is decidedly positivistic but because the analytical method is amoral and apolitical. Analytical jurisprudence does not allow the theory of law or the moral and political philosophy harboured by its practitioner to interfere with the derivation of the structural elements of law in the positive legal order. This is a methodological requirement.

Austin's practice of analytical jurisprudence was more ambitious than that of his successors. To him, analytical jurisprudence should concern itself with the coherent exposition of the principles, concepts, and notions common to the systems of positive law of all civilized European nations. Analytical jurisprudents in the English-speaking countries demurred on this point. To them, Austin had derived his data from the wrong place. Instead of seeking the highest common factor of all developed legal systems, they confine themselves to identifying, analysing, and systematizing the fundamental legal concepts embedded in a particular legal system. This accounts for the difference in their respective conceptual conclusions. Austin did not treat 'crime' as a distinct legal concept. Instead, he subsumed it under the general notion of injury or wrong. And, an elaborate, logical exposition of the latter concept (injury or wrong) evaded the distinction between criminal and penal law to which we alluded in chapter 4. *A fortiori*, it failed to reflect the distinction between criminal and penal *mens rea* to which we referred in the same chapter. Indeed, Austin eschewed the phrases *mens rea* and *actus reus* in his jurisprudential writings. However, subsequent analytical jurisprudents did not follow his example; they continued to employ these phrases. Further, by confining themselves to the language of law in systems of positive law within the common law orbit, contemporary analytical jurisprudents reached a more restrictive conceptual conclusion.

The application of the analytical method in elucidating the concept of crime under the common law revealed that it was resolvable into two elements, 'intent' and 'act.' These are the irreducible simple ideas which make up the complex notion of criminal wrong. Being a reference to bodily motion, 'act' is directly perceptible while 'intent,' which refers to the activities of the mind, is only inferentially perceptible. The analytical meaning of the concept of crime is thus inextricably intertwined with the nature of the human person, which in turn necessitates a dualistic vocabulary. In short, the concept of crime embedded in the language of the law in common law jurisdictions is intimately connected with the notion of the individual, natural person. The legal actor envisaged by the legal concept of crime is a human person.

Analysis culminates in an attempt to define the relevant concept. Accordingly, analytical criminal jurisprudence ends by formulating a definition of crime. In framing this definition, analytical criminal jurisprudents adopted the essentialist method of definition. 'Intent,' 'guilty mind,' or the mental element is regarded as the essence of crime. Consequently, the occurrence of any criminally proscribed action cannot amount to a crime unless the actor intentionally brought it about. This is the conceptual meaning of crime.

The primary function of such a delimitation is to fix once and for all the theoretical topography. This implies that an element of arbitrariness is almost always present in a given theory. The element of arbitrariness is that the establishment and recognition of a theory closes, so to speak, the workshop, and forecloses the admission of facts other than those already worked into the theory. The closing of the workshop forbids scholars working within the established conceptual framework to admit any fact that does not fit into the parameters fixed by the theory. Facts that cannot be reconciled with the postulates of the theory or included under any of the categories recognized by the paradigm are simply declared immaterial or irrelevant. In short, the acceptance of a conceptual model makes it possible for scholars to concentrate on the task of problem solving or of explicating the established theoretical framework. In either case, the postulates of the theory are taken as given: explication and problem solving refrain from recasting or re-examining the concepts and categories with which they deal.[156]

Since the analytic meaning of crime requires a subjective/cognitive standard of responsibility, the conceptual meaning of crime effectively excludes negligence. As well, it rules out strict liability in the criminal law. In other words, the scientific methodology leads to a situation in which the meaning of the fundamental legal concepts embedded in positive law become ossified. The ossification forestalls the possibility of a shift in the established paradigm. A corollary of this is that analytical criminal jurisprudence fosters the belief that the conceptual framework within which the analytical project is carried on has assumed a final and ultimate form. Such a belief stultifies and hamstrings any attempt to reorient the criminal law and make it do any job for which it was not programmed by its putative heavenly designers.

8

Beyond Analysis: The Concept as Villain

The preceding chapter showed that analytical jurisprudence aimed at systematizing existing legal knowledge, not at creating new knowledge. In pursuing that objective, it formulated a conceptual framework within which rational discourse in criminal law was to be carried on. The definitive meaning of the concept of crime formulated by analytical jurisprudence compels legal scholars to structure their ratiocination along charted and well-defined paths. In short, while analytical criminal jurisprudence set out with the avowed aim of giving an accurate description of the meaning of the fundamental terms and words found in the corpus of positive criminal law, it ended by using the ascertained meaning to discipline or structure thought in criminal law. To put it another way, it evolved a paradigm. The pivotal element in the established paradigm is the notion of 'fault,' in the quintessential sense of an intention on the part of the actor to bring about the legally proscribed act.

As originally understood, this requirement was said to have been laid down by nature herself.[1] It is impossible to quibble with this explanation, for it gained currency in intellectually sophisticated societies enamoured with the distinction between the dictates of natural law and those of conventional laws. While the requirements of the former were regarded as unchangeable, changeless, or immutable, the latter were not. In truth, history does not show that that specific mental element has always been a prerequisite for incurring legal liability. What history shows is that intentionally or wilfully inflicted harm has been invariably denounced, abhorred, and resented more than accidentally or negligently caused harm.[2] Be that as it may, analytical criminal jurists have detached this requirement from nature and/or morality. Instead, they have installed it as an invariable element or feature of developed systems of positive law. Hence, analytical criminal jurisprudents know this moral requirement simply as a principle or rule of law or, more banally, as the mental element in crime. As we saw in the last chapter, the combined result of the conceptual mode of ordering and the essentialist method of definition was that analytical criminal jurists regard the mental element – intention or reck-lessness – as the essence of crime. And, if we identify, as analytical criminal jurisprudence seems to do, criminal with penal law, then it will follow that criminal liability based on negligence and strict liability offences are, at best, exceptions to the principle of no liability without fault. Analytical criminal jurists have consistently taken this stand. They have been using their own par-adigm 'to argue in that paradigm's defense.'[3]

This chapter argues that the questions of the validity of negligence as a basis of liability and of the legitimacy of strict liability offences raise moral rather than formal or conceptual issues. Put differently, such questions are not invita-tions to inquire into what, conceptually speaking, is or what logically could be, given the postulates of a particular moral or political philosophy. Rather, they are about what (rationally) is, given the totality of our legal experience. The 'conceptualist sting,'[4] however, compels analytical criminal jurists to address these questions *as if* they raise conceptual or formal issues. It is suggested here that moral puzzles are not susceptible to conceptual solutions, or, rather, that the only moral riddles that can be solved by the conceptualist are those that are analogous to the ones already taken cognizance of, or are embedded in, the established conceptual framework. By confining legal scholarship to con-ceptual analysis and systematization of positive law, analytical legal philosophy effectively limits the imagination.

The limited imagination arises principally from the fact that analytic legal philosophy is infected with conceptualism.[5] This makes analytical jurispru-dence oblivious of empirical factors which might otherwise necessitate re-formation of a particular concept. Rather than take cognizance of such 'new' experiences of life, the analytical jurist consigns them to the realm of the con-tingent and bids us to be content with displaying and celebrating the harmoni-ous unity of the group of notions which together comprise a conceptual whole. When conceptualism is combined with pure rationalism, the analytical jurist is apt to imagine that concepts are ontological entities with eternal con-tent. If, on the other hand, conceptualism is coupled with practical rational-ism, then the analyst is apt to hold that concepts are permanent intellectual structures with determinate content. The two positions converge in that both share the conviction that analysis of concepts yields certain knowledge. In reality, like Cowper and his fire at twilight, conceptualism creates what it sees. Presumably, it creates neither life nor the forms of life disclosed by experience.

As noted in the last chapter, it was legal history that supplied the materials on which the analytical method was brought to bear. As soon as a conceptual order is established, a concept assumes an independent life of its own. This makes exposition possible, and it proceeds untrammelled by the practical context within which the concept lives. In this way, conceptual thinking becomes immune to historical and/or empirical environmental changes generated by forms or patterns of life subsequent to the formulation of the relevant concept. In short, conceptualism confines the pursuit of knowledge within an established paradigm and neglects its improvement. Or, more accurately, conceptualism accords epistemic finality and superiority to the web of established intellectual constructs; it is concerned with conservation rather than innovation or renewal. Consequently, any mention of the possibility of conceptual reformulation would be barren and empty talk to the conceptualist.

To be sure, history has not stood still since analytical jurisprudence established a conceptual framework for the criminal law. To cite a few examples, the actors on the legal scene are no longer only the simple individual human or anthropological entities assumed by the moral conception of crime. Specifically, corporate actors have come to dominate the legal world.[6] As legal persons, corporations hardly possess the characteristics of personhood pre-supposed by the established conceptual framework.[7] Thus, unless the established paradigm is allowed to dictate the terms of the debate, the generalized account of criminal responsibility fostered by analytical jurisprudence is unhelpful to resolve the theoretical problems raised by such new legal actors. Nor is it helpful on such nuanced issues as the appropriate mental element in different species of the same crime, such as homicide[8] or, to take another example, whether battered women should be criminally liable for killing their tormentors. In short, it is futile to treat such questions as whether 'negligence' can ground liability in the criminal law or whether the strict liability offence is legitimate or whether corporation aggregates are amenable to the criminal law as conceptual matters. They are not. The following discussion focuses on the limitations of analytical criminal jurisprudence by elaborating on the first two of the above-mentioned issues, namely, the legitimacy of negligence and strict liability offences. We can state our conclusion right away: it is not *intrinsically* 'ill-legal' to base responsibility for crimes on negligence or to have strict liability offences on the statute books. Of course, to say this is neither to advocate *criminal* liability for negligence nor to countenance strict *criminal* liability. On the contrary, it merely insists on the fact that resort to substantive in contradistinction to formal morality is absolutely necessary in order to avoid the cul-de-sac generated by the conceptual framework established by analytical criminal jurisprudence.

The Limitations of Analytical Criminal Theory

Negligence and the Criminal Law

The issue here is: Can negligence be a basis for liability in the criminal law? This question is treated by analytical *criminal*[9] jurists as a conceptual one. Not surprisingly, the semantic and logical answer is usually in the negative. It runs as follows. Criminal liability is essentially liability to punitive sanction.[10] Liability to punitive sanction requires 'some affirmative state of mind with respect to the particular act or consequence.'[11] Negligence is not even a state (or, if it is, it is only a negative state) of mind. Therefore, negligence is not and cannot be a ground for liability in the criminal law.

The argument is perfectly logical, but, although logic has a place in the law,[12] it is now over a century since Oliver Wendel Holmes, Jr reminded the legal world that 'the life of the law has not been logic.'[13] Law takes its sustenance from life, not logic;[14] the former is bigger than the latter.[15]

The logical elaboration of legal concepts is akin to morphology: it makes legal concepts indifferent to life. Although the formulation of the concept of crime was determined solely by logical analysis and the desire for systematization, the preceding chapters have shown that its actual formation was not. Rather, its formation was influenced by a particular moral and political theory which impressed a principle of ordering on the existing forms of life. This shaped subsequent legal practices which were in turn ultimately coordinated into legal theory. In short, it may be that, as G.P. Fletcher recently pointed out,[16] a general moral or political theory is needed to support the normative claims of the criminal law such as the requirement of fault for liability. However, this need not be so, for, as was emphasized in chapter 7, the analytical jurisprudential enterprise is not necessarily dependent on this or that school or theory of or about law or any particular moral and political theory. The normative claims of the law, including the criminal law, can be free-standing. At any rate, having cast the concept of crime into a logical mould, analytical criminal jurisprudence is oblivious of the moral and political theory which undergird its formation. Consequently, it can only reiterate ad nauseum the normative claims of the criminal law without reference to the forms of life and the moral or political theory which underlie its formation.

In the nineteenth century, the legal intellectual outlook was permeated by a positivistic ethos. But the moral and political theory that shaped the positive legal knowledge to which the analytical method was applied was itself informed by an essentially pre-industrial and predominantly Christian moral outlook. Thus, although analytical criminal theory evolved in an industrial age, it mirrored the forms of life and morality that were captured or envisaged by a different age. One does not need to be a historian to know that the moral outlook reflected in the institutionalized conception of crime is fundamentally different from what obtained in industrial and post-industrial societies.

As has been repeatedly pointed out, there is scarcely any doubt that the concept of criminal *mens rea*, as it developed under the common law, excluded negligence.[17] With the exception of its role as a basis for liability in homicide – manslaughter – negligence had no place in criminal law until towards the end of the nineteenth century. It was only then that lawmakers began making 'inroads on the reluctance of our criminal law to penalise carelessness.'[18] Obviously, this legislative innovation came several decades after analytical jurisprudence had persuaded most minds of the necessity for a logical science of law. Thus, in spite of such legislative inroads, criminal theory persists in denying a place for negligence in the criminal law. It will be suggested that this is driven by conceptualism and the desire for conceptual purity. It will be further suggested that the desire for conceptual purity blinds analytical criminal jurists to factors which might commend negligence as a basis for liability. Specifically, the 'natural antipathy evoked whenever the issue of negligence as a basis of criminal responsibility is raised in modern times,'[19] or the reluctance of juries to convict for negligent behaviour,[20] is attributable to at least three probable factors.

The first factor is the hiatus caused in legal practices by the abandonment, in the period before the transition to modern times, of the last vestigial traces of the compensatory aspects of criminal law. This is coupled with the fact that since criminal conviction entailed dire consequences – capital punishment and forfeiture – the loss of the compensatory aspect of the legal sanction probably made people averse to negligence. As noted in chapter 4, the medieval mind was convinced that negligence was blameworthy; indeed, Thomas Aquinas explicitly maintained that negligence was a sin.[21] But it is also true that medieval jurists at no time subscribed to the belief that negligence could be the basis for incurring the extraordinary degree of punishments which followed conviction in criminal proceedings.[22] Indeed, the forms of daily intercourse in pre-modern society afforded little opportunity for cases in which damnable injury could be caused by negligent acts or omissions.[23]

The second factor is what might be called 'the Crusoean' cast of modern moral and political philosophy: this outlook delayed the appearance of a 'man-Friday' on the legal topography until the third quarter of the nineteenth century. The third, and perhaps the most important, factor is that the scientific aspirations of the analytic approach blinds us from seeing that analytical jurisprudence itself rests on legal history. As well, by limiting the range of issues that could be raised in criminal theory to those allowed by the established paradigm, it effectively ruled out the possibility of revising the concept of crime. Specifically, the question of responsibility for the consequences of one's acts or omissions has been reduced to a whirligig game of formalism in which the players wield scalpels animated by remorseless logic. These three factors will be considered seriatim.

The Demise of the Compensatory Function of the Criminal Process and the Consequent Aversion to Negligence

In chapter 1 we alluded to the fact that the legal sanction served multiple purposes in pre-modern or unsophisticated legal regimes; the purpose of the legal sanction ranged from punitive to compensatory functions. This was especially so in Anglo-Saxon and early Anglo-Norman England. In this chapter, the loss of compensatory aspect of the criminal process will be adduced as one of the main reasons why the criminal sanction came to be regarded as purely punitive, and why negligence was not ordinarily considered as a sufficient basis for invoking the criminal sanction.

As was noted in chapter 3, the ascension of the King's Peace meant that compensation for breach of the peace of lesser legal authorities ceased. As well, the bifurcation of wrongs into civil and criminal wrongs, with the consequence that the former became 'common pleas' while the latter became 'pleas of the Crown,' implied that the payment of monetary compensation to the victim or the kin of the victim of criminal wrongs was no longer feasible. However, the right to monetary compensation in felonies such as homicide was not immediately extirpated. Traditionally,[24] the monetary compensation so payable, the *wergild*, was not a penalty but a reparation to the bereaved family – a satisfaction due to the survivors of the deceased. For a long time after the Norman Conquest, the *wergild* for homicide continued to be extracted. The right was kept alive and was indirectly enforced through 'the appeal of death'; it was actively prosecuted into early modern times.[25] However, by the seventeenth century the appeal of death had fallen into disuse even though it was not formally abolished until 1819.[26]

The appeal was not foreclosed unless the public prosecution had led to a conviction and execution. Generally speaking,[27] it remained available and could be used to secure compensation from the offender or to secure greater punishment of the offender in the ensuing trial if there had been no public prosecution or if the public prosecution had resulted in acquittal or pardon or conviction for manslaughter. The justices encouraged the appeal of death,[28] and, since a successful prosecution involved dire consequences, the threat of an appeal of death was naturally sufficient to induce the offender to compose with the victim's survivor. As Daniel Ernst[29] says,

[T]he results of a successful appeal were sufficiently grave to bring a killer to terms with a widow or heir. If he was found guilty in an appeal of murder, the killer was attainted and executed. If he was convicted of manslaughter, the killer could plead benefit of clergy and escape hanging, but he still suffered the consequences of attainder: forfeiture of chattels and corruption of blood. If the killer had been grossly negligent in causing death, courts could instruct juries to return murder or manslaughter convictions. Thus, in 1664, Justice Kelyng wrote that workmen who killed accidentally while 'doing nothing but what is usual with workmen to do' were guilty only of misadventure, whereas workers who killed by throwing rubbish or timber from a rooftop into the streets of London were guilty of manslaughter, for 'being in London there is a continual concourse of people passing up and down the streets.'

Incidentally, the possibility of conviction in the circumstances indicated in the last part of the above passage is evidence that the negligent act was strongly disapproved. Indeed, as the same passage shows, if the negligence in homicide cases was gross, the killer was likely to be made to suffer the ordinary felon's penalty. The same point has been noted by Sayre.[30] Thus, although negligence was not formalized until the nineteenth century, in pre-modern times moral blame attached to negligent wrongdoing. But the present point is not that negligence was discountenanced; rather, it is that judges encouraged the appeal probably because, among other factors, it was an effective means of vindicating the survivors' right to compensation. In other words, the appeal that savoured more of criminal than of civil prosecution must have prolonged the view that the criminal process served compensatory as well as punitive functions. But when the appeal fell into desuetude, and was eventually abolished, the criminal process lost this last remnant of its compensatory and conciliatory functions. It was ineluctable that the criminal sanction (whether capital or pecuniary mulct) would come to be perceived as purely punitive. This must have occasioned a change in the official and lay attitude to negligent acts and omissions, at least as far as the criminal process was concerned.

The Crusoean-orientation of the Modern Outlook

Intellectual history suggests that the notion that 'negligence' is sufficient to ground legal liability is inextricably interwined with a moral or political theory which postulates that individuals owe one another a duty of care. In most cases this means no more and no less than a duty to take such care as is necessary and sufficient to ensure that the results flowing from ordinarily legitimate or perfectly legal activity do not cause injury to others. As already noted, the common law was undoubtedly influenced in the course of its development by moral and political philosophy. But, again as already noted, English law has never been a slave to any particular abstract speculation about the nature and basis of law. On the contrary, it has remained consistently close to life.[31]

Anglophone societies have neither worn the same colour of life through all the ages nor been subjected to the superintendence of a single or unified moral and political philosophy. As a result, while law, like the chameleon, has remained the same entity throughout the ages, it has, like the chameleon, reflected the changing colour of its surroundings. In the nascent feudal society of the Anglo-Saxons as well as the full-fledged feudal society of early Anglo-Norman times, the law mirrored the social circumstances in which it functioned. In the later-medieval period, when the common law really took shape, the law also reflected the colour of the times. Medieval society was imbued with a deep sense of duty to one's neighbours. Hence, as we saw in chapter 5, the law regulated the activities of craftsmen, artificers, and tradesmen for the purpose of ensuring that they exercised their skills with assiduity and that they plied their trade in such a way as to avoid causing harm to others. Thus, in pre-modern times, town governments prohibited 'noxious factories, restricted noisy or unsavoury trades to special areas, and abated "coal-smoke nuisances"; they prevented river pollution and obstruction of the roadway, and insisted that each man should clean the pavement in front of his house.'[32]

As was also noted in the same chapter, the medieval regulative ideal was discarded during the second half of the eighteenth century. Again, as that chapter makes clear, this was made possible by a shift from the corporatist outlook promoted by medieval moral and political philosophy to the individualistic outlook supported by modern moral and political philosophy. The momentous change came in the seventeenth century when John Locke propounded the highly influential moral and political theory which revolved around the idea of natural right. Under the influence of Locke's political philosophy, at first imperceptibly and later noticeably, the traditional corporatist system crumbled. In its place was substituted the conception of society as a fictitious entity made up of a collection of disparate individuals assiduously seeking and promoting their own self-interest. The triumph of the atomistic conception of society institutionalized a individualistic moral, political, and legal outlook. Specifically, the focus on the individual made it possible for moral and political theorists to cease talking altogether about duties, whether natural or positive. Instead, they shifted their attention, and concentrated all their energies, on the protection of the natural rights of man generally and, particularly, the protection and furtherance of the right of property – what J.S. Mill uncharitably called 'the castle of unreason.'[33] By the second half of the eighteenth century, modern moral and political philosophy had been transformed and formalized into the doctrines of a new political economy.[34]

The 'moral conscience' of an individualistic society was markedly different from that of the earlier corporatist society.[35] The spirit of economic individualism did not subscribe to the moral idea that '[one] must not seek without restraint [one's] own profit and well-being but must be *careful* that in so doing [one] does not injure others.'[36] There were no neighbours but only travellers along the same path. Such a moral conscience could hardly have a place for 'negligence' as a basis for legal liability. Indeed, it was not until more than two decades into the nineteenth century that negligence began to emerge as an organizing unit in the civil branch of the law.[37] That development was necessitated by 'the luxuriant crop of "running down" actions reaped from the commercial prosperity of the late eighteenth and early nineteenth centuries.'[38] In other words, it was not until the propensity of the new forms of life – the explosion in industrial and commercial activities – to inflict injury on people in a random fashion that it dawned on the modern legal mind that carelessness could be an independent basis for incurring legal liability. However, the impact of the new consciousness was not immediately felt beyond the civil branch of the law. To complete the Crusoean analogy, a 'man-friday' did not appear on the penal landscape at the time it did on the civil.

Prescriptive Result of Descriptive Analysis

As we saw in chapter 7, the analytical jurist follows a definite procedure: he first identifies a word or term as a concept and then aspires to render its content in purely descriptive and morally neutral vocabulary. Conceptual analysis revealed that the content of the concept of crime is another concept, namely, the concept of intentional wrong. Further analysis of the latter concept showed its descriptive content to be 'intent' and 'act.' 'Intent' and 'act' exist only as particulars. Since analytical jurisprudence is informed by the conviction that concepts have universal contents, analytical criminal jurisprudence has had to isolate the universal content of 'crime.' It has done so by proffering a definitive meaning of crime.

The definition is best expressed in a paraphrase: crime means an intentional or reckless violation of duty imposed by that species of public law known as the criminal law. This definition is not only 'topic-neutral' but also agnostic. It is 'topic-neutral' because it is not restricted to a particular type or species of crimes. It is agnostic because it tells us what crime *means*, whatever the prevailing socio-economic and political system and irrespective of whether any of its defining properties subserves any particular moral or political value. Whether this conceptual meaning protects, furthers, or impedes such moral and political values as 'liberty,' 'freedom,' 'autonomy,' or the more mundane economic value of 'efficiency' and the like is beyond the pale of analytical jurisprudence. The most cursory look at contemporary criminal legal literature would show that the neutral definition of crime is, implicitly or explicitly, the basis of theorizing in criminal law.

The analytical approach constrains the jurisprudential question that can properly be asked in relation to any given legal concept. As with the concept of law itself, the question in criminal jurisprudence is a narrow one: 'What is crime?' Of course, that question receives the very short and ready-made answer furnished by conceptual analysis. In this way, the role of theory in criminal law is effectively confined to the simple task of elucidating the principal words and terms found in the definition of crime. As we saw in the preceding chapter, the moral conception of crime that crystallized in the seventeenth and eighteenth centuries under the common law was purged and snuffed of its moral underpinnings and then elevated into the legal concept of crime in the nineteenth century. It limits the meaning of criminal wrong to intentional or reckless violation of legal duty or obligation. Thus, the word 'negligence' does not occur in the definition of the concept of crime. In short, although the avowed role of analytical criminal jurisprudents was merely to act as the midwife who delivers the descriptive content of the concept of crime, analytical jurisprudents end up *prescribing* the content of the concept.

Since 'crime' is defined as an intentional or reckless violation of a legal duty imposed and designated as such by public law, and since semantic or linguistic analysis of the word 'negligence' would reveal that it is a distinct notion that can be included neither under intention nor recklessness,[39] it follows as a matter of inexorable logic that a negligent act or omission cannot amount to a crime. In this way, the question of answerability for the harmful consequences of one's acts or omissions in the criminal law is narrowed down to the simple issue of ascertaining whether an alleged criminal conduct exhibits the presence of intention or recklessness. This movement from description to prescription effectively rules out the possibility that negligence might be an acceptable independent basis of liability for crimes.

From an historical point of view, the loss of negligence as a possible basis of liability for crimes is an accident due to the advent of intellectual sophistication; it is not due to any palpable change in what may be called the untrammelled naturalism that prevailed in the unsophisticated societies such as Anglo-Saxon and early Anglo-Norman England. As we saw in chapter 4, legal sophistication came hand-in-hand with a natural law-based moral and political philosophy. The philosophy of law derived from the latter made legal liability track culpability. Ordinarily, culpability encompassed intention, recklessness, and negligence, but the distinction between criminal and penal laws necessitated the further delimitation of culpability in criminal law and its restriction to intention or recklessness. The end result of this process of refinement was perpetuated by its being incorporated into the corpus of the positive laws of 'civilized' communities.

Analytical jurisprudence gave its imprimatur to the result of this historical accident. As practised in the Anglo-American legal world, analytical criminal jurisprudence itself seldom aspires to attain a level of abstraction that transcends the ordinary requirements of positive criminal law. Nevertheless, the contemporary natural rights perspective reinforces the analytical position by maintaining that in the criminal law 'the right of the individual is to be held accountable only for those consequences of his act that were originally present in his will.'[40] To attempt to elaborate on the somewhat cryptic phrase 'consequences that were originally present in his will' means crossing ground already covered while explicating the analytic meaning of criminal guilt.[41] But it is important to emphasize that the position reached via the analytical route is confirmable and confirmed on philosophical grounds as well. Put differently, the contemporary natural-rights perspective is so closely linked with the analytic bent that it is impossible to separate the two. Both are mired in conceptualism. The analytic and the natural rights philosophers regard crime as a distinct and separate form with a content of its own – a content that unreservedly excludes negligence.

As in many other areas of study, the strength and attraction of the analytical approach in criminal jurisprudence is its power to generate substantive principles, thus making possible the articulation of a coherent body of criminal law. Its weakness lies in dogmatizing about the meaning of crime. 'Crime' is first and foremost a moral and social concept. Like any other moral or social concept, it (or its equivalents) is a compendious linguistic or formal label used in many societies to distinguish between countenanced and discountenanced acts or tolerable and intolerable effects of human actions. Such discountenanced acts might be caused intentionally, recklessly, negligently, absentmindedly, or in various other conceivable moral circumstances. As was emphasized in chapter 2, unsophisticated societies and, indeed, popular morality in sophisticated societies did not single out any of these as the sole basis for ascribing legal liability. On the contrary, unsophisticated societies and popular morality simply attached liability commensurate with the degree of responsibility manifested in the action. But 'crime' is also a product of 'the philosophy of an imperial intellect,' not in a pejorative sense but in the profound sense of the intellect that *defines*.[42] The defining intellect did not mirror popular morality; rather, it made liability follow culpability. As already severally noted, it is the dictates of the latter that require a resolute exclusion of negligence from the purview of the criminal law. In sum, the exclusion of negligence from the criminal sphere is a conceptual necessity; it is not warranted by any moral, social, or political imperative.

The desire for conceptual purity and the consequential exclusion of negligence from the purview of the criminal law is sometimes disguised in deterministic discourse. For instance, in explaining why negligence is probably not a proper basis for incurring criminal liability, Glanville Williams wrote that some people could not help being negligent: 'Some people are born feckless, clumsy, thoughtless, inattentive, with a bad memory or a slow reaction time.'[43] M. Kelman[44] has underscored the deterministic assumptions of the author of this sentence. Another leading analytical criminal jurist, Jerome Hall, was more direct and emphatic in maintaining that the negligent actor could not help being so. According to him,

negligent acts are like natural forces, and the damages should lie where they fall ... the insensitivity which one ascribes to certain inadvertent harmdoers ... has very deep roots. It has become part of the 'structure of personality' which had its origin in childhood and in a vast number of other experiences. In other words ... the personality pattern has become fixed in the adult. His present attitudes are not matters of choice; hence there is no warrant for punishing him on ... traditional moral ground.'[45]

At this juncture, it is pertinent to reiterate that the criminal law postulates freedom of the will.[46] As well, contrary to Oliver Wendell Holmes's[47] notion of an objective standard of responsibility, the notion of legal responsibility presupposes that the agent had the capacity and could have exercised that capacity to avoid the wrongful act. If an agent lacked such a capacity because of congenital defects or insufficient experience, then the issue of negligence cannot be made out. In most cases, the relevance of the capacity to avoid the wrongful act is obscured by the fact that it arises directly in legal proceedings primarily in the form of such excuses (defences) as insanity, automatism, and the like. In brief, deterministic explanation is as inappropriate in explaining away negligent actions as it is in describing intentional or reckless acts. For, if deterministic discourse is appropriate in describing the negligent actor, there is no reason why it cannot be 'used in describing purposeful criminals: people are born vicious or are rendered malicious by environmental factors.'[48] Resort to deterministic explanation with regard to why negligent acts ought not to be penalized is a counterpane which shields from view the fact that the exclusion of negligence is dictated solely by the need to maintain the conceptual purity of crime. The culprit here is the formal, concept of crime which forms the background against which such outlandish explanations are proffered. The fact is that analytical criminal jurisprudence leaves no room for the possibility of revising the concept of crime in any or such a way as will make it accommodate negligent acts. This, then, is the principal reason for excluding negligence from the realm of the law of crimes: the conceptualist's delineation of the proper scope of criminal law is the villain. The next section considers the same issue with regard to the so-called 'strict liability offences.'

Strict Liability Offences and Criminal Theory

The offences for which liability can be strict tend to be what are designated and variously called 'public welfare offences,' 'regulatory offences,' 'civil offences,' 'quasi-criminal offences,' 'police or administrative offences,' and so on.[49] In contemporary criminal jurisprudence, it is axiomatic that these offences are not real offences or true crimes.[50] This conviction is in no way confined to scholars; it pervades judicial pronouncements as well. For instance, in the Canadian case of *Sault Ste. Marie*,[51] Dickson, J. (as he then was) explicitly maintained that 'regulatory offences' are not real crimes. He said:

[Here] the court is concerned with offences variously referred to as 'statutory,' 'public welfare,' 'regulatory,' 'absolute liability,' or 'strict liability,' which are not criminal in any real sense, but are prohibited in the public interest (*Sherras* v. *De Rutzen*) ... They relate to such everyday matters as traffic infractions, sales of impure food, violations of liquor laws, and the like ... the distinction between the true criminal offence and the public welfare offence is one of prime importance.[52]

It is implausible to deny that a set of offences amounts to real or true crimes without having a concrete conception of what is a true crime. Unfortunately, in the above passage Justice Dickson left no clue other than the enigmatic assertion that regulatory offences relate to everyday matters and are prohibited in the public interest.[53] However, the distinction parallels the one between *mala in se* and *mala prohibita*. As noted in chapter 5, the latter distinction was exploded in legal theory at the same time that the analytical approach was adopted in jurisprudence. Moreover, while it lasted, the distinction did not have enduring legal ramifications. The question then arises: Why is the regulatory offence not considered a real offence? This question admits of at least three different answers: sociological/ideological, historical, and conceptual. The first has been extensively discussed in the literature;[54] there is no need to touch on it here. We will confine ourselves to the other two answers, the historical and the conceptual, in that order.

The Historical Explanation

Possible historical answers are scattered in earlier chapters of this book, especially the sections that dealt with the distinction between *mala in se* and *mala prohibita* and the re-emergence of regulatory laws in the nineteenth century.[55] Nevertheless, it is necessary to deal directly with the issue here.

The historical explanation goes back to the hostile attitude of the common law mind to the Norman conquerors. In spite of the fact that the common law developed after the conquest, the resentment felt by the English people to the conquering Normans gave birth to the stabilizing myth which regarded the common law as being of immemorial origin. Coupled with the serenade with natural law philosophy,[56] the myth fostered the subsumption under the rubric of *mala prohibita* acts that were not punishable by the common law but that were prohibited by and for the convenience of the kings.[57]

That identification remained largely a political classification until about the first half of the eighteenth century when Sir William Blackstone unwittingly confounded criminal jurisprudence by making the rather sweeping assertion that laws which created *mala prohibita* did not bind the conscience. According to Blackstone, the only obligation in conscience with regard to such offences was to submit to the penalty, if levied.[58] As pointed out elsewhere,[59] Blackstone's influence was more intellectual than practical. Despite the fact that the philosophical basis for the distinction was shattered in the nineteenth century, the shadow he cast on the law facilitated the assimilation of acts prohibited in the name of social expediency into the *mala prohibita* category.[60] It also led to the egregious conclusion that such offences are not real or true crimes.

Broadly speaking, the distinction between the 'true' criminal and the civil offence has been maintained on three different grounds at three different stages. First, in pre-modern times, the distinction rested on the perceived difference between acts contrary to nature and acts forbidden by convention. Second, the distinction has been used to discriminate between acts forbidden by a superior legislature (God) and acts forbidden by inferior legislatures (state). Third, the distinction has been employed to mark off acts that constitute serious threats to the socio-economic and political order and acts that, though injurious, are incidental to or the inevitable by-product of the prevailing socio-economic and political order. It is in the last sense that the distinction is made in modern times.

The modern usage began in the nineteenth century. As we saw in chapter 6, after a period of eclipse regulatory laws re-emerged in the latter part of that century. The abandonment of the regulative ideal in the eighteenth century was the result rather than the cause of a new and individualist moral, political, and economic outlook. Unlike the erstwhile mercantilist policy, the new outlook identified 'public interest with material productivity, which was to be achieved primarily through private initiative encouraged by government support.'[61] The encouragement was not to be in the nature of conferring monopolistic powers on some individuals and in governmental regulation of economic pursuits, as was the case in the previous epoch, but in allowing the maximum display of the spirit of individual liberty in the pursuit of socio-economic activities. The new science of political economy, founded on the principle of natural liberty and the freedom of action of individuals, regarded monopolistic powers and/or governmental intervention or regulation as an anathema. The ruling notion was that, through the impersonal regulative activities of the 'invisible hand,' private interest would be harmonized with public interest.

The morality engendered by the new socio-economic order prevented parliamentarians[62] from regarding as *morally* wrong such monopolistic economic *practices* as forestalling, regrating and engrossing,[63] food adulteration (economic[64] and not-so-economic), using false weights and measures, and so on. Nor was the impact of the new outlook limited to purely industrial activities. It also had reverberating sociological implications. For instance, although laws that protected the female gender from all manner of sexual aggression date back to early times,[65] commercial morality did not see much wrong in trafficking on a vast scale in young girls for the purpose of prostitution.[66] Child labour was not viewed with the disapprobation it deserved.[67] Sickness, maimings, and deaths resulting from seemingly unavoidable industrial accidents, food poisonings, environmental pollution, and excessively long hours of labour were perceived as normal accompaniments of industrial and commercial growth. A perverse Darwinian attitude counselled against interference with the iron law of nature.[68] The role of law had been transformed from that of fostering and supporting social cohesion to that of facilitating overall economic growth.[69]

When the Leviathan finally rose from its slumber and started to regulate and control the ways and manners that such socio-economic activities should be carried out, the offences so created were quickly subsumed under the rubric of *mala prohibita* offences as defined by William Blackstone. Unlike Blackstone's limited use of the category, however, several legal conclusions flowed from this classification. First, such offences are not common law offences, and they relate to things indifferent in themselves. Second, they relate to positive, not natural duties. Third, unlike common law offences, *mens rea*, that is, intention or recklessness, is not an indispensable element in such offences. Lastly, the modern doctrine of parliamentary sovereignty ensured that, as long as it makes it intention clear, Parliament had the power to dispense with the requirement of *mens rea* in such offences. In that case, all that was required for liability was the unlawful act.

Initially, attempts were made by business and trading interests to prevail on the legislature to make *mens rea* a necessary element in such offences. Although the courts were hesitant, they eventually sailed with the winds. It was widely known that people were indifferent to the new prohibitions, for most cared only for their own 'advantage and mastery without regard to equity.'[70] Neither intention nor recklessness nor negligence was a formal requirement for liability; liability was strict. As Ingelborg Paulus succinctly states, 'the history of nineteenth century public welfare legislation clearly show that the public welfare offence was not necessarily nor typically one of negligence, but was typically an offence committed for the maximisation of gain or the achievement of a competitive advantage.'[71] Later, the business community came to see regulatory legislation as a weapon which could be put to strategic competitive use or be manipulated to legalize the demands of industry and commerce, and so it embraced or rather 'captured' the regulatory regime.[72] Despite almost a century of the modern regulatory regime, business morality has hardly changed.[73]

What motivated the creation of strict liability offences was the knowledge that people could not care less whether their acts and omissions gave rise to breaches of the legal duty imposed by regulatory laws. Although the legislature cannot create crimes *ex post facto,* the typical criminal statute is almost invariably *ex post facto* an outrageous or injurious act. With the exception of such apparently irreconcilable English cases as *Prince*[74] and *Hibbert*[75] which were decisions of a mongrel criminal jurisprudence – mongrel, because the judges were dancing between the two poles of common law and statute – almost all instances of strict liability involve offences that are known to be treated cavalierly by the populace. For instance, the American[76] and English[77] cases that upheld strict liability in indictments for bigamy[78] were decided at a time when, under the tempestuous influence of wild social speculations, the institution of monogamous marriage was being undermined. We may not be free to speculate on the case of *Larsonneur*,[79] which has been justly castigated as 'the acme of strict injustice.'[80] But the written word has a way of depriving the reader of insight into moral and social sentiments which played significant roles in some legal decisions.

Once experience showed that ordinarily people did not care whether their actions gave rise to the harmful results which the law sought to prevent, and that sometimes they took active steps to mock the law, the sovereign political authority knew that it was pointless to require proof of intention, recklessness, or negligence in establishing responsibility with respect to such offences. The new morality did not recognize the wrongness of the acts criminalized by regulatory laws; the only obligation men recognized was a political one, namely, to submit to the penalty, if levied. So it is far from illuminating to say merely that 'all history reveals is that strict liability arrived and remained.'[81] Strict liability offences are not the product of an arbitrary exercise of legislative powers by parliamentary authorities inebriated with unlimited legal powers. As well, they are not the handiwork of a limpid bench occupied by chicken-hearted men who bowed to the behests of an uncompromising Leviathan. Both the legislatures' actions and the courts' decisions merely reflected the 'changing social attitudes and philosophico-legal currents'[82] of the time. The fact is that ethics had ossified at the entrepreneurial stage but law, like the traveller, has always had to prepare for the morrow[83] – no matter how pleasant the previous day's peregrinations had been.

The mischief here is caused by a system of criminal law which has abolished the distinction between *mala in se* and *mala prohibita* but which still unconsciously allows its intellectual impact to intrude into legal discourse. The insistence on distinguishing between the real and regulatory offences rests on the influence of these Latin phrases. Lord Devlin, for instance, said that 'real crimes are sins with legal definitions and that the criminal law is at its best when it sticks closely to the content of the sin.'[84] P.J. Fitzgerald was content with the assertion that adherence to the view that crimes could properly be classified into *mala in se* and *mala prohibita* did not necessarily commit us to any doctrine of absolute values in morals.[85] H.M. Hart,[86] no less than Jerome Hall,[87] assumed that the distinction is basically sound. The courts piously adhere to it, and law reform commissions insist that the distinction between the real and the regulatory offence is recognized by ordinary persons and should be maintained.[88] Thus, the distinction between *mala in se* and *mala prohibita* has metamorphosed into the distinction between 'the traditionally anti-social acts recognized and penalized as such in the historically given legal materials and recently penalized infringements of newly or partially recognized social interests.'[89] But, unlike the former, the latter distinction has jurisprudential implications: with regard to such offences, liability can be strict. This brings us to the conceptual reasons for demarcating real from regulatory offences.

The Conceptual Explanation

The conceptual explanation can be stated briefly: strict liability offences do not fulfil the formal requirements of the conceptual meaning of crime. It is hardly necessary to elaborate on this point for, as we saw in chapter 7, the essentialist definition of crime rules out strict liability in criminal law. Instead, we will make some general remarks.

The term 'regulatory offences' is not an altogether happy appellation, for two reasons. First, the criminal law isolates and identifies some activities or results or effects of human, social, economic, or political activities that are so insufferable that they ought to be publicly disapproved. Through the exercise of public power, such activities or the results or effects of such activities are designated crimes and are prohibited by the law. This serves as a notice to citizens that they should not engage in such harmful activities or that they should guard against the injurious results or effects of such activities. As H.L.A. Hart puts it, the general aim of the criminal law is 'to announce to society that these actions are not to be done and to secure that fewer of them are done.'[90] All offences, therefore, would appear to be regulatory.

The term 'regulatory offences' is a misnomer for another reason. It gives the impression that this class of offences is of a different metaphysical character from the so-called real crimes. The distinction between the 'real crime' and the 'quasi-crime' springs from a kind of metaphysical pathos to which, according to Arthur Lovejoy,[91] philosophers are particularly susceptible. Lovejoy called this pathos 'eternalistic,' that is, the notion of changelessness, immutability, and the like. It was manifested in criminal jurisprudence, and was particularly noticeable, in the distinction between *mala in se* and *mala prohibita*. Although the distinction was put to some constitutional or political use, it was largely philosophical in nature; it had moral and political but not jurisprudential ramifications. The philosophical basis for the distinction was shattered by juridical positivists. But, even if this had not happened, the nature of analytical criminal jurisprudence was such that it could not have taken cognizance of the distinction. In fact, regulatory offences and/or strict liability offences were nonexistent at the time Austin delineated the lineaments of analytical jurisprudence. When, in the course of the nineteenth century, regulatory statutes began to be enacted, the conviction that the offences created by such statutes differed from traditional offences brought back memories of the bifurcated model. Crimes were once more divided into common law and statutory offences. Unlike the earlier model, however, the new model had jurisprudential ramifications: while common law crimes invariably required *mens rea*, the latter did not necessarily require such a mental element.

The thrust of the foregoing discussion is that the insistence on a rigid distinction between the 'real' and the so-called regulatory offences is the result of an intellectual tradition fostered by commercial and industrial morality – a morality which insists that 'regulatory' offences cannot be real crimes. Ethics petrified at the entrepreneurial stage and this, in turn, impoverished positive criminal law. Strict liability offences are the direct result of the conceptual impoverishment occasioned in positive criminal law by the ossification, at the time of the emergence of the entrepreneurial state, of what Roscoe Pound called 'pioneer modes of thought.'[92]

Conclusion

Analytic concepts are agnostic. This means that they hold or are supposed to hold irrespective of the socio-economic and political order in which they function. The above analysis has underscored the fact that the concept of crime is antagonistic to both strict liability offences and negligence as a basis for liability. Although it is not altogether advisable to separate them, antagonism to strict liability in the criminal law can be accounted for on at least two grounds, one historical, the other logical. The historical explanation is that the strict liability offence developed after the moral conception of crime crystallized. Since it was this conception that was elevated into the concept of crime, it is not surprising that strict liability is repugnant to the analytic meaning of the concept of crime.

Hostility to 'negligence' can also be explained on historical as well as logical grounds. Although the pre-modern mind believed that 'negligence' was blameworthy and could ground punishment, it was a firmly entrenched view that negligence could not ground the condign punishments which followed criminal conviction. However, it is surmised that the retention of the appeal of blood prolonged the perception of the criminal process as serving punitive as well as compensatory or conciliatory functions. A corollary of this is that the demise of the appeal, by cementing the notion that the criminal law is strictly punitive, excluded negligence. Further, it is not implausible to suggest that the Crusoean cast of the modern period contributed to the exclusion of negligence from the sphere of the criminal law. Thus, on the one hand, the exclusion of strict liability and negligence from the purview of the criminal law can be explained historically, and on the other, it is a logical consequence of the basic premises of the legal concept of crime: the theoretical closure effected by analytical criminal jurisprudence rules them out.

The historical explanation contrasts sharply with the logical explanation. Whereas history shows that the content of crime changes with time, place, and circumstances, the conceptual meaning of crime is static, in both form and content. Like any other concept, it is a clear and distinct idea which can be fleshed out and built into a systematic whole. Far from being robust entities, concepts are exceedingly lean creatures that hang on 'the one among the many,'[93] that is to say, essences.

Because it claims knowledge of arcane essences, conceptual thinking is contemptuous of contingencies whether moral, political, social, or economic. Conceptually speaking, crime is a synthetic given with an invariable content of its own. Hence, analytical criminal jurisprudence is not embarrassed by the fact that negligence can be and has been accorded a role, albeit a limited role, in the criminal laws of sophisticated legal systems. Nor is it embarrassed by the fact that strict liability offences have become an integral part of the criminal laws in mature legal systems. Instead, it perceives them as aberrations or rather impurities which ought to be excised from the corpus of the criminal law. Thus, while historical analysis can find a place for strict liability offences and negligence in the criminal law, the analytic or conceptual or scientific – all interchangeable terms – position takes a head-in-the-sand position and insists that they are alien to the criminal law. It is because analytical criminal jurisprudence reduces 'the criminal law to a single formula for determining when conduct ought to be treated as criminal'[94] that it can be reconciled neither with strict liability offences nor with negligence.

Conclusion:
A Leap over Rhodes

The thrust of the last chapter was that, since the advent of analytical jurisprudence in the nineteenth century, criminal theory has not advanced beyond affirming and tinkering with the moral conception of crime. Specifically, the institutionalized conception of crime is hostile to strict liability offences as well as liability based on negligence. In spite of the readiness of positive law to embrace these phenomena, analytical criminal jurisprudence adamantly opposes and thwarts any attempt to fit them into the lattice of the criminal law. This is so despite the fact that history reveals cogent reasons why the law in many jurisdictions has been sympathetic to these notions. Instead of giving them theoretical backing, analytical criminal jurisprudence perceives such substantive reasons as covert ways of introducing impurities into the realm of the criminal law. It sees its task as that of sieving such impurities like these from the cream of criminal law.

Analytical criminal jurisprudence claims to have fathomed the real meaning of crime, and it fastens on intention or recklessness as the element that distinguishes crime from other juristic concepts and categories. Consequently, it decrees that the word 'crime' can be used in the indicated sense only, that is, to denote intentional or reckless breach of legal duty or obligation, and nothing else. In so doing, analytical criminal jurisprudence appears to have turned the central question in criminal theory, 'what is crime?' into 'a battle over names.'[1] For the analytical stance comes to this: any system of criminal law that embraces anything other than what analytical criminal jurisprudence says crime means *ipso facto* ceases to be about criminal law and practice. But this is not necessarily so. The contrary position depends on two strategic moves made by analytical criminal jurisprudence.

The first move was made when analytical criminal jurisprudence converted the moral conception of crime into *the* concept of crime. The notion of wrong embodied in the moral conception of crime was a simple and straightforward one, namely, that of intentional wrongdoing. Since it was the same notion that was incorporated into the common law, analytical criminal jurisprudence ought to have treated the concept of crime under the common law as no more and no less than what it is, namely, the concept of intentional wrong. That way, it would have been impossible to confuse 'the thing,' the idea, with the linguistic label used to describe it. The second strategic move was made when analytical criminal jurisprudence invested the moral conception of crime with the power of eminent domain within that branch of public law called the criminal law.

The utilization of the word 'crime' to signify intentional or reckless breach of legal duty and obligation is an act of illegitimate linguistic appropriation which does not suffice to confer the right to decree this usage. For, unlike concepts that are intellectual constructs and that serve as scientific reference points since they are invested with permanent meanings, ordinary words neither have 'absolute permanent meanings'[2] nor are they integral parts of the thought they express. Rather, words are instruments of expression, and the particular letters that make up a word have no logical relation to the thought it expresses any more than a proper name necessarily reveals the character of its bearer. This is a by-product of the conventional nature of language in general, and legal language is not an exception. In short, 'the idea'[3] summed up in the word 'crime' can be descried, described, and preserved without having recourse to the services of that word.[4]

The pertinent question is whether the analytical position captures the totality or merely a part of available legal experience. For it is only if the analytical position reflects all available legal experience that it can pretend to decide what the law is. This chapter makes two brief points: first, that it is by the strategy of resorting to a truncated legal history that analytical criminal jurisprudence is able to maintain that its position captures the totality of available legal experience; second, that the framework of analytical jurisprudence makes it impossible for criminal theory to transcend the formal requirements of positive criminal law. The analytical jurisprudential position reflects only a part of legal experience.

Unless analytical jurisprudence is allowed to determine what constitutes the totality of legal experience, the view of history held by analytical jurisprudents cannot be determinative on this issue. The analytical jurist sees legal history as consisting essentially of the sum total of the finite and definite intellectual constructs (concepts) resident in ample and mature systems of positive law. If we call 'ample and mature' systems of positive law 'sophisticated legal orders,' and 'all legal systems uninfluenced by Greek science'[5] 'unsophisticated' or 'primitive,' a sophisticated legal system can be described simply as any positive system of law that exhibits such finite and definite intellectual constructs. Put differently, analytical jurisprudence concerns itself primarily with the ways in which the distinctions it regards as permanent intellectual constructs manifest themselves in a particular legal system, and also with the manner in which such distinctions have been utilized to systematize the materials of a given legal order.

This enables analytical jurisprudence in general, and analytical criminal jurisprudence in particular, to insist that rationality begins and ends with the charting of the web of concepts found in ample and mature systems of positive law. Such an approach implies that analytical jurisprudence accords universal validity to the distinctions, notions, and terms found in sophisticated legal systems. This is unobjectionable in itself. What is objectionable, however, is that analytical jurisprudence favours the conceptual conclusions fashioned in sophisticated legal systems over those of unsophisticated or primitive legal orders. Indeed, it would be prepared to go a step farther and deny that the latter possessed recognizably rational legal notions. Of course, a quick look at history shows that concepts are originally the product of analysis, and that they were first extracted and then transplanted from one sophisticated (sometimes dead, as was the case with the Roman law in Europe) legal system to other (living) legal jurisdictions. In fact, it is the role of such concepts in their new homes that transforms those other systems into structured systems of law.

We emphasized in the preceding chapter that the conceptualism underlying analytical jurisprudence makes scholars regard certain concepts as some sort of absolute monarchies whose domain are coextensive with the particular area of the law in which they function. In such cases, it is the meaning of a concept that fixes the boundaries of the relevant area of the law. As already noted, this is what happened in criminal jurisprudence. Thus, the role of the concept of crime is to preside over and rule exclusively within the domain of the criminal law. A corollary of this is that analytical criminal jurisprudence condemns its practitioners to an endless recycling of the particular legal conclusions embodied in what it takes to be the peak of rationality. In the best tradition of dogmatizing, analytical criminal jurisprudence insists that its 'judgment is fittest to be the intellectual standard.'[6] Such dogmatism is concealed by the innocuous, descriptive label, conceptual analysis, under which the analytical enterprise operates.

It is not easy to see that it is the abbreviated legal history with which analytical jurisprudence works that enables it to focus entirely on 'specie-fied knowledge.' By 'specie-fied knowledge' I mean the manifestations of the fossilized idea of law in different areas of the law such as tort and crime. That analytical jurisprudence indeed focuses on 'specie-fied knowledge' is obscured by the tendency of analytical jurisprudence to treat those species, for species they are, as genuses. At the expense of repetition, 'wrong' is the genus from which the species 'crime' was derived. As was amply demonstrated by John Austin,[7] in sophisticated legal systems the genus 'wrong' connotes intentional, rash (reckless?), or negligent breach of legal duty or obligation. It was the differentiation necessitated by the moral conception of crime – which was synonymous with the common law concept of crime – that limited the notion of wrong in the criminal law to intentional or reckless violation of legal duty or obligation. This contrasts sharply with the unitary and undifferentiated connotation of wrong in unsophisticated legal orders, which had strict liability at one end of the spectrum and liability for intentional acts at the other. By confining itself to the point at which the idea of wrong had been particularized, that is, differentiated into civil and criminal wrongs, and the latter had been further delimited to intentional or reckless wrongs, analytical criminal jurisprudence is able to maintain that negligent acts as well as strict liability offences do not and cannot fall within the purview of the criminal law. It strengthened its position by the simple expedient of discounting the period in which the same notions gained a foothold in modern law.

The realization of the fact that analytical jurisprudence converted what are essentially species into genera should cleanse us of the conceit that the legal notions of sophisticated societies are necessarily superior to those found in unsophisticated legal regimes. For the alleged superiority of the former consists solely in the fact of specification, and the alleged inferiority of the latter consists in nothing other than the fact that it shunned specialization. Yet it is partly the absence of specialization and partly the absence of sophistication that made it possible for 'primitive' legal thought to embrace the totality of legal experience. In short, to juxtapose the idea of wrong in unsophisticated legal regimes with the same idea embedded in sophisticated legal systems is to put back into the haystack the hay scattered first by a natural law-based moral and political philosophy, part of which was subsequently gathered and bound together by analytical jurisprudence. This will have the added advantage of bringing to the fore, and preserving, the 'unalterable truth'[8] contained in analytical criminal jurisprudence while dispensing with the problems involved in installing the moral conception of crime as an absolute monarchy which rules the kingdom of the law of crimes. All that this requires is a proper assessment of the role of history in the formation or the ascertainment of the proper function of the analytic essence of the legal concept of crime. This can be quickly disposed of.

The previous chapters have shown that the criminal law was profoundly influenced, shaped, and moulded by a myriad of political, economic, moral, and social factors. From an historical point of view, it is futile to attempt to account for the rules of criminal law by having recourse to the general principle of liability laid down by analytical criminal jurisprudence. But to say that the existing rules of criminal law cannot be accounted for by the general principle proffered by analytical criminal jurisprudence is not to say that there are no universal principles. Nor is it to say that the existing rules of criminal law cannot be evaluated by universal principles. However, the analytical jurist's faith in the essentialist method of definition,[9] which regards *mens rea* as the essence of crime, makes it impossible to articulate such universal principles. Or, rather, it allows us to articulate only such universal principles as are dictated solely by its own terms. Nevertheless, the analytical jurist's insistence that fundamental legal concepts have essences (whether nominal or real) cannot be denied. For, if concepts have determinate contents, and if, as pointed out earlier, legal concepts are species rather than genera, then there must reside in each species a basis for differentiating one from another. Clearly, this is no more than an analytic or taxonomic concession which underscores the fact that concepts have fixed, appropriate, and determinate contents.

Although it cannot be gainsaid that legal concepts have essences in the analytical sense, it is submitted that there is another, non-analytic sense in which concepts have essences. This is the ethical sense. It is somewhat tautologous to say that law is a human not a natural science. Of course, as we noted in chapter 7, the analytical method is morally and politically neutral formally. However, the formal neutrality of the analytical method does not mean that the materials on which it is brought to bear are themselves morally and politically neutral. Rather, 'formal neutrality' merely underscores the methodological requirement that philosophical analysis of law and legal concepts should not be prejudiced by the theory of or about law or a(ny) particular moral or political theory the jurist happens to embrace. Another way of putting it is to say, as one of the most ardent legal positivists in the twentieth century so wisely conceded, that law has a 'minimum content of natural law.'[10] Of course, by their very nature, concepts are not physical entities.

There can be no doubt that the analytical method is utilized in both human and natural sciences and that, as was demonstrated in chapter 7, it is capable of revealing the formal components or descriptive contents of legal concepts. However, when it comes to determining the normative element of concepts, the analytical method is prostrate. If the analytical legal philosopher is confronted with such enigmatic questions, he would shield the analytical position by making one or all of the following three moves. First, he would object to the question being raised at all, for he would say that it is meaningless. Second, he would state that it would lead to infinite regress. And, third, in flagrant breach of the injunctions of analytic philosophy, he would seek refuge in the postulates of one or another theory of or about law or moral and political philosophy. The inability of the analytical jurist to answer such questions is not due to any deficiency in analytical philosophy itself. Rather, it is because the analytical method is not suited for the task.

Hans Kelsen[11] has rightly pointed out that the science of law is a science of 'ought.' All 'oughts' are 'internal statements couched in the normative language.'[12] While, as legal positivism proclaims, the legal 'oughts' in particular systems of positive law may not necessarily be moral 'oughts,' 'the normative language is common to both law and morals.'[13] This suggests that law is normative. The pertinent question, then, is not the scholastic one as to whether law and other fundamental legal concepts have normative contents, but how to identify and isolate their normative elements. In other words, unless one regards the analytical approach and legal positivism as Siamese twins, the separation of law and morals necessitated by the analytical method (in contradistinction to that necessitated by legal positivism) does not entail the conclusion that law and legal concepts are devoid of normative contents.

The domain of the normative is not so much what formally 'is' as what rationally 'is.' Unlike the latter, the former is liable to vary from one legal jurisdiction to another or with theories/theorists of or about law. We saw in chapter 7 that, in conformity with modern epistemological orientation, analytical jurisprudence assumes empirical foundation for legal knowledge. As well, we saw that Austin confined the philosophy of law to the identification and analysis of the concepts in, and the systematization of the materials of, developed systems of positive law. But positive systems of law in general, and developed systems of positive law in particular, seldom speak explicitly the normative language. Consequently, the analysis of the language of developed systems of positive law can hardly be expected to lead to normative conclusions. In other words, analytical jurisprudence is concerned exclusively with the description of the formal elements of law and legal concepts; it is in no way concerned with the normative content of these structures. Indeed, it denies that the concept of law and other fundamental legal concepts have any normative content.

Since analytical jurisprudence is concerned with law and legal concepts as they are formally in developed systems of positive law, and not with law and legal concepts as they are normatively, its tentacles cannot reach beyond the former to the latter. To state the case differently, while analytical jurisprudence is competent to determine the formal contents of legal concepts, it is not competent to determine their normative contents. Indeed, it is futile to seek the normative content of the concept of law and other legal concepts embedded in positive systems of law in their formal properties. This requires elaboration.

We saw in chapter 7 that Austin outlined the program for analytical jurisprudence at the same time that he revived the classical Roman lawyers' notion that the matter of jurisprudence is positive law, and not divine or natural law. The question of the meaning of the concept of positive law has always been debated by two rival schools of law, juridical positivism and juridical naturalism, or legal positivists and natural law–natural right theorists respectively. While juridical positivism postulates that law derives, mediately or immediately, from the will of the sovereign, whoever that may be at any given time in any given polity, juridical naturalism postulates that law is 'the human child of a divine parent.'[14] We are not here concerned with the details of this debate. It suffices to reiterate that, while the analytical approach is not incompatible with these opposed schools of law, intellectual sanity requires that we keep philosophical inquiry into law and legal concepts separate and distinct from the concept of law and other legal concepts fostered by schools or theories of or about law.

As positivists, Bentham and Austin insisted on the separation of law and morals, on law as it is and law as it ought to be. As analytical jurists, however, they insisted not so much on the separation of law and morals as on distinguishing the exposition of law as it is in positive system(s) of law from the exposition of the same phenomenon as it would be if it conformed with a particular moral or political standard. That is, as analytical jurists, they insisted on freeing legal philosophy from the trammels of theories of or about law. But their main target was juridical naturalism. It is an astonishing paradox that they failed to see the inconsistency involved in their positivistic insistence on separating law and morals prior to analysing law.

H.L.A. Hart[15] has suggested that, had Bentham published in his lifetime his *Of Laws in General*[16] (or *The Limits of Jurisprudence Defined*[17]), that book, rather than Austin's work, would have been regarded as the fountainhead of English jurisprudence. He further suggested that in that event analytical jurisprudence 'would have advanced far more rapidly and bloomed into more fertile ways than it has since Bentham.'[18] It may well be that Bentham would have been early recognized as the father of analytical jurisprudence, but it is doubtful that that would have made any difference to the progress of jurisprudence in the English-speaking world since the second half of the nineteenth century.

Bentham had described legal concepts as the names of 'fictitious entities,'[19] and he delineated the boundary of philosophical inquiry into any subject by stipulating that 'to find the limits of any subject, nothing more can be done than to ascertain the real or semi-real entities, the substances or motions or situations it relates to.'[20] By 'real or semi-real entities, substances or motions or situations' Bentham meant things that are 'either *perceptible* or *inferential*: perceptible either *impressions* or *ideas*; inferential, either *material*, i.e., *corporeal*, or *immaterial*, i.e., *spiritual*.'[21] As R. Harrison notes,[22] in this scheme of things, 'what we now think of as mental states are regarded as individual objects, or entities.' Further, Bentham linked exposition with empiricist epistemology,[23] and he enunciated a method – *paraphrasis* – for analysing legal concepts.[24] According to him, the ideas annexed to legal concepts, 'fictitious entities,' spring from 'real entities': 'The ideas annexed to ... words ... are ideas copied immediately from the impressions made by real entities, the ideas annexed to the words and phrases, *act of will*, sign of an act of the will, physical act or act of the body, event, circumstance etc. are either like the former, ideas copied immediately from impressions made by real entities or copies of the sensible affections of determinate real entities.'[25] It has been pointed out that Bentham's aim was to demystify the law by producing and deploying 'a completely neutral, descriptive, account' of law and legal concepts 'shorn of any normative elements. It is expository rather than censorial jurisprudence.'[26] Bentham is indeed the grandfather of analytical jurisprudence.

Among other things, chapter 7 showed that the content of the concept of crime is another concept, namely, the concept of intentional unlawful act. If one accepts Bentham's delimitation of the scope of philosophical inquiry into legal concepts, and if one couples the resolutive with the compositive aspect of analysis, then, as soon as one reaches the 'real entities' to which the concept of crime relates, all that needs be done is to coordinate them into conceptual formulation. The conceptual formulation will express the meaning or 'import' of the word. As we have seen, the concept of intentional unlawful act is resolvable into two 'real entities,' namely, 'intent' and 'act.' Hence, analytical criminal jurisprudence defines crime as an intentional act which breaches a duty imposed by the species of law called the criminal law in mature systems of positive law.

But to accept, without demur, Bentham's delimitation of the scope of philosophical inquiry is implicitly to embrace the empiricist epistemology which underlies his pronouncement. Specifically, the structural contents of legal concepts are not necessarily limited to or by the 'ideas copied immediately from the impressions made by real entities.' The contrary position betrays the incompleteness of an amoral philosophy of law. The point can be made clearer if we first outline the nature of concepts and then distinguish between the two analytic contexts in which they function.

Concepts are forms of thought. As forms, they are units of understanding; as thought, they are the understanding of forms. One might put it differently: concepts are forms with determinate content. Or, put differently still, concepts are categories of thought while content is the substance of these self-same categories.

The structural content of concepts may be divided into two: material and immaterial. Material contents are 'items which are real, that is, either directly perceptible or knowable by inference based on perception,'[27] or what Bentham called 'real entities.' The immaterial contents of concepts are items that are neither directly perceptible nor knowable by inference based on perception. We shall call the material components of concepts the 'formal' concept, and the immaterial components the 'pure' concept. The union of the two is 'the concept.'

We can now refer to the two distinctive analytic contexts in which concepts function. The first is 'the context of the thing being investigated or the context in which the concepts *originally* were used.'[28] In the case of legal concepts, this is the framework of expounding the ideas – things that explain why the thing being investigated is as it is and cannot be otherwise[29] – immanent in positive law. The second context is the 'theoretical context in terms of which [a concept] is being analyzed or treated as an object of study, of analysis.'[30] In the case of legal concepts, this is the framework of expounding 'the *conceptions* and rules of law in general, as distinct from the law of a particular state,'[31] without any attempt to discern transhistorical legal ideas.

We have already noted that positive systems of law, especially developed systems of positive law, eschew the normative language. When legal concepts function within the theoretical context of a philosophy of law which limits itself to the analysis of the language of developed systems of positive law, and which fixes the terminal point of philosophical inquiry into legal concepts at the 'real or semi-real entities to which they relate,' the notion of the concept as a union of material and immaterial elements atrophies. In other words, analytical jurisprudence denies the dual character of concepts; it denies the reality of immaterial things – things that are neither directly perceptible nor knowable by inference based on perception. In this way, analytical jurisprudence forecloses the possibility of winning the 'pure' concept or 'the *form* of rationality'[32] immanent in the concepts embedded in positive systems of law. Analytical jurisprudence shortens the intellectual vision.

Although linguistic analysis facilitates the process, 'the form of rationality' immanent in the concepts embedded in positive law does not consist of analytically recoverable 'things.' According to the principle of 'adaequatio,'[33] they are discernible only by the rational intellect. In other words, the normative elements of concepts are perceptible only by the rational intellect, that is to say, they are rationally discernible things. On this view, which is at least as old as Plato and Aristotle,[34] the difference between the subject of the natural and that of the human sciences is not one between fact and value. Rather, the distinction is between moral and natural objects which are both *facts* capable of being unravelled by the intellect.

I submit that juridical concepts have essences of an ethical variety. Unlike the analytic essence, the function of such essences is not the descriptive one of marking off one concept from another but the discriminatory one of determining what ought or ought not to be practised. It cannot be over-emphasized that it is not the office of the analytic intellect to play this discriminatory role; rather, it falls within the province of the rational intellect.

In relation to the criminal law, the normative aspect of *free will* is the idea that we ought not to regard a legal person as a *responsible agent* unless that person, insofar as human knowledge is concerned, has the capacity for free action. The normative aspect of *act* is the idea that we ought not to regard a legal person as *an actor* unless, at the time of the action, the agent who had and could have exercised the capacity to conform his actions with his legal duties and obligations instead exercised (or omitted to exercise) that capacity in a way that is causally linked to the *actus reus*. And the normative aspect of *mens rea* is the idea that we ought not to impose condign or extra-ordinary sanction on a responsible actor for breach of a legal duty or obligation unless the action or omission was intentional or at least reckless. A close attention to the totality of legal experience attests to the fact that the normative rule mentioned in the preceding sentence is the notion, the unalterable truth, reflected in, or the portion of legal experience captured by, analytical criminal jurisprudence. It is the sole, *nameless* tenant in the gigantic edifice constructed and maintained by analytical criminal jurisprudence.

Each of these normative rules is 'designed to preserve the ordinary standards of human legislation against perversely rigorous misunderstanding of penal laws.'[35] But none of them warrants the exclusion of negligence or strict liability offences from the purview of that branch of public law known as the criminal law. That seemingly inevitable result is dictated solely by the inordinate or imperial ambitions of analytical criminal jurisprudence.

Whatever may be said against the 'folk-psychology' that underlies the criminal law,[36] the *ideas* expressed in the normative rules mentioned above are not some gaudy relics of obscurant metaphysics. Rather, they are 'ethical statements [which] should be regarded as warrants addressed to any potential givers of behests and reproaches, and not to the actual addressees of such behests and reproaches, i.e., not as personal action-tickets but as impersonal injunction-tickets, not imperatives, but "laws" that only such things as imperatives and punishments can satisfy. Like statute laws they are to be construed not as orders, but as licenses to give and enforce orders.'[37] They are *laws* of law-making, law interpretation, and law application. By singling out intention or recklessness as *the* essence of crime, analytical criminal jurisprudence has befuddled reason. The resultant maudlin sentimentality makes it impossible for criminal theory to grasp the totality of legal experience. Hence, analytical criminal jurists insist that negligence and the strict liability offence fall outside the sphere of the criminal law. Delimiting the notion of wrong in the way stipulated by analytical criminal jurisprudence unduly curtails legal experience. It fails to traverse the gamut of legal experience; what is more, it constrains our moral sensibilities and shrinks the intellectual horizon.

At the end of one of his essays, H.L.A. Hart opined that we cannot 'know how strict "strict" liability really is or how absolute "absolute" prohibition really is, or how "subjective" negligence is, till we see what the courts do with [them] in practice.'[38] The courts have been handling these notions for more than a century now. There is scarcely any doubt that the standard of responsibility for negligent acts or omissions and strict/absolute liability offences is constrained by the demands of rationality. Indeed, it would be interesting to ascertain to what extent the conclusions reached in this book parallel developments in some common law jurisdictions, notably Canada, where, since the inception of the Charter of Rights and Freedoms,[39] the courts have been wielding constitutional provisions like an anvil to forge a link between 'the principles of fundamental justice'[40] and the criminal laws.[41] But such an inquiry is beyond the scope of the present work. Our goal has been to explore the possibility of solving or dissolving two of the perennial problems in criminal jurisprudence, namely, the legitimacy of negligence and strict liability offence *within* the theoretical framework of penal law.

Notes

Introduction: Criminal Law or the Law of Crimes

1 Mark DeWolfe Howe, 'The Positivism of Mr. Justice Holmes,' *Harvard L.R.* 64 (1950–1) 529 at 538.
2 See John Salmond, *The Law of Torts*, 6th ed. (London: Sweet and Maxwell 1924).
3 See Percy H. Winfield, *The Province of the Law of Tort* (Cambridge: Cambridge University Press 1931).
4 'The only direct utility of legal history ... lies in the lesson that each generation has an enormous power of shaping its own law ... the study of legal history would ... teach them that they have free hands': F.W. Maitland, in a letter to Dicey, cited in C.H.S. Fifoot, *F.W. Maitland: A Life* (1971), quoted in D. Sugarman, 'Legal Theory, the Common Law Mind and the Making of the Textbook Tradition,' in *Legal Theory and Common Law,* ed. William Twinning (London: Basil Blackwell 1986) at 42.
5 Arthur O. Lovejoy, *The Great Chain of Being* (Cambridge, Mass.: Harvard University Press 1936) at 324.

1: The Idea of Wrong in Anglo-Saxon Law I

1 R. Pound, 'A New School of Jurists,' *University of Nebraska Studies* 4 (1904) 248 at 250. Prominent historical jurists who fall into this 'new school' include Sir Henry Maine and Sir Paul Vinogradoff. See Henry Maine, *Ancient Law: Its Connection with the Early History of Society and Its Relation to Modern Ideas*, 10th ed. (London: John Murray 1885); H. Maine, *Early Law and Custom* (New York: Henry Holt 1883); Paul Vinogradoff, *Outlines of Historical Jurisprudence*, 2 vols. (Oxford: Oxford University Press 1920).
2 G.W. Bartholomew, 'The Ancient Codes and Modern Science,' *Univ. of Tasmania L.R.* 1 (1958–63) 429.

3 J. Boorstin, 'Tradition and Method in Legal History,' *Harvard L.R.* 54 (1941) 424.

4 F. Pollock and F.W. Maitland, *History of English Law before the Time of Edward I*, 2nd. ed., 2 vols. (Cambridge: Cambridge University Press 1923).

5 F.W. Maitland, *Domesday Book and Beyond: Three Essays in the Early History of England* (Cambridge: Cambridge University Press 1897) at 225, 356.

6 Ibid. at 356.

7 Ibid.

8 D. Millon, 'Positivism in the Historiography of the Common Law,' *Wisconsin L.R.* (1989) 669 at 711. For instance, 'we are [so] accustomed to considering it one of the demands of justice that no one shall be punished for any action except such as he himself has committed, and which deserves to be branded as willful or at any rate negligent [that] when we come across laws which ... allow one member of a family to be punished for what another member of the family has done ... we are in the habit of regarding this as symptomatic of an undeveloped sense of justice.': Jos Andenaes, 'Determinism and Criminal Law,' *J. of Cr. Law, Crim. & Police Science* 47 (1956) 406 at 411.

9 Millon, supra n.8 at 672.

10 Glanville Williams, *Criminal Law, The General Part*, 2nd ed. (London: Steven and Sons 1961) at 30.

11 David J. Seipp, 'The Structure of English Common Law in the Seventeenth Century,' in *Legal History in the Making: Proceedings of the Ninth British Legal History Conference, 1989)* ed. W.M. Gordon and T.D. Fergus (London: Hambledon 1991) 61 at 83.

12 'We have learned from authors worthy of confidence that entire nations have been, on their own admissions, pirates and brigands; "for the ancients, piracy was not something strange and unexpected, but something reputable," Didymus says in his comment on Homer. Ariston, as quoted by Aulus Gellius, affirms: "Among the ancient Egyptians ... all acts of theft were permitted and went unpunished." This same Gellius says that even among the Lacademonians ... there was both a right and custom of theft. And in truth, the Romans themselves, who are held up as having displayed examples of virtue for the entire world, how did they acquire for themselves honors, triumphs, glory, and an immortal memory for their own name, if not from robbery and rapine by which they laid the entire world to waste? What else is that great "virtue" so celebrated among them with so many panegyrics, what else is it, I ask, but violence and wrong?': J. Locke, *Questions Concerning the Law of Nature*, trans. R. Horwitz et al., (Ithaca, N.Y., and London: Cornell University Press 1990) at 185–7. For the modern period, see, *inter alia*, C.H. Karraker, *Piracy Was a Business* (1953); J.H. Parry, *Europe and a Wider World 1415–1715* (London: Hutchinson University Library 1949); J.H. Parry, *The Age of Reconnaissance*, 2nd ed. (London: Weindenfeld and Nicholson 1966).

13 '[A]nthropologists are able to show by empirical observation that no society tolerates indiscriminate lying, stealing or violence within the in-group, and indeed, the last six of the Ten Commandments, which require respect for parents and prohibits killing, adultery, stealing, perjury, and fraud, have some counterpart in every known culture': Harold J. Berman, *The Interaction of Law and Religion* (Nashville, Tenn.: Abingdon Press 1974) at 37.

14 Even Cesare Lombroso, whose racial-based criminology led to the idea of the criminal as an anthropological type, did not find a single case where intra-group homicide was a pastime: C. Lombroso, *Crime: Its Causes and Remedies*, trans. H.P. Horton (Montclair, N.J.: Patterson Smith 1968) at 21–42.

15 'Ages' here is used descriptively to denote the conditions that obtained in a given society at a given period. It is not used in any sense associated with the grand though not grandiose theory of the successive ages or stages of society. The most elaborate and, perhaps, the most fruitful of such theories is that identified with the Scottish Enlightenment of which Adam Smith is the most widely known representative. See, for example, Adam Smith, *Lectures on Jurisprudence*, ed. R.L. Meek et al. (Oxford: Clarendon Press 1978) i, 27–32; P. Stein, 'The Four Stage Theory of the Development of Societies,' in *The Character and Influence of the Roman Civil Law: Historical Essays* (Hambledon Press 1988) at 395–409.

16 G. Post, *Studies in Medieval Legal Thought* (Princeton: Princeton University Press 1964) at 556.

17 Edward Jenks, 'The Development of Teutonic Law,' in *Select Essays in Anglo-American Legal History*, 3 vols. (Boston: Little, Brown 1907) 1 at 63.

18 Ibid. at 38: 'The Criminal is the man who endeavours to return to a state of things which society has once practised, but has condemned as the result of experience ... The murderer, the thief, the bigamist, are unfortunate survivals from a bygone age.'

19 Ibid. Emphasis added.

20 Charles P. Segal, 'Nature and the World of Man in Greek Literature,' *Arion* 2 (1963) 19 at 26–7: '[T]he moral and physical, the religious and secular aspects of human life were not yet separated ... Even in the more rationalistic systems of early natural philosophy the coherence and vitality of the world persists. Here the world is a *kosmos* ... Here too there is a close coherence between the physical processes of nature and the moral demands of human life. Physical and moral demands are essentially the same.' See also Richard Tarnas, *The Passion of the Western Mind* (New York: Ballantine Books 1991) at 17. Or, as Simpson succinctly puts it, 'the further back one goes into legal history the less useful is the conceptual distinction between the "is" and the "ought"': A.W.B. Simpson, 'The Analysis of Legal Concepts,' *Law Quarterly Rev.* 80 (1964) 535 at 548n33.

21 H.J. Berman, *Law and Revolution: The Formation of the Western Legal Tradition* (Cambridge, Mass.: Harvard University Press 1983) at 181, 187; Gerhard O.W.

Mueller, 'Tort, Crime and the Primitive,' *J. of Cr. Law., Crim. & Police Science* 46 (1955–6), 303, 309–11.

22 Israel Drapkin, *Crime and Punishment in the Ancient World* (Toronto: Lexington Books 1989) 186. See also H. Maine, supra n. 1 at 372.

23 'What is clear is that one has no business expecting of any primitive culture that its law shall have achieved the official and doctrinal unity *allegedly* found in the modern state ... Against such background of the problems which force law-men to devise law ways, law-concepts, and law rules, many of the "contrasts" between primitive law and modern lose much of their seeming contrast; and they gain understandability thereby. There is, for instance, the conception that primitive law runs much more heavily to "tort," i.e., private wrong, than to "crime," or public wrong. Viewed purely as a matter of procedure, there is truth in this. But it is when viewed as a matter of substance and function that the truth takes on its needed perspective. The fact is that in any group or culture any wrong concerns the whole to some extent at the same time that it gives concern to the more particularly aggrieved. If it did not concern the whole, the aggrieved would be looked upon as an aggressor, not as a redresser, when he undertakes his redress.' Llewellyn and Hoebel, *The Cheyenne Way* (1941) at 60, cited in Gerhard O.W. Mueller, 'Tort, Crime and the Primitive,' *Journal of Cr. Law, Crim. & Police Science* 46 (1955–6) 303 at 320.

24 W.H. Greenleaf, *Order, Empiricism and Politics: Two Traditions of English Political Thought, 1500–1700* (Oxford: Oxford University Press 1964) at 12.

25 W.S. Holdsworth, *Historians of Anglo-American Law* (Hamden, Conn.: Archon Books 1966) at 69.

26 P. Stein, *Legal Evolution: The Story of an Idea* (Cambridge: Cambridge University Press 1980) at 122.

27 H. Butterfield, *The Whig Interpretation of History* (London: G. Bell 1963).

28 See, for example, J. Laurence Laughlin, 'The Anglo-Saxon Legal Procedure,' in *Essays in Anglo-Saxon Law* (Boston: Little, Brown 1876) at 262; George E. Howard, 'On the Development of the King's Peace and the English Local Peace-Magistracy,' *University of Nebraska Studies* 1 (1888–92) 235.

29 W.H. Greenleaf, *The British Political Tradition*, 2 vols. (London: Methuen 1983) 2 (*The Ideological Heritage*) at 21ff.; George A. Feaver, 'The Political Attitudes of Sir Henry Maine,' *Journal of Politics* (1965) 290.

30 See J.W. Burrow, *A Liberal Descent: Victorian Historians and the English Past* (Cambridge: Cambridge University Press 1981).

31 Supra n.28 at 262. 'Far back in the dimmest ages of the Teutonic foreworld the historical student discerns a period when all wrongs were avenged by the stroke of the broad-sword. The right ... of vengeance was handed on from father to son, and the circle widened from kinsman to kinsman, till the terrible blood-feud was like to destroy a tribe or even a nation. Then at some period far back in the ages, the idea

was conceived of exorcising the spirit of revenge by the wand of pecuniary compensation.': T. Hodgkin, *The History of England: From the Earliest Times to the Norman Conquest*, in vol. 1 of *The Political History of England*, ed. M. Hunt and R.L. Poole (London: Longmans, Green 1906) at 227.

32 Drapkin, supra n.22 at 9.

33 R.R. Cherry, *Lectures on the Growth of Criminal Law in Ancient Communities* (London: MacMillan 1890) at 8.

34 Shakespeare makes the Prince of Verona say: 'Three civil brawls, bred of an airy word, / By thee, old Capulet, and Montague, / Have thrice disturb'd the quiet of our streets, / And made Verona's ancient citizens, / By their grave beseeming ornaments, / To wield old partisans, in hands as old, / If ever you disturb our streets again, / Your lives shall pay the forfeit of the peace.' *Romeo and Juliet*, Act 1, Sc. 1, lines 88–95.

35 F. Boas, *The Mind of Primitive Man* (1938; rep. Westport, Conn.: Greenwood Press 1983).

36 Pollock and Maitland, supra n.4 at 27: 'The very slight and inconspicuous part which procedure takes in the written Anglo-Saxon laws is enough to show that they are mere superstructures on a much larger base of custom. All they do is to regulate and amend in details now this branch of customary law, now another.'

37 W.W. Lehman, 'The First English Law,' *Journal of Legal History* (1985) 1.

38 See B. Snell, *The Discovery of the Mind: The Greek Origins of European Thought*, trans. T.G. Rosenmeyer (Oxford: Basil Blackwell 1953) at 165–7; W. Sombart, *The Quintessence of Capitalism: A Study of the History and Psychology of the Modern Business Man*, trans. M. Epstein (London: T. Fisher Unwin 1915) at 265: '[A]ll early peoples had [a] double-barrelled morality, with one code of conduct towards the tribesman and another towards the stranger'; F. Boas, supra n.35 at 202; H. Spencer, *The Principles of Ethics*, 2 vols. (New York: D. Appleton 1903) 1: at 322: '[F]rom the earliest times ... rude tribes and civilized societies ... had had continually to carry on external self-defence and internal cooperation – external antagonism and internal friendship. Hence, their members have acquired two different sets of sentiments and ideas, adjusted to these two kinds of activity.'

39 Caesar, *Commentaries on the Gallic War*, trans. T. Rice Holmes (London: MacMillan 1908) Bk. vi, 23.

40 S.T. 1–2, qu. 94, Art. 4, cited, in W. Lloyd, *Natural Law and Justice* (Cambridge, Mass.: Harvard University Press 1987) at 285, n.47.

41 How should we interpret the actions of the African Biddoomah tribe 'who neither cultivate the ground nor rear flocks or herds [and] who adopted as a religious creed that God having withheld from them corn and cattle, which the nations around enjoy, has given in their stead strength and courage, to be employed in taking these good things from all in whose possession they may be found'?: Hugh Murray, *The African Continent* (London: T. Nelson and Sons 1853) at 187. Or, to move back to Europe,

how should we explain the rapine, violence, and destruction fostered by the bellicose religious beliefs of the Teutonic nations. For their ancient religious beliefs had no ties with the 'pure and benevolent virtues of life.' Instead, their religious beliefs 'sanctified all the horrors of war, and connected all the hopes, energies, and passions of humanity with its continual prosecution': S. Turner, *The History of the Anglo-Saxons: From the Earliest Period to the Norman Conquest* 7th ed., 3 vols. (London: Longmans 1852), 1: at 200.

42 Locke, *Questions Concerning the Law of Nature*, supra n.12 at 221. The passage continues: 'That is, there exists no moment in time when it is lawful to allow anything such as stealing, murder, or other things of this kind without committing a crime. And, thus, to deprive a person of his wealth and property by force or fraud is an action which constitutes of itself a perpetual offense; nor can anyone pollute himself with another's blood without incurring guilt. We are forever bound to refrain from these actions and others of this kind.'

43 E. Becker, 'The Problem of Legal Analysis,' *Yale L.J.* 54 (1945) 809.

44 H.L.A. Hart, *The Concept of Law* (Oxford: Oxford University Press 1962) at 188.

45 Ibid. at 195.

46 John T. Noonan, Jr, *Persons and Masks of the Law* (New York: Farrar, Strauss and Giroux 1976) at 20: 'By masks, I mean, a legal construct suppressing the humanity of a participant in the process,' cited in D. Granfield, *The Inner Experience of Law* (Washington: Catholic University of America 1988) at 36.

47 Aristotle, *Politics*, Bk. 1, 5, 1254a–1255b.

48 See, for example, John H. Hopkins, *A Scriptural, Ecclesiastical and Historical View of Slavery: From Abraham to the Nineteenth Century* (1864; rep.; New York: W.I. Pooley 1964); Thomas R.R. Cobb, *An Historical Sketch of Slavery from the Earliest Periods* (1858; rep. Mnemosyne 1969).

49 Whether or not slavery existed in pre-migration Germany (see E.A. Thompson, 'Slavery in Early Germany,' in *Slavery in Classical Antiquity*, ed. M.I. Finley, [Cambridge: W. Heffer and Sons 1960 at 192–203]), slavery, as a political and social institution, existed and was fully recognized in England until the twelfth century: Pollock and Maitland, supra n.4, 1: at 35; David Pelteret, 'Slave Raiding and Slave Trading in Early England,' *Anglo-Saxon England 9 (1981)* 99. Page goes so far as to say that 'Anglo-Saxon England was a slave society': R.I. Page, *Life in Anglo-Saxon England* (New York: Putnam's Press 1970) at 51.

50 '[T]he power of lords over their slaves was not absolute. If the owner beat out a slave's eye or teeth, the slave recovered his liberty; if he killed him he paid a fine to the King': John Reeves, *History of the English Law, 2nd ed.*, 5 vols. (1787; rep. Rothman Reprints 1961) 1: at 6. '[E]ven the thrall had personal rights of some sort.': Pollock and Maitland, supra n.4, 1: at 35. In sophisticated societies, 'laws that prohibit the maltreatment of slaves are not based on claims made by slaves, but on

claims originating from slaveholders, or from the general interest of society (which do not include the interests of slaves)': J. Rawls, *Political Liberalism* (New York: Columbia University Press 1993) at 33.

51 Anne Stick, *Injustice for All* (Penguin Books 1978) at 76: 'Divine law authority took various forms. Rulers claimed to be either gods on earth (Egypt from about 3000 B.C.), the representatives of gods on earth (Mesopotamia, about 2000 B.C.), or to become gods on death (Rome, about 27 B.C.) ... Consequences, however, were in effect the same: not only divine right to rule, but divine mandate for those political, religious, and legal institutions that each ruler declared one with himself.'

52 See, for example, Caesar's *Commentaries*, Bk. vi, 21, 22.

53 C. Kingsley, *Lectures Delivered in America 1874* (Philadephia: Jos H. Coates 1875) at 131.

54 See *inter alia*, Arthur O. Lovejoy, *The Great Chain of Being* (Cambridge, Mass.: Harvard University Press 1936); E.M.W. Tillyard, *The Elizabethan World Picture: A Study of the Idea of Order in the Age of Shakespeare, Donne and Milton* (New York: Vantage Books 1967); Alice Chandler, *A Dream of Order: The Medieval Ideal in Nineteenth Century English Literature* (Lincoln: University of Nebraska Press 1970).

55 Hodgkin, supra n.31 at 214.

56 H. Berman, Jr, 'The Background of the Western Legal Tradition in the Folklaw of the Peoples of Europe,' *University of Chic. L.R.* 45 (1978) 551 at 570; '[T]he Church was more than a spiritual force; it was a feudal system with its land grants, laws, courts, and secular officials. The bishops were great landlords ... The Church supported the feudal system which was emerging in England ... The Church was an important part of the feudal system.': C.R. Jefferey, 'The Development of Crime in Early English Society,' *Journal of Cr. Law. Crim. & Police Science* 47 (1956–7) 647 at 653.

57 P.H. Winfield, *The Chief Sources of English Legal History* (New York: Burt Franklin 1925) at 44.

58 David Hume, Essay XI, 'On the Populousness of Ancient Nations,' in *Philosophical Works, Vol. III*, ed. T.H. Green and T.H. Gros (1886; rep. 1964) at 414: '[T]he first page of Thucydides is ... the commencement of real history.'

59 See, for example, A.S. Diamond, *The Evolution of Law and Order* (London: Watts 1951).

60 de Tocqueville was so struck with the similarity between Tacitus's description of the political institutions, manners, and laws of Germanic tribesmen and the mode of life of some Native American Indians that he wrote that 'in what we usually call the German institutions ... I am inclined to perceive only barbarian habits, and the opinion of savages in what we style feudal principles': *Democracy in America*, trans. Henry Reeve (New York: Alfred A. Knopf 1966) 1: at 344.

61 Steven Bassett, 'In Search of the Origins of Anglo-Saxon Kingdoms,' in *The Origins of Anglo-Saxon Kingdoms* ed. S. Bassett (Leicester University Press 1989) at 3–27.

62 D.V.J. Fisher, *The Anglo-Saxon Age* (London: Longman 1973) 86ff.; F.M. Stenton, *Anglo-Saxon England*, 3rd ed. (Oxford: Clarendon Press 1971) at 112ff.; William A. Chaney, 'Paganism to Christianity in Anglo-Saxon England,' *Harv. Theological Rev.* 53 (1960) 197.

63 Sally F. Moore, 'Legal Liability and Evolutionary Interpretation: Some Aspects of Strict Liability, Self-Help and Collective Responsibility,' in *The Allocation of Responsibility*, ed. Max Gluckman (Manchester University Press 1972) at 32–55.

64 Pollock and Maitland, supra n.4, 1: at 43.

65 Turner, supra n.41 at 183.

66 P. Wormald, 'Charters, Laws and the Settlement of Disputes in Anglo-Saxon England,' in *The Settlement of Disputes in Early Medieval Europe*, ed. W. Davies and P. Fouracre (Cambridge University Press 1986) 149–168, at 164; 'The Laws show a King who already governed his people, and the fact of causing part of the customary law to be written down associated him more clearly than before with its administration and enforcement': Fisher, supra n.62 at 133.

67 Ine 9; Alfred 42; IV Aethelred 4(1); II Edmund 7.

68 F.L. Attenborough, ed., *The Laws of the Earliest English Kings* (1922) (rep.; New York: Russell and Russell 1963); A.J. Robertson, ed., *The Laws of the Kings of England From Edmund to Henry I* (Cambridge: Cambridge University Press 1925). All references are to these collections of Anglo-Saxon laws.

69 *The wer* or *wergild* was a money payment made to a family group if a member of that family was killed or in some other way injured. The *wite* was a public fine payable to a lord or king, and the *bot* was a general payment of compensation for injuries less than death: C.R. Jeffery, 'The Development of Crime in Early English Society,' *Journal of Cr. Law. Crim. & Police Science* 47 (1956–7) 647.

70 Aethelberht 9, 90; Wihtred 10, 13, 15, Ine 3; Alfred 25.

71 Lehman, supra n.37 at 21.

72 Charles M. Radding, *The Origins of Medieval Jurisprudence: Pavia and Bologna, 850–1150* (New Haven, Conn.: Yale University Press 1988) at 22.

73 Aethelberht 33.

74 Aethelberht 34, 35; Alfred 70.

75 Aethelberht 41, 42; Alfred 46.

76 Aethelberht 48, 49.

77 Aethelberht 54, 55; Alfred 56–60, 64.

78 Aethelberht 56.

79 Aethelberht 57, 58.

80 Alfred 49.

81 Alfred 44, 45, 47, 51.

82 Ine 69.

83 Aethelberht 27, 28, 32.

84 Ine 58: the horn of an ox is worth 10 pence; Ine 59: a cow's horn is worth 2 pence, the tail of an ox a shilling, a cow's tail 5 pence, the eye of an ox 5 pence, and a cow's eye a shilling.

85 Aethelberht 2, 3, 5.

86 Ine 45; Alfred 40.

87 Alfred 7.

88 Alfred 3.

89 Alfred 3.

90 The 'nudities of a nation,' to borrow Daniel Defoe's phrase: (*A Tour Through England and Wales*, vol. 1) are seldom found in standard history books. For a short account of the 'darker side of Anglo-Saxon life,' see Page, supra n.49 at 7ff.

91 Until the tenth century, powerful individuals and/or kindred could still abort the law. 'Aethelstan [923?–939?] was the first English King to deal in legislation with lords who "maintained" their men in defiance of right and justice': F.M. Stenton, supra n.62 at 354. See III Aethelstan 6: 'If any man is so rich, or belongs to so powerful a kindred that he cannot be punished, and moreover is not willing to desist from his wrongdoing, you shall cause him to be removed to another part of your kingdom ... whatever his station in life, whether he be noble or commoner.' IV Aethelstan 3: 'And if anyone is so rich or belongs to so powerful a kindred, that he cannot be restrained from crime or from protecting and harbouring criminals, he shall be led out of his native district with his wife and children, and all his goods, to any part of the kingdom which the king chooses, be he noble or commoner, whoever he may be – with the provision that he shall never return to his native district. And henceforth, let him never be encountered by anyone in that district; otherwise he shall be treated as a thief caught in the act.' Also, V Aethelstan 1.

92 'The prefaces in the collection of Anglo-Saxon laws indicate ... the sort of share which the leading men of Church and State had in the royal legislation. Laws are passed in the name and by the authority of the King.': T. Hodgkin, supra n.31 at 219. 'Before they were promulgated, all the law was customary law, depending upon traditions accepted by the older and more important members of the community and in particular by the paramount chief or King and his advisers and counsellors': A.W.B. Simpson, 'The Law of Ethelbert,' in *On the Laws and Customs of England: Essays in Honor of Samuel E. Thorne*, ed. Morris S. Arnold et al. (Chapel Hill: University of North Carolina Press 1981) at 8.

93 *Leges Henrici Primi*, ed. L.J. Downer (Oxford: Clarendon Press 1972) Cl. 6,4: '[T]here is so much perversity in human affairs and so much profusion of evil that the precise truth of the law or a settled statement of the legal remedy can rarely be found, but to the greater confusion of all ... a new trick for inflicting injury is

devised, as if too little damage follows from what has been done before, and he who does most harm to most people is valued the most highly.'

94 Stenton, supra n.62 at 222.
95 Hlothehere and Eadric 16; Ine 25; III Edmund 5.
96 Ine 56: 'If anyone buys any sort of beast, and then finds any manner of blemish in it within 30 days, he shall send it back to its former owner ... or the former owner shall swear that he knew of no blemish in it when he sold it him.'
97 IV Edgar 7–11; I Aethered 3.
98 II Aethelred 2–4.
99 II Canute 24.
100 'The first official statement of the attitude of the government towards the currency occurs in the laws of Athelstan [2 Athelstan 14]: 'We declare that there shall be one coinage throughout the King's dominions and that there shall be no minting except in a port. And if a minter be convicted of striking bad money, the hand with which he was guilty shall be cut off and set up on the mint-smithy.': F.M. Stenton, supra n.62 at 535–6.
101 II Canute 9.
102 See G.O.W. Mueller, 'Tort, Crime and the Primitive,' *Journal of Cr. Law, Crim. & Police Science* 46 (1955) 303.
103 Moore, supra n.63 at 55.
104 Ibid.
105 See for example, A.S. Diamond, supra n.59 at 142–3.
106 See Lehman, supra n.37.
107 See Simpson, supra n.92. Pollock and Maitland, supra n.4, 1: at 11–12.
108 Ibid. at 17.
109 Lehman, supra n.37 at 21; A. Kiralfy, 'Law and Right in English Legal History,' *Journal of Legal History* 6 (1985) 49.
110 Diamond, supra n.59 at 143 n.1.
111 Ibid. at 142.
112 H. Maine, *Early Law and Customs* (New York: Henry Holt 1883) at 163; H. Berman, Jr,'The Background of the Western Legal Tradition in the Folklaw of the Peoples of Europe,' *Univ. of Chic. L.R.* 45 (1978) 551.
113 'The Church's recognition of the institution of kingship led to development in political thought': Page, supra n.49 at 51. 'Even in the weakest of hands the royal power was upheld by a religious sanction against all other powers in the State.' Stenton, supra n.62 at 546.
114 Page, supra n.49 at 52.
115 Lehman, supra n.37 at 13.
116 Maine, *Early Law and Custom*, supra n.1 at 170.
117 Kiralfy, supra n.109; Simpson, supra n.92 at 5.

118 See Lehman, supra n.37 at 12: 'Today we might believe that those decisions are the expression, after hearing everyone who wanted to speak of the competing claims, of a subconscious kneaded by long life in a culture or we might posit a human structure for the perception of right. But we cannot ... deny that in history rules have been but the experience of ages of judging generalized. Law is synthetic.'

119 Simpson, supra n.92 at 15. There is no doubt that the taking of gold in compensation for blood must have been initially repulsive to the unsophisticated mind. See Vinogradoff, supra, n.1, 1: at 312.

120 L.O. Pike, *A History of Crimes in England, 1873–76* 2 vols. (rep. New Jersey: Patternson Smith 1968), 1: at 74–5: '[O]ne of the most important points in which rulers of England before the Norman Conquest differed from the primitive Germans of Tacitus was the use of coin ... the Germans when free from external influence, had no cities, no trade, no objects of barter except flocks and herds, nothing but live stock with which they could even pay a penalty.'

121 Vinogradoff, supra n.1, vol. 2 at 312.

122 Hodgkin, supra n.31 at 218.

123 Vinogradoff, vol. I, supra n.1 at 355.

124 Moore, supra n.63 at 67.

125 Lehman, supra n.37 at 11.

2:   The Idea of Wrong in Anglo-Saxon Law II

1 J.H. Wigmore, 'Responsibility for Tortious Acts: Its History,' *Harvard L.R.* 7 (1894) 315.

2 H. Maine, *Ancient Law: Its Connection with the Early History of Society and Its Relation to Modern Ideas*, 10th ed. (London: John Murray 1885)

3 F. Pollock and F.W. Maitland, *History of English Law Before the Time of Edward I*, 2nd ed., 2 vols. (Cambridge: Cambridge University Press 1923), 1: at 54, 2: at 470.

4 John P.S. McLaren, 'The Origins of Tortious Liability: Insights from Contemporary Tribal Societies,' *U.T.L.J.* 25 (1975) 42 at 45.

5 H. Maine, *Early Law and Custom* (New York: Henry Holt 1883) at 198.

6 McLaren, supra n.4 at 45.

7 Ibid.

8 Ibid. at 46. (Emphasis in the original.)

9 G. MacCormack, 'Standards of Liability in Early Law,' *Juridical Review* (1985–6) 166 at 170.

10 P.H. Winfield, 'The Myth of Absolute Liability,' *L.Q.R.* 42 (1926) 37.

11 Ibid. at 40.

12 Wigmore, supra n.1.

13 Pollock and Maitland, supra n.3; William Holdsworth, *The History of English Law,*

7 vols. (London: Methuen 1923) 2: at 43ff.; E. Levitt, 'The Origin of the Doctrine of Mens Rea,' *Illinois L.R.* 17 (1922–3) 116; P.E. Raymond, 'The Origin and Rise of Moral Liability in Criminal Law,' *Oregon L.R.* 15 (1935–6) 93.

14 E. Levitt, 'Extent and Function of the Doctrine of Mens Rea,' *Illinois L.R.* 17 (1922–3) 578; P.H. Winfield, supra n.10; F. Sayre, 'Mens Rea,' *Harvard L.R.* 45, 974; G.O.W. Mueller, 'On Common Law Mens Rea,' *Minnesota L.R.* (1957–8) 1043.

15 Levitt, 'The Origin of the Doctrine of Mens Rea,' supra n.13 at 135.

16 O.W. Holmes, Jr, *The Common Law*, (1883 rep. Cambridge, Mass.: Belknap Press 1963); N. Isaacs, 'Fault and Responsibility,' *Harvard L.R.* 31 (1917–18) 954.

17 McLaren, supra n.4.

18 MacCormack, supra n.9.

19 Moore, 'Legal Liability and Evolutionary Interpretation: Some Aspects of Strict Liability, Self-Help and Collective Responsibility,' in *The Allocation of Responsibility* ed. Max Gluckman (Manchester: Manchester University Press 1972) at 32–55.

20 F.P. Pollock, *Oxford Lectures* (rep.; New York: Books for Library Press 1972) at 70.

21 '[T]he act of the individual affected not only himself but the whole community who were his kinsmen; so that when society began to effect a settlement the matter was conducted not between individuals who may have been the person directly concerned but between the heads of the communities, acting for the individual members both as leaders and as sureties for good faith': J.W. Jeudwine, *Tort, Crime and Police*, (London: Williams and Norgate 1917) at 24; 'All freemen, noble or simple, looked to their kindred as their natural helpers and avengers.': F.P. Pollock, *The Expansion of the Common Law* (London: Stevens 1904) at 150.

22 C.R. Jeffery, 'The Development of Crime in Early English Society,' *Journal of Cr. Law. Crim. & Police Science* 47 (1956–7) 647 at 655.

23 '[T]here is no department of criminal law as such away from what we class as civil matters; the regulation of all social affairs, from the gravest murder, to the small breach of contract or the careless tieing of a dog, was the subject of a local police law of which the procedure and the remedies were indifferently applicable to all ... there was no criminal law so called, and certainly no civil law, the penalties for the abuses of civil rights being of the same nature as those for what we call crime': Jeudwine, supra n.21 at 24, 26.

24 H. Potter, *An Introduction to the History of English Law* (London: Sweet and Maxwell 1923) at 93.

25 Levitt, supra n.13, 117 at 127.

26 'The Church brought with it moral ideas which were to revolutionize English law. Christianity had inherited from Judaism an outlook upon questions which was strictly individualistic. The salvation of each separate soul was dependent upon the actions of the individual and this contrasted sharply with the custom of English tribes

which looked less to the individual than to the family group of which the individual formed a part': T.F.T. Plucknett, *A Concise History of the Common Law*, 4th ed. (London: Butterworth 1948) at 9.

27 H.R. Loyn, 'Kinship in Anglo-Saxon England,' in *Anglo-Saxon England*, ed. Peter Clemoes (Cambridge: Cambridge University Press 1974) no. 3 at 207: 'In Anglo-Saxon England kindreds were not given enough time to develop into full-fledged land-owning institutions ... The legal being of the kindred depended greatly on the active tutelage of the King, personal lordship, and territorial organization. Even the blood-feud itself failed to reach that stage in formal institutional growth, untrammelled by superior folk-principles, that it achieved elsewhere in other communities.'

28 '[T]here is general agreement that later Anglo-Saxon England had become a land of lordly estates cultivated by the labours of a dependent peasantry': D.J.V. Fisher, *The Anglo-Saxon Age 410–1042* (London: Longmans 1973) at 125; T. Hodgkin, *The History of England from the Earliest Times to the Norman Conquest*, vol. 1, *The Political History of England*, ed. M. Hunt and R.L. Poole (London 1906); F.M. Stenton, *Anglo-Saxon England*, 3rd ed. (Oxford: Clarendon Press 1971) at 112ff.

29 W. Stubbs, *Lectures on Early English History*, ed. A. Hassall (London: Longmans 1906) at 19. 'As a *society* feudalism refers to a system of personal dependence with a military class occupying the higher levels in the social scale, and with a subdivision of rights in real property corresponding to this system of personal dependence. As a *legal* system feudalism means a body of institutions creating obligations of service and duty – a military service on the part of the vassal and an obligation of protection on the part of the lord with regard to the vassal': Jeffery, supra n.22 at 649.

30 See chapter 1, n.69.

31 MacCormack, supra n.9 at 166.

32 See, *inter alia*, J. Hall, *General Principles of Criminal Law*, 2nd ed. (Indianapolis: Bobb-Merrill 1960); H. Packer, 'Mens Rea and the Supreme Court,' *Supreme Court Rev.* (1962) 107; G.O.W. Mueller, 'Mens Rea and the Law without It,' *W. Virg. L.R.* 58 (1955–6) 34; P. Brett, *An Inquiry into Criminal Guilt* (London: Sweet and Maxwell 1963).

33 H.L.A. Hart, 'Varieties of Responsibility,' *L.Q.R.* 83 (1967) 346; rep. *Punishment and Responsibility* (Oxford: Oxford University Press 1968), chapter 9. For a more recent attempt to clarify the concept of responsibility but a less helpful one for our purposes, see Meir Dan-Cohen, 'Responsibility and the Boundaries of the Self,' *Harvard L.R.* 105 (1992) 959 at 962–5.

34 Ibid. at 358.

35 Moore, supra n.19 at 55.

36 H.L.A. Hart, supra n.33 at 352.

37 MacCormack, supra n.9 at 167.

38 McLaren, supra n.4 at 92.

39 See particularly *Leges Henrici Primi*, ed. L.J. Downer (Oxford: Oxford University Press 1972) 90, 10, 11, 11(a)–(d).

40 Winfield, supra n.10 at 41.

41 Hart, supra n.33 at 350.

42 A.W.B. Simpson, 'The Law of Ethelbert,' in *On the Laws and Customs of England: Essays in Honor of Samuel E. Thorne*, ed. Morris S. Arnold et al. (Chapel Hill: University of North Carolina Press 1981) 3: at 7; W.J.V. Windeyer, *Lectures on Legal History*, 2nd ed. (Law Books of Australasia 1957) at 18: 'No good purpose is really served by seeking to apply to a primitive system of law the technical terms of later days, which are based on a distinction which it does not know.'

43 Moore, supra n.19 at 62.

44 *Leges Henrici Primi*, supra n.39, 90, 11d. (at 285).

45 Levitt, supra n.25 at 135.

46 *Leges Henrici Primi*, 90 ll(b).

47 Ibid. 90 ll(c).

48 Pollock and Maitland, supra n.3, 1: at 54.

49 W.W. Lehman, 'The First English Law,' *Journal of Legal History* 1 (1985) at 17.

50 S. Turner, *The History of the Anglo-Saxons: From the Earliest Period to the Norman Conquest*, 7th ed. (London: Longmans 1852) vol. 1 at 184.

51 McLaren, supra n.4 at 69.

3: The Idea of Wrong under the Common Law I

1 For the different senses which the 'common law' can assume, see Morris L. Cohen, 'The Common Law in the American Legal System: The Challenge of Conceptual Research,' *Law Library Journal* 81 (1989) 13–32.

2 Matthew Hale, *The History of the Common Law of England*, ed. Charles M. Gray (Chicago: University of Chicago Press 1971).

3 F.W. Maitland and Francis C. Montaigne, *A Sketch of English Legal History* (London: G.P. Putnam's Sons 1915) at 2: 'Hardly a rule remains unaltered, and yet the body of law that now lives among us is the same body that Blackstone described in the eighteenth, Coke in the seventeenth, Littleton in the fifteenth, Bracton in the thirteenth, Glanvill in the twelfth. This continuity, this identity, is very real to us.'

4 George E. Howard, 'On the Development of the King's Peace and the English Local Peace-Magistracy,' *University of Nebraska Studies* 1 (1888–92) 235.

5 R. Pound, *Criminal Justice in America* (New York: Holt 1930) at 83; F.P. Pollock, *Oxford Lectures* (1890; rep. London: MacMillan 1970) at 70–1; 'Other persons as well as the King have their *grio* or *mund;* if it is broken compensation must be made to them. The Church had its peace, or rather the Churches have their peaces ... The

sheriff has his peace, the lord of a soken.': F. Pollock and F.W. Maitland, *History of English Law before the Time of Edward I*, 2nd ed., 2 vols. (Cambridge: Cambridge University Press 1923), 2: at 453. For a comparative study of the idea of peace, see Jack K. Weber, 'The King's Peace: A Comparative Study,' *Journal of Legal History* 10 (1989) 129.

6 D. Feldman, 'The King's Peace, the Royal Prerogative and Public Order: The Roots and Early Development of Binding Over Powers,' *Cambridge L.J.* 47 (1988) 101, 107.

7 'In [the] sanctity of the homestead we have one of the earliest securities for order ... Every man was entitled to peace in his own house. The brawler or trespasser in another's homestead broke the owner's peace and owed him special amends. We find this in the very earliest collection of ordinances, dating in substance at least from the first quarter of the seventh century ... The peace of the house is broken not only by slaying but by quarelling.': Pollock, supra n.5 at 70–1.

8 Feldman, supra n.6.

9 Ibid. at 106: 'These safe conducts were granted to the royal justices, officials, diplomats and others, including traders. Breach of the hand-grith was not to be redeemed by any payment, and was a most serious offence.' Or, as Pollock says, 'under the West Saxon rule, where the King's power was first consolidated ... we find that breaking the peace of the king's house is a graver matter than anything yet mentioned before the time of Ine [tenth century]': *Oxford Lectures,* supra n.5 at 72.

10 Ibid. at 83.

11 The phrase is Pollock's, ibid. at 66.

12 F.M. Stenton, *Anglo-Saxon England*, 3rd ed. (Oxford: Clarendon Press 1971) at 492–9.

13 Feldman, supra n.6 at 107.

14 J.W. Jeudwine, *Tort, Crime and Police* (London: Williams and Norgate 1917) at 101.

15 Pollock and Maitland, supra n. 5. 2: at 453.

16 Richard W. Kaeuper, *War, Justice and Public Order: England and France in the Later Middle Ages* (Oxford: Clarendon Press 1988) at 153.

17 Ibid. at 140.

18 Pollock, supra n.5 at 87.

19 G.W. Keeton, *The Norman Conquest and the Common Law* (London: Benn 1966) at 175; Adam Smith, *Lectures on Jurisprudence*, ed. R.L. Meek et al. (Oxford: Clarendon 1978) at 106–10.

20 Pollock, supra n.5 at 90; Pollock and Maitland, supra n.5, 1: at 465; Keeton, supra n.19 at 175.

21 T.F.T. Plucknett, *A Concise History of English Law*, 4th ed. (London: Butterworths 1948) at 398.

22 See infra.

23 Harold J. Berman, *Law and Revolution: The Formation of the Western Legal Tradition* (Cambridge, Mass.: Harvard University Press 1983) at vii.

24 Kaeuper, supra n.16.

25 L.O. Pike, *A History of Crimes in England 1873–76* (rep.; Montclair, N.J.: Patternson Smith 1968), 1: at 133; Kaueper, supra n.16 at 159.

26 Berman, supra n.23; C.R. Jefferey, 'The Development of Crime in Early English Society,' *Journal of Cr. Law, Crim. & Police Science* 47 (1956–7) 647 at 653.

27 Plucknett, supra n.21 at 9.

28 F. Barlow, *The Norman Conquest and Beyond* (London: Hambledon Press 1983) at 6.

29 Berman, supra n.23 at 183.

30 M.H. Kerr, *Catholic Church and Common Law: Three Studies in the Influence of the Church on English Law* (University of Toronto, PhD Thesis 1991) at 16. However, The Leges Henri Primi LXXV explicitly mentioned 'penance.'

31 J. Kemble, *The Anglo-Saxons in England*, vol. 2 at 516, cited in Jeffrey, supra n.26 at 664. '[T]he Church sought both to legalize morality and to moralize legality ... on the one hand, standards of right and wrong were reinforced by legal procedures and legal sanctions; on the other hand, a divine righteousness was attributed to legal standards': Harold J. Berman, *The Interaction of Law and Religion* (Nashville: Abingdon Press 1974) at 61.

32 Berman, supra n.23 at 181.

33 Sir Matthew Hale, *The History of the Common Law of England*, ed. Charles M. Gray (Chicago: University of Chicago Press 1971) at 21; Keeton, supra n.19 at 177. See also Berman, supra n.23 at 185.

34 Pollock and Maitland, supra n.5, 2: at 452.

35 Ibid.

36 Ibid.

37 See Kaueper, supra n.16 at 145ff.

38 L.J. Downer, ed., *Leges Henrici Primi* (Oxford: Clarendon Press 1972).

39 'Felony was a vivid but imprecise word, signifying something cruel, fierce, wicked, base; at law felonies could be recognized by their consequences. The felon's condemnation to lose life or limb and to forfeit his land to his lord. By the thirteenth century felonies had become ... commensurate with the bootless crimes of Canute ... the imprecise moral attitude in the word felony perhaps helped to develop a concept of criminal liability. Felony implied a certain venom, malice, premeditation, in the felon': Alan Harding, *A Social History of English Law* (Penguin Books 1966) at 63.

40 Pollock and Maitland, supra n.5, 2: at 466.

41 F.B. Sayre, 'Mens Rea,' *Harv. L.R.* 45 (1945) 974 at 989.

42 Pollock and Maitland, supra n. 5, 1: at 78.

43 The following discussion is based on H. Rashdall, *The Universities of Europe in the*

Middle Ages, rev. ed., ed. F.M. Powicke and A.B. Emden, 3 vols. (London: Oxford University Press 1936), 1: at 31ff.; H.D. Hazeltine, 'Roman and Canon Law in the Middle Ages,' in *Cambridge Medieval History*, 8 vols., 5: at 697–762; Harold J. Berman, supra n.23 at 123–55; R.R. Bolgar, *The Classical Heritage and Its Beneficiaries* (Cambridge: Cambridge University Press 1958) chapter 4; Stig Stromholm, *A Short History of Legal Thinking in the West* (Stockholm: Norstedts Forlag 1985) at 97–131; Nathan Schachner, *The Medieval Universities* (London: George Allen and Unwin 1938) chapters 2, 15.

44 Ibid. at 123.
45 Hazeltine, supra n.43 at 757.
46 Berman, supra n.23 at 121: '[T]he law that was first taught and studied systematically in the West was not the prevailing law; it was the law contained in an ancient manuscript which had come to light in an Italian library toward the end of the eleventh century. The manuscript reproduced the enormous collection of legal materials, which had been compiled under the Roman Emperor, Justinian about 534 A.D.'
47 Hazeltine, supra n.43 at 736.
48 J. Kerr Wylie, 'Roman Law as an Element in European Culture,' *S.A.L.J.* (1948) 14; D.R. Kelly, *The Human Measure: Social Thought in the Western Legal Tradition* (Cambridge, Mass.: Harvard University Press 1990) at 113.
49 W. Ullmann, *The Medieval Idea of Law As Represented by Lucas de Penna* (London: Methuen 1946) at 4.
50 Ibid. at 1. 'It was due to their efforts that the Roman legal technique came to be adapted to serve the needs of the medieval and modern world, and to form the basis of a juridical science which was, and is, essentially European in spirit ... The Commentators were no mere idle theorists, but wrote with a constant eye to practice. They were ... jurists in the highest and best sense of the word.': Wylie, supra n.48 at 203.
51 Ullmann, supra n.49.
52 Berman, supra n.23 at 150.
53 It will be noticed that this brief survey does not touch on the canonists. This is not because I am oblivious of the significant role played by canon law but because I want only to emphasize the influence of classical legal science. For studies that *emphasize* the influence of the canonists, see, for example, Berman, supra n.23; Kerr, supra n.30; J.M.B. Crawford and J.F. Quinn, *The Christian Foundations of Criminal Responsibility*, in *Toronto Studies in Theology*, vol. 40 (Queenston: Edwin Mellen Press 1991).
54 Pollock and Maitland, supra n.5, 1: at 77: 'the Normans had no written law to bring with them to England, and we may safely acquit them of much that could be called jurisprudence.'
55 Hazeltine, supra n.43 at 738.

56 D. Knowles, *The Evolution of Medieval Thought* (London: Longmans 1962).

57 Ibid. at 89. '[The scholastic] method which was first fully developed in the early 1100s both in law and theology presupposes the absolute authority of certain books, which are to be comprehended as containing an integrated and complete body of doctrine; but ... it also presupposes that there may be both gaps and contradiction within the text; and it sets as its main task the summation of the text, the closing of the gaps within it, and the resolution of the contradictions': Berman, supra n.23 at 131.

58 P. Wilson, *Second-Hand Knowledge: An Inquiry into Cognitive Authority* (Westport, Conn. Greenwood Press 1983) at 15: '[C]ognitive authority is influence on one's thoughts that one would consciously recognize as proper ... The authority's influence on us is thought proper because he is thought credible, worthy of belief.' See, further, Hans Georg-Gadamer, *Truth and Method* (New York: Seabury Press 1975) at 248–51.

59 Sir Paul Vinogradoff, *Roman Law in Medieval Europe*, 3rd ed. (Oxford: Oxford University Press 1961) at 57; Berman, supra n.23 at 132: '[I]n law, the scholastic method took the form of analyzing and synthesizing the mass of doctrines, many of them in conflict with others, found in the law of Justinian as well as in secular authorities ... the written text as a whole, the Corpus Juris Civilis, ... was accepted as sacred, the embodiment of reason.'

60 Rashdall, supra n.43 at 119.

61 Vinogradoff, supra n.59 at 62.

62 Berman, supra n.23 at 289.

63 W. Ullmann, supra n.49 at 4.

64 G. Post, *Studies in Medieval Legal Thought* (Princeton: Princeton University Press 1964) at 528ff.

65 Berman, supra n.23 at 273.

66 Post, supra n.64 at 557.

67 Ibid. at 552.

68 Otto von Gierke, *Political Theories of the Middle Ages*, trans. F.W. Maitland (Cambridge: Cambridge University Press 1900) at 74. 'Men supposed ... that before the State existed, the *Lex Naturalis*, already prevailed as an obligatory statute, and that immediately or mediately from this flowed those rules of right to which the State owed even the possibility of its own rightful origin. And men also taught that the highest power on earth was subject to the rules of Natural Law. They stood above the Pope and above the Kaiser, above the Ruler and above the sovereign people, nay, above the whole Community of mortals. Neither statute nor act of government, neither resolution of the people not custom could break the bounds that thus were set. Whatever contradicted the eternal and immutable principles of Natural Law was utterly void and would bind no one' (at 75).

69 See, generally, Berman, supra n.23 at 181ff.; Ullmann, supra n.49 at 142–62; Crawford and Quinn, supra n.53.

70 Vinogradoff, supra n.59 at 97; Hazeltine, supra n.43 at 759; T.F.T. Plucknett, 'The Relations Between Roman Law and English Common Law Down to the Sixteenth Century: A General Survey,' *U.T.L.J.* 3 (1939) 24 at 44; Berman, supra n.23 at 123. In Sir Henry Maine's poignant phrase, the European nations built the 'debris of Roman law into their walls': *Ancient Law: Its Connection with the Early History of Society and Its Relation to Modern Ideas*, 10th ed. (London: John Murray 1885).

71 David J. Seipp, 'Roman Legal Categories in the Early Common Law,' in *Proceedings of the Eighth British Legal History Conference, 1987,* ed. T.G. Watkin (London: Hambledon Press 1989) at 10; David J. Seipp, 'Bracton, the Year Books, and the Transformation of Elementary Legal Ideas in the Early Common Law,' *Law & Hist. Rev.* 7 (1989) 175 at 179.

72 R.H. Helmholz, *Canon Law and the Law of England* (London: Hambledon Press 1987) at 1.

73 F.W. Maitland, *The Collected Papers*, 3 vols. ed. H.A.L. Fisher (Cambridge: Cambridge University Press 1911), 1: at 322.

74 Pollock and Maitland, supra n.5, 1: at 132; Ralph V. Turner, 'Who Was the Author of Glanvill? Reflections on the Education of Henry II's Common Lawyers,' *Law & Hist. Rev.* 8 (1990) 97.

75 H. Brunner, *The Sources of the Law of England* (Edinburgh: T. and T. Clark 1888) at 26.

76 George W. Woodbine, 'Roman Elements in Bracton,' *Yale L.J.* 31 (1921–2) at 828.

77 Sir Paul Vinogradoff, 'The Roman Elements in Bracton's Treatise,' *Yale L.J.* 32 (1923) 751.

78 Bracton, *On the Laws and Customs of England*, 4 vols. trans. Samuel E. Thorne (Cambridge, Mass.: Belknap Press 1968), 2: at 20.

79 See, J. Rawls, *A Theory of Justice* (Cambridge, Mass.: Harvard University Press 1971) at 5–6; R. Dworkin, *Taking Rights Seriously* (Cambridge, Mass.: Harvard University Press 1977) at 134–6.

80 Fritz Schulz, *Classical Roman Law* (Oxford: Clarendon 1951) at 579.

81 Maine, supra n.70 at 402.

82 Ibid. R.R. Cherry, *Lectures on the Growth of Criminal Law in Ancient Communities* (London: MacMillan 1890).

83 W.J.V. Windeyer, *Lectures on Legal History*, 2nd ed. (Law Books of Australasia 1957) at 19.

84 Jeudwine, supra n.14 at 84.

85 Pollock and Maitland, supra n.5, 2: at 458.

86 Helmholz, supra n.72 at 143–4.

87 Glanvill, *The Treatise on the Laws and Customs of the Realm of England Commonly Called Glanvill*, ed. Hall (London: Thomas Nelson and Sons 1965).
88 Ibid. I.1.
89 Bk. XIV.
90 Bracton, supra n.78.
91 Anna E. Wilhelm-Hovijbergh, *Peccatum: Sin and Guilt in Ancient Rome* (Gronningen and Djakarta: J.B. Wolters 1954) at 38.
92 Ibid. at 30.
93 Maine, supra n.70 at 381.
94 Ullmann, supra n.49 at 148.
95 It cannot be overemphasized that the medieval philosophy of law owed as much to Christianity as it did to classical sources. Indeed, 'the central theme of medieval culture was the Christian faith': S. Painter, *A History of the Middle Ages, 284–1500*, (New York: Alfred A. Knopf 1953) at 430.
96 R. Pound, *Law and Morals* (University of North Carolina Press 1926) at 31.
97 M. Horwitz, 'History and Theory,' *Yale L.J.* 96 (1987) 1825; W.E. Hocking, 'Ways of Thinking about Right: A New Theory of the Relation Between Law and Morals,' in *Law: A Century of Progress 1835–1935*, 3 vols. (New York: State University of New York Press) 2: at 242.
98 T.A. Green, *Verdict According to Conscience* (Chicago: University of Chicago Press 1985) at 28ff.
99 Naomi D. Hurnard, 'The Jury of Presentment and the Assize of Clarendon,' *Eng. Hist. Rev.* 56 (1941) 374.
100 Green, supra n.98 at 52.
101 Ed. Meynial, 'Roman Law,' in *The Legacy of the Middle Ages* ed. G.C. Crump and E.F. Jacob (Oxford: Clarendon Press 1926) at 370.
102 W. Ullmann, supra n.49 at 142.
103 Ibid.
104 Ibid. at 142.
105 Ibid. at 144.
106 Ibid. See also Walter Ullmann, 'Some Medieval Principles of Criminal Procedure,' *Juridical Review* 59 (1947) 1.
107 Ibid. at 146.
108 Ibid. at 147.
109 Ibid. at 144.
110 Ibid.
111 Ibid. at 147.
112 Ibid.
113 Ibid.

114 Adam Smith, *The Theory of Moral Sentiments*, ed. D.D. Raphael and A.L. Macfie (Oxford: Clarendon Press 1976) at 312.

115 Jeremy Bentham, *Introduction to the Principles of Morals and Legislation*, ed. J.H. Burns and H.L.A. Hart (London: Athlone Press 1970) at 114.

116 Jeremy Bentham, *The Limits of Jurisprudence Defined*, ed. Charles W. Everett (New York: Columbia University Press 1945) at 292.

117 Ullmann, supra n.49 at 144. (Emphasis in the original.)

118 de Penna stipulates two conditions of imputability: that the wrongful act be performed by a human agent, and that it be performed under circumstances in which the agent is free from psychical or physical compulsion. See Ullmann, supra n.49 at 149.

119 Moore's thoroughgoing consequentialist ethics did not prevent him from conceding that motives are relevant to moral judgments: '[I]n our moral judgments we actually do, and ought to, take account of motives; and indeed ... it marks a great advance in morality when men do begin to attach importance to motives and are not guided exclusively, in their praise or blame, by the "external" nature of the act done or by its consequences ... it is quite certain that when a man does an action which has bad consequences from a good motive, we do tend to judge him differently from a man who does a similar action from a bad one; and also that when a man does an action which has good consequences from a bad motive we may nevertheless think badly of him for it ... and it is right and proper that a man's motives should thus influence our judgment.': G.E. Moore, *Ethics* (London: Oxford University Press 1912) at 114.

120 Ullmann, supra n.49 at 149.

121 Ibid. at 149.

122 Ibid. at 150. The last sentence in the passage further underscores the point made earlier that de Penna was concerned mainly with the moral quality of the act and that he used 'motive' and 'intention' interchangeably.

123 Ibid.

124 Ibid. at 149.

125 Green, supra n.98.

126 Pollock and Maitland, supra n.5, 2: at 478.

127 H.G. Richardson, 'Studies in Bracton,' *Traditio* 6 (1948) 61 at 70.

128 Green, supra n.98 at 28.

129 The general nature of medieval scholarship was such that the intellectual class was able to combine a hodgepodge of ideas derived from variegated sources into a workable encyclopedic body of knowledge: '[T]he modern mind separates its ideas into categories, scientific, ethical, philosophical, and theological and counts it a virtue to keep its concepts clearly defined. To later antiquity and to the Middle Ages, the segregation of ideas in this manner would have been incomprehensible. All

learning was not only ethical and theological in outlook but it was also always encyclopedic': Frederick B. Artz, *The Mind of the Middle Ages, A.D. 200–1500: A Historical Survey*, 3rd rev. ed. (Chicago: University of Chicago Press 1980) at 233.

130 Richardson, supra n.127 at 71.

131 Brown, 'The Emergence of the Psychical Test in Guilt in Homicide 1200– 1550,' *University of Tasmania L.R.* 1 (1958–63) 231 at 233.

132 Green, supra n.98 at 85. See, further, Naomi H. Hurnard, *The King's Pardon for Homicide* (Oxford: Clarendon Press 1969).

133 Ibid. at 85.

134 Ullmann, supra n.49 at 156.

135 Ibid. at 153.

136 Ibid. at 150–3.

4:   The Idea of Wrong under the Common Law II

1 D.R. Kelley, *The Human Measure: Social Thought in the Western Legal Tradition* (Cambridge, Mass.: Harvard University Press 1990) at 164: '[T]he science of law has always claimed to be universal, but in reality have [*sic*] developed along specific and even local lines.'

2 See A. Levitt, 'The Origin of the Doctrine of Mens Rea,' *Illinois L.R.* 17 (1922–3) 115 at 136; J.M.B. Crawford and J.F. Quinn, *The Christian Foundations of Criminal Responsibility* (Queenston, N.Y.: Edwin Mellen Press 1991) at 40.

3 D.R. Kelley, supra n.1 at 176. The renaissance in the twelfth century that set the people of Europe into frenzied intellectual activity was not national but 'supranational.' See D. Knowles, *The Evolution of Medieval Thought* (London: Longmans 1962); Harold J. Berman, *Law and Revolution: The Formation of the Western Legal Tradition* (Cambridge, Mass.: Harvard University Press 1983).

4 David J. Seipp, 'Roman Legal Categories in the Early Common Law,' in *Proceedings of the Eighth British Legal History Conference, 1987* ed. T.G. Watkin (London: Hambledon Press 1989) at 9.

5 Richard A. Posner, '"Conventionalism": The Key to Law as an Autonomous Discipline?' *U.T.L.J.* 30 (1988) 333 at 347.

6 H.L.A. Hart, 'Bentham and The Demystification of the Law,' *Modern L. Rev.* 36 (1973), 28; rep. *Essays on Bentham* (Oxford: Clarendon Press 1982).

7 See *inter alia*, Walter Ullmann, *Law and Politics in the Middle Ages*, (New York: Cornell University Press 1975); G. Post, *Studies in Medieval Legal Thought* (Princeton: Princeton University Press 1964); *The Legacy of the Middle Ages*, ed. G.C. Crump and E.F. Jacob (Oxford: Clarendon Press 1926); M. Hortwiz, 'History and Theory,' *Yale L.J.* 96 (1987) 1825; R. Pound, *Law and Morals* (Chapel Hill: University of North Carolina Press 1926).

8 *Fowler v. Padget* (1798), 7 Term. Rep. 509; 101 E.R. 1103 at 1106 (K.B.).

9 Downer, L.J., ed., *Leges Henrici Primi* (Oxford: Oxford University Press 1972), S.5.28b.

10 P.E. Raymond, 'The Origin and Rise of Moral Liability in Anglo-Saxon Criminal Law,' *Oregon L.R.* 15 (1936) 93, 110.

11 H.D.J. Bodenstein, 'Phases in the Development of Criminal Mens Rea,' *South African L.J.* 36 (1919) 323.

12 R.R. Cherry, *Lectures on the Growth of Criminal Law in Ancient Communities* (London: MacMillan 1890) at 1. Bentham, to whom every infraction of the law is an offence, made the point succinctly when he first distinguished between civil and criminal offenses, and then expressly denied any 'correspondency' between criminal and penal law: '[A]ny offence may be deemed a civil offence to which there seems to be no need of annexing any extraordinary species or degree of punishment ... On the other hand, every offence to which it seems to be necessary to annex any extraordinary species or degree of punishment may be termed ... a criminal offence or misdemeanor. Is it then true ... that whatever part of the law goes to make up the description of a criminal offence, belongs to the penal or criminal branch of law? Here ... the correspondency must fail. In many articles it is a part only of what belongs to the description of a criminal offence that can be included with any degree of propriety or convenience within this latter branch. For wherever the directory part of any law of which the conminatory part threatens an extraordinary degree of punishment runs out into details, those forming long and separate titles, those titles carrying nothing that belongs to punishment upon the face of them it must be aggregated to the civil branch of the law. The necessity of this will appear the more manifest in the instances where we see an offence which by the change or edition of a single circumstance may be attended with such diversity of effects as in the one case shall rank it under the head of civil, in the other, under the head of criminal offences. The circumstances ... is of one sort, a circumstance respecting the state of the offender's mind with reference to the obnoxious event, a circumstance relative to intentionality and consciousness.': Jeremy Bentham, *The Limits of Jurisprudence Defined*, ed. Charles W. Everett (New York: Columbia University Press 1945) at 292.

13 2 Bracton at 289. To the classical lawyers, 'delictum meant an offence from which resulted *iure civili*, a penal obligation (*obligatio ex delicto*) and a penal action (*civilis actio poenalis*), and they sometimes used the term *maleficium* instead of *delictum*. Such that *delictum* (*maleficium*) and *obligatio ex delicto* were confined to *ius civile*. They reserved the term *crimen* (crime) for 'an offence which was punished by public criminal law': Fritz Schulz, *Classical Roman Law* (Oxford: Clarendon 1951) at 572.

14 Crawford and Quinn, supra n.2 at 134.

15 See Bodenstein, supra, n.11.

16 For a recent summary, see C.L. Ten, *Crime, Guilt and Punishment: A Philosophical Introduction* (Oxford: Clarendon Press 1987) at 100–10.

17 See Jerome Hall, *General Principles of Criminal Law*, 2nd ed. (Indianapolis: Bobb-Merrill 1960).

18 'The men who first undertook the task [of distinguishing between *dolus* and *culpa*] were the Italian jurists of the thirteenth and following centuries under the influence of the revived study of the Roman Law. The Italian jurists who were the first to pay special attention to the different forms of *mens rea* in criminal law, and became the fathers of modern science of criminal law were not the Glossators but the post-Glossators or Commentators': Bodenstein, supra, n.11 at 327, 337; William W. Bassett, 'Canon Law and the Common Law,' *Hastings L.J.* 29 (1978) 1383 at 1413; Berman, supra n.3 at 181ff.

19 Jeremy Bentham, supra n.12 at 291.

20 Ibid.

21 M.H. Kerr, *Catholic Church and Common Law: Three Studies in the Influence of the Church on English Law* (University of Toronto, PhD Thesis 1991) at 197.

22 John Austin, *Lectures on Jurisprudence*, 3rd rev. ed., ed. R. Campbell, 2 vols. (London: John Murray 1869), 1: at 445.

23 Jeremy Bentham, *Introduction to the Principles of Morals and Legislation*, ed. H.L.A. Hart and J.H. Burns (London: Anthone press 1970) at 94.

24 Ibid.

25 John Austin, supra n.22.

26 Jeremy Bentham, supra n.23 at 57. To the Greeks, 'negligence' denoted 'carelessness which though less culpable than deliberate wrongdoing nevertheless might merit blame. The same attitude is to be found in Aquinas. "Negligence," claims Aquinas, "denotes a lack of due solicitude. Now every lack of a due act is sinful; wherefore it is evident that negligence is a sin"': P.J. Fitzgerald, 'Crime, Sin and Negligence,' *Law Quarterly Rev.* 79 (1963) 351 at 367. To the Romans, it meant 'lack of foresight, which is blameworthy because an ordinary prudent man would not have lacked it,' 'lack of care in doing acts which might be injurious to others' or 'not foreseeing what a diligent man could and ought to have foreseen': Bodenstein, supra n.11 at 333.

27 D.A. Stroud, *Mens Rea* (London: Sweet and Maxwell 1911) at 11.

28 Adam Smith, *Lectures on Jurisprudence*, ed. R.L. Meek et al. (Oxford: Clarendon Press 1978) at 103.

29 Bodenstein, supra n.11 at 330. (Emphasis added.)

30 Ibid.

31 Austin, supra n.22, vol. 1 at 355.

32 Indeed, Austin subsequently realized that he had erred in assimilating indirect intention into *dolus*, and he corrected himself. Austin, ibid. at 445 and 480.

33 Pollock and Maitland, *History of English Law before the Time of Edward I*, 2nd. ed., 2 vols. (Cambridge: Cambridge University Press 1923).

34 F.B. Sayre, 'Mens Rea,' *Harvard L.R.* (1945) 974 at 997.

35 Pollock and Maitland, supra n.33, 1; T.A. Green, *Verdict According to Conscience* (Chicago: University of Chicago Press 1985) at 56.

36 Sayre, supra n.34.

37 Bodenstein, supra n.11 at 330.

38 J.M. Kaye, 'Early History of Murder and Manslaughter,' *L.Q.R.* 83 (1967) 365.

39 Naomi D. Hurnard, *The King's Pardon for Homicide* (Oxford: Clarendon Press 1969).

40 Sayre, supra n.34 at 997.

41 Jerome Hall, supra n.17.

42 See generally, Green, supra n.35.

43 Coke, *Third Institute*, 51.

44 Ibid. at 55. See also Hale, *History of the Pleas of the Crown*, 2 vols. (London: Professional Books 1971), 1: at 449: '[M]urder and manslaughter differ not in the kind or nature of the offence, but only in the degree, the former being the killing of a man of malice prepense, the latter upon a sudden provocation and falling out.'

45 Ibid., 47. (Emphasis added.)

46 Sayre, supra n.34.

47 D. Agretelis, '"Mens Rea" in Plato and Aristotle,' *Issues in Criminology* 1 (1965–6) 19.

48 *Collected Papers*, 3 vols. (Cambridge: Cambridge University Press 1911), 1: at 328.

49 Augustines, 'Ben Sermones,' No. 180 C. 2 (2 *Library of the Fathers* 1937), cited in P.E. Raymond, supra n.10 at 110.

50 C.R. Jeffery, 'The Development of Crime in Early English Society,' *J. of Cr. Law, Crim. & Police Science* 47 (1956–7) 647 at 664.

51 See chapter 6 infra.

52 Bodenstein, supra n.11.

53 H. Packer, 'Mens Rea and the Supreme Court,' *Supreme Ct. Rev.* (1962) 107 at 108.

54 John Andenaes, 'Determinism and Criminal Law,' *Journal of Cr. L. Crim. & Pol. Science* 47 (1956) 406; Alan Norrie, 'Freewill, Determinism and Criminal Justice,' *Legal Studies* 3 (1983) 60.

55 'The man of the Renaissance was a fallen creature, unable to save himself from the consequences of his original and his inevitably recurrent sin, because his nature was such that when he would do good evil was present with him and sure to prevail. His environment was also ruined. His companionship was with creatures of his own kind and was detrimental to him and to them. Science and religion agreed on these points': H. Craig, *The Enchanted Glass* (Oxford: Basil Blackwell 1960) at 113.

56 H.L.A. Hart, 'Prolegomenon to the Principles of Punishment,' in *Punishment and Responsibility* (Oxford: Clarendon Press 1968) at 6.
57 Evidence Act 1851 and Criminal Evidence Act 1898.
58 See, for example, A. Levitt, 'Extent and Function of the Doctrine of Mens,' *Illinois L.R.* 17 (1922–3) 578 at 585.
59 See, for example, O.W. Holmes, Jr, *The Common Law* (1883; rep. Cambridge, Mass.: Belknap Press 1963).
60 Sayre, supra n.34 at 1004.
61 G.O.W. Mueller, 'Mens Rea and the Law without It,' *W. Virg. L.R.* 58 (1955–6) 34 at 41.
62 P. Brett, *An Inquiry into Criminal Guilt* (London: Sweet and Maxwell 1962).
63 George P. Fletcher, *Rethinking Criminal Law* (Toronto and Boston: Little, Brown 1978).
64 Ibid. at 458.
65 M.S. Moore, 'The Moral and Metaphysical Sources of the Criminal Law,' *Nomos XXVII (Criminal Justice)* (1985) ll at 14.
66 Owen M. Fiss, 'The Supreme Court 1978 Term – Forward: The Forms of Justice,' *Harv. L.R.* 93 (1979) 1 at 22.

5: Crimes and the Common Law Mind

1 'Criminalization' here means 'the redefinition of a number of acts as being not primarily conflicts between private individuals but also directed against the State ... criminalisation was a long process going on from the 12/13th centuries well into the 19th century': P. Spirenburg, 'Theory and the History of Criminal Justice,' in *Crime and Criminal Justice in Europe and Canada*, ed. L.A. Knafla (Waterloo, Ont.: Wilfried Laurier University Press 1981) at 322. See also J.H. Baker, 'The Refinement of English Criminal Jurisprudence 1500–1848,' ibid., at 18.
2 Paul Lucas, 'Ex Parte Sir William Blackstone, "Plagiarist": A Note on Blackstone and the Natural Law,' *Am. J. of Legal Hist.* 7 (1963) 142.
3 Joseph M. Levine, *Humanism and History: Origins of Modern English Historiography* (Ithaca, N.Y.: Cornell University Press 1987) at 192.
4 H.F. Jolowicz, 'Political Implications of Roman Law,' *Tulane L.R.* 22 (1947) 62; Myron P. Gilmore, *Argument from Roman Law in Political Thought, 1200–1600* (Cambridge: Harvard University Press 1941).
5 Daniel R. Coquillette, 'Legal Ideology and Incorporation I: The English Civilian Writers, 1523–1607,' *Bos. Univ. L.R.* 61 (1981) 1 at 76–87.
6 Peter Goodrich, '*Ars Bablativa*: Ramism, Rhetoric, and the Genealogy of English Jurisprudence,' in *Legal Hermeneutics, History, Theory, and Practice* ed. G. Leyh (Berkeley: University of California Press 1992) at 52; Peter Goodrich, 'Poor Illiter-

ate Reason: History, Nationalism and Common Law,' *Social and Legal Studies* 1 (1992) 7; Christopher Hill, *Intellectual Origins of the English Revolution* (Oxford: Clarendon Press 1966) 225–65 (on Sir Edward Coke), esp. at 257n.3., Harold J. Berman, 'Origins of Historical Jurisprudence,' *Yale L.J.* 103 (1994) 1651 at 1680.

7 J.G.A. Pocock, *The Ancient Constitution and the Feudal Law* (Cambridge: Cambridge University Press 1957). '[O]riginating in Elizabeth's reign, its development accelerated during the constitutional upheavals of the seventeenth century and it acquired the principal elements which were to characterise its continuing ascendancy after 1688': Janice Lee, 'Political Antiquarianism Unmasked: The Conservative Attack on the Myth of the Ancient Constitution,' *Bulletin of the Inst. of Historical Research* 55 (1982) 166.

8 Richard Hooker, *Of the Laws of Ecclesiastical Polity*, ed. George Edelen (Cambridge, Mass.: Harvard University Press 1977) at 108, cited in D.R. Kelly, *The Human Measure: Social Thought in the Western Legal Tradition* (Cambridge, Mass.: Harvard University Press 1990) at 172.

9 '[In the seventeenth century] ... the common law is pictured invested with a halo of dignity, peculiar to the embodiment of the deepest principles and the highest expression of human reason and of the law of nature implanted by God in the heart of man ... It is the common law which men set up as the object of worship. They regard it as the symbol of ordered life and discipline activities ... And the common law is the perfect ideal of law; for it is natural reason developed and expounded by the collective wisdom of many generations. By it Kings reign and princes decree judgment. By it are fixed the relations of the estates of the realm, and the fundamental laws of the Constitution. Based upon usage and almost supernatural wisdom its authority is above, rather than below that of Acts of Parliament or royal ordinances.': F.N. Figgis, *The Divine Right of Kings*, 2nd ed. (Cambridge: Cambridge University Press 1922) at 229–30. See, further, George L. Mosse, *The Struggle for Sovereignty in England: From the Reign of Queen Elizabeth to the Petition of Right* (East Lansing: Michigan State College Press 1950) at 139–74.

10 C.P. Rodgers, 'Humanism, History and the Common Law,' *J. of Legal Hist.* 6 (1985) 136.

11 D.R. Kelley, 'History, English Law and the Renaissance,' *Past and Present* 65 (1974) 24 at 32.

12 1 *Blackstone Commentaries* 16.

13 3 *Coke Institutes* 181: '[W]hatsoever offence is contrary to the ancient and fundamental laws of the realm, is punishable by law ... that offence which is contrary to the ancient and fundamental laws of the realm is *malum in se*.' According to Berman, it was 'the Canonists [who] invented the category of *mala in se* to describe acts that are sinful regardless of intention, but, in fact, they are acts whose intention is also invariably sinful': Harold J. Berman, *Law and Revolution: The Formation of the*

Western Legal Tradition (Cambridge, Mass. Harvard University 1983) at 598 n.47.

14 Berman, ibid. at 441, points out that regular legislation was not considered to be part of the function of the political authorities until after the Norman Conquest.

15 John G. Bellamy, *Criminal Law and Society in Late Medieval and Tudor England* (New York: St Martin's Press 1984), passim; J.B. Post, 'Local Jurisdictions and Judgment of Death in Later Medieval England,' *Cr. Justice Hist.* (1983) 1 at 10.

16 3 *Institutes*, preface.

17 'At no period in English history do we see any antagonism between the common lawyers and the Parliament. On the contrary, the lawyers recognize it not only as a court, but as "the highest court which the king has," in which relief could be given which could be given nowhere else, in which powers could be exercised which neither the king nor any other body in the state could exercise, in which the errors of their own courts could be redressed.': W.S. Holdsworth, *A History of English Law*, 3rd ed. (London: Methuen 1923) vol. 2 at 430.

18 T.F.T. Plucknett, *Legislation of Edward I* (Oxford: Clerendon Press 1949) at 8.

19 A plethora of terms such as 'Assizes,' 'Establishment,' 'Provisions,' 'Ordinances,' 'Proclamations' were used to designate statutes in pre-modern period. See T.F.T. Plucknett, *Statutes and Their Interpretation in the First Half of the Fourteenth Century* (Cambridge: Cambridge University Press 1922) at 31–4.

20 This should not be construed as a manifestation of the distinction between criminal and penal laws made in the preceding chapter. Unlike that general distinction, the distinction between offences created by parliamentary statutes and those created by penal statutes is peculiar to the common law. For examples of penal statutes, see 3 *Coke Institutes* 191, 194.

21 3 *Coke Institutes*, preface.

22 R.T. Vann, 'The Free Anglo-Saxons: A Historical Myth,' *Journal of the Hist. of Ideas* 19 (1958), 259; A.S. Seaberg, 'The Norman Conquest and the Common Law: The Levellers and the Argument from Continuity,' *Historical Journal* 24 (1981) 791.

23 4 *Blackstone Commentaries*, chapter 33.

24 Ibid.

25 3 *Coke Institutes*; Pollock and Maitland, *History of English Law before the Time of Edward I*, 2nd ed., 2 vols. (Cambridge: Cambridge University Press 1923), 1: at 101; F.M. Stenton, *Anglo-Saxon England*, 3rd ed. (Oxford: Clarendon Press 1971) at 684.

26 4 *Commentaries*, chapter 33 at 408.

27 In the acerbic language of *The Anglo-Saxon Chronicle*, the Conqueror 'made great protection for the game. And imposed laws for the same ... He preserved the harts and boars, And loved the stags as much as if he were their father.' *The Anglo-Saxon Chronicle*, ed. D. Whitelock (New Brunswick; N.J.: Rutgers University Press 1961) at 165, cited in Charles R. Young, 'English Royal Forests under the Angevin Kings,' *J. of British Studies* 12 (1972), 1 at 2.

28 It included the following: the clearing of land; cutting of wood, burning, hunting; the carrying of bow and spears in the forest, the wretched practice of hambling dogs; anyone who does not come to aid in the deer-hunt; anyone who lets loose the livestock which he has kept confined; buildings in the forest; failure to obey summonses; the encountering of anyone in the forest with dogs; and the finding of hide or flesh: *Leges Henrici Primi*, ed. L.J. Downer (Oxford: Clarendon Press 1972) 17, 2. at 121.

29 4 *Blackstone Commentaries* 416.

30 Ric. 2, c. 13 (1379). For a discussion of the various goals of game laws, see Thomas A. Lund, 'British Wildlife Law before the American Revolution, Lessons From the Past,' *Michigan L.R.* 74 (1975) 49.

31 C. Kirby and E. Kirby, 'The Stuart Game Prerogative,' *English Historical Rev.* 46 (1931) 239.

32 22 & 23 Car. 2, c. 25 (1671).

33 F. Barlow, *The Norman Conquest and Beyond* (London: Hambledon Press 1983) at 14, tells the anecdote about how this came about. See, also, Young, supra n.27.

34 P.B. Munsche, *Gentlemen and Poachers* (New York: Cambridge University Press 1981), at 10. 'The reason they give is that this prohibition is made to prevent the lower sort of people from spending their time on such an unprofitable employment but the real reason is ... the delight the great take in hunting and the great inclination they have to screw all they can out of their hands': Adam Smith, *Lectures on Jurisprudence* ed. R.L. Meek et al. (Oxford: Clarendon Press 1978) at 24.

35 See, *inter alia*, Munsche, supra n.34; E.P. Thompson, *Whigs and Hunters: The Origins of the Black Act* (New York: Pantheon Books 1975); D. Hay, 'Poaching and the Game Laws on Cannock Case,' in *Albion's Fatal Tree,* ed. D. Hay et al. (New York: Pantheon Books 1975); B. Inglis, *Poverty and the Industrial Revolution* (Hodder and Stoughton 1971) at 243–6; D.M. Stenton, *English Society in the early Middle Ages, 1066–1307,* 4th ed. (Penguin 1965) at 100–22.

36 Hay, supra n.35 at 191. In Blackstone's words, both the forest and the game laws were 'founded upon the same unreasonable notion of permanent property in wild creatures; and both productive of the same tyranny to the commons: but with this difference, that the former laws established only one mighty hunter throughout the land, the game laws have raised a little Nimrod in every manor': 4 *Commentaries* 418.

37 *Leges Henrici Primi* 17.1.

38 See, generally, P.B. Munsche, supra n.34; Peter J. Cook, 'The Demise of the Game Law System: A Study in Attitudes,' *Holdsworth L. Rev.* 8 (1983) 121.

39 The belief that 'public morality' refers to a pervasive or monolithic morality is, perhaps, an illusion. See, *inter alia*, J.S. Mill, *On Liberty*, ed. G. Himmelfarb (Penguin 1985) at 65–6; A.V. Dicey, *Law and Public Opinion in England during the Nineteenth Century*, 2nd ed. (London: MacMillan 1962) at 3, 10; J. Hall, 'Prolegomena to

a Science of Criminal Law,' *Univ. of Penn. L.R.* 89 (1940) 549; R.C. Fuller, 'Morals and the Criminal Law,' *J. of Cri. Law & Cr.* 32 (1942) 624.

40 Prevention of Cruelty to Animals, 5 and 6 Will. 4, c. 59; 12 & 13 Vict., c. 92. Although statutes that protected animals qua property may have indirectly afforded protection against cruelty to animals, no pre-nineteenth century statute was made for the express purpose of preventing cruelty to animals: J.E.G. de Montmorency, 'State Protection of Animals at Home and Abroad,' *L.Q.R.* 18 (1902) 31.

41 W. Stubbs, *Lectures on Early English History*, ed. A. Hassall (London: Longmans 1906) at 338.

42 R. Pound, *The Spirit of the Common Law* (Francestown, N.H.: Marshall Jones 1931) at 87.

43 'It was one of the fundamental assumptions of the Middle Ages that society and indeed the whole universe was hierarchical. The various classes which made up the population ... were seen as occupying fixed and interconnected positions within this hierarchy, the stability of which was maintained by the forces of custom and law': Frances J. Shaw, 'Sumptuary Legislation in Scotland,' (1979) *Juridical Review* (1979) 81 at 108–9.

44 See, generally, R. Pound, *Interpretations of Legal History* (Cambridge: Cambridge University Press 1923) at 30–1.

45 W.J. Ashley, *An Introduction to English Economic History and Theory*, 3rd ed. 1894) at 6, cited in Jerome Hall, *Theft, Law and Society* (Boston: Little, Brown 1935) at 333.

46 3 *Cambridge Economic History*, ed. M.M. Postan et al. (Cambridge: Cambridge University Press 1963) at 419.

47 F. Elizabeth Baldwin, *Sumptuary Legislation and Personal Regulation in England*, vol. 49, *Johns Hopkins University Studies in History and Political Science* (Baltimore: Johns Hopkins University Press 1926).

48 Ibid. at 22.

49 Ibid. at 23.

50 37 Edw. III, c. 8. The first sumptuary laws attempted to regulate the number of courses that the English people could have for dinner. 'The act was entitled "tatutum de Cibariis Utendis" and was passed on October 15, 1336, in the tenth year of Edward's reign': Baldwin, supra n.47 at 24.

51 Ibid. at 53.

52 Holdsworth attested to this when he wrote: 'In the course of my studies in legal history, I have been struck by the fact that many of the rules of English law have an economic origin': W.S. Holdsworth, 'A Neglected Aspect Between Economics and Legal History,' *Economic History Rev.* 1 (1927) 114.

53 'Medieval society has been defined as "a democracy founded upon the principle of aristocracy." Each man's place was appointed to him in a common scheme; he must,

in general, be content to live in that state of life unto which it had pleased God to call him at his birth. When the people of the Middle Ages rebelled against authority, it was against the misuse of these fixed conditions, not with any hope of changing the conditions. Since each man's place in life was thus fixed by social custom, it was heresy for him to attempt to rise above his class either in his manner of living or in his dress.': Baldwin, supra n.47 at 23.

54 Ibid. at 30.

55 3 *Cambridge Economic History* supra n.46 at 421.

56 Joan Kent, 'Attitudes of Members of the House of Commons to the Regulation of "Personal Conduct" in Late Elizabethan and Early Stuart England,' *Bulletin of the Institute of Historical Research* 46 (1973) 41.

57 Coke's comment on laws regulating apparel is: 'The best mean to repress costly apparel and the excess thereof, is by example; for if it would please great men to show good example and to wear apparel of the cloth and other commodities wrought within the realm, it would best cure this vain and consuming ill, which is a branch of prodigality.': 3 *Coke Institute* 199.

58 4 *Blackstone Commentaries* 170. It should be noted, however, that this reservation was expressed in the context of the fact that the government of England consisted of both monarchy and democracy, and that while luxury was necessary in the one it was ruinous to the other.

59 19 & 20 Vict, c. 64 (1856). 1 Jac. 1, c. 25 (1604) repealed all apparel laws.

60 J.E. Starrs, 'The Regulatory Offense in Historical Perspective,' in *Essays in Criminal Science*, ed. G.O.W. Mueller (London: Sweet and Maxwell 1961) at 254.

61 Ibid.

62 Ibid.

63 W.S. Holdsworth, *A History of English Law*, 3rd ed., 7 vols. (London: Methuen 1923), 2: at 444.

64 Starrs, supra n.60 at 255.

65 Baldwin, supra n.47 at 250 surmised that this was due to the emergence of the modern spirit: 'By the beginning of the seventeenth century, the medieval fondness for regulation was commencing to die out. Perhaps, the legislators had learned that such laws were very difficult to enforce. Some far-sighted writers seem to have recognized that acts like the statutes of apparel not only interfered too much with the daily life of the people and were burdensome, oppressive, and therefore liable to stir up discontent, but also that they might prove a positive hindrance and discouragement to trade and manufactures. Probably some such train of reasoning on the part of the lawmakers was responsible for the gradual decline of sumptuary legislation in England after the close of the Tudor period. Certainly that decline cannot be accounted for by any decrease in extravagance, or by the disappearance of fantastic fashions.'

66 Pollock and Maitland, supra n.25, 2: at 453.
67 'Attitude' here means 'the view taken of particular actions by those involved with them or their consequences, whether that view be favourable or unfavourable, weak or strong, ambiguous or unambiguous; whether it be directed to a particular action or some class of actions in general': T.C. Curtis and F.M. Hale, 'English Thinking about Crime 1530–1620,' in *Crime and Criminal Justice in Europe and Canada*, supra n.1 at 111.
68 S. Dowell, *A History of Taxation and Taxes in England*, 4 vols. (1884; rep. New York: Augustus M. Kelley 1965) 1: at 7–10.
69 R.W. Kaeuper, *War, Peace and Justice* (Oxford: Clarendon Press 1988) at 153.
70 'Pecuniary penalties recovered from crimes, trespasses and offences of all sorts afforded a considerable revenue more particularly during the times of the Norman Kings when justice was administered mainly on account of the profits. Amerciaments – fines assessed on offenders who were in *misericordia regis* at the mercy of the King – and compositions for offences, real or supposed, formed another source of revenue for the King': Dowell, supra n.68 at 26. See also Pollock and Maitland, supra n.25, 2: at 453; Kaeuper, supra n.69 at 20.
71 'Purveyance' is 'the right to impress carriages and horses for the service of the King in removing his household or in the conveyance of timber, baggage and goods.' 'Preemption' is 'the right to purchase provisions and other necessaries for the royal household at an appraised value.' 'Prisage' is 'the right to take a cask or two casks, according to the amount of the cargo, from wine-laden ships on their arrival at a port.' see Dowell, supra n.68.
72 Ibid. at 24.
73 Ibid. at 59.
74 Ibid. Also, James F. Willard, *Parliamentary Taxes on Personal Property, 1290–1334* (Cambridge, Mass.: Medieval Academy of America 1934) (rep; New York: Kraus 1970).
75 Dowell, supra n.68 at xxxiii.
76 F.P. Pollock, 'English Law before the Norman Conquest,' in *The Expansion of the Common Law* (London: Stevens 1904) at 155.
77 Dowell, supra n.68 at 60.
78 Roger Schofield, 'Taxation and the Political Limits of the Tudor State,' in *Law and Government Under the Tudors*, ed. C. Cross et al. (Cambridge: Cambridge University Press 1988) at 255.
79 See, *inter alia*, J.R. Maddicott, 'The English Peasantry and the Demands of the Crown, 1294–1341,' *Past and Present* (1975), supplement no. 1; Alan Rogers, 'Clerical Taxation under Henry IV, 1399–1413,' *Bulletin of the Institute of Hist. Research* (1973) 123; G.L. Harriss, 'Aids, Loans and Benevolences,' *Historical Journal* 6 (1963) 1; K.B. McFarlene, 'War, the Economy and Social Change,' in *England in the Fifteenth Century: Collected Essays* (London: Hambledon Press 1981) at 139 ff.

80 Opposition to taxes and taxation played significant roles in such upheavals as the insurrection of the 'Peasants' in 1380, Cade's Rebellion in 1450, and the Yorkshire and Durham Revolts in 1488. *Bates Case* (1606) arose from a merchant's refusal to pay new duty levied by the King on imported currant: Dowell, supra n.68 at 99, 117, 129, 186.

81 'Another ancient source of revenue in England consisted in exactions of toll at the ports from merchants importing or exporting goods. The origin of these exactions is unknown; but the reason for their existence is clear. The merchant, in those predatory times when every one was so ready and eager to fleece him ... willingly paid, on entering the kingdom and on taking his merchandise out of it, toll to the King for the necessary safeguard for himself and his merchandise ... in port, on land and on the seas. The toll was ... in the nature of a premium paid to the King for insurance': Dowell, ibid. at 75. 'As early as circa 673–85 the Kings of Kent had their *wicgerefa*, their port reeve whose job ... almost certainly included the collection of tolls. The Mercian Kings of the eighth century were granting exemption from tolls, and therefore collecting them, at the ports of the south-east coast. Under Ethelred ... we have an elaborate tariff setting out the tolls paid at London': J.R. Maddicott, 'Trade, Industry and the Wealth of King Alfred,' *Past & Present* 135 (1992) 164 at 167.

82 Ibid. Also W. Kennedy, *English Taxation 1640–1799: An Essay on Policy and Opinion* (1913; rep. New York: Augustus Kelly 1968) at 10.

83 Madicott, supra n.79.

84 L.O. Pike, *A History of Crimes in England 1873–76* (rep. New Jersey: Patterns Smith 1968) at 265; A. Hyatt Verrill, *Smugglers and Smuggling* (London: George Allen and Unwin 1924); Dowell, supra n.68 at 174.

85 W.A. Cole, 'Trends in Eighteenth Century Smuggling,' *Economic Hist. Rev.* 10 (1957) 395; John Styles, 'Our Traitorous Money-Makers: The Yorkshire Coiners and the Law,' in *An Ungovernable People* ed. J. Brewer and John Styles (New Brunswick, N.J.: Rutgers University Press 1980) at 172–249; C. Winslow, 'Sussex Smugglers,' in *Albion's Fatal Tree*, ed. D. Hay et al. (New York: Pantheon Books 1975) at 119–66; H.N. Shore, *Smuggling Days and Smuggling Ways* (London: Cassell 1892); Clive Borrell and Brian Cashinella, *Crime in Britain Today* (London: Routledge and Kegan Paul 1975) at 120–30; Dave McIntosh, *The Collectors: A History of Canadian Customs and Excise* (Toronto: NPC Press 1984) at 215–88; Hoh-Cheung and L.H. Mui, 'Smuggling and the British Tea Trade before 1784,' *American Hist. Rev.* 74 (1968) 442. Smuggling has been known ever since political authorities started to prohibit the importation or exportation of specific goods, and it was in no way confined to disreputable persons. Indeed, smuggling had served imperial/national purposes. For instance, the silk-culture of Greece and the Levant owed its origin to monks' smuggling the jealously guarded eggs of the silk-worm, hidden in a bamboo cane, to Justinian: *Silks, Spices and Empire*, ed. Owen and Eleanor Lattimore (New

York: Delacorte Press 1968) at 18–21; C. Raymond Beazley, *The Dawn of Modern Geography*, 3 vols. (1897; rep. New York: Peter Smith 1949), 1 at 96.

86 G.S.A. Wheatcroft, 'The Attitude of the Legislature And the Courts to Tax Avoidance,' *Modern L.R.* 18 (1955) 209 at 214.

87 25 Edw. 3, statute 5, c. 2.

88 'Forestalling, ingrossing, and regrating was the offence of buying up large quantities of any article of commerce for the purpose of raising the price. The forestaller intercepted goods on their way to market and bought them up so as to be able to command what price he chose when he got to the market. The ingrosser or re-greator – for the two words had much the same meaning – was a person who, having bought goods wholesale, sold them again wholesale': J.F. Stephen, *A History of the Criminal Law of England*, 3 vols. (London: Stevens 1883), 3: at 199; 6 Edw. VI, c. 4.

89 See Hawkins, *Pleas of the Crown* (London: Professional Books 1973) 234–42.

90 Ibid.

91 E.P. Cheyney, *An Introduction to the Industrial and Social History of England* (New York: MacMillan 1908) at 231; E. Lipson, *The Growth of English Society* (London: A.C. Black 1949) at 34; F. Bradshaw, *A Social History of England* (London: Clive University Tutorial Press 1918) at 179; Stephen, supra n.88 at 192.

92 See 3 *Cambridge Economic History*, supra n.46 at 421ff.

93 Holdsworth, *A History of English Law*, 2: at 468.

94 3 *Cambridge Economic History*, supra n.46 at 422; Alan S.C. Ross, 'The Assize of Bread,' *Econ. Hist. Rev.* (Series 2) 9 (1956–7) 332.

95 3 *Cambridge Economic History* supra n.46; Stenton, supra n.35 at 181. 'The interest of the dealers ... in any particular branch of trade or manufactures, is always in some respects different from, and even opposite to, that of the public. To widen the market and to narrow the competition, is always the interest of the dealers. To widen the market may frequently be agreeable enough to the interest of the public; but to narrow the competition must always be against it, and can serve only to enable the dealers, by raising their profits above what they would naturally be, to levy, for their own benefit, an absurd tax upon the rest of their fellow citizens.': Adam Smith, *The Wealth of Nations* (Cannan's ed., Vol. 1 at 250), cited in W.A. Lewis, 'Monopoly and the Law,' *Modern L.R.* 6 (1943) 97 at 101.

96 Ibid.

97 Pike, supra n.84 at 237.

98 Ibid. at 423; Walton H. Hamilton, 'The Ancient Maxim: "Caveat Emptor,"' *Yale L.J.* 40 (1931) 1133.

99 E.P Cheyney, supra n.91 at 224; Bradshaw, supra n.91 at 80; E.P. Thompson, 'The Moral Economy of the English Crowd in the Eighteenth Century,' *Past and Present* 50 (1971) 76.

100 M.W. Beresford, 'The Common Informer, the Penal Statutes and Economic Regulation,' *Econ. Hist. Rev.* 10 (2nd Series) (1957) 221.

101 L.A. Clarkson, 'English Economic Policy in the Sixteenth and Seventeenth Centuries: The Case of the Leather Industry,' *Bulletin of the Institute of Hist. Research,* 38 (1965) 147.

102 25 Hen. 8, c. 2 (1533), 4 Statutes of the Realm, 263.

103 Starrs, supra n.60 at 246.

104 Pike, supra n.84 at 106.

105 3 *Coke Institutes* 195; 9 Edw. 3, c. 1 (1533); 25 Edw. 3, c. 4, 12; 6 R.2, 10, 11 Ric. 27, 1 H. 4 17 {Hawkins I, 235}

106 Lipson, supra n.91 at 75. See, generally, H.M. Robertson, *Aspects of the Rise of Economic Individualism* (Cambridge: Cambridge University Press 1933).

107 K.B. MacFarlane, 'Bastard Feudalism,' in *England in the Fifteenth Century,* supra n.79 at 23.

108 Berman, supra n.13, chapter 12; Pike, supra n.84 at 130.

109 Bradshaw, supra n.91 at 77.

110 Lipson, supra n.91 at 34; T.H. Marshall, 'Capitalism and the Decline of the English Gilds,' *Cambridge Hist. Journal* 3 (1929) 23.

111 Thompson, supra n.99 at 136.

112 Pike, supra n.84 at 213.

113 The classical economist Adam Smith argued that the laws against forestalling 'endeavoured to annihilate a trade of which the free exercise is not only the best palliative of the inconveniences of a dearth, but the best preventative of a calamity,' and he likened fear of this type of commercial practice to fear of witchcraft, that is, both were non-existent evils: *The Wealth of Nations,* Bk. iv. c. 5 (1880 ed.) at 109, cited in W.F. Dana, '"Monopoly" Under the Anti-Trust Act,' *Harvard L.R.* 7 (1893) 338 at 346. See also D. Hay, 'The Criminal Prosecution in England And Its Historians,' *Modern L.R.* 47 (1984) 1.

114 12 Geog. 3, c. 71 (1772).

115 7 & 8 Vict., c. 24 (1844). See, generally, D. Hay, supra n.113.

116 Holdsworth, supra n.63, 2: at 444–5.

117 D.E.C. Yale, 'Hobbes and Hale on Law, Legislation and the Sovereign,' *Cambridge L.J.* 31 (1972) 21; P.S. Atiyah and R.S. Summers, *Form and Substance in Anglo-American Law* (Oxford: Clarendon Press 1987) at 227–9; 240–5. Cf: J.H. Hexter, 'Hobbes and the Law,' *Cornell L.R.* 15 (1980) 471.

118 J.N.J. Palmer, 'Evils Merely Prohibited,' *British J. of Law and Soc.* 3 (1976), 1.

119 While some writers claim that the distinction between *mala in se* and *mala prohibita* could be traced, like many other ideas, to the Greeks, others suggest that we owe the distinction to ecclesiastical sources. See, 'The Distinction Between Mala Prohibita and Mala in Se in Criminal Law,' [Notes], *Col. L.R.* 30 (1930) 74; R.

Pound, *Law and Morals*, 2nd ed. (Chapel Hill: University of North Carolina Press 1926) at 73; Berman, supra n.13 at 598; Aristotle, *Nicomachean Ethics*, Bk. 5, c. 7.

120 Ibid.

121 J. Bentham, *An Introduction to the Principles of Morals and Legislation* ed. J.H. Burns and H.L.A. Hart (London: Athlone Press 1970) at 307. Cf: John Austin, *Lectures on Jurisprudence,* 4th ed., ed. R. Campbell (London: John Murray, 1873), Lecture VI at 273–80.

122 Neil MacCormick, *Legal Right and Social Democracy* (Oxford: Clarendon Press 1982) at 30.

123 'The Distinction Between Mala Prohibita and Mala in Se in Criminal Law,' supra n.119.

124 G.L. Postema, *Bentham and the Common Law Tradition* (Oxford: Clarendon Press 1986) at l.

125 F.W. Maitland, *The Constitutional History of England* (Cambridge: Cambridge University Press, 1968) at 303; J.R. Spencer, 'Public Nuisance: A Critical Examination,' *Cambridge L.J.* 48 (1989) 55 at 63; Carolyn A. Edie, 'Tactics and Strategies: Parliament's Attack upon the Royal Dispensing Power, 1597–1689,' *Am. J. of Legal Hist.* 29 (1985) 189 at 199: 'There were limits upon the crown's power. The King could grant dispensations only to statute not common law, and in theory only to penal statutes, that is, statutes carrying penalties which he could forgo. But he could dispense only with penalties assigned the crown; he could not forgo a penalty due a subject. Nor could he dispense if in doing so he allowed one subject to dispossess another, do another injury, or deprive another or recourse to a private suit or action. He was not expected to dispense with any statute enacted *pro bono publico*, intended to safeguard the health, welfare or safety of the public. *He could not license what was regarded as intrinsically evil,* malum in se, *whether it was an act such as murder, arson, or the engrossment of crops, or a thing, such as noisome dump, a dangerous bridge or some other public nuisance. He had only a power to permit a subject to do or have legally what otherwise was prohibited by statute,* malum prohibitum.' (Emphasis added.)

126 'The Distinction Between Mala Prohibita and Mala in Se in Criminal Law,' supra n.119.

127 Ibid.

128 Ibid. at 76; Spencer, supra, n.125; Carolyn A. Edie, 'Revolution and the Rule of Law: The End of the Dispensing Power, 1689,' *Eighteenth Century Studies* 10 (1977) 434.

129 Ibid. at 76.

130 Ibid.

131 3 *Coke Institutes*, Introduction.

132 1 Wm. & Mary 2, c. 2 (1689).

133 Spencer, supra n.125 at 64; Edie, supra n.128.

134 Stephen A. Siegel, 'The Aristotelian Basis of English Law 1450–1800,' *N.Y.U.L. Rev.* 56 (1981) 18.

135 Leslie Stephens, *English Utilitarians*, vol. 1 at 240, cited in R. Cross, 'Blackstone v. Bentham,' *Law Quarterly Rev.* 96 (1976) 516 at 517.

136 See, for example, D. Lieberman, *The Province of Legislation Determined: Legal Theory in 18th Century Britain* (Cambridge: Cambridge University Press 1989) at 31ff.; Gerald J. Postema, supra n.124; Michael Lobban, *The Common Law and English Jurisprudence, 1760–1850* (Cambridge: Cambridge University Press 1991) at 27ff.; J.M. Finnis, 'Blackstone's Theoretical Intentions,' *Natural Law Forum* (1964) 163.

137 1 *Blackstone Commentaries* 44 (First Edition).

138 Ibid. at 54.

139 Ibid.

140 Ibid.

141 Lucas, supra n.2 at 155.

142 4 *Commentaries* 42.

143 See, for example 1 *Commentaries* 54, 57; 4 *Commentaries* 8, 9, 29.

144 See supra nn.126–31 and accompanying text.

145 'The Distinction Between Mala Prohibita and Mala in Se in Criminal Law,' supra n.119 at 77.

146 Lucas, supra n.2.

147 1 *Commentaries* 58.

148 J. Bentham, *A Comment on the Commentaries and a Fragment on Government*, ed. J.H. Burns and H.L.A. Hart (London: Athlone Press 1977) at 88.

149 C.K. Allen, *Legal Duties* (rep. Aaelen: Scientia 1977) at 239.

150 Basil Williams, *The Whig Supremacy 1714–1760*, 2nd ed. (Oxford: Clarendon Press 1962).

151 Thomas Hobbes, *Leviathan*, ed. W.G. Pogson-Smith (Oxford: Clarendon Press 1909); but also see Shirley R. Letwin, 'Hobbes and Christianity,' *Daedalus* (1976) 1; David Hume, *An Enquiry Concerning Human Understanding*, ed. Eric Steinberge (Indianapolis: Hacket Publishing 1977) at 72–90; Jean-Jacques Rosseau, *The Social Contract*, ed. M. Cranston (Penguin 1968) at 182–7; Joseph Priestley, *A History of the Corruptions of Christianity* (1872 ed.) at 293–301; R.P. Kraynack, 'John Locke: From Absolutism to Toleration,' *American Pol. Sc. Rev.* 74 (1980) 53.

152 F.A. Hayek, *The Constitution of Liberty*, (London: Routledge and Kegan Paul 1960) at 168.

153 A.D. Kriegel, 'Liberty and Whiggery in Early 19th Century England,' *Journal of Modern Hist.* 52 (1980) 253.

154 D. Hay, 'Property, Authority and the Criminal Law,' in *Albion's Fatal Tree*, supra

n.85; E.P. Thompson, *Whigs and Hunters: The Origin of the Black Act* (London: Penguin 1975). After the revolution, 'the primary goal of law and politics was ... the preservation and advantage of propertied interests': Neal Wood, *The Politics of Locke's Philosophy* (Berkeley: University of California Press 1983) at 11.

155 It is not infrequently remarked that Christianity is part of the common law. See, for example 4 *Commentaries* 52; John C.H. Wu, *Fountain of Justice* (London: Sheed and Ward 1955) at 64–5. For judicial statements to the same effect, see, for example, *De Costa* v. *De Paz* (1743) 2 Swans. 532, 36 E.R. 715; *Bowman* v. *Secular Society Ltd.* [1971] A.C. 406. Or: '[E]ven if Christianity be not part of the law of England, yet the common law has its roots in Christianity,' per Lord Hodson, *Shaw* v. *D.P.P.* [1961] 2 W.L.R. 897 at 939. Cf: Bradley S. Chitton, 'Cliobernetics, Christianity and the Common Law,' *Law Library Journal* 83 (1991) 315 (emphasizing that the explicit incorporation of Christianity into the common law occurred in the seventeenth century).

156 Lord Coke and Chief Justice Hale, among others, 'would have repudiated all arbitrary government whatsoever, whether by King or Parliament; Filmer had declared that any government in England must be both arbitrary and royal; for Hobbes it must be arbitrary but not necessarily royal; for many Whigs a century later it must be arbitrary and cannot be royal ... after 1689 and the revolution settlement which marked the final triumph of the Whigs, the arbitrary power of Hobbes and Filmer was for the first time "engrafted into the English Constitution" ... and vested in the national assembly ... For the Whigs the only real sovereign must be Parliament. By the mid-eighteenth century this Whig conception of sovereign Parliament had hardened into orthodoxy.': B. Bailyn, *The Ideological Origins of the American Revolution* (Cambridge, Mass.: Belknap Press 1967) at 201.

157 Gerald R. Cragg, *Reason and Authority in the Eighteenth Century* (Cambridge: Cambridge University Press 1964).

158 See, for example, Adam Smith, supra n.34 at 105.

159 C.H.S. Fifoot, *English Law and Its Background* (London: G. Bell and Sons 1932) at 115.

160 Lucas, supra n.141.

161 This is evident from chapter 33, Bk. Four.

162 D.R. Nolan, 'Sir W. Blackstone and the New American Republic: A Study of Intellectual Impact,' *N.Y.U.L. Rev.* 51 (1976) 731. Cf: Craig E. Klafter, 'The Americanization of Blackstone's Commentaries,' in *Essays on English Law and the American Experience,* ed. Elizabeth A. Cawthon and David E. Narret (College Station, Texas: A & M University Press 1994) 42–65.

163 S.F.C. Milson, 'The Nature of Blackstone's Achievement,' *Oxf. Journal of Legal Studies* 1 (1981) 1.

164 David Sugarman, 'Legal Theory, the Common Law Mind and the Making of the

Text-book Tradition,' in *Legal Theory and Common Law*, ed. William Twining (Oxford: Basil Blackwood 1986) at 26.

165 Ibid.

166 1 *Commentaries* 39–40 (First Ed.).

167 Ibid. 41.

168 Ibid. 42.

169 Ibid. at 55: '[W]ith regard to things in themselves indifferent ... [they] become either right or wrong, just or unjust, duties or misdemeanors, according as the municipal legislator sees proper for promoting the welfare of the society and for effectually carrying on the purposes of civil life ... Thus our own common law had declared that the goods of the wife do instantly upon marriage become the property and right of the husband; and our statute law has declared all monopolies a public offence: yet that right, and this offence, *have no foundation in nature; but are merely created by the law, for the purposes of civil society.'* (Emphasis added.)

170 See, generally, J. Bentham, supra n.121, chapters 1 and 2.

171 E. Halevy, *The Growth of Philosophic Radicalism* (London: Faber and Faber 1928) at 19; Postema, supra n.124 at 165.

172 Bentham, supra n.121 at 11.

173 Ibid.

174 Ibid. at 12–13.

175 Joseph W. Singer, 'The Legal Rights Debate in Analytical Jurisprudence from Bentham to Hohfeld,' *Wisconsin L.R.* (1982) 975 at 1016.

176 A.P. D'Entreves, 'On The Nature of Political Obligation,' *Philosophy* 43 (1968) 309.

177 Bentham, supra n.148 at 63–8; 79–87.

178 Ibid. at 89.

179 Ernest Nagel, 'Impressions and Appraisals of Analytic Philosophy in Europe,' *Journal of Philosophy* 33 (1936) 5.

180 Brendan Edgeworth, 'Legal Positivism and the Philosophy of Language: A Critique of H.L.A. Hart's "Descriptive Sociology,"' *Legal Studies* 6 (1986) 115.

181 John Austin, *Lectures on Jurisprudence*, 4th ed., ed. Robert Campbell (London: Athlone Press 1970), 1: at 85.

182 Ibid., vol. 2: at 582.

183 Ibid., vol. 1: at 501.

184 Ibid.

185 Ibid. 2: at 591. 'The distinction of crimes, made by the Roman Law into crimes *juris gentium* and crimes *jure civili*, tallies with the distinction of crimes made by modern writers into *mala in se* and *mala prohibita*. Offences against human rules which obtain universally, are (according to these writers) *mala,* or offences *in se,* inasmuch as they *would be* offences against the law of Nature or the Deity, although

they were not offences against rules of human position. But offences against human rules which only obtain partially, are *not*, according to those writers, offences against laws of nature. Or at least, they would not be offences against laws of the Deity if they were not offences against positive law or morality. And therefore they are *mala*, or offences, *quia prohibita*, or they take their quality of offences from human prohibitions and injunctions.' It appears that Sir William Blackstone is the archetype of the modern writers referred to by Austin.

186 Ibid. at 590–1: '[I]f an offence would be mischievous on the whole, although the violated law were itself useless or pernicious, it might be styled *malum prohibitum*, or *malum quia prohibitum*. The act would *be* malum (or an offence against the Law of God as well as the Law of Man) merely *because* the breach of the useless or mischievous prohibition might lead to violations of beneficent obligations. If the breach of the useless or mischievous law would not be mischievous (with reference to the sum of its consequences) it would not be *malum* at all.

According to the principle of Utility, the distinction (if worth taking) would therefore stand thus: *Mala in se* are offences against useful laws: *Mala prohibita*, or *quia prohibita*, are mischievous offences against laws which are themselves useless or mischievous.

Innocuous offences against useless or mischievous laws are not *mala*: In other words, they are not pernicious; and therefore are not violations of the Law of God or Nature.'

187 Ibid.

188 H. Kelsen, *General Theory of Law and State* (Cambridge, Mass.: Harvard University Press 1945) at 52.

6:   The Re-emergence of Regulatory Offences

1 F.B. Sayre, 'Public Welfare Offences,' *Col. L.R.* 33 (1933) 55.

2 Robert S. Summers, 'Two Types of Substantive Reasons: The Core of a Theory of Common Law Justification,' *Cornell L.R.* 63 (1978) 707 at 716: 'A ... substantive reason is a reason that derives its justificatory force from moral, economic, political, institutional, or other social considerations.'

3 Maurice W. Thomas, *The Early Factory Legislation: A Study in Legislative and Administrative Evolution* (London: Thames Bank Publishing 1948) at 223.

4 C.A. Cooke, 'Adam Smith and Jurisprudence,' (1935) 51 *Law Quarterly Rev.* 51 (1935) 326.

5 Sir Ernest Barker, 'Reflections on English Political Theory,' *Political Studies* 1–2 (1953–4) 6 at 11; Robin P. Malloy, 'Invisible Hand or Sleight of Hand? Adam Smith, Richard Posner and the Philosophy of Law and Economics,' *Kansas L.R.* 36 (1988) 209.

6 *The Wealth of Nations*, 2 vols. (Cannan ed., 2: at 184), cited in C.A. Cooke, 'Adam Smith and Jurisprudence,' supra n.4 at 328.

7 See, generally, Adam Smith, *Lectures on Jurisprudence*, ed. R.L. Meek et al. (Oxford: Clarendon Press 1978) and *The Theory of Moral Sentiments* (Oxford: Clarendon Press 1976).

8 B. Inglis, *Poverty and the Industrial Revolution* (London: Hodder and Stoughton 1971) at 147.

9 D. Winch, *Adam Smith's Politics: An Essay in Historiographical Revision* (Cambridge: Cambridge University Press 1978) at 167.

10 Guido De Ruggiero, *The History of European Liberalism*, trans. R.G. Collingwood 1959), cited in Ronald D. Rotunda, *The Politics of Language* (Iowa City: University of Iowa Press 1986) at 23.

11 N. MacCormick, *Legal Right and Social Democracy* (Oxford: Clarendon Press 1982) at 75.

12 H.L.A. Hart, *The Concept of Law* (Oxford: Oxford University Press 1961) at 191.

13 E.P. Thompson, 'The Moral Economy of the Eighteenth Century English Crowd,' *Past and Present* 50 (1971) at 90; F. Bradshaw, *A Social History of England* (London: Clive University Tutorial Press 1918) at 284; A.N. Whitehead, *Adventures of Ideas* (Cambridge: Cambridge University Press 1933) at 43.

14 Thurman W. Arnold, *The Symbols of Government* (New Haven: Yale University Press 1935) at 77.

15 Harold Perkin, 'Individualism versus Collectivism in Nineteenth Century Britain: A False Antithesis,' *J. of British Studies* 17 (1977) 105 at 109.

16 F.A. Hayek, *Law, Legislation and Liberty*, 3 vols. (Chicago: University of Chicago Press 1981), 3: at 166.

17 See, generally, Inglis, supra n.8 passim. The resultant morally dessicated and impoverished political economist is described by *The Times* thus: '[A] political economist is an animal with limited brains, and altogether destitute of bowels. With moral principles or results he never ventures to trouble himself ... The human race with such a philosophy are but necessary incumbrances to spinning jennies': *The Times*, 11 May 1836, cited in Thomas, supra n.3 at 90.

18 P.W.J. Bartrip, 'State Intervention in Mid-19th Century Britain: Fact or Fiction?' *J. of British Studies* 23 (1983) 63.

19 S. Checkland, *British Public Policy 1776–1939* (Cambridge: Cambridge University Press 1983) at 49: '[T]he emerging industrial pattern was entirely without state surveillance of any kind until the beginning of the nineteenth century. Men, women and children were wholly in the hands of their employers so far as conditions of work were concerned.' See also Checkland, *The Rise of Industrial Society in England, 1815–1885* (London: Longmans, Green 1964) at 122.

20 *Capitalism and the Historians,* ed. F.A. Hayek (Chicago: University of Chicago

Press 1954); Lloyd R. Sorenson, 'Some Classical Economists, Laissez-faire and the Factory Acts,' *J. of Economic Hist.* (1952) 247; W. Woodruff, 'Capitalism and The Historians: A Contribution to the Discussion on the Industrial Revolution in England,' *J. of Economic Hist.* 16 (1956) 1; Mark Blaug, 'The Classical Economists and the Factory Acts: A Re-Examination,' *Quarterly J. of Econ.* (1958) 211.

21 Health and Morals of Apprentices Act, 42 Geo. 3, c. 73.

22 59 Geo. 3, c. 66.

23 B.L. Hutchins and A. Harrison, *A History of Factory Legislation*, 3rd ed. (1926; rep. New York: Augustus M Kelley 1966) at 16; Blaug, supra n.20 at 212: '[T]he history of factory legislation in England begins with Peel's Bill of 1819. An earlier Act of 1802, regulating the labor of parish apprentices was an extension of the Poor Laws not a factory act; *no new power of the state was at issue.* Peel's Bill ... did raise the question of state interference in private industry ... There was opposition to the bill, particularly in the House of Lords in the form of an appeal to "that great principle of political economy that labour ought to be left free"' (Emphasis added.)

24 Checkland, supra n.19.

25 The Act prohibited the employment in cotton mills of children under nine years of age; limited the working hours of persons under sixteen years of age to twelve hours a day and restricted the working hours between five a.m. o'clock in the morning and nine p.m. Further, it stipulated that one half-hour should be allowed for breakfast and one full hour for dinner. It also directed that the factory premises be washed with quicklime and water twice a year.

26 Inglis, supra n.8 at 122.

27 W.G. Carson, 'The Institutionalization of Ambiguity: Early British Factory Acts,' in *White-Collar Crime: Theory and Research*, ed. Gilbert Geiss and Ezra Stotland (Beverly Hills: Sage Publications 1980) at 153.

28 *Parliamentary Papers* 1833, vol. 20, para. 32.

29 Ibid.

30 Ibid. para. 64.

31 The supporters of the Act had realized this. 'We repeat,' they declared, 'without watchfulness and exertion ... the present law ... will become a dead letter. For there are arrayed against it powerful interests which must defeat it unless an agency be created adequate to enforce it. There is the interest of the parents, who, it is proved, cares only for the wages of his child, and who will do everything in his power to evade any provision made for its physical and moral improvement if that improvement costs any portion, however small, of the child's wages. There is the interest of the workman on whom the care required by the law ... imposes considerable trouble and some expense. There is the interest of the master to whom the strict observance of the regulations ... must cause still more trouble and expense. There is the interest of the advocate for imposing restriction on adult labour who, in order to demonstrate

that there is no true remedy for the evils of the factory system ... will do anything in his power to counteract the working of a measure, the direct and immediate object of which is limited to the regulation of the labour, the protection of the health and the security of the education of the young': *London and Westminster Review* (October 1836), 206, cited in Thomas, supra n.3 at 73.

32 *Parliamentary Papers*, supra n.28, para. 64.

33 P. Gaskell, *The Manufacturing Population of England* (London: Baldwin and Cradock 1833); W. Bowden, *Industrial Society in England Towards the End of the Eighteenth Century*, 2nd ed. (London: Frank Cass and 1965).

34 *Parliamentary Papers*, supra n.28 para. 26. The passage continued: 'Young persons of more advanced age, speaking of their own feelings when younger, give to the Commissioners such representations as the following: 'Many a time has been so tired that she could hardly take off her clothes at night or put them on in the morning,' 'Looks at the long hours as a great bondage,' 'Thinks they are no better than the Israelites in Egypt, and their life is no pleasure to them,' 'Are the hours to be shortened?,' earnestly demanded one of these girls of the Commissioner who was examining her 'for they are too long.' The truth of the account given by the children of the fatigue they experience ... is confirmed by ... their parents ... adult operatives, overlookers, managers and proprietors.'

35 Ibid. para. 65.

36 Ibid. para. 67.

37 Ibid. para. 68.

38 Carson, supra n.27; Howard P. Marvel, 'Factory Regulation: A Re-interpretation of Early English Experience,' *J. of Law and Economics* 20 (1977) 379.

39 *Parliamentary Papers*, supra n.28, para. 68.

40 In penalizing violations of its provisions, s.7 of the 1819 Act employed one of those myriad words and phrases which, as modern scholarship says, implied *mens rea* in statutory offences. See J.L1.J. Edwards, *Mens Rea in Statutory Offences* (London: Macmillan 1955).

41 Checkland, supra n.19 at 247.

42 Marvel, supra n.38 at 382: '[T]here is evidence to suggest that it was completely ignored in Scotland. The Scots manufacturers successfully lobbied to replace the altogether too diligent ... Leonard Horner with the lethargic James Stuart [as Inspector].' See also P.W.J. Bartrip, 'British Government Inspection 1832–1875: Some Observations,' *Historical Journal* 25 (1982) 605.

43 Carson, supra n.27 at 159.

44 Hutchins and Harrison, supra n.23 at 73.

45 Ibid. at 74.

46 *Parliamentary Papers*, 9 (1841) at 565.

47 Ibid. at 578–9.

48 *Parliamentary Debates* 73 (1844) at 1074.
49 Ibid.
50 See, for example, I. Paulus, *The Search for Pure Food* (London: Martin Robertson 1974)
51 *Parliamentary Debates*, 15 (1833) at 1165.
52 P. Devlin, *The Enforcement of Morals* (Oxford: Oxford University Press 1965) at 26.
53 T. Ingman, 'The Rise and Fall of the Doctrine of Common Employment,' *Juridical Review* (1978) 106.
54 Paulus, supra n.50; I. Paulus, 'Strict Liability: Its Place in Public Welfare Offences,' *Cr. L. Quarterly* 20 (1977/78) 445 at 451.
55 C. Emsley, *Crime and Society in England, 1750–1900* (London: Longman 1987); Inglis, supra n.8 at 409–10.
56 A.E. Dingle, '"The Monster Nuisance of All": Landowners, Alkali Manufacturers and Air Pollution 1828–64,' *Econ. Hist. Rev.* 35 (1982) 529; John P.S. McLaren, 'Nuisance Law and the Industrial Revolution – Some Lessons from Social History,' *Oxf. Journal of Legal Studies* 3 (1983) 155.
57 Hart, supra n.12.
58 Paulus, supra n.54; F. Sayre, supra n.1. Cf: Richard G. Singer, 'The Resurgence of Mens Rea III: The Rise and Fall of Strict Criminal Liability,' *Boston C.L.R.* 30 (1988–9) 337.

7: Analytical Jurisprudence and the Criminal Law

1 W.L. Morison, 'Some Myth About Positivism,' *Yale L.J.* 68 (1958) 212 at 232.
2 E. Campbell, 'German Influences in English Legal Education Jurisprudence in the 19th Century,' *Univ. of Western Australia Annual L.R.* 4 (1957–9) 357, 363.
3 Richard A. Cosgrove, 'The Reception of Analytical Jurisprudence: The Victorian Debate on the Separation of Law and Morality, 1860–1900,' *Durham Univ. Journal* 74 (1981) 47.
4 M.H. Hoeflich, 'Transatlantic Friendships and the German Influence on American Law in the First Half of the 19th Century,' *Am. J. of Comp. Law* 35 (1987) 599 at 611. For a brief description of the legal intellectual climate in Germany at the time of Austin's visit, see Andreas B. Schwarz, 'John Austin and the German Jurisprudence of His Time,' *Politica* (1934) 178; Michael Lobban, 'Was There a Nineteenth Century "English School of Jurisprudence?"' *J. of Legal Hist.* 16 (1995) 34.
5 See chapter 3.
6 Gaius Noster, the author of Gaius's *Institute* – a pre-Justinian, second-century text which was discovered in 1816 and was published in 1820. It was Gaius who delineated the Roman system of jurisprudence that was later codified by Justinian: 'In contrast to the naturalistic or mathematical ... strategy of starting with general

principles and reasoning from them, Gaianism gave prominence and priority to the human aspect, to what from the 12th Century onward would be termed "positive law," and then advanced, empirically in a sense, to higher degrees of rationality and universality.' Donald R. Kelley, 'Gaius Noster: Substructures of Western Social Thought,' *Am. Hist. Rev.* (1979) 619 at 624.

7 For a brief discussion of the differences between the philosophical outlook of the classical and the post-classical Roman lawyers, see Fritz Pringsheim, 'The Inner Relationship Between English and Roman Law,' *Cambridge L.J.* 5 (1933–5) 347; H.F. Jolowicz, 'Academic Elements in Roman Law,' *L.Q.R.* 48 (1932) 171.

8 A.G. Chloros, 'Some Aspects of the Social and Ethical Elements in Analytical Jurisprudence,' *Juridical Rev.* 67 (1955) 79; Campbell, supra n.2; M.H. Hoeflich, 'John Austin and Joseph Story: Two Nineteenth Century Perspectives on the Utility of the Civil Law for the Common Lawyer,' *Am. J. of Legal Hist.* 29 (1985) 36; Michael Lobban, *The Common Law and English Jurisprudence, 1760–1850* (Cambridge: Cambridge University Press 1991) chapter 8; Lobban, supra n.4

9 P. Stein, *Legal Evolution: The Story of an Idea* (Cambridge: Cambridge University Press 1980) at 123.

10 John Austin, *Lectures on Jurisprudence*, 4th ed., 2 vols., ed. R. Campbell (London: John Murray 1873), 2 at 1108.

11 Ibid. at 1115. (Emphasis added.)

12 '[G]eneral jurisprudence, or the philosophy of positive law, is ... concerned directly with principles and distinctions which are common to various systems of particular and positive law; and which each of those various systems inevitably involves, let it be worthy of praise or blame, or let it accord or not with an assumed measure or test. Or (changing the phrase) general jurisprudence ... is concerned with law as it necessarily *is*, rather than with law as it *ought* to be: with law as it be, *be it good or bad*, rather than with law as it must be, *if it be good*': *Lectures*, I: at 33.

13 *Lectures*, 2: at 1110: '[I]t will be impossible, or useless, to attempt an exposition of these principles notions and distinctions, until by careful analysis, we have accurately determined the meaning of certain leading terms which we must necessarily employ; terms which recur incessantly in every department of the science: which, whithersoever we turn ourselves, we are sure to encounter. Such, for instance, are the following: Law, Right, Obligation, Injury, Sanction: Person, Thing, Act, Forbearance. Unless the import of these are determined at the outset, the subsequent speculations will be a tissue of uncertain talk.'

14 Austin wrote: 'By a careful analysis of leading terms, law is detached from morals, and the attention of the student of jurisprudence is confined to the distinctions and divisions which relate to law exclusively.' See *Lectures*, 2: at 1111.

15 Robert S. Summers, 'The New Analytical Jurists,' *N.Y.U.L. Rev.* 41 (1966) 861 at 888: '[A]nalytical jurisprudence is a discipline, not a doctrine, let alone a doctrine

about the nature of law, and its problems include many besides this one.' See also Wilfrid E. Rumble, *The Thought of Austin* (London: Athlone Press 1985) at 3: '[A]nalytical jurisprudence ... entails the "clarification of the meaning of law, the identification of the characteristic structure of a legal system, and the analysis of pervasive and fundamental legal notions." Analytical jurisprudence is thus an *approach* to the study of law. As such it is consistent with various non-positivist conceptions of law or its relationship to morality.' (Emphasis in the original.)

16 J. Rawls, *A Theory of Justice* (Cambridge, Mass.: Harvard University Press 1971) at 130; Joseph Raz, *The Morality of Freedom* (Oxford: Oxford University Press 1986) at 14.

17 H.L.A. Hart, 'Analytical Jurisprudence in Mid-20th Century: A Reply to Professor Bodenheimer,' *Univ. of Penn. L.R.* 104 (1957) at 954. (Emphasis in the original.)

18 Gerald J. Postema, *Bentham and the Common Law Tradition* (Oxford: Clarendon Press 1986) at 331.

19 Ernest Nagel, 'Impressions and Appraisals of Analytic Philosophy in Europe,' *Journal of Philosophy* 33 (1936) 5 at 9. (Emphasis in the original). Pre-World War II analytical jurists thus 'believe[d] in a descriptive theory of the fundamental structures of positive law as a possible and philosophically interesting task, which is neutral between controversial political and ideological options and alternative moral systems': J.S. Brito, 'Hart's Criticism of Bentham in Contemporary Concepts of Law,' *Archives for Phil of Law and Social Philosophy* (supplement no. 1, Pt. 4) (1983) 531 at 532. Post-World War II analytical jurists retained the formal neutrality of the previous era. A newer strain in analytical legal philosophy, which sought to reunite legal philosophy with modern moral and political philosophy, emerged in the 1970s, beginning with Rawls, *A Theory of Justice*, supra n.16. The new strain was promptly challenged by advocates of classical moral and political philosophy. By the 1980s, the jurisprudential landscape had become a bedlam of interpretive legal philosophies such as liberal 'democratic' or 'conservative,' economic analysis of law, feminist analysis of law, critical legal studies, law and literature, and so on. See Gary Minda, *Postmodern Legal Movements: Law and Jurisprudence at Century's End* (New York: New York University Press 1995).

20 Postema, supra n.18 at 332.

21 See, for example, ibid.

22 Bentham, *Essay on Language*, 321, cited in Ross Harrison, *Bentham* (London: Routledge and Kegan Paul 1983) at 65.

23 Ibid.

24 Austin, *Lectures*, 2: at 1111.

25 H.L.A. Hart, *The Concept of Law* (Oxford: Oxford University Press 1961) at 202.

26 A.G. Chloros, 'Some Aspects of the Social and Ethical Element in Analytical Jurisprudence,' *Juridical Rev.* 67 (1955) 79; Postema, supra n.18 at 332.

27 David Lyons, 'Founders and Foundations of Legal Positivism,' review of H.L.A. Hart, *Essays on Bentham: Studies in Jurisprudence and Political Theory* (Oxford: Clarendon Press 1982), and of W.L. Morison, *John Austin* (Stanford, Calif.: Stanford University Press 1982) *Mich. L.R.* 82 (1984) 722 at 728–9; H.L.A. Hart, introduction to John Austin, *The Province of Jurisprudence Determined and the Uses of Jurisprudence* (London: Weidenfeld and Nicolson 1954) at xv.

28 See Ronald Dworkin, *Law's Empire* (Cambridge. Mass.: Harvard University Press 1986) at 92: '[A] legal philosopher ... begins his work enjoying a fairly uncontroversial preinterpretive identification of the domain of law, and with tentative paradigms to support his argument and embarrass competitors.'

29 Chloros, supra n.26.

30 George P. Fletcher, *Rethinking Criminal Law* (Toronto: Little, Brown 1978) at 449.

31 '[P]articular jurisprudence, or the science of particular law [is] the science of any ... system of positive law as now actually obtains, or once actually obtained, in a specifically determined nation, or specifically determined nations': Austin, *Lectures*, 1: at 33; 'With us, Jurisprudence is the science of what is essential to law, combined with the science of what it ought to be. It is particular or universal. Particular Jurisprudence is the science of any actual system of law, or of any portion of it. The only practical jurisprudence is particular': 2: at 1112.

32 Michael Corrado, *The Analytic Tradition in Philosophy: Background and Issues* (Chicago: American Library Association 1975) at 38; Nagel, supra n.19 at 6.

33 Timothy M.S. Baxter, *The Cratylus: Plato's Critique of Naming* (New York: E.J. Brill 1992) at 76.

34 On Austin's empiricism, see Wilfrid Rumble, 'John Austin and His 19th Century Critics: The Case of Sir Henry Sumner Maine,' *N.I.L.Q.* (1988) 119; Rumble, supra n.15 at 96ff.; Morison, supra n.27 at 179–207. On the *nature* of Austin's empiricism, see Bichenbach, 'Empiricism and Law,' review of Morison, supra n.27, *U.T.L.J.* 35 (1985) 94; Robert N. Moles, *Definition and Rule in Legal Theory* (London: Basil Blackwell 1987) at 30–4; Lobban, supra n.8. It should be emphasized, however, that there is 'no necessary connection between empiricism and analytic philosophy': J.O. Urmson, 'The History of Philosophical Analysis,' in *The Linguistic Turn*, ed. Richard Rorty (Chicago: University of Chicago Press 1967) at 295.

35 '[I]n the positive systems of Law which are worthy of accurate examination (in the positive systems, that is, of all civilized European Nations) *common* distinctions and principles, though they take very various forms, are sufficiently numerous to constitute the subject of a science. Accordingly, these are the subjects of the universal Jurisprudence which is the purpose of the *Lectures* to expound' – catalogue description by Austin of his course of lectures (Second Statement by the Council of the University of London Explanatory of the Plan of Instruction, 1828), cited in Wilfrid E. Rumble, 'Divine Law, Utilitarian Ethics, and Positivist Jurisprudence: A Study of

the Legal Philosophy of John Austin,' *Am. J. of Jurisprudence* 24 (1979) 139 at 155 (rep. *The Thought of John Austin* supra n.15, 60–107 at 75).

36 As Austin emphatically puts it, his aim is to 'show, not what is law here or there, but what is law' everywhere, or, more accurately, what is law in all civilized European Nations: *Lectures*, 1 at 33.

37 This universalistic claim probably derives from Aristotle, *Analytica Posteriora*. See A.W.B. Simpson, 'The Rise and Fall of the Legal Treatise: Legal Principles and the Forms of Legal Literature,' *Univ. of Chic. L.R.* 48 (1981) 632 at 642; 'Legal Iconoclasts and Legal Ideals,' Univ. of Cincinnati *L.R.* 58 (1990) 819 at 834.

38 David Sugarman, 'Legal Theory, the Common Law Mind and the Making of the Textbook Tradition,' in *Legal Theory and Common Law*, ed. William Twining (London: Basil Blackwell 1986) 26–61 at 43.

39 Ibid. 'Austinian jurisprudence was taken as the most sophisticated defence of the common law credo that the law of the land was the measure of justice. In analytical jurisprudence ... there was a tendency to equate the good with the existent: the law (and English society) had become normative concepts.'

40 Edgar Bodenheimer, 'Modern Analytical Jurisprudence and the Limits of Its Usefulness,' *Univ. of Penn. L.R.* 104 (1956) at 1083.

41 Sugarman, supra n.38 at 31.

42 See chapter 3.

43 '[T]he terms "public" and "private" may be applied indifferently to all Law. Which is as much as to say, that the distinction ... is a distinction without a difference.' *Lectures*, 1 at 416, 2: at 778–87.

44 Ibid., 2 at 1109.

45 C.S. Kenny, *Outlines of Criminal Law*, 15th ed. (Cambridge: Cambridge University Press 1936) at 15.

46 G. Williams, 'The Definition of a Crime,' (1955) *Current Legal Problems* 107 at 123, 130: 'We must distinguish, primarily, not between crimes and civil wrongs but between criminal and civil proceedings ... a crime is an act capable of being followed by criminal proceedings having a criminal outcome and a proceeding or its outcome is criminal if it has certain characteristics which mark it as criminal ... the legal quality of criminality is the product of our minds.'

47 *Lectures*, 1 at 417. Also at 517–18.

48 Ibid. at 354.

49 Ibid.

50 Ibid. at 422.

51 Ibid. at 427.

52 Ibid. at 426.

53 Ibid. at 427.

54 Ibid. at 432.

55 Ibid. at 433.

56 Ibid.

57 P. Brett, *An Inquiry into Criminal Guilt* (London: Sweet and Maxwell 1963).

58 H.L.A. Hart, *Punishment and Responsibility* (Oxford: University Press 1968) at 101.

59 C.T. Sistare, 'On the Use of Strict Liability in Criminal Law,' *Canadian Journal of Phil.* 17 (1987) 395. Although Colvin formulated the same idea rather too narrowly, he emphasized that the requirement is fundamental in criminal law: E. Colvin, *Principles of Criminal Law* (Toronto: Carswell 1986) at 27–8. See also J.Ll.J. Edwards, 'Automatism and Criminal Responsibility,' *Modern L.R.* 21 (1958) 375. For a criticism of Edwards's article, see 'Acts of Will and Responsibility,' in supra n.58 at 94–5. Hart, in an earlier article ('The Ascription of Responsibility and Legal Rights,' *Proc. of Arist. Society* 49, 171) confused the requirement of 'voluntariness' with the mental element of an offence. See G.O.W. Mueller, 'On Common Law Mens Rea,' *Minn. L.R.* 42 (1957–8) 1043. Traces of the confusion are discernible even in 'Acts of Will and Responsibility.' Hart later repudiated the earlier article: *Punishment and Responsibility* supra n.38 [preface]. For a recent critique of Hart's approach, see K.W. Saunders, 'Voluntary Acts and the Criminal Law: Justifying Culpability Based on the Existence of Volition,' *Univ. of Pittsburgh L.R.* 49 (1988) 443 (stating that 'volition' is logically a necessary but not a sufficient condition for finding *mens rea*). See, more comprehensively, Michael S. Moore, *Act and Crime: The Philosophy of Action and Its Implications for Criminal Law* (Oxford: Clarendon Press 1993).

60 Austin, *Lectures*, 1: at 433.

61 Ibid.

62 Ibid. at 434.

63 Ibid. at 434.

64 Ibid. at 450–3.

65 Ibid. at 435, 436.

66 Ibid. at 436: 'You hate me mortally: And, in order that you may appease that painful and importunate feeling, you shoot me dead. Now here you *intend* my death ... my death is the *end* of the act, and of the volition which precedes the act. Nothing but that consequence would accomplish the purpose, which (speaking with metaphysical precision) is the end of the act and the volition ... Again: You shoot me, that you may take my purse. I refuse to deliver my purse, when you demand it. I defend my purse to the best of my ability. And, in order that you may remove the obstacle which my resistance opposes to your purpose, you pull out a pistol and shoot me dead. Now here you *intend* my death, and you also *desire* my death. But you desire it as a *mean*, and not as an end. Your desire of my death is not the ultimate *motive* suggesting the volition and the act. Your ultimate motive is your desire of my purse ... Lastly: You shoot at Sempronius or Styles, at Titius or Nokes, desiring and intending to kill him. The death of Styles is the *end* of your volition and act. Your desire of his death, is the

ultimate motive to the volition. You contemplate his death, as the probable consequence of the act. But when you shoot at Styles, I am talking with him, and am standing close by him. And, from the position in which I stand with regard to the person you aim at, you think it not unlikely that you may kill *me* in your attempt to kill *him*. You fire, and kill me accordingly. Now here you *intend* my death, without *desiring* it. The *end* of the volition and act, is the death of Styles. *My* death is neither desired as an *end*, nor is it desired as a *mean*: *My* death *subserves not* your end: you are not a bit the nearer to the death of Styles, by killing *me*. But, since you contemplate my death as a probable consequence of your act, you *intend* my death although you *desire* it not.'

67 Ibid. at 439.

68 Ibid. at 440.

69 Ibid. at 440–1; 444.

70 Ibid. at 441.

71 Ibid.

72 Ibid. at 443.

73 Ibid. at 457–72.

74 Ibid. at 473.

75 Ibid.

76 Ibid.

77 Ibid. at 479.

78 Ibid. at 423.

79 Ibid. at 474. (Emphasis added.)

80 Ibid.

81 Ibid. at 476.

82 Ibid.

83 Ibid. at 479. The difficulties encountered in applying Roman law taxonomy had led Bentham to counsel writers to discard *dolus* and to use *culpa*: *Introduction to the Principles of Morals and Legislation*, at 95n.

84 Ved Mehta, *Fly and the Fly Bottle* (Boston: Little, Brown 1962) at 269; W. Lucy, 'Controversy in the Criminal Law,' *Legal Studies* 8 (1988) 217.

85 Fletcher, supra n.30 at 396.

86 Ibid.

87 See supra n.17 and text.

88 Geoffrey Samuel, 'Science, Law and History: Historical Jurisprudence and Modern Legal Theory,' *N.I.L.Q.* 41 (1990) 1 at 18.

89 Hart, supra n.27 at xv.

90 See, for example, J.F. Stephen, 'English Jurisprudence,' *Edinburgh Review* 114 (1861) 246 at 297: 'History without analysis is a mere curiosity, and analysis without history is blind,' cited in Rumble, supra n.34, 119 at 148.

91 Sir Fitzjames Stephens, *A History of the Criminal Law of England*, 3 vols. (London: Stevens 1883).

92 John Roach, 'Liberalism and the Victorian Intelligentsia,' *Cambridge Historical Journal* 13 (1957) 58.

93 Stephen, supra n.91, 1: at 4.

94 Pollock and Maitland, *The History of English Law before the time of Edward I*, 2nd ed., 2 vols. (Cambridge: Cambridge University Press 1923), 2 at 573.

95 Stephen, supra n.91.

96 See, infra, chapter 8.

97 Geoffrey Samuel, supra n.88 at 18: '[c]riminal policy is simply trapped within the limitations of its own theoretical structures, themselves the result of a history some-what badly understood in terms of research and indicators ... The twentieth century is witnessing "ideological chaos" because philosophers, in trying to abandon history, are in truth "neolithic" in their attachment to historical premises – in their attachment to the concept of the individual person.'

98 R. Pound, *Law and Morals*, 2nd ed. (Chapel Hill: University of North Carolina Press 1926) at 31.

99 See, particularly, Williams, supra n.46.

100 J.M. Kaye, 'The Early History of Murder and Manslaughter,' *L.Q.R.* 83 (1967) 365.

101 T. Hobbes, *De Cive* (1651), ed. H. Warrender (Oxford: Clarendon Press 1983) at 177; T. Hobbes, *Leviathan*, ed. W.G. Pogson-Smith (Oxford: Clarendon Press 1909), Part I, Chap. 15, Para. 79.

102 G. Himmerfarb, *Victorian Minds* (New York: Alfred Knopf 1961) at 97.

103 *De Cive*, supra n.101 at 178.

104 *Leviathan*, Part II, Chap. 27, Para. 151. (Emphasis added.)

105 4 *Commentaries* 20.

106 'Words,' he wrote, 'are wise men's counters, they do but reckon by them: but they are the mony of fooles, that value them by the authority of an Aristotle, a Cicero, or a Thomas [Aquinas] or any other doctor whatsoever, if but a man': *Leviathan* Part I, Chap. 4, Para. 15.

107 'For cause of the Will to doe any particular action, which is called Volitio, they [the Schoolmen] assign the Faculty, that is to say, the Capacity in generall, that men have, to will sometimes one thing, sometimes another, which is called Voluntas; making the Power the cause of the Act: As if one should assign for cause of the good or evill Acts of men, their Ability to doe them': *Leviathan,* Part 4, Chap. 46, Para 375.

108 *Leviathan*, Part I, Chap. 5, Para. 22: '[T]he Light of humane minds is Perspicuous Words, but by exact definitions first snuffed, and purged from ambiguity; Reason is the pace; Encrease of Science, the way; and the Benefit of man-mind, the end. And in the contrary, metaphors and senselesse and ambiguous words are like *ignes fatui*; and reasoning wandering amongst innumerable absurdities.'

109 A. MacIntyre, 'The Antecedents of Action,' in A. MacIntyre, *Against the Self-Images of the Age* (New York: Schocken Books 1972) at 191–210.

110 *Leviathan*, Part I, Chap. 6, Para. 28.

111 Ibid. Para. 29.

112 F.P. Pollock, *A First Book of Jurisprudence* (New York: Burt Franklin, Research and Source Works, Series 452 ed.) at vii: 'I have learned much from Hobbes and hold acquaintance with his work at first hand indispensable for all English speaking men who may give any serious consideration to the theoretical part of either politics or law.' Also: 'In jurisprudential perspective, the land [U.K.] has been ruled ... by a sovereign Parliament cut to the specifications of Thomas Hobbes. Parliament is a sovereign with no juridical bounds whatever to its power, a sovereign whose corporate words are law, whatever words it chooses to speak ... [But] whatever jurisprudential theory says, we know, as Coke did, that in England the sovereign is not under man but under the law.': J.H. Hexter, 'Hobbes and the Law,' *Cornell L.R.* 15 (1980) 471 at 490.

113 Austin, *Lectures*, 1: at 33.

114 H. Packer, 'Mens Rea and the Supreme Court,' *Supreme Court Rev.* (1962) 107.

115 J.C. Smith and B. Hogan, *Criminal Law*, 4th ed. (London: Butterworths 1978) at 39.

116 Hart, supra n.57 at 108.

117 Glanville Williams, *Criminal Law: The General Part*, 2nd ed. (London: Steven and Sons 1961); Turner, supra n.45; Smith and Hogan, supra n.115.

118 J. Hall, *General Principles of Criminal Law*, 2nd ed. (New York: Bobbs-Merrill 1960) at 113.

119 See, for example, D.J. Birch, 'The Foresight Saga: The Biggest Mistake of All?' *Cr. L.R.* (1988) 4.

120 W.S. Holdsworth, *Some Lessons From Our Legal History* (New York: MacMillan 1928) at 94.

121 J. Griffith, 'Is Law Important?' *N.Y.U.L. Rev* 54 (1979) 339 at 367.

122 O.W. Holmes, Jr, 'The Path of the Law,' *Harvard L.R.* (1897) 457. 'Political writers,' wrote Hume, 'have established it as a maxim that in contriving any system of government, and fixing the several checks and controuls of the Constitution every man ought to be supposed a knave, and to have no other end, in all his actions, than private interest': 'On the Independency of Parliament,' in *Philosophical Works*, ed. T.H. Green and T.H. Grose (Cambridge, Mass.: Belknap Press 1963) 1: at 117.

123 J.W.C. Turner, 'The Mental Element in Crimes at Common Law,' *Cambridge L.J.* 6 (1936–8) 31 at 42.

124 John E. Stannard, 'A Tale of Four Codes: John Austin and the Criminal Law,' *N.I.L.Q.* 41 (1990) 293.

125 See, for example, John E. Stannard, 'Subjectivism, Objectivism and the Draft

Criminal Code,' *L.Q.R.* 101 (1985) 540; Gerald H. Gordon, 'Subjective and Objective Mens Rea,' *Cr. L.Q.* 17 (1974–5) 353.

126 See, for example, George P. Fletcher, 'The Theory of Criminal Negligence: A Comparative Analysis,' *U. Pa. L.R.* 119 (1971) 401.

127 H.L.A. Hart, 'Mens Rea, Negligence and Criminal Responsibility,' in *Punishment and Responsibility* supra n.58.

128 [Note], 'Negligence and the General Problem of Criminal Responsibility,' *Yale L.J.* 81 (1972) 949 at 976.

129 H. Wechsler, 'Culpability and Crime: The Treatment of Mens Rea in the Model Penal Code,' *Annals* 339 (1962) 24; Herbert L. Packer, 'Mens Rea and the Supreme Court,' *Supreme Court Rev.* (1962) 107.

130 Against: J.W.C. Turner, supra n.123; Jerome Hall, 'Negligent Behavior Should be Excluded from Penal Liability,' *Columbia L.R.* 63 (1963) 632; 'Negligence and the General Problem of Criminal Responsibility' – [Note], supra n.127; Robert P. Fine and M. Cohen, 'Is Criminal Negligence a Defensible Basis for Penal Liability?' *Buffalo L.R.* 16 (1967) 749; John Delmonte, 'Negligence: A Reappraisal of Its Validity as a Basis for Criminal Liability and Sanction,' *South Texas L.J.* 20 (1979) 179; Peter E. Salvatori, 'Criminal Law – Criminal Negligence – Punishment,' *Canadian Bar Rev.* 58 (1980) 660; Richard G. Singer, 'The Resurgence of Mens Rea III – The Rise and Fall of Strict Criminal Liability,' *Boston College L.R.* 30 (1988–9) 337. For: James M. Brady, 'Punishment for Negligence: A Reply to Professor Hall,' *Buffalo L.R.* 22 (1973) 107; L. Westerfield, 'Negligence in the Criminal Law: A Historical and Ethical Refutation of Jerome Hall's Arguments,' *Southern. Univ. L.R.* 5 (1978/9) 181.

131 Alan W. Mewett and Morris Manning, *Criminal Law*, 2nd ed. (Toronto: Butterworths 1985) at 104: 'While the concept of *mens rea* as it exists today is a more complex concept ... the original meaning has never been wholly abandoned, and it is to that historical meaning that courts should be directed in order to ensure that there is never a weakening of the requirements of a blameworthy state of mind'; John C. Smith, 'Subjective or Objective? Ups and Downs of the Test of Criminal Liability in England,' *Villanova L.R.* 27 (1981–2) 1179; Richard G. Singer, supra n.130 at 407: '[T]he "subjectivist bug" [should be] allowed to regain its rightful position in the criminal law'; Rollin M. Perkins, 'Criminal Liability Without Fault: A Disquieting Trend,' *Iowa L.R.* 68 (1983) 1067.

132 Stephen, supra n.91, vol. 2: at 94–5. See also F.B. Sayre, 'Mens Rea,' *Harvard L.R.* (1945) 974.

133 J. Bentham, *The Limits of Jurisprudence Defined*, ed. Charles W. Everett (New York: Columbia Press 1945) at 58.

134 Harrison, supra n.22 at 58.

135 Supra n.133.

136 'A realist view about minds grants that there really are mental states, that in any taking of inventory of the furniture of the universe mental states must be included just as surely as tables and chairs.' Michael S. Moore, 'The Moral and Metaphysical Sources of the Criminal Law,' *Nomos: Criminal Justice* 27 (1985) 11 at 47 n.31.

137 G. Ryle, *The Concept of Mind* (London: Hutchinson Press 1949)

138 Brett, supra n.57.

139 Fletcher, supra n.30.

140 Hyman Gross, *A Theory of Criminal Justice* (New York: Oxford University Press 1979).

141 Moore, supra n.136 at 31.

142 Michael S. Moore, supra n.136 at 40: '[B]ehaviorism can[not] sustain the rejection of the subjective mental states of belief, desire, and willing ... none of the forms of skepticism [about the reality of mental state] should shake the realist intuition that "the state of a man's mind is as much a fact as the state of his digestion." Persons really possess the mental states of belief and desire, really will (cause) the movements of their bodies, and nothing from contemporary legal theory, philosophy, or psychology should convince us otherwise.'

143 John H. Randall, Jr, 'The Development of the Scientific Method in the School of Padua,' *Journal of the Hist. of Ideas* 1 (1940) 177.

144 C.K. Odgen and I.A. Richards, *The Meaning of Meaning*, 8th ed. (New York: Harcourt Brace and World 1923) at 100: 'Words ... always symbolize thought and the conceptualist is apt to imply that the very special case of the construct or concept imagined for the purpose of an attempted scientific reference or classification, and then itself examined, can be generalized.'

145 Hobbes, *Leviathan,* Part 4, Chap. 46, Para. 371. (Emphasis added.)

146 Karl. R. Popper, *The Open Society and Its Enemies*, 2 vols. 5th ed. (London: Routledge and Kegan Paul 1966), 2: at 9.

147 The maxim *actus non facit reum nisi mens sit rea* is patently essentialist.

148 *Lectures*, 1: at 474. (Emphasis in the original.)

149 C.T. Cistare, 'On the Use of Strict Liability in Criminal Law,' *Canadian J. of Phil.* 17 (1987) 395; M. Kelman, 'Strict Liability: An Unorthodox View,' in *Encyclopedia of Crime and Justice*, 4 vols., ed. Sanford H. Kadish (New York: Free Press, 1983), 4: at 1512–18. R.A. Wasserstrom, 'Strict Liability in the Criminal Law,' *Stanford L.R.* 12 (1959–60) 731; P. Brett, 'Strict Responsibility: Possible Solutions,' *Modern L.R.* 37 (1974) 417; James B. Brady, 'Strict Liability Offenses: A Justification,' *Cr. L. Bulletin* (1972) 217; Laurie L. Levenson, 'Good Faith Defenses: Reshaping Strict Liability Crimes,' (1993) 78 *Cornell L.R.* 401 (strict liability crimes are acceptable, as long as 'good faith defenses' are available); Steven S. Nemerson, 'Criminal Liability Without Fault: A Philosophical Perspective,' [Note]

Col. L.R. 75 (1975) 1517 (strict liability 'for certain rigidly circumscribed classes of offenses' only).

150 Packer, supra n.114; Levenson, supra n.149 at 403n.7.

151 G.O.W. Mueller, 'Mens Rea and the Law without It,' W. Virg. *L.R.* 58 (1955–6) 34 at 50.

152 Hall, supra n.118 at 336; Brett, supra n.57 at 103; *Our Criminal Law* (Law Reform Commission of Canada 1976) at 22; Singer, supra n.130; Alan Salzman, 'Strict Criminal Liability and the United States Constitution: Substantive Criminal Law and Due Process,' *Wayne L.R.* 24 (1978) 1571.

153 Wasserstrom, supra n.149 at 743.

154 For an excellent exploration of this issue, see Bruce Chapman and Michael J. Trebilcock, 'Punitive Damages: Divergence in Search of a Rationale,' *Alabama L.R.* 40 (1989) 741.

155 C. Archibald, 'The Constitutionalisation of the General Part of Criminal Law,' *Can Bar Rev.* 67 (1988) 403; C.P. Erlinger, 'Mens Rea, Due Process and the Supreme Court: Toward a Constitutional Doctrine of Substantive Criminal Law,' *Am. J. of Cr. Law* 9 (1981) 163; James J. Hippard, Sr, 'The Constitutionality of Criminal Liability Without Fault: An Argument For a Constitutional Doctrine of Mens Rea,' *Houston L.R.* 10 (1974) 1039.

156 See Thomas S. Kuhn, *The Structure of Scientific Revolutions*, 2nd ed. (Chicago: University of Chicago Press 1970).

8:   Beyond Analysis: The Concept as Villain

1 See, for example, *Bishop Commentaries on the Criminal Law* (Williams S. Hein 1986), 1. 1: 'The essence of an offence is the wrongful intent, without which it cannot exist ... it is the doctrine of the law superior to all other doctrines because first in nature from which the law itself proceeds, that no man is to be punished as a criminal unless his intent is wrong.'

2 A contemporary of Plato, Demostheme, is reported to have penned the following lines: 'Among people I find this sort of distinction universally observed. If a man has gone wrong wilfully, he is visited with resentment and punishment. If he has erred unintentionally, pardon takes the place of punishment. This distinction will be found not only embodied in our statutes, but laid down by nature herself in her unwritten laws and in the moral sense of men.' *De Corona* 274–5, cited in J.M. Kelly, *A Short History of Western Legal Theory* (Oxford: Clarendon Press 1991) at 34.

3 Thomas S. Kuhn, *The Structure of Scientific Revolutions*, 2nd ed. (Chicago: University of Chicago Press 1970) at 94.

4 See chapter 7.

5 In chapter 5, 'conceptualism' was used to denote the belief that the operative con-

cepts in a system of thought 'correspond to elements of the real world.' That was a truth claim. We are not here concerned with such claims. In this and the next chapter, the word will be employed in two other senses. First, it will be used to describe the conviction which sustains the analytic bent in legal philosophy generally, namely that concepts are not simply tools but *finite* and *definite* implements already gathered together and contained in a toolbox, in this case the positive law of 'civilized' communities. Secondly, it will be used to denote the conviction that *some* concepts, 'crime' among them, rule exclusively in specific areas of the law. It is in the latter sense that the word 'criminal' is used in the phrase 'analytical criminal jurisprudence.' It will be clear from the context in which sense the word is being used.

6 '[T]he modern institutional landscape is one of firms, associations and partnerships all using the facade of corporate legal personality ... and this is a structure which, institutionally, does not lend itself to the traditional Christian morality which still lies at the heart of the concept of law': Geoffrey Samuel, 'Science, Law and History: Historical Jurisprudence and Modern Legal Theory,' *N.I.L.Q.* 41 (1990) 1 at 18.

7 Michael S. Moore, 'The Moral and Metaphysical Sources of the Criminal Law,' *Nomos: Criminal Justice* 27 (1985) 11 at 12: '[M]oral agency [is] coextensive with personhood, so that all and only persons are moral agents; aggregates of persons (corporations), and members of the human species that lack certain distinctive features of personhood (as the insane and the very young lack rationality) are not moral agents, on this view.' Susan Wolf, 'The Legal and Moral Responsibility of Organizations,' 267 at 279: '[O]rganizations lack souls ... As long as the criminal law continues to include among its functions the expression of moral blame, the application of criminal law should be restricted to persons and other beings that have ... souls.' Cf: Steven Walt and William S. Laufer, 'Why Personhood Doesn't Matter: Corporate Criminal Liability and Sanctions,' *Am. J. Crim. Law* 18 (1991) 263 at 269: '[W]hether corporations are persons is an empirical matter. The issue does not depend on whether it makes *sense* to say that corporations act or have intentions ... finding that an entity is a person does not require investigation into the entity's underlying "hardware." A finding of rationality constrains the attribution.' See, further, John C. Coffee, Jr, '"No Soul to Damn, No Body to Kick": An Unscandalized Inquiry into the Problem of Corporate Punishment,' *Michigan L.R.* 79 (1981) 386; Leslie J. Moran, 'Corporate Criminal Capacity: Nostalgia for Representation,' *Social and Legal Studies* 1 (1992) 371.

8 See Caroline Fennell, 'Intention in Murder: Chaos, Confusion and Complexity,' *N.I.L.Q.* 41 (1990) 325.

9 The emphasis on the word 'criminal' here is meant to exclude analytical jurists such as H.L.A. Hart whose approach to the question of responsibility in the law transcends the threshold of strict conceptual analysis. See H.L.A. Hart, *Punishment and Responsibility* (Oxford: Oxford University Press 1968), chapter 6.

10 See J. Hall, *General Principles of Criminal Law*, 2nd ed. (New York: Bobbs-Merrill 1960) 325.

11 R.A. Wasserstrom, 'Strict Liability in the Criminal Law,' *Stanford L.R.* 12 (1959–60) 731 at 743.

12 Morris R. Cohen, 'The Place of Logic in the Law,' *Harvard L.R.* 29 (1915–16) 622.

13 O.W. Holmes, Jr, *The Common Law* (1883) at 1.

14 Of course, 'a logical science of law can help us digest our legal material, but we must get our food before we can digest it. The law draws its sap from feelings of justice and social need.': Cohen, supra n.12 at 628.

15 E.F. Schumacker, *A Guide for the Perplexed* (New York: Harper and Row 1977) at 123.

16 George P. Fletcher, *Rethinking Criminal Law* (Boston: Little, Brown 1978) at 395.

17 See chapter 4.

18 P.J. Fitzgerald, 'Crime, Sin and Negligence,' *L.Q.R* 79 (1963) 351 at 362.

19 J.Ll.J. Edwards, 'The Criminal Degrees of Knowledge,' *Modern L.R.* 17 (1954) 294 at 312.

20 Fitzgerald, supra n.18 at 363.

21 Ibid. at 367.

22 See chapter 4.

23 In the medieval period, 'negligence' arose principally within the context of the principal means of transportation and shooting. Judicial attitude varied depending on the context. In accidental homicide cases such as those involving carts and ploughs, 'thirteenth-century courts ... systematically acquitted, [for, among other reasons] more often than not the victim, rather than the driver, had failed to use care ... [However] in shooting accidents and other cases where the slayer was more likely to have been the negligent party, the pardon requirement was maintained,' apparently to prevent spurious cases of accidental shooting. In subsequent centuries, the requirement of pardon in such cases was relaxed. Two centuries later, and following the invention of firearm and increase in homicides involving its use, the courts became more strict in requiring pardon in shooting accidents generally: Thomas A. Green, *Verdict According to Conscience* (Chicago: University of Chicago Press 1985) at 87, 124.

24 See chapter 1.

25 Daniel R. Ernst, 'The Moribund Appeal of Death: Compensating Survivors and Controlling Jurors in Early Modern England,' *Am. J. of Legal Hist.* 28 (1984) 64 at 170: 'In early modern times survivors could and did use the appeal to remedy wrongful death when the public prosecution of a malefactor had not foreclosed their suits.'

26 Ibid. 59 Geo. 3, Ch. 46 (1819).

27 At common law the results of prosecution on an indictment foreclosed a subsequent prosecution for the same offence, but there was always solicitude, on the part of judges and Parliament alike, for the right of appeal. 4 *Blackstone Commentaries* 329:

'[I]n favour of appeals, a general practice was introduced, not to try any person on an indictment of homicide, till after the year and day, within which appeals may be brought, were past; by which time it often happened that the witnesses die, or the whole was forgotten. To remedy which inconvenience, the statute 3 Hen VII, c.1 enacts, that indictments shall be proceeded on, immediately, at the king's suit, for the death of a man, without waiting for bringing an appeal; and that the plea, of *autrefois acquit* on an indictment, shall be no bar to the prosecuting of any appeal.'

28 When the appeal of death and therefore the right to compensation was threatened by the pleas of *autrefois acquit, autrefois attaint,* or *autrefois convict,* the justices resorted to a strategy that effectively protected the appeal. See supra n.27. 'The justices' deference to the appeal took two forms. First, if an indictment and an appeal were pending for the same crime, justices stayed proceedings on the indictment as long as the appellor actively prosecuted the killer. Second, in 1482 the royal justices resolved that "if a man is indicted of the death of a man, the person indicted shall not be arraigned within the year for the same felony at the King's suit, so that the suit of the party may be saved"': Ernst, supra n.25 at 173.

29 Supra n.25 at 170.

30 F.B. Sayre, 'Mens Rea,' *Harvard L.R.* 45, 974.

31 W.S. Holdsworth, *Some Lessons From Our Legal History* (New York: Macmillan 1928).

32 Poole, *Medieval England* (rev. ed. 1958) at 252–3, cited by J.E. Starrs, 'The Regulatory Offense in Historical Perspective,' in *Essays in Criminal Science*, ed. G.O.W. Mueller (London: Sweet and Maxwell 1961) at 244.

33 J.S. Mill, 'Austin on Jurisprudence,' in *Collected Works of John Stuart Mill* ed. John M. Robson (Toronto: University of Toronto Press 1984) 2: at 168.

34 Pierre Manent, *An Intellectual History of Liberalism*, trans. Rebecca Balinsky (Princeton: Princeton University Press 1994) at 46.

35 See, generally, B. Inglis, *Poverty and The Industrial Revolution* (Hodder and Stoughton 1971), passim; A.D. Kriegel, 'Liberty and Whiggery in Early 19th Century England,' *Journal of Mod. Hist.* 52, 253. In the United States, 'in the latter part of the nineteenth century, the doctrine of natural rights was given new vigor by the vogue of Spencer's philosophy. Spencer objected even to laws securing the public health at the expense of individual freedom. He conceived it wrong even to compel an owner to clean up his premises in order to safeguard epidemics ... this mode of thought was eagerly taken up both by those bred in an atmosphere of pioneer distrust of interference with everyone doing as he liked, and by those who feared that the regime of private property would be weakened ... the whole emphasis was on rights as contrasted with duties.': R. Pound, *Criminal Justice in America* (New York: H. Holt 1930) at 131–2; R. Pound, *Interpretations of Legal History* (Cambridge: Cambridge University Press 1923) at 147.

36 P. Devlin, *The Enforcement of Morals* (London: Oxford University Press 1965) at 26. (Emphasis added.)

37 P.H. Winfield, 'The History of Negligence in the Law of Torts,' *L.Q.R.* 42 (1926) 184 at 185.

38 C.H.S. Fifoot, *History and Sources of the Common Law* (1949) 164, cited in Morton J. Horwitz, *The Transformation of American Law, 1780–1860* (Cambridge, Mass.: Harvard University Press 1977) at 88.

39 See, particularly, Hall, supra n.10.

40 J.S. Prichard and Alan Brudner, 'Tort Liability for Breach of Statute: A Natural Rights Perspective,' *Law & Philosophy* 2 (1983) 89 at 111.

41 See chapter 7.

42 John H. Newman, *The Idea of a University* (1852; rep. London: Longmans Green 1929) at 461: 'The philosophy of an imperial intellect ... is based, not so much on simplification as on discrimination. It's true representative defines, rather than analyzes.'

43 Glanville Williams, *Criminal Law: The General Part,* 2nd ed. (London: Stevens and Sons 1961), S.43.

44 M. Kelman, 'Interpretive Construction in the Substantive Criminal Law,' *Stanford L.R.* 33 (1981) 591 at 652.

45 Hall, supra n.10 at 136, 138.

46 John Andenaes, 'Determinism and Criminal Law,' *Journal of Cr. Law, Crim. & Police Sc.* 47 (1956) 406.

47 Holmes, Jr, supra n.13.

48 Kelman, supra n.44.

49 For an extended reference, see C. Howard, *Strict Responsibility* (London: Sweet and Maxwell 1963) at 1n.3.

50 R. Perkins, *Criminal Law*, 2nd ed. (New York: Foundation Press 1969) at 784ff.; F. Sayre, 'Public Welfare Offenses,' *Col. L.R.* 33 (1933) 55; Law Reform Commission of Canada, *Studies in Strict Liability* (Ottawa: Supplies and Services 1974).

51 (1978) 2 S.C.R. 1299.

52 Ibid. at 1302, 1309.

53 Some scholars have undertaken the difficult task of stating an ostensive criteria for identifying regulatory offences. For instance, according to J.E. Starrs, these are: (1) concrete damage is unnecessary; (2) guilty intent is not required; (3) an act and an omission to act are punished; (4) the penalty is usually a light monetary fine; (5) widespread public injury is probable; (7) an act not universally or even popularly deemed reprehensible is prohibited; and (8) an act by which no dangerous personality is revealed is punished': Starrs, supra n.32. See also Sayre, supra n.50.

54 See, *inter alia*, E.H. Sutherland, *White Collar Crime* (Westport, Conn.: Greenwood

Press 1949); Terrence Morris, 'The Social Toleration of Crime,' in *Changing Concepts of Crime and Its Treatment*, ed. H.J. Klare (New York: Pergamon Press 1966) at 13–34; W.G. Carson, 'The Institutionalization of Ambiguity: Early British Factory Acts,' in *White-Collar Crime: Theory and Research*, ed. Gilbert Geiss and Ezra Stotland (Beverley Hills: Sage Publications 1980) 142–73; Barry Feld, 'The Political Economy of Corporate Regulation: The Structural Origins of White Collar Crime,' in *Law and Society: Sociological Perspectives on Criminal Law*, ed. J.M. Inverarity et al. (Boston: Little, Brown 1983) at 216–42; R.C. Fuller, 'Morals and the Criminal Law,' *Jour. of Cr. Law & Crim.* 32 (1942) 624; S.H. Kadish, 'Some Observations on the Use of Criminal Sanctions in Enforcing Economic Regulations,' *Univ. of Chic. L.R.* 30 (1963) 423; H.V. Ball and Lawrence M. Friedman, 'The Use of Criminal Sanctions in the Enforcement of Economic Legislation: A Sociological View,' *Stanford L.R.* 17 (1964–5) 197; W.G. Carson, 'Some Sociological Aspects of Strict Liability and the Enforcement of Factory Legislation,' *Modern L.R.* 33 (1970) 396; Neil Sargent, 'Law, Ideology and Corporate Crime: A Critique of Instrumentalism,' *Can. J. of Law and Society* 4 (1989) 39.

55　See chapters 5 and 6.

56　See D.R. Kelley, *The Human Measure: Social Thought in the Western Legal Tradition* (Cambridge, Mass.: Harvard University Press 1990) at 165–86.

57　See chapter 5.

58　I *Commentaries* 58.

59　See chapter 5, n.162.

60　See R. Pound, *The Ideal Element in Law* (Calcutta: Calcutta University Press 1958) at 31.

61　R.C.B. Risk, 'The Law and the Economy in Mid-Nineteenth Century Ontario: A Perspective,' in *Essays in the History of Canadian Law*, ed. David H. Flaherty (Toronto: University of Toronto Press 1981) 88 at 105.

62　After the parliamentary Reform Acts of 1832–48, the rulers of England were what Alfred Whitehead called 'pure liberals'; they did not deem it the proper function of the government to attempt to remedy the moral and social evils created by the boom in commercial and industrial activities. See A.N. Whitehead, *Adventures of Ideas* (Cambridge: Cambridge University Press 1933) at 43.

63　See chapter 5.

64　Defined as 'non-harzardous adulteration that degrades the general quality of a good as perceived by consumers': Donna J. Wood, 'The Strategic Use of Public Policy: Business Support for the 1906 Food and Drug Act,' *Bus. Hist. Rev.* 59 (1985) 403 at 408. For an informative discussion of three of the fierce legal battles fought by pure-food activists and the business world, see James H. Young, 'Three Southern Food and Drug Cases,' *Journal of Southern Hist.* 49 (1983) 1.

65　Constance B. Backhouse, 'Nineteenth Century Canadian Rape Law, 1800–92,' in

Essays in the History of Canadian Law, ed. David H. Flaherty (Toronto: University of Toronto Press 1983), 2: at 200–47.

66 See Fredrick K. Grittner, *White Slavery: Myth, Ideology and American Law* (New York: Garland 1990); John McLaren, 'White-Slavers: The Reform of Canada's Prostitution Laws and Patterns of Enforcement 1900–1920,' *Criminal Justice History* 8 (1987) 53; John McLaren, 'The Canadian Magistracy and the Anti-White Slavery Campaign 1900–1920,' in *Canadian Perspectives on Law and Society: Issues in Legal History*, ed. W. Wesley Pue and Barry Wright (Ottawa: Carleton University Press 1988) at 329–53.

67 See chapter 6.

68 Inglis, supra n.35, passim. Cf: Charles Darwin, *The Origin of Species* (1859), ed. J.W. Burrow (Penguin 1987) at 119: '[L]ighten any check, mitigate the destruction ever so little, and the number of the species will almost instantaneously increase to any amount. The face of Nature may be compared to a yielding surface, with ten thousand sharp wedges packed close together and driven inwards by incessant blows, sometimes one wedge being struck, and then another with greater force.'

69 Morton J. Horwitz, 'The Rise of Legal Formalism,' *Am. J. of Legal Hist.* 19 (1975) 251, rep. *The Transformation of American Law 1780–1860*, supra n.38.

70 A. Linton Davidson, *The Genesis and Growth of Food and Drug Administration in Canada* (Ottawa: Department of National Health and Welfare 1949) at 97.

71 I. Paulus, 'Strict Liability: Its Place in Public Welfare Offences,' *Cr. L.Q.* 20 (1977/78) 445 at 460; R.M. Jackson, 'Absolute Prohibition in Statutory Offences,' *Camb. L.J.* (1938) 83.

72 H.W. Wiley, *The History of a Crime Against the Food Law* (rep. New York: Arno Press 1976); Gabriel Kolko, *The Triumph of Conservatism* (New York: Free Press 1963); Carman D. Baggarley, *The Emergence of the Regulatory State in Canada, 1867–1939*, Technical Report no. 15 (Economic Council of Canada, 1981); Wood, supra n.64.

73 See, *inter alia*, Joseph C. Goulden, *The Million Dollar Lawyers* (New York: Putnam's Sons 1977); C. Borrell and B. Cashinells, *Crime in Britain Today* (London: Routledge and Kegal Paul 1975); P. Brodeur, *Outrageous Misconduct: The Asbestos Industry on Trial* (New York: Pantheon Books 1985).

74 [1874–80] All E.R. 881, 44 L.J.M.C. 122.

75 (1869) L.R. 1 C.C.R. 184, 38 L.J.M.C. 61.

76 See G.O.W. Mueller, 'Mens Rea and the Law Without It,' *W. Virg. L.R.* 58 (1955–6) 34 at 48.

77 See W.T.S. Stallybrass, 'The Eclipse of Mens Rea,' *Law Quarterly Rev.* 52 (1936) 60 at 65.

78 At common law bigamy was not a crime. It was made a felony in 1603 by 1 James 1, c. 11.

79 (1933) 149 L.T. 542, 24 Cr. App. Rep. 74.

80 Hall, supra n.10 at 329n.14.

81 *Studies in Strict Liability* (Law Reform Commission of Canada) at 171.

82 Mueller, supra n.76 at 44.

83 Consider the fireside reflections of some criminal law scholars. Mueller, supra n.76 at 35, 36 states that 'the sphere of crime is no longer that body of disapproved conduct which is a cultural heritage of a people and known to every sane adult to be so. The law stepped faster, too fast to be absorbed into the body of the rules of ethics, of culture. The law have grown fast; ethics have grown barely.' Hall, supra n.10 at 331, writes '[T]he public welfare enactments are relatively new. They represent adaptations to an intricate economy, including an impersonal market ... the modern regulations are not strongly supported by the mores. Their occurrence does not arouse the resentment directed at the perpetrators of traditional crimes.'

84 Devlin, supra n.36 at 27.

85 Fitzgerald, supra n.18 at 354.

86 H.M. Hart, 'The Aims of the Criminal Law,' *Law & Contemporary Problems* 23 (1958) 401.

87 J. Hall, 'Prolegomena to a Science of Criminal Law,' *Univ. of Penn. L.R.* 89 (1940–1) 549 at 566. This is so in a limited sense. 'The unfortunate effect of the *mala in se-mala prohibita doctrine*,' Hall wrote, 'when interpreted as an application of the natural law-convention distinction, has been the setting up of a rigid dichotomy between traditional harms and the mass of petty misdemeanors which were accordingly declared completely un-moral. A truer interpretation ... is provided by the notion of "continuum" which suggests a range in morality from the major moral principles to the least of ethical norms ... None of such law is morally indifferent.' Cf: Hall, supra n.10 at 341.

88 See, for example, Law Reform Commission of Canada, *Our Criminal Law*; *Law Commission Report No. 143* (London: Her Majesty's Stationery Office 1986).

89 R. Pound, *Law and Morals*, 2nd ed. (Chapel Hill: University of North Carolina Press 1926) at 74.

90 H.L.A. Hart, 'Prolegomenon to the Principles of Punishment,' in supra n.9 at 6.

91 Arthur O. Lovejoy, *The Great Chain of Being* (Cambridge, Mass.: Harvard University Press 1936) at 6.

92 Pound, supra n.35 at 204.

93 Jerome Hall, *Law, Social Science and Criminal Law* (Littleton, Colo.: Fred B. Rothman 1982) at 263.

94 Fletcher, supra n.16 at xxii.

Conclusion: A Leap over Rhodes

1 Plato, *Cratylus* 438, 439, *The Dialogues of Plato*, 4 vols., trans. B. Jowett, 1

(New York: Random House 1937): 'But if this is a battle of names, some of them asserting that they are like the truth, others contending that *they* are, how or by what criterion are we to decide between them? ... The knowledge of things is not to be derived from names ... No; they must be studied and investigated in themselves.' (Emphasis in the original.)

2 Rodolfo Sacco, 'Legal Formants: A Dynamic Approach to Comparative Law,' *Am. J. Comp. Law* 39 (1991) 1 at 12.

3 In the sense in which it was succinctly put by R. Stammler, 'Fundamental Tendencies in Modern Jurisprudence,' *Mich. L.R.* 21 (1922–3) 623 at 639: '"The idea" signifies the concept of the absolute totality of all conceivable experiences.' However, I would substitute the word 'available' for 'conceivable' in this quotation.

4 As Locke succinctly puts it, 'if we but separate the Idea under consideration from the sign that stands for it, our Knowledge goes equally on in the discovery of real Truth and Certainty, whatever Sounds we make use of': Locke, *Essay Concerning Human Understanding*, IV, Chap. IV, 9.27–30.

5 Morris L. Cohen, 'The Place of Logic in the Law,' *Harvard L.R.* 29 (1915–16) 622 at 624.

6 Joseph Glanvill, *The Vanity of Dogmatizing: The Three Versions*, ed. Stephen Medcalf (Harvester Renaissance Library I, Harvester Press 1970), III, 31.

7 See chapter 7.

8 Mark DeWolfe Howe, 'The Positivism of Mr. Justice Holmes,' *Harvard L.R.* 64 (1950–1) 529 at 534.

9 See chapter 7.

10 H.L.A. Hart, *The Concept of Law* (Oxford: Oxford University Press 1961) at 189–95.

11 Hans Kelsen, *General Theory of Law and State*, trans. Anders Wedberg (Cambridge, Mass.: Harvard University Press 1946).

12 Hart, supra n.10 at 199.

13 Ibid.

14 Kelsen, supra n.11 at xv.

15. H.L.A. Hart, 'Bentham's *Of Laws in General*,' in *Essays on Bentham* (Oxford: Clarendon Press 1982), chapter 5, 105 at 108.

16. Bentham, *Of Laws in General*, ed. H.L.A. Hart (London: Athlone Press 1970).

17 The version of *Of Laws in General* edited and published in 1945 by Charles W. Everett.

18 Hart, supra n.15.

19 Everett, supra n.17 at 58.

20 Ibid. at 85.

21 *Chrestomathia* III, 126n, cited in R. Harrison, *Bentham* (London: Routledge and Kegan Paul 1983) at 56. (Emphasis in the original.) On the whole, Bentham eliminated the 'immaterial' or 'spiritual' altogether: See James E. Crimmins, *Secular Util-*

itarianism: Social Science and the Critique of Religion in the Thought of Jeremy Bentham (Oxford: Clarendon Press 1990), passim.

22 Harrison, ibid.

23 'If it be true that our ideas are derived all of them from our senses and that the only way of rendering any of our ideas clear and determinate is to trace it up to the sensible objects in which it originates the only method that can be taken for explaining them to the purpose is the method ... of paraphrasis': *Of Laws in General*, supra n.16 at 294.

24 'To define or ... expound a word, is to resolve, or make a progress towards resolving, the idea belonging to it into simple ones.' 'For expounding the words ... that abound so much in ethics and jurisprudence ... the only method by which any instruction can be conveyed is ... the method [of] *paraphrasis*.' Further, 'a word may be said to be expounded by paraphrasis when not that *word* alone is translated into other words, but some whole *sentence* of which it forms a part is translated into another sentence; the words of which latter are expressive of such ideas as are *simple*, or are more immediately resolvable into simple ones than those of the former.' Jeremy Bentham, *A Comment on the Commentaries and A Fragment on Government,* ed. J.H. Burns and H.L.A. Hart (London: Athlone Press 1977) at 495 nn.1(4), (5), (6). Elsewhere, Bentham described the method of paraphrasis thus: 'By the word paraphrasis may be designated that sort of exposition which may be afforded by transmuting into a proposition, having for its subject some real entity, a proposition which has not for its subject any other than a fictitious entity': Bentham, *Logic* VIII, 246, cited in Harrison, supra n. 21 at 58. For an extensive discussion, see ibid., chapter 4.

25 Bentham, supra n.16 at 251–2.

26 Harrison, supra n.21 at 98; H.L.A. Hart, 'Bentham and the Demystification of the Law,' in supra n.15; Gerald J. Postema, *Bentham and The Common Law Tradition* (Oxford: Clarendon Press 1986).

27 Harrison, supra n. 21 at 58.

28 Ulrich Verster, *Philosophical Arguments* (Oxford: Academic Publications 1992) at 154. (Emphasis added.)

29 Aristotle, *Analytica Posteriora,* Bk. I, 2 10. 71b.

30 Verster, supra n.28.

31 Henry Sidgwick, *Philosophy: Its Scope and Relations* (London: MacMillan 1902) at 25. (Emphasis added.)

32 G.W.F. Hegel, *The Philosophy of Right* (preface), trans. T.M. Knox, vol. 46 of *Great Books of the Western World* (Encyclopaedia Britannica 1952).

33 This principle 'defines knowledge as *adaequatio rei et intellectus* – the understanding of the knower must be *adequate* to the thing to be known': E.F. Schumacher, *A Guide for the Perplexed* (New York: Harper and Row 1977) at 39.

34 Ralph Cudworth, *A Treatise Concerning Eternal and Immutable Morality* (1731; rep. New York: Garland Publishing 1976), passim.

35 W. Kneale, *The Responsibility of Criminals* (Oxford: Clarendon Press 1967) at 13.

36 See, for example, Andrew E. Lelling, 'Eliminative Materialism, Neuroscience and the Criminal Law,' *Univ. of Penn. L.R.* 141 (1993) 1471; Richard A. Posner, *The Problems of Jurisprudence* (Cambridge, Mass.: Harvard University Press 1991).

37 G. Ryle, *The Concept of Mind* (London: Hutchinson Press 1949) at 128.

38 H.L.A. Hart, 'Acts of Will and Responsibility,' in H.L.A. Hart, *Punishment and Responsibility* (Oxford: Oxford University Press 1968) at 112.

39 Schedule B, Canada Act 1982, c. 11.

40 Ibid. s.7.

41 See Christopher P. Manfredi, 'Fundamental Justice in the Supreme Court of Canada: Decisions under s.7 of the Charter of Rights and Freedoms, 1984–1988,' *American J. of Comp. Law* 38 (1990) 653; W.J. Blacklock, 'The Post-Vaillancourt Era,' *Crown's Newsletter* 3 (1991) 1; Graeme G. Mitche, 'Significant Developments in Criminal Charter Jurisprudence, 1993–4,' *Cr. L.Q. 37* (1995) 461 at 463–73.

Bibliography

Agretelis, D. '"Mens Rea" in Plato and Aristotle.' *Issues in Criminology* 1 (1965–6) 19.

Allen, C.K. *Legal Duties.* Oxford: Clarendon Press 1931.

Andenaes, J., 'Determinism and Criminal Law." *J. of Cr. Law, Crim. & Police Science* 47 (1956) 406.

Anderson, J.W. *The Illiterate Anglo-Saxon.* Cambridge: Cambridge University Press 1946.

Archibald, C. 'The Constitutionalization of the General Part of Criminal Law.' *Can. Bar Rev.* 67 (1988) 403.

Aristotle. *Analytica Posteriora.*

Arnold, Thurman W. *The Symbols of Government.* New Haven, Conn.: Yale University Press 1935.

Artz, Frederick B. *The Mind of the Middle Ages, A.D. 200–1500: A Historical Survey.* 3rd ed. Chicago: University of Chicago Press, 1980.

Atiyah, P.S., and R.S. Summers. *Form and Substance in Anglo-American Law.* Oxford: Clarendon Press 1987.

Attenborough, F.L. *The Laws of the Earliest English Kings.* New York: Russell and Russell 1963.

Austin, John. *Lectures on Jurisprudence*, 2 vols., 3rd and 4th eds. Ed. R. Campbell. London: John Murray 1869, 1873.

Backhouse, Constance B. 'Nineteenth Century Canadian Rape Law, 1800–92.' In *Essays in the History of Canadian Law*, ed. David H. Flaherty. Toronto: University of Toronto Press 1981.

Baggarley, Carman D. *The Emergence of the Regulatory State in Canada, 1867–1939.* Technical Report no. 15, Economic Council of Canada 1981.

Bailyn, B. *The Ideological Origins of the American Revolution.* Cambridge, Mass.: Belknap Press 1967.

Baldwin, F. Elizabeth. *Sumptuary Legislation and Personal Regulation in England.* Vol.

49, Johns Hopkins University Studies in History and Political Science. Baltimore: Johns Hopkins University Press 1926.

Ball, H.V., and Lawrence M. Friedman, 'The Use of Criminal Sanctions in the Enforcement of Economic Legislation: A Sociological View.' *Stanford L.R.* 17 (1964–5) 197.

Barker, Ernest, 'Reflections on English Political Theory.' *Political Studies* 1–2 (1953–4) 6.

Barlow, F. *The Norman Conquest and Beyond.* London: Hambledon Press 1983.

Bartholomew, G.W. 'The Ancient Codes and Modern Science.' *Univ. of Tasmania L.R.* 1 (1958–63) 429.

Bartrip, P.W.J. 'State Intervention in Mid-19th Century Britain: Fact or Fiction?' *J. of British Studies* 23 (1983) 63.

Bassett, William W. 'Canon Law and the Common Law.' *Hastings L.J.* 29 (1978) 1383.

Baxter, Timothy M.S. *The Cratylus: Plato's Critique of Naming.* New York: E.J. Brill 1992.

Becker, E. 'The Problem of Legal Analysis.' *Yale L.J.* 54 (1945) 809.

Bellamy, John G. *Criminal Law and Society in Late Medieval and Tudor England.* New York: St Martin's Press 1984.

Bentham, Jeremy. *The Limits of Jurisprudence Defin*ed. Ed. Charles W. Everett. New York: Columbia University Press 1945.

– *An Introduction to the Principles of Morals and Legislation.* Ed. H.L.A. Hart and J.H. Burns. London: Anthone Press 1970.

– *A Comment on the Commentaries and A Fragment on Government.* Ed. J.H. Burns and H.L.A. Hart. London: Athlone Press 1977.

Beresford, M.W. 'The Common Informer, the Penal Statutes and Economic Regulation.' *Econ. Hist. Rev.* 2nd Ser., 10 (1957) 221.

Berman, Harold J. *Law and Revolution: The Formation of the Western Legal Tradition.* Cambridge, Mass.: Harvard University Press 1983.

– 'Origins of Historical Jurisprudence.' *Yale L.J.* 103 (1994) 1651.

Bichenbach, Jerome E. 'Empiricism and Law.' Review of W.L. Morison, *John Austin.* Stanford: Stanford University Press 1982. *U.T.L.J.* 35 (1985) 94.

Birch, D.J. 'The Foresight Saga: The Biggest Mistake of All?' *Cr. L.R.* (1988) 4.

Blacklock, W.J. 'The Post-Vaillancourt Era.' *Crown Newsletter* 3 (1991) 1.

Blackstone, Sir William. *Commentaries.* 4 vols.

Blaug, Mark. 'The Classical Economists and the Factory Acts: A Re-Examination.' *Quarterly J. of Econ.* (1958) 211.

Boas, F. *The Mind of Primitive Man* (1938; rep. Westport, Conn.: Greenwood Press 1983.

Bodenheimer, Edgar. 'Modern Analytical Jurisprudence and the Limits of Its Usefulness.' *Univ. of Penn. L.R.* 104 (1956) 1080.

Bodenstein, H.D.J. 'Phases in the Development of Criminal Mens Rea.' *S.A.L.J.* 36 (1919) 323.

Bolgar, R.R. *The Classical Heritage and Its Beneficiaries.* Cambridge: Cambridge University Press 1958.

Boorstin, J. 'Tradition and Method in Legal History.' *Harvard L.R.* 54 (1941) 424.

Borrell, C., and B. Cashinells. *Crime in Britain Today.* London: Routledge and Kegan Paul 1975.

Bowden, W. *Industrial Society in England towards the End of the Eighteenth Century.* 2nd ed. London: Frank Cass 1965.

Bracton. *On the Laws and Customs of England.* 4 vols. Trans. Samuel E. Thorne. Cambridge, Mass.: Belknap Press 1968.

Bradshaw, F. *A Social History of England.* London: Clive University Tutorial Press 1918.

Brady, James M. 'Punishment for Negligence: A Reply to Professor Hall.' *Buffalo L.R.* 22 (1973) 107.

Brett, P. *An Inquiry into Criminal Guilt.* London: Sweet and Maxwell 1963.

– 'Strict Responsibility: Possible Solutions.' *Modern L.R.* 37 (1974) 417.

Brewer, J., and John Styles, eds. *An Ungovernable People.* New Brunswick, N.J.: Rutger's University Press 1980.

Brodeur, P. *Outrageous Misconduct.* New York: Pantheon Books 1983.

Brown, B. 'The Emergence of the Psychical Test in Guilt in Homicide, 1200–1550.' *Univ. of Tasmania L.R.* 1 (1958–63) 231.

Brunner, H. *The Sources of the Law of England.* Edinburgh: T. and T. Clark 1898.

Burrow, J.W. *A Liberal Descent: Victorian Historians and the British Past.* Cambridge: Cambridge University Press 1981.

Butterfield, H. *The Whig Interpretation of History.* London: G. Bell 1963.

Caesar, *Commentaries on the Gallic War.* Trans. T. Rice Holmes. London: Macmillan 1908.

Campbell, E. 'German Influences in English Legal Education and Jurisprudence in the 19th Century.' *University of Western Australia Annual L.R.* 4 (1957–9) 357.

Carson, W.G. 'The Institutionalization of Ambiguity: Early British Factory Acts.' In *White-Collar Crime: Theory and Research.* Ed. Gilbert Geiss and Ezra Stotland. Beverly Hills: Sage Publications 1980.

Chandler, Alice. *A Dream of Order: The Medieval Ideal in Nineteenth Century English Literature.* Lincoln: University of Nebraska Press 1970.

Chaney, William A. 'Paganism to Christianity in Anglo-Saxon England.' *Harv. Theological Rev.* 53 (1960) 197.

Chapman, Bruce, and Michael J. Trebilcock. 'Punitive Damages: Divergence in Search of a Rationale.' *Alabama L.R.* 740 (1989) 41.

Checkland, S. *The Rise of Industrial Society in England, 1815–1885.* London: Longmans, Green 1964.

– *British Public Policy, 1776–1939.* Cambridge: Cambridge University Press 1983.

Cherry, R.R. *Lectures on the Growth of Criminal Law in Ancient Communities.* London: MacMillan 1890.

Cheyney, E.P. *An Introduction to the Industrial and Social History of England.* New York: Macmillan 1908.

Chitton, Bradley S. 'Cliobernetics, Christianity and the Common Law.' *Law Library Journal* 83 (1991) 315.

Chloros, A.G. 'Some Aspects of the Social and Ethical Elements in Analytical Jurisprudence.' *Juridical Rev.* 67 (1955) 79.

Clarkson, L.A. 'English Economic Policy in the Sixteenth and Seventeenth Centuries: The Case of the Leather Industry.' *Bulletin of the Institute of Hist. Research,* 38 (1965) 147.

Clemoes, Peter. *Anglo-Saxon England.* Cambridge: Cambridge University Press 1974. Volume 3.

Coffee, John C. '"No Soul to Damn, No Body to Kick": An Unscandalized Inquiry into the Problem of Corporate Punishment.' *Mich. L.R.* 79 (1981) 386

Cohen, Morris L. 'The Common Law in the American Legal System: The Challenge of Conceptual Research.' *Law Library Journal* 81 (1989) 13.

Cohen, Morris R. 'The Place of Logic in the Law.' *Harvard L.R.* 29 (1915–6) 622.

Coke, Sir Edward. *Third Institute.*

Cole, W.A. 'Trends in Eighteenth Century Smuggling.' *Econ. Hist. Rev.* 10 (1957) 395.

Colvin, Eric. *Principles of Criminal Law.* Toronto: Carswell 1986.

Cook, Peter J. 'The Demise of the Game Law System: A Study in Attitudes.' *Holdsworth L.R.* 8 (1983) 121.

Cooke, C.A. 'Adam Smith and Jurisprudence.' *L.Q.R.* 51 (1935) 326.

Coquillette, Daniel R. 'Legal Ideology and Incorporation I: The English Civilian Writers, 1523–1607.' *Bos. Univ. L.R.* 61 (1981) 1.

Corrado, Michael. *The Analytic Tradition in Philosophy: Background and Issues.* Chicago: American Library Association 1975.

Cosgrove, Richard A. 'The Reception of Analytic Jurisprudence: The Victorian Debate on the Separation of Law and Morality 1860–1900.' *Durham University Journal,* 74 (1981) 47.

Cragg, Gerald R. *Reason and Authority in the Eighteenth Century.* Cambridge: Cambridge University Press 1964.

Craig, H. *The Enchanted Glass.* Oxford: Basil Blackwell 1960.

Crawford, J.M.B., and J.F. Quinn. *The Christian Foundations of Criminal Responsibility.* Vol. 40, *Toronto Studies in Theology.* Queenston, N.Y.: Edwin Mellen Press 1991.

Cudworth, R. *A Treatise Concerning Eternal and Immutable Morality.* (1731; rep. New York: Garland Publishing 1976).

Dan-Cohen, Meir. 'Responsibility and the Boundaries of the Self.' *Harv. L.R.* 105 (1992) 959.

Davidson, A. Linton. *The Genesis and Growth of Food and Drug Administration in Canada.* Ottawa: Department of National Health and Welfare 1949.

Davis, W., and P. Fouracre, eds. *The Settlement of Disputes in Early Medieval Europe.* Cambridge: Cambridge University Press 1986.

Delmonte, John. 'Negligence; A Reappraisal of Its Validity as a Basis for Criminal Liability and Sanction.' *South Texas L.J.* 20 (1979) 179.

de Montmorency, J.E.G. 'State Protection of Animals at Home and Abroad.' *L.Q.R.* 18 (1902) 31.

D'Entreves, A.P. 'On The Nature of Political Obligation.' *Philosophy* 43 (1968) 309.

Devlin, P. *The Enforcement of Morals.* London: Oxford University Press 1965.

Diamond, A.S. *The Evolution of Law and Order.* London: Watts 1951.

Dicey, A.V. *Law and Public Opinion in England during the Nineteenth Century.* 2nd ed. London: Macmillan 1962.

Dingle, A.E., '"The Monster Nuisance of All": Landowners, Alkali Manufacturers and Air Pollution 1828–64.' *Econ. Hist. Rev.* 35 (1982) 529.

Dowell, S. *A History of Taxation and Taxes in England.* 3rd ed., vols. 1 and 2 (1884; rep. New York: Augustus M. Kelley 1965.

Downer, L.J. Ed. *Leges Henrici Primi.* Oxford: Clarendon Press 1972.

Drapkin, Israel. *Crime and Punishment in the Ancient World.* Toronto: Lexington Books 1989.

Dworkin, R. *Taking Rights Seriously.* Cambridge: Mass.: Harvard University Press 1977.

– *Law's Empire.* Cambridge, Mass.: Harvard University Press 1986.

Edgar, Harold. 'Mens Rea.' In *Encylopaedia of Criminal Justice* 4 vols., 3: 1029.

Edgeworth, Brendan. 'Legal Positivism and the Philosophy of Language: A Critique of H.L.A. Hart's "Descriptive Sociology."' *Legal Studies* 6 (1986) 115.

Edwards, J.Ll.J. 'The Criminal Degrees of Knowledge.' *Modern L.R.* 17 (1954) 294.

– *Mens Rea in Statutory Offences.* London: Macmillan 1955.

– 'Automatism and Criminal Responsibility.' *Modern L.R.* 21 (1958) 375.

Emsley, C. *Crime and Society in England, 1750–1900.* London: Longman 1987.

Erlinger, C.P. 'Mens Rea, Due Process and the Supreme Court: Toward a Constitutional Doctrine of Substantive Criminal Law.' *Am. J. of Cr. Law* 9 (1981) 163.

Ernst, Daniel R. 'The Moribund Appeal of Death: Compensating Survivors and Control- ling Jurors in Early Modern England.' *Am. J. of Legal Hist.* 28 (1984) 64.

Feaver, George A. 'The Political Attitudes of Sir Henry Maine.' *Journal of Politics* (1965) 290.

Feld, Barry. 'The Political Economy of Corporate Regulation: The Structural Origin of

White Collar Crime.' In *Law and Society: Sociological Perspectives on Criminal Law*. Ed. J.M. Inverarity et al. Boston: Little, Brown 1983.

Feldman, D., 'The King's Peace, the Royal prerogative and Public Order: The Roots and Early Development of Binding Over Powers.' *Cambridge L.J.* 47 (1988) 101.

Fennell, Caroline. 'Intention in Murder: Chaos, Confusion and Complexity.' *N.I.L.Q.* 41 (1990) 325.

Fifoot, C.H.S. *English Law and Its Background*. London: G. Bell and Sons 1932.

Figgis, F.N. *The Divine Right of Kings*. 2nd ed. Cambridge: Cambridge University Press 1922.

Fine, Robert P., and M. Cohen. 'Is Criminal Negligence a Defensible Basis for Penal Liability?' *Buffalo L.R.* 16 (1967) 749.

Fisher, D.J.V. *The Anglo-Saxon Age, 410–1042*. London: Longmans 1973.

Fiss, Owen M. 'The Supreme Court 1978 Term – Forward: The Forms of Justice.' *Harvard L.R.* 93 (1979) 1.

Fitzgerald, P.J. 'Crime, Sin and Negligence.' *L.Q.R.* 379 (1963) 51.

Fletcher, George P. 'The Theory of Criminal Negligence: A Comparative Analysis.' *U. Pa. L.R.* 119 (1971) 401.

– *Rethinking Criminal Law*. Toronto and Boston: Little, Brown 1978.

Fuller, R.C. 'Morals and the Criminal Law.' *J. of Crim. Law, Crim. & Pol Science* 32 (1942) 624.

Gaskell, P. *The Manufacturing Population of England*. London: Baldwin and Cradock, 1833.

Gierke, Otto von. *Political Theories of the Middle Age*. Trans. F.W. Maitland. Cambridge: Cambridge University Press 1900.

Gilmore, Myron P. *Argument from Roman Law in Political Thought, 1200–1600*. Cambridge, Mass.: Harvard University Press 1941.

Glanvill. *The Treatise on the Laws and Customs of the Realm of England*. Ed. G.D.G. Hall. London: Thomas Nelson and Sons 1965.

Glanville, Joseph. *The Vanity of Dogmatizing: The Three 'Versions.'* Ed. Stephen Medcalf. Harvester Press 1970.

Gluckman, Max. *The Allocation of Responsibility*. Manchester: Manchester University Press 1972.

Goodrich, Peter, '*Ars Bablativa*: Ramism, Rhetoric, and the Genealogy of English Jurisprudence.' In *Legal Hermeneutics, History, Theory, and Practice*. Ed. G. Leyh. Berkely: University of California Press 1992.

– 'Poor Illiterate Reason: History, Nationalism and Common Law.' *Social and Legal Studies* 1 (1992) 7.

Gordon, Gerald H. 'Subjective and Objective Mens Rea.' *Cr. L.Q.* 17 (1974–5) 353.

Green, T.A. *Verdict According to Conscience*. Chicago: University of Chicago Press 1985.

Greenleaf, W.H. *Order, Empiricism and Politics: Two Traditions of English Political Thought 1500–1700*. Oxford: Oxford University Press 1964.

Griffith, J. 'Is Law Important?' *N.Y.U.L. Rev.* 54 (1979) 339.

Grittner, Fredrick K. *White Slavery: Myth, Ideology and American Law*. New York: Garland Publications 1990.

Gross, Hyman. *A Theory of Criminal Justice*. New York: Oxford University Press 1979.

Hale, Matthew. *The History of the Common Law of England*. Ed. Charles M. Gray. Chicago: University of Chicago Press 1971.

Hall, J. *General Principles of Criminal Law*. 2nd ed. Indianapolis: Bobb-Merrill 1960.

– 'Negligent Behavior Should Be Excluded from Penal Liability.' *Col. L.R.* 63 (1963) 632.

– *Law, Social Science and Criminal Law*. Littleton, Colo.: Fred B. Rothman 1982.

Harding, Alan. *A Social History of English Law*. London: Penguin Books 1966.

Harrison, Ross. *Bentham*. London: Routledge and Keagan Paul 1983.

Harriss, G.L. 'Aids, Loans and Benevolences.' *Hist. Journal* 6 (1963) 1.

Hart, H.L.A. 'Philosophy of Law and Jurisprudence in Britain.' *Am. J. of Comp. Law* 2 (1953) 355.

– 'Analytical Jurisprudence in Mid-20th Century: A Reply to Professor Bodenheimer.' *Univ. of Penn. L.R.* 104 (1957) 952.

– *The Concept of Law*. Oxford: Oxford Univ. Press, 1961.

– *Punishment and Responsibility*. Oxford: Oxford University Press, 1968.

– 'The Ascription of Responsibility and Legal Rights.' *Proc. of Arist. Society* 49, new series (1948–9) 171.

– 'Bentham and the Demystification of the Law.' *Modern L.R.* 36 (1973) 28.

Hart, H.M. 'The Aims of the Criminal Law.' *Law & Contemporary Problems* 23 (1958) 401.

Hawkins. *Pleas of the Crown*, 2 vols. London: Professional Books 1973.

Hay, D. 'Poaching and the Game Laws on Cannock Case.' In *Albion's Fatal Tree*. Ed. D. Hay et al. New York: Pantheon Books 1975.

– 'Property, Authority and the Criminal Law.' In *Albion's Fatal Tree*.

– 'The Criminal Prosecution in England and Its Historians.' *Modern L.R.* 47 (1984) 1.

Hay, D. et al., eds. *Albion's Fatal Tree*. New York: Pantheon Books 1975.

Hayek, F.A. *Capitalism and the Historians*. Chicago: University of Chicago Press 1954.

– *The Constitution of Liberty*. London: Routledge and Kegan Paul 1960.

– *Law, Legislation and Liberty*. Vol. 3. Chicago: University of Chicago Press 1981.

Hazeltine, H.D. 'Roman and Canon Law in the Middle Ages.' In *Cambridge Medieval History*, 8 vols. vol. 5. Cambridge: Cambridge University Press 1936.

Helmholz, R.H. *Canon Law and The Law of England*. London: Hambledon Press 1980.

Hexter, J.H., 'Hobbes and the Law.' *Cornell L.R.* 15 (1980) 471.

Himmerfarb, G. *Victorian Minds*. New York: Alfred Knopf 1961.

Hippard, James J., Sr 'The Constitutionality of Criminal Liability Without Fault: An Argument for a Constitutional Doctrine of Mens Rea." *Houston L.R.* 10 (1974) 1039.

Hobbes, T. *Leviathan.* Ed. W.G. Pogson-Smith. Oxford: Clarendon Press 1909.

– *De Cive.* (1651) Ed. H. Warrender. Oxford: Clarendon Press 1983.

Hocking, W.E. 'Ways of Thinking about Right: A New Theory of the Relation Between Law and Morals.' In *Law: A Century of Progress, 1835–1935,* 3 vols. vol. 2. New York: University Press 1935.

Hodgkin, T. *The History of England from the Earliest Times to the Norman Conquest.* Vol. 1, *The Political History of England.* Ed. M. Hunt and R.L. Poole. London: 1906.

Hoeflich, M.H. 'John Austin and Joseph Story: Two Nineteenth Century Perspectives on the Utility of the Civil Law for the Common Lawyer.' *Am. J. of Legal Hist.* 29 (1985) 36.

– 'Transatlantic Friendships and the German Influence on American Law in the First Half of the 19th Century.' *Am. J. of Comp. Law* 35 (1987) 599.

Hoh-Cheung, and L.H. Mui. 'Smuggling and the British Tea Trade before 1784.' *American Hist. Rev.* 74 (1968) 441.

Holdsworth, W.S. *A History of English Law.* 3rd. ed. Vol. 2. London: Methuen 1923.

– 'A Neglected Aspect Between Economics and Legal History.' *Economic Hist. Rev.* 1 (1927) 114.

– *Historians of Anglo-American Law.* New York: Columbia University Press 1928.

– *Some Lessons From Our Legal History.* New York: Macmillan 1928.

Holmes, O.W., Jr. *The Common Law.* 1883; rep. Cambridge, Mass.: Belknap Press 1963.

– 'The Path of the Law.' *Harvard L.R.* (1897) 457.

Horwitz, M. 'History and Theory.' *Yale L.J.* 97 (1987) 1825.

Horwitz, Morton J. *The Transformation of American Law, 1780–1860.* Cambridge, Mass.: Harvard University Press 1977.

Howard, C. *Strict Responsibility.* London: Sweet and Maxwell 1963.

Howard, George E. 'On the Development of the King's Peace and the English Local Peace-Magistracy.' *University of Nebraska Studies* 1 (1888-92) 235.

Howe, Mark D. 'The Positivism of Mr. Justice Holmes.' *Harvard L.R.* 64 (1950–1) 529.

Hume, David. *Philosophical Works,* 4 vols. Ed. T.H. Green and T.H. Gross. 1882; rep. Aalen: Scientia Verlag 1964.

Hurnard, Naomi D. 'The Jury of Presentment and the Assize of Clarendon.' *Eng. Hist. Rev.* 56 (1941) 374.

Hurnard, Naomi H. *The King's Pardon for Homicide.* Oxford: Clarendon Press 1969.

Hutchins, B.L., and A. Harrison. *A History of Factory Legislation.* 3rd ed. (1926; rep. New York: Augustus M. Kelly, 1966).

Inglis, B. *Poverty and the Industrial Revolution.* London: Hodder and Stoughton 1971.

Ingman, T. 'The Rise and Fall of the Doctrine of Common Employment.' *Juridical Rev.* (1978) 106.

Isaacs, N. 'Fault and Responsibility.' *Harvard L.R.* 31 (1917–18) 954.

Jackson, R.M. Absolute Prohibition in Statutory Offences. *Cambridge L.J.* (1938) 83.

Jefferey, C.R. 'The Development of Crime in Early English Society.' *J. of Cr. Law, Crim. & Police Science* 47 (1956–7) 647.

Jeudwine, J.W. *Tort, Crime and Police.* London: Williams and Norgate 1917.

Jolowicz, H.F. Academic Elements in Roman Law. *L.Q.R.* 48 (1932) 171.

– 'Political Implications of Roman Law.' *Tulane L.R.* 22 (1947) 62.

Kadish, S.H. 'Some Observations on the Use of Criminal Sanction in Enforcing Economic Regulations.' *Univ. of Chic. L.R.* 30 (1963) 423.

Kaeuper, Richard W. *War, Justice and Public Order.* Oxford: Clarendon Press 1988.

Kaye, J.M. 'The Early History of Murder and Manslaughter.' *L.Q.R.* 83 (1967) 365.

Keeton, G.W. *The Norman Conquest and the Common Law.* London: Benn 1966.

Kelley, D.R. 'History, English Law and the Renaissance.' *Past and Present* 65 (1974) 24.

– 'Gaius Noster: Substructures of Western Social Thought.' *Am. Hist. Rev.* (1979) 619.

– *The Human Measure: Social Thought in the Western Legal Tradition.* Cambridge, Mass.: Harvard University Press 1990.

Kelly, J.M. *A Short History of Western Legal Theory.* Oxford: Clarendon Press 1991.

Kelman, M. 'Interpretive Construction in the Substantive Criminal Law.' *Stan. L.R.* 33 (1981) 591.

– 'Strict Liability: An Unorthodox View.' In *Encyclopaedia of Crime and Justice*, 4 vols. Ed. Sanford H. Kadish. Volume 4. New York: Free Press 1983.

Kelsen, Hans. *General Theory of Law and State.* Cambridge, Mass.: Harvard University Press 1945.

Kennedy, W. *English Taxation, 1640–1799: An Essay on Policy and Opinion* (1913; rep. New York: Augustus Kelly 1968).

Kenny, C.S. *Outlines of Criminal Law.* 15th ed. Cambridge: University Press 1936.

Kent, Joan. 'Attitudes of Members of the House of Commons to the Regulation of "Personal Conduct" in Late Elizabethan and Early Stuart England.' *Bulletin of the Institute of Hist. Research* 46 (1973) 41.

Kerr, M.H. *Catholic Church and Common Law: Three Studies in the Influence of the Church on English Law.* University of Toronto, PhD Thesis 1991.

Kingsley, C. *Lectures Delivered in America 1874.* Philadephia: Jos H. Coates 1875.

Kirby, C., and E. Kirby. 'The Stuart Game Prerogative.' *English Historical Rev.* 46 (1931) 239.

Klafter, Craig E. 'The Americanization of Blackstone's Commentaries.' In *Essays on English Law and the American Experience.* Ed. Elizabeth A. Cawthon and David E. Narret. College Station, Texas: Texas A & M University Press 1994.

Kneale, W. *The Responsibility of Criminals.* Oxford: Clarendon Press 1967.

Knowles, D. *The Evolution of Medieval Thought.* London: Longmans 1962.

Kolko, Gabriel. *The Triumph of Conservatism.* New York: Free Press 1963.

Kriegel, A.D. 'Liberty and Whiggery in the Early 19th Century England.' *Journal of Modern Hist.* 52 (1980) 253.

Kuhn, Thomas S. *The Structure of Scientific Revolution.* 2nd ed. Chicago: University of Chicago Press 1970.

Lattimore, Owen, and Eleanor Lattimore, eds. *Silks, Spices and Empire.* New York: Delacorte Press 1968.

Lee, Janice. 'Political Antiquarianism Unmasked: The Conservative Attack on the Myth of the Ancient Constitution.' *Bulletin of the Inst. of Historical Research* 55 (1962) 166.

Lehman, W.W. 'The First English Law.' *Journal of Legal Hist.* (1985) 1.

Lelling, Andrew E. 'Eliminative Materialism, Neuroscience and the Criminal Law.' *Univ. of Penn. L.R.* 141 (1993) 1471.

Levine, Joseph M. *Humanism and History: Origins of Modern English Historiography.* Ithaca, N.Y.: Cornell University Press 1987.

Levitt, E. 'Extent and Function of the Doctrine of Mens Rea.' *Illinois L.R.* 17 (1922–3) 578.

Lieberman, D. *The Province of Legislation Determined: Legal Theory in 18th Century Britain.* Cambridge: Cambridge University Press 1989.

Lipson, E. *The Growth of English Society.* London: A.C. Black 1949.

Lobban, Michael. *The Common Law and English Jurisprudence, 1760–1850.* Cambridge: Cambridge University Press 1991.

– 'Was There a 19th Century "English School of Jurisprudence?"' *J. of Legal Hist.* 16 (1995) 34.

Locke, J. *Questions Concerning the Law of Nature.* Trans. R. Horwitz et al. Ithaca, N.Y.: Cornell University Press 1990.

Lombroso, C. *Crime: Its Causes and Remedies.* Trans. H.R. Horton. Montclair. N.J.: Patterson Smith 1968.

Lovejoy, Arthur O. *The Great Chain of Being.* Cambridge, Mass.: Harvard University Press 1936.

Lucas, Paul. 'Ex Parte Sir William Blackstone, "Plagiarist": A Note on Blackstone and the Natural Law.' *Am. J. of Legal Hist.* 17 (1963) 42.

Lucy, W. 'Controversy in the Criminal Law.' *Legal Studies* 8 (1988) 217.

Lyons, David. 'Founders and Foundations of Legal Positivism.' 82 *Mich. L.R.* 722 (1984). Review of H.L.A. Hart, *Essays on Bentham: Studies in Jurisprudence and Political Theory.* Oxford: Clarendon Press 1982, and of W.L. Morison, *John Austin.* Stanford, Calif.: Stanford University Press 1982.

MacCormack, G. 'Standards of Liability in Early Law.' *Juridical Rev.* (1985–6) 166.

MacCormick, Neil. *Legal Right and Social Democracy.* Oxford: Clarendon Press 1982.

Maddicott, J.R. 'The English Peasantry and the Demands of the Crown, 1294–1341.' *Past & Present*, supplement no. 1 (1975).

– 'Trade, Industry and the Wealth of King Alfred.' *Past & Present* 135 (1992) 164.

Maine, H. *Early Law and Customs*. New York: Henry Holt 1883.

– *Ancient Law: Its Connection with the Early History of Society and Its Relation to Modern Ideas*. 10th ed. London: John Murray 1885.

Maitland, F.W. *Domesday Book and Beyond*. Cambridge: Cambridge University Press 1897.

– *The Collected Papers*. Ed. H.A.L. Fisher. Cambridge: Cambridge University Press 1911.

– *The Constitutional History of England*. Cambridge: Cambridge University Press 1968.

Maitland, F.W., and Francis C. Montaigne. *A Sketch of English Legal History*. London: G.P. Putnam's Sons 1915.

Malloy, Robin P. 'Invisible Hand or Sleight of Hand? Adam Smith, Richard Posner and the Philosophy of Law and Economics.' *Kansas L.R.* 36 (1988) 209.

Manent, Pierre. *An Intellectual History of Liberalism*. Princeton: Princeton University Press 1994.

Manfredi, Christopher P. 'Fundamental Justice in the Supreme Court of Canada: Decisions Under s.7 of the Charter of Rights and Freedoms, 1984–1988.' *Am. J. of Comp. Law* 38 (1990) 653.

Marshall, T.H. 'Capitalism and the Decline of the English Gilds.' *Cambridge Hist. Journal* 3 (1929) 23.

Marvel, Howard P. 'Factory Regulation: A Re-interpretation of Early English Experience.' *J. of Law and Economics* 20 (1977) 379.

McIntosh, Dave. *The Collectors: A History of Canadian Customs and Excise*. Toronto: NPC Press 1984.

McLaren, John P.S. 'The Origins of Tortious Liability: Insights from Contemporary Tribal Societies.' *U.T.L.J.* 25 (1975) 42.

– 'Nuisance Law and the Industrial Revolution – Some Lessons From Social History.' *Oxf. Journal of Legal Studies* 3 (1983) 155.

– 'White-Slavers: The Reform of Canada's Prostitution Laws and Patterns of Enforcement, 1900–1920.' *Criminal Justice History* 8 (1987) 53.

– 'The Canadian Magistracy and the Anti-White Slavery Campaign, 1900–1920.' In *Canadian Perspectives on Law and Society: Issues in Legal History*. Ed. W. Wesley Pue and Barry Wright. Ottawa: Carleton University Press 1988.

Mehta, Ved. *Fly and the Fly Bottle*. Boston: Little, Brown 1962.

Mendelsohn, S. *The Criminal Jurisprudence of the Ancient Hebrews*. 2nd ed. New York: Herman Press 1968.

Mewett, Alan W., and Morris Manning. *Criminal Law*. Toronto: Butterworths 1978.

Mill, J.S. *On Liberty*. Ed. G. Himmelfarb. Penguin 1985.

Millon, D. 'Positivism in the Historiography of the Common Law.' *Wisconsin L.R.* (1989) 669.

Milson, S.F.C. 'The Nature of Blackstone's Achievement.' *Oxf. Journal of Legal Studies* 1 (1981) 1.

Minda, Gary. *Postmodern Legal Movements: Law and Jurisprudence at Century's End.* New York: New York University Press 1995.

Moles, Robert N. *Definition and Rule in Legal Theory.* London: Basil Blackwell 1987.

Moore, G.E. *Ethics.* London: Oxford University Press 1912.

Moore, Michael S. 'The Moral and Metaphysical Sources of the Criminal Law.' *Nomos XXVIII (Criminal Justice)* (1985) 11.

– *Act and Crime: The Philosophy of Action and Its Implications for Criminal Law.* Oxford: Clarendon Press 1993.

Moran, Leslie J. 'Corporate Criminal Capacity: Nostalgia for Representation.' *Social and Legal Studies* 1 (1992) 37

Morison, W.L. 'Some Myth about Positivism.' *Yale L.J.* 68 (1958) 212.

– *John Austin.* Stanford, Calif.: Stanford University Press 1982.

Mosse, George M. *The Struggle for Sovereignty in England.* East Lansing: Michigan State College Press 1950.

Mueller, Gerhard O.W. 'Mens Rea and the Law without It.' *W. Virg. L.R.* 58 (1955–6) 34.

– 'Tort, Crime and the Primitive.' *J. of Cr. Law, Crim. & Police Science* 46 (1955–6) 303.

– 'On Common Law Mens Rea.' *Minn. L.R.* 42 (1957–8) 1043.

Munsche, P.B. *Gentlemen and Poachers.* New York: Cambridge University Press, 1981.

Murray, Hugh. *The African Continent.* London: T. Nelson and Sons 1853.

Nagel, Ernest. 'Impressions and Appraisals of Analytic Philosophy in Europe.' *Journal of Philosophy* 33 (1936) 5.

Nermerson, Steven S. 'Criminal Liability Without Fault: A Philosophical Perspective.' [Note], *Col. L.R.* 75 (1975).

Newman, John Henry. *The Idea of a University* (1852). Rep. London: Longmans, Green 1929.

Nolan, D.R. 'Sir W. Blackstone and the New American Republic: A Study of Intellectual Impact.' *N.Y.U.L. Rev.* 751 (1976) 31.

Noonan, John T., Jr. *Persons and Masks of the Law.* New York: Farrar, Strauss and Giroux, 1976.

Norrie, Alan. 'Freewill, Determinism and Criminal Justice.' *Legal Studies* 3 (1983) 60.

Odgen, C.K., and I.A. Richards. *The Meaning of Meaning.* 8th ed. New York: Harcourt, Brace and World 1923.

Packer, H. 'Mens Rea and the Supreme Court.' *Supreme Ct. Rev.* (1962) 107.

Page, R.I. *Life in Anglo-Saxon England.* New York: Putnam's Press 1970.

Painter, S. *A History of the Middle Ages, 284–1500*. New York: Alfred A. Knopf 1953.

Palmer, J.N.J. 'Evils Merely Prohibited.' *British J. of Law and Soc.* 3 (1976) 1.

Paulus, I. *The Search for Pure Food*. London: Martin Robertson 1974.

– 'Strict Liability: Its Place in Public Welfare Offences.' *Cr. L. Quarterly* 20 (1977–8) 445.

Perkin, Harold. 'Individualism versus Collectivism in Nineteenth Century Britain: A False Antithesis.' *J. of British Studies* 17 (1977) 105.

Perkins, R. *Criminal Law*. 2nd ed. New York: Foundation Press 1969.

Pike, L.O. *A History of Crimes in England, 1873–76*. Vol. 1 New Brunswick, N.J.: Patterson Smith 1968.

Plato, *Cratylus*. In *The Dialogues of Plato*. Trans. B. Jowett. Vol. 1. New York: Random House 1937.

Plucknett, T.F.T. *Statutes and Their Interpretation in the First Half of the Fourteenth Century*. Cambridge: Cambridge University Press 1922.

– 'The Relations between Roman Law and English Common Law Down to the Sixteenth Century: A General Survey.' *U.T.L.J.* 3 (1939) 24.

– *A Concise History of English Law*. 4th ed. London: Butterworths 1948.

– *Legislation of Edward I*. Oxford: Clarendon Press 1949.

Pocock, J.G.A. *The Ancient Constitution and The Feudal Law*. Cambridge: University Press 1957.

Pollock, F.P. *The Expansion of the Common Law*. London: Stevens 1904.

– *Oxford Lectures*. New York: Books for Library Press 1972.

Pollock, F.P., and F.W. Maitland, *The History of English Law before the Time of Edward I*. 2 vols., 2nd ed. Cambridge: Cambridge University Press 1923.

Popper, K.R. *The Open Society and Its Enemies*. 2 vols., 5th ed. London: Routledge and Kegan Paul 1966.

Posner, Richard A. '"Conventionalism": The Key to Law as an Autonomous Discipline?' *U.T.L.J.* 30 (1988) 333.

– *The Problems of Jurisprudence*. Cambridge, Mass.: Harvard University Press 1991.

Post, G. *Studies in Medieval Legal Thought*. Princeton: Princeton University Press 1964.

Post, J.B. 'Local Jurisdictions and Judgment of Death in Later Medieval England.' *Cr. Justice Hist.* (1983) 1.

Postan, M.M., et al., eds. *Cambridge Economic History*. Vol. 3 Cambridge: Cambridge University Press 1963.

Postema, Gerald J. *Bentham and the Common Law Tradition*. Oxford: Clarendon Press 1986.

Potter, H. *An Introduction to the History of English Law*. London: Sweet and Maxwell 1923.

Pound, R. 'A New School of Jurists.' *University of Nebraska Studies* 4 (1904) 248.

– *The Spirit of the Common Law*. Boston: Marshall Jones 1921.

- *Interpretations of Legal History.* Cambridge: Cambridge University Press 1923.
- *Law and Morals.* Chapel Hill: University of North Carolina Press 1926.
- *Criminal Justice in America.* New York: Holt 1930.

Prichard, J.S., and Alan Brudner. 'Tort Liability for Breach of Statute: A Natural Rights Perspective.' *Law & Phil.* 2 (1983) 89.

Pringsheim, Fritz. 'The Inner Relationship between English and Roman Law.' *Cambridge L.J.* 5 (1933–5) 347.

Radding, Charles M. *The Origins of Medieval Jurisprudence: Pavia and Bologna, 850–1150.* New Haven, Conn.: Yale University Press 1988.

Randall, John H., Jr. 'The Development of the Scientific Method in the School of Padua.' *J. of the Hist. of Ideas* 1 (1940) 177.

Rashdall, H. *The University of Europe in the Middle Ages.* Vol. 1, rev. ed., F.M. Powicke and A.B. Emden, eds. Oxford: Oxford University Press 1936.

Rawls, John. *A Theory of Justice.* Cambridge, Mass.: Harvard University Press 1971.

Raymond, P.E. 'The Origin and Rise of Moral Liability in Criminal Law.' *Oregon L.R.* 15 (1935–6) 93.

Richardson, H.G. 'Studies in Bracton.' *Traditio* 6 (1948) 61.

Risk, R.C.B. 'The Law and the Economy in Mid-Nineteenth Century Ontario: A Perspective.' In *Essays in the History of Canadian Law.* Ed. David H. Flaherty. Toronto: University of Toronto Press 1981.

Roach, John. 'Liberalism and the Victorian Intelligentsia.' *Cambridge Hist. Journal* 13 (1957) 58.

Robertson A.J. *The Laws of the Kings of England from Edmund to Henry I.* Cambridge: Cambridge University Press 1925.

Robertson, H.M. *Aspects of the Rise of Economic Individualism.* Cambridge: Cambridge University Press 1933.

Rodgers, C.P. 'Humanism, History and the Common Law.' *J. of Legal Hist.* 6 (1985) 136.

Rogers, Alan. 'Clerical Taxation under Henry IV, 1399–1413.' *Bulletin of the Institute of Hist. Research* (1973) 123.

Rotunda, Ronald D. *The Politics of Language.* Iowa City: University of Iowa Press 1986.

Rumble, Wilfrid E. 'Divine Law, Utilitarian Ethics, and Positivist Jurisprudence: A Study of the Legal Philosophy of John Austin.' *Am. J. of Jurisprudence* 24 (1979) 139.

- *The Thought of John Austin.* London: Anthlone Press 1985.
- 'John Austin and His 19th Century Critics: The Case of Sir Henry Sumner Maine.' *N.I.L.Q.* (1988) 119.

Ryle, G. *The Concept of Mind.* London: Hutchinson Press 1949.

Sacco, Rodolfo. 'Legal Formants: A Dynamic Approach to Comparative Law.' *Am. J. Comp. Law* 39 (1991) 1.

Salvotori, Peter E. 'Criminal Law – Criminal Negligence – Punishment.' *Canadian Bar Rev.* 58 (1980) 660.

Salzman, Alan 'Strict Criminal Liability and the United States Constitution: Substantive Criminal Law and Due Process.' *Wayne L.R.* 24 (1978) 1571.

Samuel, Geoffrey. 'Science, Law and History: Historical Jurisprudence and Modern Legal Theory.' *N.I.L.Q.* 41 (1990) 1.

Sargent, Neil. 'Law, Ideology and Corporate Crime: A Critique of Instrumentalism.' *Can. J. of Law & Society* 34 (1989) 9.

Saunders, K.W. 'Voluntary Acts and the Criminal Law: Justifying Culpability Based on the Existence of Volition.' *Univ. of Pittsburgh L. Rev.* 49 (1988) 443.

Sayre, F.B. 'Public Welfare Offences.' *Col. L.R.* 33 (1933) 55.

– 'Mens Rea.' *Harvard L.R.* 45 (1945) 974.

Schachner, Nathan. *The Medieval Universities.* London: George Allen and Unwin 1938.

Schofield, Roger. 'Taxation and the Political Limits of the Tudor State.' In *Law and Government under the Tudors.* Ed. C. Cross et al. Cambridge: Cambridge University Press 1988

Schulz, Fritz. *Classical Roman Law.* Oxford: Clarendon Press 1951.

Schumacher, E.F. *A Guide for the Perplexed.* New York: Harper and Row 1977.

Schwarz, Andreas B. 'John Austin and the German Jurisprudence of His Time.' *Politica* (1934) 178.

Seaberg, A.S. 'The Norman Conquest and the Common Law: The Levellers and the Argument from Continuity.' *Historical Journal* 24 (1981) 791.

Segal, Charles P. 'Nature and the World of Man in Greek Literature.' *Arion* 2 (1963) 19.

Seipp, David J. 'Bracton, the Year Books and the Transformation of Elementary Legal Ideas in the Early Common Law.' *Law & Hist. Rev.* 7 (1989) 175.

– 'Roman Legal Categories in the Early Common Law.' In *Proceedings of the Eighth British Legal History Conference, 1987.* Ed. T.G. Watkin. London: Hambledon Press 1989.

Shaw, Frances J. 'Sumptuary Legislation in Scotland.' 1979 *Juridical Rev.* (1979) 81.

Siegel, Stephen A. 'The Aristotlean Basis of English Law 1450–1800.' *N.Y.U.L. Rev.* 56 (1981) 18.

Simpson, A.W.B. 'The Rise and Fall of the Legal Treatise.' *Univ. of Chic. L.R.* 48 (1981) 632.

– 'Legal Iconoclasts and Legal Ideals.' *Univ. of Cincinatti L.R.* 58 (1990) 819.

Singer, Joseph W. 'The Legal Rights Debate in Analytical Jurisprudence from Bentham to Hohfeld.' *Wisconsin L.R.* (1982) 975.

Singer, Richard G. 'The Resurgence of Mens Rea III – The Rise and Fall of Strict Criminal Liability.' *Boston C.U.L.R.* 30 (1988–9) 337.

Sistare, C.T. 'On the Use of Strict Liability in Criminal Law.' *Canadian Journal of Phil.* 17 (1987) 395.

Smith, Adam. *The Theory of Moral Sentiments.* Ed. D.D. Raphael and A.L. Macfie. Oxford: Clarendon Press 1976.

– *Lectures on Jurisprudence.* Ed. R.L. Meet et al. Oxford: Clarendon Press 1978.

Smith, J.C., & B. Hogan. *Criminal Law.* 4th ed. London: Butterworths 1978.

Smith, John C. 'Subjective or Objective? The Ups and Downs of the Test for Criminal Liability in England.' *Villanova L.R.* 27 (1981–2), 1179.

Snell, B. *The Discovery of the Mind: The Greek Origins of European Thought.* Trans. T.G. Rosenmeyer. Oxford: Basil Blackwell 1953.

Sombart, W. *The Quintessence of Capitalism: A Study of the History and Psychology of the Modern Business Man.* Trans. M. Epstein. London: T. Fisher Unwin 1915.

Sorenson, Lloyd R. 'Some Classical Economists, Laissez-faire and the Factory Acts.' *J. of Economic Hist.* (1952) 247.

Spencer, Herbert. *The Principles of Ethics.* Vol. 1. New York: D. Appleton 1903.

Spencer, J.R. 'Public Nuisance: A Critical Examination.' *Cambridge L.J.* 48 (1989) 55.

Stallybrass, W.T.S. 'The Eclipse of Mens Rea.' *L.Q.R.* 52 (1936) 60.

Stammler, R. 'Fundamental Tendencies in Modern Jurisprudence.' *Mich. L.R.* 21 (1922–3) 623.

Stannard, John E. 'Subjectivism, Objectivism and the Draft Criminal Code.' *L.Q.R.* 101 (1985) 540.

– 'A Tale of Four Codes; John Austin and the Criminal Law.' *N.I.L.Q.* 41 (1990) 293.

Starrs, J.E. 'The Regulatory Offense in Historical perspective.' In *Essays in Criminal Science.* Ed. G.O.W. Mueller. South Hackensack, N.J.: F.B. Rothman 1961.

Stein, P. *Legal Evolution: The Story of an Idea.* Cambridge: Cambridge University Press 1980.

Stenton, F.M. *Anglo-Saxon England.* 3rd ed. Oxford: Clarendon Press 1971.

Stephen, J.F. *A History of the Criminal Law of England.* 3 vols. London: Stevens 1883.

Stick, Anne. *Injustice For All.* Penguin 1978.

Stromholm, Stig. *A Short History of Legal Thinking in the West.* Stockholm: Norstedts Forlag 1985.

Stubbs, W. *Lectures on Early English History.* Ed. A. Hassal. London: Longmans 1906.

Sugarman, David. 'Legal Theory, the Common Law Mind and the Making of the Text-book Tradition.' In *Legal Theory and Common Law.* Ed. William Twining. London: Basil Blackwell 1986

Summers, Robert S. 'The "New" Analytical Jurists.' *N.Y.U. L.R.* 41 (1966) 861.

– 'Two Types of Substantive Reasons: The Core of a Theory of Common Law Justification.' *Cornell L.R.* 63 (1978) 707.

Sutherland, E.H. *White Collar Crime.* Westport, Conn.: Greenwood Press 1949.

Ten, C.L. *Crime, Guilt and Punishment.* Oxford: Clarendon Press 1987.

Terrence, Morris, 'The Social Toleration of Crime.' In *Changing Concepts of Crime and Its Treatment*, 13–34. Ed. H.J. Lare. New York: Pergamon Press 1966.

Thomas, Maurice W. *The Early Factory Legislation*. London: Thames Bank 1948.

Thompson, E.P. 'The Moral Economy of the English Crowd in the Eighteenth Century.' *Past & Present* 50 (1971) 76.

– *Whigs and Hunters: The Origin of the Black Act*. London: Penguin 1975.

Tillyard, E.M.W. *The Elizabethan World Picture*. New York: Vantage Books 1967.

Turner, J.W.C. 'The Mental Element in Crimes at Common Law.' *Cambridge L.J.* 6 (1936–8) 31.

Turner, S. *The History of The Anglo-Saxons from the Earliest period to the Norman Conquest*. 7th ed. Vol. 1. London: Longmans 1852.

Twining, William, ed. *Legal Theory and Common Law*. Oxford: Basil Blackwood 1986.

Ullmann, W. *The Medieval Idea of Law: As Represented by Lucas de Penna*. London: Methuen 1946.

– *Law and Politics in the Middle Ages*. New York: Cornell University Press 1975.

Urmson, J.O. 'The History of Philosophical Analysis.' In *The Linguistic Turn*. Ed. Richard Rorty. Chicago: University of Chicago Press 1967.

Vann, R.T. 'The Free Anglo-Saxons: A Historical Myth.' *J. of the Hist. of Ideas* 19 (1958) 259.

Vinogradoff, Sir P. *Outlines of Historical Jurisprudence*. 2 vols. Oxford: Oxford University Press 1920.

– *Roman Law in Medieval Europe*. 3rd ed. Oxford: Oxford University Press 1961.

Walt, Steven, and William S. Laufer, 'Why Personhood Doesn't Matter: Corporate Criminal Liability and Sanctions.' *Am. J. Crim. Law* 18 (1991) 263.

Wasserstrom, R.A. 'Strict Liability in the Criminal Law.' *Stanford L.R.* 12 (1959–60) 731.

Weber, Jack K. 'The King's Peace: A Comparative Study.' *J. of Legal Hist.* 10 (1989) 12.

Westerfield, L. 'Negligence in the Criminal Law: A Historical and Ethical Refutation of Jerome Hall's Arguments.' *Southern Univ. L.R.* 5 (1978–9) 181.

Wheatcroft, G.S.A., 'The Attitude of the Legislature and the Courts to Tax Avoidance.' *Modern L.R.* 18 (1955) 209.

Whitehead, A.N. *Adventures of Ideas*. Cambridge: Cambridge University Press 1933.

Wigmore, J.H. 'Responsibility for Tortious Acts: Its History.' *Harvard L.R.* 7 (1894) 315.

Wiley, H.W. *The History of a Crime Against the Food Law*. Rep. New York: Arno Press 1976.

Wilhelm-Hovijbergh, Anna E. *Peccatum: Sin and Guilt in Ancient Rome*. Gronningen, Djkarta: J.B. Wolters 1954.

Willard, James F. *Parliamentary Taxes on Personal Property, 1290–1334*. New York: Kraus 1970.

Williams, B. *The Whig Supremacy, 1714–1760*. 2nd ed. Oxford: Clarendon Press 1962.

Williams, G. 'The Definition of Crime.' *Current Legal Problems* (1955) 107.

– *Criminal Law, the General Part*. 2nd ed. London: Steven and Sons 1961.

Wilson, P. *Second-Hand Knowledge: An Inquiry into Cognitive Authority*. Westport, Conn.: Greenwood Press 1983.

Winch, D. *Adam Smith's Politics: An Essay in Historiographical Revision*. Cambridge: Cambridge University Press 1978.

Windeyer, W.J.V. *Lectures on Legal History*. Sydney: Law Books of Australasia 1957.

Winfield, P.H. *The Chief Sources of English Legal History*. New York: Burt Franklin 1925.

– 'The Myth of Absolute Liability.' *L.Q.R.* 42 (1926) 37.

– *The Province of the Law of Tort*. Cambridge: Cambridge University Press 1931.

Wood, Donna J. 'The Strategic Use of Public Policy: Business Support for the 1906 Food and Drug Act.' *Bus. Hist. Rev.* 59 (1985) 403.

Wood, Neal. *The Politics of Locke's Philosophy*. Berkeley: University of California Press 1983.

Woodruff, W. 'Capitalism and the Historians: A Contribution to the Discussion on the Industrial Revolution in England.' *J. of Economic Hist.* 16 (1956) 1.

Wylie, J. Kerr. 'Roman Law as an Element in European Culture.' *S.A.L.J.* (1948) 14.

Yale, D.E.C. 'Hobbes and Hale on Law, Legislation and the Sovereign.' *Cambridge L.J.* 31 (1972) 21.

Young, James H. 'Three Southern Food and Drug Cases.' *Journal of Southern Hist.* 49 (1983), 1.

Index